THE NETWORK TROUBLESHOOTING LIBRARY

Implementing IPv6

THE NETWORK TROUBLESHOOTING LIBRARY

Implementing IPv6

Mark A. Miller, P.E.

M&T Books
A Division of MIS:Press, Inc.
A Subsidiary of Henry Holt and Company, Inc.
115 West 18th Street
New York, New York 10011

Printed in the United States of America

Library of Congress Cataloging-in-Publication Data

Miller, Mark 1955–
Implementing IPv6: migrating to thge next generation Internet protocol / Mark Miller.
p. cm.
ISBN 1-55851-579-8
1. TCP/IP (Computer netowrk protocol) I. Title.
TK5105.585.M55 1997 97-46336
004.6'2--dc21 CIP

10 9 8 7 6 5 4 3 2 1

Associate Publisher: Paul Farrell
Managing Editor: Shari Chappell
Editor: Debra Williams Cauley
Technical Editor: John S. Thompson
Production Editor: Maya Riddick
Copy Edit Manager: Karen Tongish
Copy Editor: Annette Devlin

Contents-in-Brief

Contents

Appendices

Table of Illustrations

Preface

It should come as no surprise that the Internet is growing, and that some enhancements will be required to keep this vital communication system well tuned into the twenty-first century. These enhancements were originally called Internet Protocol, *next generation*, or IPng, and have now become formalized as IP version 6, or IPv6. This, the eighth volume of the *Network Troubleshooting Library*, provides network managers with some practical advice on implementing this new protocol.

My engineering nature finds a certain thrill in watching a new system come from concept to prototype to product. And the IPv6 development process has not been an exception. In order to better understand the IPv6 and related protocols, we built a test lab, much like many of you will do. We were able to learn alongside the software developers as they strove to develop products, and we strove to implement and integrate their work. I am sure that we all learned a lot during the process.

Bay Networks, Inc., Digital Equipment Corporation, FTP Software, Inc., and Wandel & Goltermann, Inc. provided equipment for our IPv6 test lab. Special thanks to Dimitry Haskin, Tom Meehan, and Robert MacFarlane from Bay; John Barenys, Jim Bound, Nancy Cappuccio, Liz Kratoska, and Bob Nusbaum from Digital; Bill Andrews, Shishir Belbase, Chip Sparling, and J.D. Stanley from FTP Software; and Eugene Cookmeyer, John Kern, Brian Kirkham, and Gary Rohlke from Wandel and Goltermann. Stephen Kent graciously reviewed the section on IPv6 security.

My team at M&T Books, including Paul Farrell, Debra Williams Cauley, Annette Sroka Devlin, and Maya Riddick provided editorial support. The experience of my technical editor, Dr. John Thompson, was particularly valuable. David Hertzke of Integrated Graphic Communication assisted with some of the figures. Donna Mullen did much of the research for the appendices and managed the final production of all the figures.

As always, Holly, Nathan, and Nicholas added their support and encouragement that makes a project such as this possible. Brutus and Boomer took responsibility for the security and physical fitness aspects of the project, respectively. May your *next generation* be as fulfilling as my current one.

mark@diginet.com

November 1997

Introduction

A lot has changed since the Internet suite of protocols was developed in the early 1970s. Among these changes are virtual LANs using switching technologies, high-speed backbones using ATM and SONET technologies; real-time traffic, such as voice and video over the Internet; the World Wide Web; and electronic commerce. And many of these technologies either directly or indirectly impact the worldwide Internet. As a result, the Internet must continue to be enhanced. The protocols and processes of a generation ago may not be optimal for the networks of the twenty-first century.

In particular, the Internet Engineering Task Force, or IETF, recognized that the Internet Protocol (IP) would need some significant enhancements in order to remain the vital communications medium that it had become. That development effort was named Internet Protocol, *next generation*, or IPng, which led to what we now call IPv6. RFC 1726, the "IPng Technical Criteria," stated the following goals of that project:

First, IPng must offer an internetwork service akin to IPv4, but improved to handle the well-known and widely understood problems of scaling the Internet architecture to more end-points and an ever increasing range of bandwidths. Second, it must be desirable for users and network managers to upgrade their equipment to support IPng. At a minimum, this second point implies that there must be a straightforward way to transition systems from IPv4 to IPng. But it also strongly suggests that IPng should offer features that IPv4 does not; new features provide a motivation to deploy IPng more quickly.

The goals of this book are similar: describing the function of IPv6 and the related protocols, illustrating how they operate using case studies that were developed in our IPv6 test lab, and looking toward a transition from the existing IPv4 to the new IPv6.

This book is comprised of nine chapters, plus appendices. Chapter 1 describes the shortcomings of IPv4, the criteria for IPng, some of the IPng proposals that were put forth during the development process, and the final result: IPv6. Chapter 2 looks at the IPv6 Specification, the functions of IPv6, and the packet headers that provide these functions. Chapter 3 details one of the most significant aspects of IPv6—the new addressing architecture.

In Chapters 4 through 7, we consider enhancements to the support systems that will be required for IPv6. Chapter 4 looks at intranetwork communication and ICMPv6. Chapter 5 looks at issues surrounding support for local networks including the autoconfiguration algorithm and the IEEE EUI-64 addressing scheme. Chapter 6 discusses routing issues, and enhancements to RIP, OSPF, and BGP. Chapter 7 looks at the higher layer issues, such as operating system enhancements, application programming interfaces, and security.

Chapters 8 and 9 deal with implementation issues: network management and transition strategies, respectively.

The first round of Request for Comments (RFC) documents that specify IPv6 and the related protocols and processes were published in late 1995, and more were added in 1996. At the time of this writing, many of these RFCs are being updated as additional implementation experience is obtained. For example, RFC 1972, published in August 1996, details support for IPv6 over Ethernet networks. This RFC assumes the use of 48-bit Ethernet addresses. Subsequently, the Institute of Electrical and Electronics Engineers (IEEE) developed the EUI-64 address, a 64-bit address format for local area networks. For these (and a few other) reasons, RFC 1972 was updated. The first round of such an update is called an *Internet Draft*. After approval from the appropriate IETF working groups and the RFC editor, an Internet Draft is issued an RFC number, and a notation is made that the new RFC obsoletes a previous RFC.

In this text, every effort has been made to provide the latest information regarding IPv6. However, this is a formidable task, as the development efforts are moving quite quickly, with participants from many countries around the globe.

In the case where information in an existing RFC is likely to be revised, updated, or otherwise enhanced by new developments, this new work will be described using the term *proposed*, and a reference (shown at the end of each chapter) will be made to *both* the current RFC and any Internet Draft, noted appropriately as *work in progress*, that may revise or update that RFC.

But since all Internet information is subject to revision or enhancement, the reader is advised to consult the current listings of RFCs and Internet Drafts and obtain the most currently available information on a particular subject matter. Appendix D describes a number of ways of obtaining this information, such as the RFC and Internet Draft electronic archives, and the RFC-INFO service.

Why This Book Is for You

Unless you have recently arrived from a distant planet, you have heard of the Internet. And unless you haven't used the Internet lately, you have seen the volume of traffic increase and response times degrade as more and more firms make this transmission medium their first choice for data traffic.

But unfortunately, the protocols that run the Internet date back to the early 1970s, with the development of the Internet's predecessor, the Advanced Research Projects Agency Network, or ARPANET. At that time, the ARPANET was used for government-sponsored research and educational purposes, and commercial use was strictly prohibited. My, how times have changed. Today, it is hard to watch television for more than 10 minutes without seeing a commercial where the vendor's Web site address is given—underscoring the acceptance of the Internet as a necessary part of business communication.

This combination of increased traffic plus greater commercial use meant that the Internet protocol suite, which is anchored by the Transmission Control Protocol (TCP) and the Internet Protocol (IP), needed some significant enhancements. To compound the issue, the Internet community's research projected a near-term shortage of some types of IP addresses, raising concerns regarding the continuing expansion of the Internet. Clearly, some major work on the Internet protocol suite was in order. Internet Protocol version 6, or IPv6, answers those concerns.

Efforts to provide enhancements to these protocols have been in process for some time; however, IPv6 development got seriously underway in the last few years. At the present time, several dozen host and router vendors have developed products that include IPv6 capabilities. So, for most network managers, it is time to start thinking about a migration to the next generation. This book is designed to make that transition easier. The major topics of discussion include:

- The IPv6 Specification
- The new addressing architecture
- New protocol processes, such as autoconfiguration
- Enhancements to the routing system: RIP, OSPF, and BGP
- Host issues, such as operating system enhancements, APIs, and security
- New MIBs for managing IPv6 internetworks
- Transition strategies for moving from IPv4 to IPv6

As with other volumes in the *Network Troubleshooting Library*, the protocols discussed are illustrated with case studies that show their operation in detail. In addition, a CD-ROM is enclosed which contains the RFCs that describe, define, and document IPv6.

If you plan to be part of the next generation Internet, this book should be part of your library.

The Road to IPv6

Unless you have just recently arrived from another planet, you have been a participant (although perhaps unwillingly) in the communications and data networking explosion of recent years. In many ways, new technologies and systems have made dramatic changes in the way that people store, retrieve, and disseminate information.

On the data side of the equation, we have seen the mainframe environments of the 1970s yield to distributed computing in the 1980s, to local networks in the early 1990s, and to corporate intranetworks in the late 1990s. On the communication side of the equation, we have seen the leased lines migrate to frame relay and Asynchronous Transfer Mode (ATM) connections, and dial up circuits migrate to Integrated Services Digital Networks (ISDNs). Transmission speeds in the last two decades have increased from a few hundred bits per second to hundreds and even thousands of megabits per second.

In many cases, those underlying technologies and systems can trace their roots to the *Internet*, a network that was born in 1969 as the Advanced Research Projects Agency Network (ARPAnet), sponsored, in part, with U.S. Government research grants. Note that in this text, we will use the term *Internet* (with an upper case I) to indicate the worldwide Internet, and the term *internet* (lower case I) to indicate a private (or corporate) internetwork.

Because the ARPAnet was government sponsored, its use was limited by what became known as *acceptable use policies,* or AUPs, which, in many cases, limited transmissions on the Internet to those focused on education and research. As time passed, the Internet migrated from a research-oriented medium to a commercial communications medium; as a result, some of the rules changed.

AUPs became a thing of the past, and decency or privacy of Internet communication became issues for both technologists and legislators to wrestle with.

Regardless of the funding for the Internet—government or commercial—the end result was the same: more host connections, more users, and more traffic on the Internet. Which brings us to the topic of this book: enhancing the protocols of the Internet to keep pace with the technologies employed by the end users.

1.1 The Internet Suite of Protocols

The protocols that operate on the Internet are part of what is called the ARPA suite of protocols, now more commonly referred to as simply the *Internet* suite of protocols. The Advanced Research Projects Agency (ARPA) model of internetworking consists of four defined layers: Network Interface, Internet, Host-to-Host, and Process/Application (see Figure 1-1). Developed in the early 1970s, this model predated the Open Systems Interconnection Reference Model (OSI-RM) by several years. Like ARPA, the OSI-RM was designed to internetwork dissimilar computer systems. However, the OSI-RM efforts were focused on international standards and interoperability of a global nature, whereas the ARPA work was primarily concerned with communication between collaborators in academic, research, and government organizations. As a result, the ARPA model is considered by many to be a more pragmatic, practical approach to networking architecture.

ARPA Layer	Protocol Implementation						OSI Layer
Process / Application	File Transfer	Electronic Mail	Terminal Emulation	File Transfer	Client / Server	Network Management	Application
	File Transfer Protocol (FTP) MIL-STD-1780 RFC 959	Simple Mail Transfer Protocol (SMTP) MIL-STD-1781 RFC 821	TELNET Protocol MIL-STD-1782 RFC 854	Trivial File Transfer Protocol (TFTP) RFC 783	Sun Microsystems Network File System Protocols (NFS) RFCs 1014, 1057, and 1094	Simple Network Management Protocol (SNMP) RFC 1157	Presentation Session
Host-to-Host	Transmission Control Protocol (TCP) MIL-STD-1778 RFC 793			User Datagram Protocol (UDP) RFC 768			Transport
Internet	Address Resolution ARP RFC 826 RARP RFC 903		Internet Protocol (IP) MIL-STD-1777 RFC 791		Internet Control Message Protocol (ICMP) RFC 792		Network
Network Interface	Network Interface Cards: Ethernet, Token Ring, ARCNET, MAN and WAN RFC 894, RFC 1042, RFC 1201 and others						Data Link
	Transmission Media: Twisted Pair, Coax, Fiber Optics, Wireless Media, etc.						Physical

Figure 1-1. Comparing ARPA protocols with OSI and ARPA architectures

1.1.1 The ARPA Model of Internetworking

Let's take a brief look at the ARPA architecture and see how the Internet Protocol (IP) fits into that structure.

The first layer of the ARPA model is the Network Interface Layer, sometimes called the *Network Access Layer* or *Local Network Layer*. It connects the local host to the local network hardware. As such, it comprises the functions of the OSI Physical and Data Link Layers: It makes the physical connection to the cable system, it accesses the cable at the appropriate time (e.g., using a Carrier Sense Multiple Access with Collision Detection (CSMA/CD) or token passing algorithm), and it places the data into a frame. The *frame* is a package that encapsulates the data with information, such as the hardware address of the local host and a check sequence to assure data integrity. The frame is defined by the hardware in use, such as an Ethernet LAN or a frame relay interface into a WAN. For each of these implementations, an Internet document, known as a *Request for Comments* document, or RFC, has been published. These include Ethernet (RFC 894), IEEE 802 LANs (RFC 1042), ARCNET (RFC 1201), Fiber Distributed Data Interface—FDDI (RFC 1103), serial lines using the Serial Line Internet Protocol—SLIP (RFC 1055) or the Point to Point Protocol—PPP (RFC 1661), Packet Switched Public Data Networks—PSPDNs (RFC 877), frame relay (RFC 1490), Switched Multimegabit Data Service—SMDS (RFC 1209), and the Asynchronous Transfer Mode (ATM), defined in RFC 1438.

The Internet Layer transfers packets from one host (the computing device that runs application programs) to another host. Note that we said *packet* instead of *frame*. The packet differs from the frame in that it contains address information to facilitate its journey from one host to another through the internetwork; the address within the frame header gets the frame from host to host on the same local network. The protocol that operates the Internet Layer is known as the *Internet Protocol* (the IP in TCP/IP), and includes the version that is implemented in current networks, IP version 4, documented in RFC 791. The subject of this text, IP version 6, or IPv6, is documented in numerous RFCs, which we will discuss along the way. (Version 5 had been assigned to another protocol, the Streams Protocol, ST2. The next number available for assignment was 6, hence the next generation is called IPv6.) Also note that within the context of IPv4, the term *datagram* is used, which has its historical roots in the word *telegram*; it can be considered a synonym for *packet*.

To support the operation of IPv4, additional protocols are also required.

The *Address Resolution Protocol* (ARP) provides a way to translate between IP addresses and local network addresses, such as Ethernet, and is discussed in RFC 826. The *Reverse Address Resolution Protocol* (RARP), explained in RFC 903, provides the complementary function, translating from the local address (again, such as Ethernet) to IP addresses. (In some architectural drawings, ARP and RARP are shown slightly lower than IP to indicate their close relationship to the Network Interface Layer. In some respects, ARP/RARP overlap the Network Interface and Internet Layers.)

The *Internet Control Message Protocol* (ICMP) provides a way for the IP software on a host or gateway to communicate with its peers on other machines about any problems it might have in routing IP datagrams. ICMP, which is explained in RFC 792, is a required part of the IP implementation. One of the most frequently used ICMP messages is the Echo Request, commonly called the *Ping*, which allows one device to test the communication path to another.

As the datagram traverses the Internet, it may pass through multiple gateways and their associated local network connections. (Taken in the ARPA context, a gateway is a device which operates principally at the ARPA Internet Layer, and connects a host to a network or one network to another network. Most technical literature today uses the term *router* instead of *gateway*.) Thus there's a risk that packets may be lost or that a noisy communication circuit may corrupt data. The Host-to-Host Layer guards against these problems, however remote, and assures the reliable delivery of a datagram sent from the source host to the destination host. (Recall that one of the major objectives of the ARPA project was military communication, which, by definition, must be ultra-reliable.)

The Host-to-Host Layer defines two protocols: the *User Datagram Protocol* (UDP) and the *Transmission Control Protocol* (TCP). The minimum reliability UDP, described in RFC 768, provides minimal protocol overhead. UDP restricts its involvement to higher-layer port addresses, defining the length, and a checksum. TCP, detailed in RFC 793, defines a much more rigorous error-control mechanism. TCP (of the TCP/IP nomenclature) provides much of the strength of the Internet protocol suite. TCP provides reliable datastream transport between two host applications by providing a method of sequentially transferring every octet (8-bit quantity of data) passed between the two applications.

End users interact with the host via the Process/Application Layer. Because of the user interface, a number of protocols have been developed for this layer. As its name implies, the *File Transfer Protocol* (FTP) transfers files between two host systems. FTP is described in RFC 959. To guarantee its reliability, FTP is implemented over TCP. When economy of transmission is desired, you may use a simpler program, the *Trivial File Transfer Protocol* (TFTP), described in RFC 783. TFTP runs on top of UDP to economize the Host-to-Host Layer as well.

Electronic mail and terminal emulation are two of the more frequently used Internet applications. The *Simple Mail Transfer Protocol* (SMTP), given in RFC 821, sends mail messages from one host to another. When accessing a remote host via the Internet, one must emulate the type of terminal the host wishes to see. For example, a Digital host may prefer a VT-100 terminal, while an IBM host would rather see a 3278 or 3279 display station. The *Telecommunications Network* (TELNET) Protocol provides remote host access and terminal emulation.

As internetworks become more complex, system management requirements increase as well. A large number of vendors, including Hewlett-Packard, IBM, Microsoft, SunSoft, and others have developed network management systems that supply these needs. Common to all of these platforms is the use of a protocol, the *Simple Network Management Protocol* (SNMP), given in RFC 1157, that was originally developed to meet the needs of TCP/IP-based internets. As its name implies, SNMP uses minimal overhead to communicate between the

Manager (i.e., management console) and the Agent (i.e., the process within the device, such as a router, being managed).

1.1.2 IPv6 within the ARPA Model

In subsequent chapters we will discover that many of the enhancements found with IPv6 replace or embellish some of the protocols and supporting functions that exist to support IPv4. For example, IPv6 contains new functions, such as neighbor discovery and router discovery, that replace ARP and RARP. The ICMP functions have been enhanced, and are now called ICMPv6. The functions resident at the ARPA Host-to-Host and Process/Application layers do not change, per se, but the ways in which they are implemented may. For example, one of the new features in IPv6 provides for packet prioritization and flow labeling. In order to access this feature (at the ARPA Internet Layer), the upper-layer Application Programming Interfaces (APIs), typically resident within an operating system, such as UNIX, must be revised in order to identify the need for, and subsequently access, these enhancements. These revised functions will be considered as we proceed through this text.

1.2 The Limitations of IPv4

As the Internet made the transition from a government-sponsored to a commercially driven communications environment, some of the original operational characteristics required reexamination. For example, prior to commercial use of the Internet, widespread security of end-user communication was not required. Now, as many end users conduct business on the Internet and routinely submit their credit card information for purchases, the need for private communication sessions is enhanced.

But the most dramatic issue related to growth became the huge numbers of hosts that were connecting to the Internet, and the associated IP addresses that were being consumed by those hosts. The firm Network Wizards [1-1] does a periodic survey of both hosts and connected domains and has found these numbers growing at exponential rates, as shown in Figure 1-2. With each of those hosts needing a unique identifier, more and more addresses are therefore consumed.

And even though the current IPv4 address space can identify a theoretical 4.2 billion hosts (2^{32}), the structure of that address space, dividing it into Class A, Class B, Class C, etc. addresses, as we will study in Chapter 3, imposes some additional constraints. In short, greater growth equated to a faster consumption of the existing address space. Other related problems, such as the limited addressing hierarchy that is possible within the confines of the 32-bit IPv4 address, plus the associated limitations on routing function scaling (again, constraining the long-term growth of the Internet), were also identified.

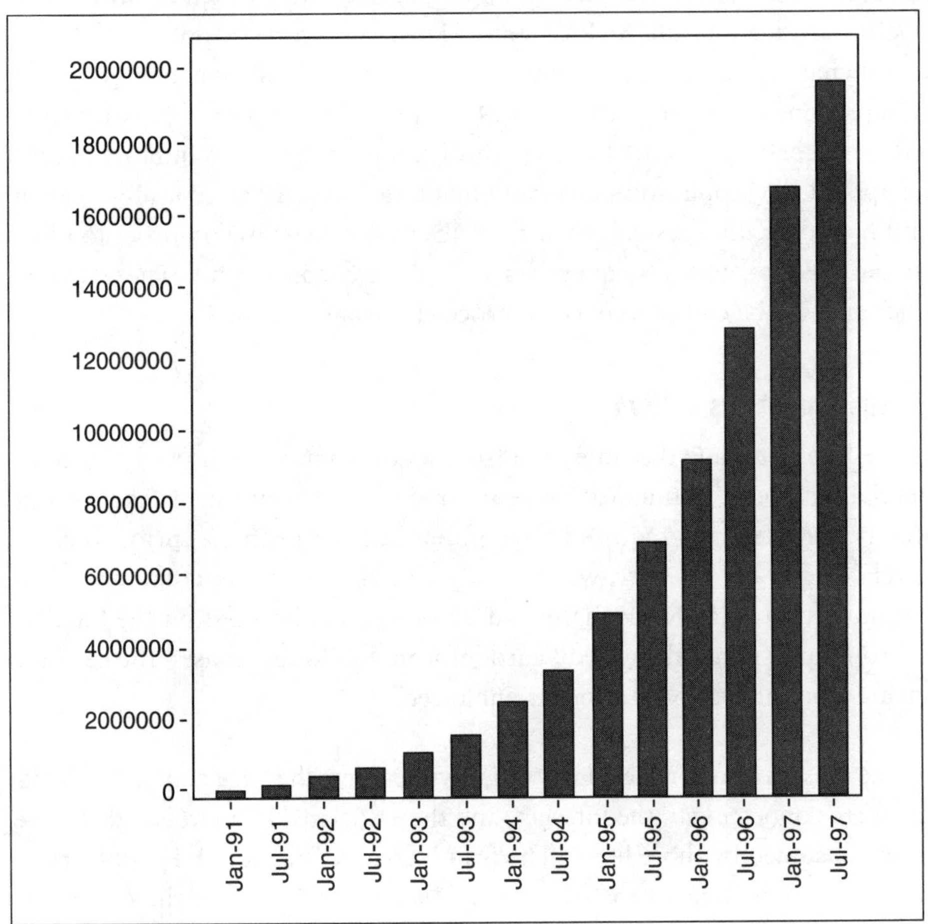

Figure 1-2. Growth of Internet hosts
(Source: Network Wizards survey, http://www.nw.com)

Anticipating this shortage of IP addresses—with the "Date of Doom" forecast for March 1994, the predicted time at which part of the current IP address space would be exhausted [1-2]—moved the Internet Engineering Task Force to act. In response to these concerns, in July 1991, the IETF began the process of researching the problem, soliciting proposals for solutions, and narrowing in on a conclusion, describing this preliminary process in RFC 1380 [1-3], published in November 1992. In addition, a new research area, called the Internet Protocol Next Generation, or IPng, Area, was commissioned by the IETF to formally study these issues.

1.3 The Criteria for IPng

In December 1993, RFC 1550 was distributed, titled "IP: Next Generation (IPng) White Paper Solicitation" [1-4]. This RFC invited any interested party to submit comments regarding any specific requirements for the IPng or any key factors that should be considered during the IPng selection process. Twenty-one responses were submitted that addressed a variety of topics, including: security (RFC 1675), a large corporate user's view (RFC 1687), a cellular industry view (RFC 1674), and a cable television industry view (RFC 1686). Many of these papers, plus a complete listing of the white paper responses, are given in Scott Bradner and Allison Mankin's book *IPng—Internet Protocol Next Generation* [1-5]. Other interested organizations, such as the Institute of Electrical and Electronics Engineers (IEEE), also supported the IPng enhancement efforts [1-6].

The IPng Area commissioned RFC 1726, "Technical Criteria for Choosing IP the Next Generation (IPng)" [1-7], to define a set of criteria that would be used in the IPng evaluation process. Seventeen criteria were noted:

- Scale—The IPng Protocol must scale to allow the identification and addressing of at least 10^{12} end systems and 10^{9} individual networks.
- Topological Flexibility—The routing architecture and protocols of IPng must allow for many different network topologies.

- Performance—A state-of-the-art, commercial-grade router must be able to process and forward IPng traffic at speeds capable of fully utilizing common, commercially available, high-speed media at the time. Hosts must be able to achieve data transfer rates with IPng that are comparable to the rates achieved with IPv4, using similar levels of host resources.
- Robust Service—The network service and its associated routing and control protocols must be robust.
- Transition—The protocol must have a straightforward transition plan from the current IPv4.
- Media Independence—The protocol must work across an internetwork of many different LAN, MAN, and WAN media, with individual link speeds ranging from a ones-of-bits per second to hundreds of gigabits per second.
- Unreliable Datagram Service—The protocol must support an unreliable datagram delivery service.
- Configuration, Administration, and Operation—The protocol must permit easy and largely distributed configuration and operation. The automatic configuration of hosts and routers is required.
- Secure Operation—IPng must provide a secure network layer.
- Unique Naming—IPng must assign all IP-Layer objects in global, ubiquitous, Internet unique names.
- Access and Documentation—The protocols that define IPng, its associated protocols, and the routing protocols must be published in the standards track RFCs, be freely available, and require no licensing fees for implementation.
- Multicast—The protocol must support both unicast and multicast packet transmission.
- Extensibility—The protocol must be extensible; it must be able to evolve to meet the future service needs of the Internet. In addition, as IPng evolves, it must allow different versions to coexist on the same network.

- Network Service—The protocol must allow the network to associate packets with particular service classes and provide them with the services specified by those classes.
- Mobility—The protocol must support mobile hosts, networks, and internetworks.
- Control Protocol—The protocol must include elementary support for testing and debugging networks.
- Private Networks—IPng must allow users to build private internetworks on top of the basic Internet infrastructure, supporting both IP-based and non–IP-based internetworks.

1.4 The IPng Development Process

Several proposals were evaluated vis-à-vis the above criteria. In January 1995, RFC 1752, "The Recommendation for the IP Next Generation Protocol" was issued [1-8]. This paper summarized the evaluations of three IPng proposals: Common Architecture for the Next Generation Internet Protocol (CATNIP) [1-9] and [1-10], Simple Internet Protocol Plus (SIPP) [1-11] and [1-12], and the TCP/UDP with Bigger Addresses (TUBA) [1-13] and [1-14]. Each of these three proposals was evaluated according to the criteria established in RFC 1726, and summarized in a table presented in RFC 1752, section 8.

1.4.1 CATNIP

The objective of the CATNIP proposal is to provide some commonality between Internet, OSI, and Novell protocols. To accomplish this, CATNIP integrates a number of Network layer protocols, including the ISO Connectionless Network Protocol (CLNP), IP, and Novell's Internetwork Packet Exchange (IPX) protocol. In addition, the CATNIP design allows a number of Transport protocols, including the ISO Transport Protocol, class 4 (TP4), Connectionless Transport Protocol (CLTP), TCP, UDP, and Novell's Sequenced Packet Exchange (SPX), to run over any of the above Network layer protocols. According to the proposal, it would be possible for a single Transport layer protocol, such as TCP, to operate over one Network layer protocol (such as IPv4) at one end of the connection, and over another Network layer protocol (such as CLNP) at the other. As documented in RFC 1752, the reviewers felt that CATNIP met five of the key criteria, did not meet two of the criteria, and had mixed reviews or an unknown conclusion on the remaining criteria.

1.4.2 SIPP

The objective of SIPP is to provide a new, evolutionary step from IPv4. As such, IPv4 functions that worked were retained, and functions that did not were removed. In addition, SIPP installation is planned as a software upgrade, and it is interoperable with the existing IPv4. SIPP revises the IP header for more efficient processing and increases the size of the IP addresses from 32 to 64 bits in length. As documented in RFC 1752, the reviewers felt that SIPP met ten of the key criteria, did not meet two of the criteria, and had mixed reviews or an unknown conclusion on the remaining criteria.

1.4.3 TUBA

The key strategy behind TUBA is to replace the existing IPv4 Network layer with the ISO CLNP. There are two benefits to this: providing for increased address space, while allowing for TCP or UDP and related upper layer applications to operate unchanged. The addresses defined for CLNP (and therefore in TUBA) are called *Network Service Access Points*, or NSAPs, which are variable-length addresses. The use of CLNP at the Network layer would be supported by existing ISO routing protocols, including the Inter Domain Routing Protocol (IDRP), the Intermediate System–to–Intermediate System (IS-IS) protocol, and the End System–to–Intermediate System (ES-IS) protocol. As documented in RFC 1752, the reviewers felt that TUBA met five of the key criteria, did not meet one of the criteria, and had mixed reviews or an unknown conclusion on the remaining criteria.

1.4.4 The Final Result

As also reported in RFC 1752, all three proposals exhibited significant problems, and CATNIP in particular was determined to be “too incomplete to be considered.” As a result of these discussions, the SIPP proposal was revised, incorporating 128-bit addresses and dealing with other concerns. The final recommendation incorporated this revised SIPP proposal, coupled with the autoreconfiguration and transition elements of TUBA, the addressing work based on the Classless Inter-Domain Routing, or CIDR (an intermediate solution to the address depletion problem), plus routing header enhancements.

Figure 1-3, developed by Steve Deering, author of the SIPP proposal, illustrates the process through which the best capabilities of CATNIP, SIPP, and TUBA became IPng. To quote from RFC 1752:

> *This proposal represents a synthesis of multiple IETF efforts with much of the basic protocol coming from the SIPP effort, the autoconfiguration and transition portions influenced by TUBA, the addressing structure based on CIDR work and the routing header evolving out of the SDRP [Source Demand Routing Protocol] deliberations.*

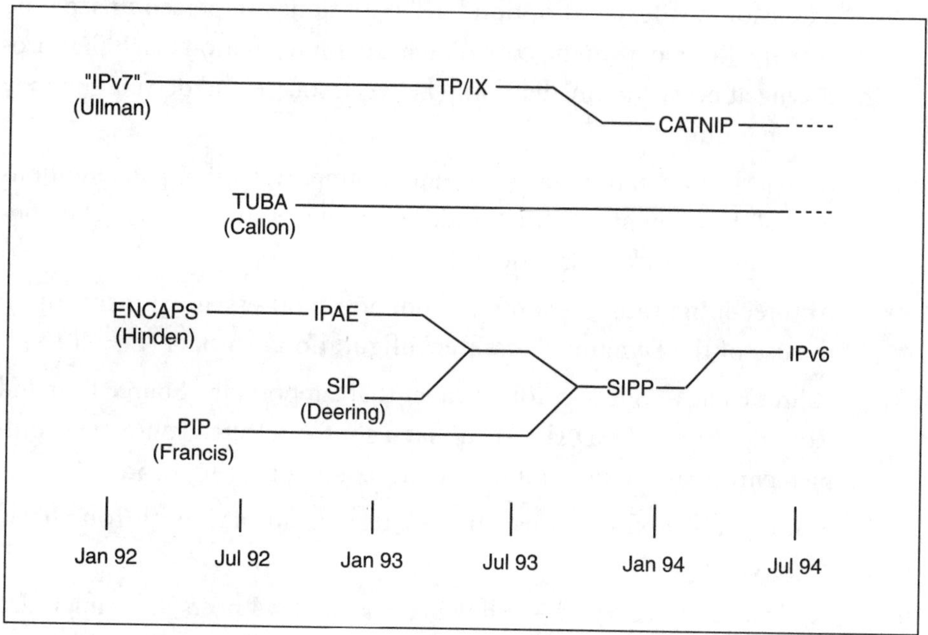

Figure 1-3. IPng candidates
(Copyright 1997 by Steven Deering. Reprinted with permission.)

1.5 Functional Capabilities of IPv6

RFC 1752 also describes the important features of IPng, formally designated IPv6. These capabilities of IPv6 include:

- Expanded addressing and routing—Increasing the IP address field from 32 to 128 bits in length, which allows for a much greater number of addressable nodes, more levels of addressing hierarchy, defining new types of addresses, etc.
- Simplified header format—Eliminating or making optional some of the IPv4 header fields to reduce the packet handling overhead, thus providing some compensation for the larger addresses. Even with the addresses, which are four times as long, the IPv6 header is only 40 octets in length, compared with 20 octets for IPv4.
- Extension headers and options—IPv6 options are placed in separate headers, located after the core IPv6 header information, such that processing at every intermediate stop between source and destination may not be required.
- Authentication and privacy—Required support in all implementations of IPv6 to authenticate the sender of a packet and encrypt the contents of that packet, as required.
- Autoreconfiguration—Support from node address assignments up to the use of the Dynamic Host Reconfiguration Protocol (DHCP).
- Source routes—Support for a header that supports the Source Demand Routing Protocol (SDRP), such that a source-selected route may complement the route determined by the existing routing protocols.
- Simple and flexible transition—A transition plan with four basic requirements:
    1. Incremental upgrade—Allowing existing IPv4 hosts to be upgraded at any time without a dependency on other hosts or routers being upgraded.

2. Incremental deployment—New IPv6 hosts and routers can be installed at any time without any prerequisites.
3. Easy addressing—When existing installed IPv4 hosts or routers are upgraded to IPv6, they may continue to use their existing address without needing a new assigned address.
4. Low start-up costs—Little or no preparation work is needed in order to upgrade existing IPv4 systems to IPv6 or to deploy new IPv6 systems.

➢ Quality of service capabilities—A new capability is added to enable the labeling of packets belonging to particular traffic "flows" for which the sender has requested special handling, such as nondefault quality of service or "real-time" service.

Thus the foreseeable exhaustion of the available IPv4 address space gave the Internet community the impetus to consider revisions to this widely deployed protocol. But other factors, such as support for real-time applications, enhanced security, and other design criteria listed above may be equally important, or possibly more important, to individual network managers.

1.6 Implementations of IPv6

Despite the functional capabilities of the new protocol, some network managers may have reservations about making the transition from the tried-and-proven IPv4 to the newly minted IPv6. Bay Networks, Inc., in their white paper *The Case for IPv6* [1-15], refutes six myths that have surfaced regarding the need to implement IPv6:

Myth #1 The only driving force behind IPv6 is the address space depletion. (Other IPv6 capabilities address current business requirements, including more scalable network architectures, improved security, integrated quality of service, mobile computing, and others, that go beyond the address space issue.)

Myth #2 Extensions to IPv4 can replicate IPv6 functionality. (Extensions cannot substitute for a protocol suite with built-in enhancements.)

Myth #3 IPv6 support for a large diversity of network devices is not an end-user or business concern. (Internet connections of conventional computers will be joined with unconventional devices in the near future, including personal digital assistants (PDAs), intelligent mobile phones, and others, which are all driven by end-user requirements. The larger IPv6 address space will be able to accommodate these more unconventional connections.)

Myth #4 IPv6 is primarily relevant to backbone routers, not end-user applications. (Support for critical end-user applications, such as autoconfiguration, security, and quality of service features, are key elements of IPv6.)

Myth #5 Asynchronous Transfer Mode (ATM) cell switching will negate the need for IPv6. (ATM is a high-speed transmission medium, implemented in many campus and corporate backbones; however, it cannot replace the need for packet routing. The integration of ATM and IPv6, rather than the replacement of one with the other, is a more likely outcome.)

Myth #6 IPv6 is something that only large telecommunications companies or the government should worry about. (IPv6 has been designed with many forward-looking capabilities. Those who invest in IPv6 now will be better positioned in the future.)

At the present time, more than two dozen router and host companies have indicated support or plans to support IPv6 in their products. Almost all of these vendors announce their plans on the IPv6 industry home page:

http://playground.sun.com/pub/ipng/html/ipng-main.html

In addition, many of the vendors have their own home pages devoted to the implementations of IPv6 within their products and the capabilities that those products currently offer.

Of special interest to IPv6 implementers is the 6bone, an experimental network running in parallel with the existing Internet. The 6bone is an outgrowth of the IETF IPv6 development work; at the time of this writing, it has connections in 27 different countries in North America, Europe, and Japan, as shown in Figure 1-4. Backbone links on the 6bone may operate using static routes or one of the IPv6-enabled routing protocols: the Routing Information Protocol—Next Generation (RIPng), or the Border Gateway Protocol version 4 (BGP4+IPv6), as shown in Figure 1-5. End users wishing to get personal experience with IPv6 before migrating the protocol to their entire internetwork may get a connection through a variety of portals.

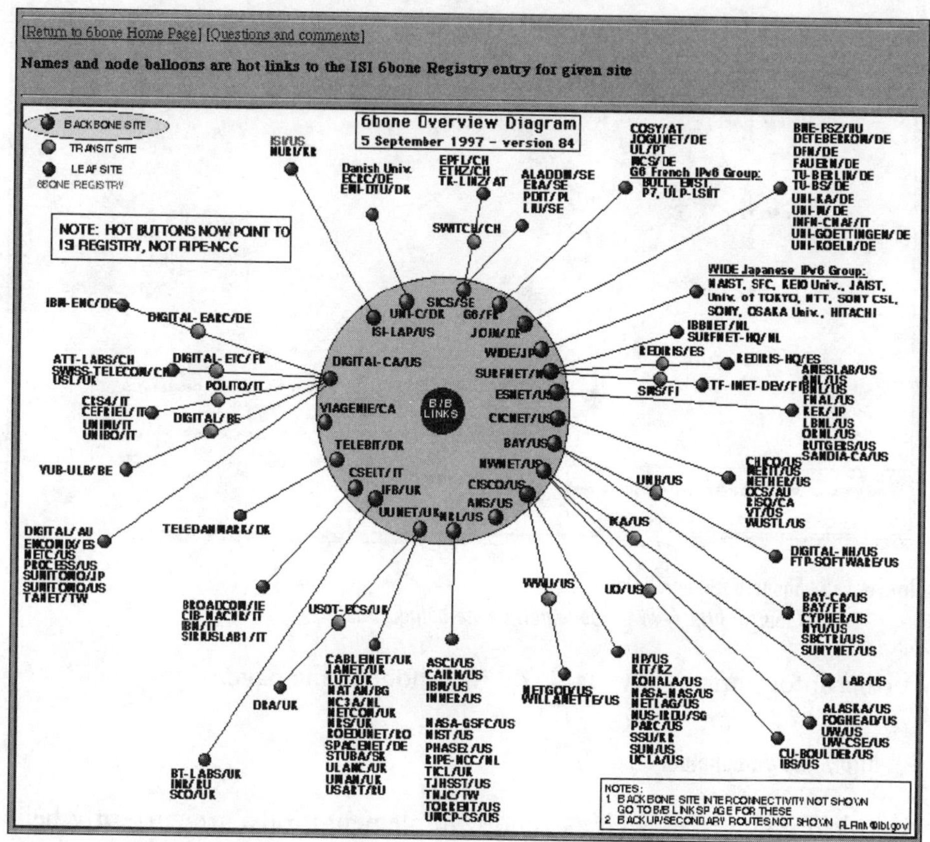

Figure 1-4. 6bone drawing
(Source: http://www.6bone.net/6bone-drawing.html)

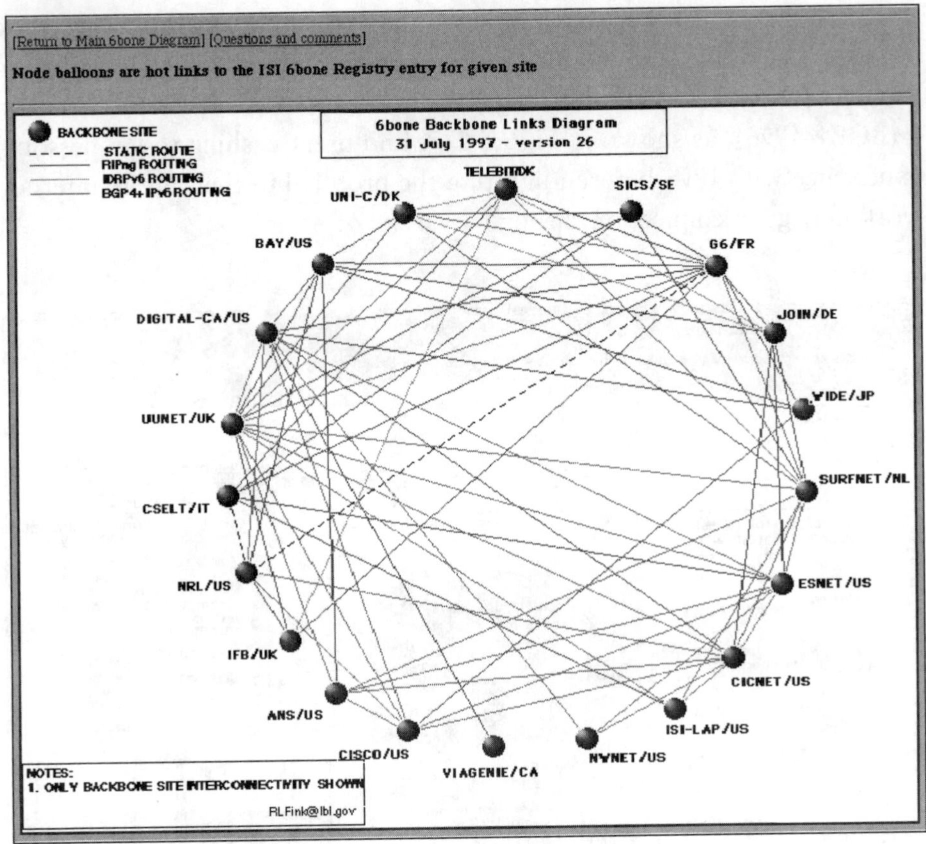

Figure 1-5. 6bone backbone links
(Source: http://www.6bone.net/6bone-bblinks.html)

Further information is available on the 6bone home page:

http://www.6bone.net

Technical updates, as well as vendor implementations, are currently being chronicled in the internetworking trade press. References [1-16] through [1-30] are examples of recent articles.

1.7 Documenting IPv6

At the present time, a number of Internet Request for Comments (RFC) documents that describe the IPng development effort, IPv6, and the related protocols have been issued. These RFCs, are included on the accompanying CD-ROM. The RFCs specific to IPv6 are:

RFC	Subject
1550	IPng White Paper Solicitation
1726	Technical Criteria for IPng
1752	Recommendation for IPng
1809	Using the Flow Label Field
1810	Report on MD5 Performance
1825	Security Architecture
1826	IP Authentication Header
1827	IP Encapsulating Security Payload (ESP)
1828	IP Authentication using Keyed MD5
1829	The ESP DES-CBC Transform
1881	IPv6 Address Allocation Management
1883	IPv6 Specification
1884	IPv6 Addressing Architecture
1885	ICMPv6 for IPv6
1886	DNS Extensions to Support IPv6
1887	IPv6 Unicast Address Allocation

RFC	Subject
1888	OSI NSAPs and IPv6
1897	IPv6 Testing Address Allocation
1924	A Compact Representation of IPv6 Addresses
1933	Transition Mechanisms for IPv6 Hosts and Routers
1970	Neighbor Discovery for IPv6
1971	IPv6 Stateless Address Autoconfiguration
1972	Transmitting IPv6 over Ethernet Networks
1981	Path MTU Discovery for IPv6
2019	Transmitting IPv6 over FDDI Networks
2023	IPv6 over PPP
2030	Simple Network Time Protocol (SNTP) for IPv4, IPv6 and OSI
2073	IPv6 Provider-based Unicast Address Format
2080	RIPng for IPv6
2133	Basic Socket Interface Extensions for IPv6
2147	TCP and UDP over IPv6 Jumbograms
2185	Routing Aspects of IPv6 Transition

In addition, many Internet Drafts have been written regarding IPv6 functionality and are in various stages of completion. Keywords to look for in the Internet Draft titles include:

- ipv6 (Internet Protocol version 6)
- ipngwg (IP Next Generation Working Group)
- ipsec (IP Security)
- ngtrans (Next Generation Transition)

Much of the work of the IPv6 working groups is available through their mailing lists. These mailing lists include:

- ipng@sunroof.eng.sun.com (IPv6 General Discussion Mailing List)
- 6bone@isi.edu (6bone Discussion List)
- ipv6imp@munnari.oz.au (IPv6 Implementers Discussion List)
- ipsec@tis.com (IP Security Discussion List)
- ngtraus@sunroof.eng.com (Transition Discussion List)

To subscribe to the IPv6 General Discussion list, send email to:

```
majordomo@sunroof.eng.sun.com
```

With the following line in the message body:

```
subscribe ipng
```

Subscriptions to the other lists can be made in a similar manner by substituting the desired list name in the appropriate places in the email message.

Information on how to obtain RFCs and Internet Drafts electronically is given in Appendix D.

1.8 Outlining Our Study of IPv6

This volume of the *Network Troubleshooting Library* will retain two characteristics of the series: the architecture will be explored one layer (or one function) at a time, and as this is done, case studies will be used to illustrate the protocols in operation.

We will begin our journey through the world of IPv6 by first looking at the IPv6 packet specification in Chapter 2, and comparing it with the existing IPv4. In Chapter 3, we will examine the IPv6 addressing architecture in detail. Chapter 4 will be devoted to issues relating to ICMPv6, which provides communication within an IPv6 network. Chapter 5 will discuss autoconfiguration ("plug and play") for IPv6, along with other effects that IPv6 presents to local and wide area networks. Chapter 6 will discuss effects on the routing process and protocols, and Chapter 7 will consider effects on the host processes, such as the upper layers, operating systems and security aspects of IPv6. Chapter 8 looks at IPv6 network management issues, and Chapter 9 will consider implementation strategies. The appendices that follow provide reference information on IPv6-related parameters, documentation, and product implementations.

For consistency, all case studies have been captured using a Wandel & Goltermann, Inc.'s Domino Internetwork Analyzer. The test network for all of these case studies consists of workstations running FTP Software Inc.'s Secure Client and Network Access Suite software supporting IPv6, plus routers from Bay Networks, Inc. and Digital Equipment Corp. that have been enhanced to support IPv6. Both workstations and routers maintain IPv4 functionality for backward compatibility with the installed base.

In this text, every effort has been made to provide the latest information regarding IPv6. However, this is a formidable task, as the development efforts are moving quite quickly, with participants from many countries around the globe. In the case where information in an existing RFC is likely to be revised, updated or otherwise enhanced by new developments, this new work will be described using the term *proposed*, and a reference (shown at the end of each chapter) will be made to *both* the current RFC and any Internet Draft, noted appropriately as *work in progress*, that may revise or update that RFC.

But since all Internet information is subject to revision or enhancement, the reader is advised to consult the current listings of RFCs and Internet Drafts, and obtain the most currently-available information on a particular subject matter. Appendix D describes a number of ways of obtaining this information, such as the RFC and Internet Draft electronic archives, and the RFC-INFO service.

Roll up your sleeves and get ready for the next generation!

1.9 References

[1-1] The Internet Domain Survey is produced periodically by the firm Network Wizards. Current information is available at http://www.nw.com.

[1-2] Mankin, Allison. "The Trillion Node Internet: An Update on IPv6." *ComNet 1996* Conference Proceedings, January 1996.

[1-3] Gross. P., and P. Almquist. "IESG Deliberations on Routing and Addressing." RFC 1380, November 1992.

[1-4] Bradner, S., and A. Mankin. "IP: Next Generation (IPng) White Paper Solicitation." RFC 1550, December 1993.

[1-5] Bradner, Scott O., and Allison Mankin, editors. *IPng—Internet Protocol Next Generation*. Reading, MA: Addison-Wesley Publishing Company, 1996.

[1-6] Special issue: The Future of the Internet Protocol. *IEEE Network Magazine*, May 1993.

[1-7] Partridge, C., and F. Kastenholz. "Technical Criteria for Choosing IP The Next Generation (IPng)." RFC 1726, December 1994.

[1-8] Bradner, S., and A. Mankin. "The Recommendation for the IP Next Generation Protocol." RFC 1752, January 1995.

[1-9] McGovern, M., and R. Ullman. "CATNIP: Common Architecture for the Internet." RFC 1707, October 1994.

[1-10] McGovern, Michael, and Robert Ullmann. "The CATNIP: Purrposed Common Architecture for the Internet." *ConneXions* (May 1994): 18–27.

[1-11] Hinden, R. "Simple Internet Protocol Plus White Paper." RFC 1710, October 1994.

[1-12] Hinden, Robert M. "Simple Internet Protocol Plus (SIPP) Overview." *ConneXions* (May 1994): 34–48.

[1-13] Callon, R. "TCP and UDP with Bigger Addresses (TUBA)." RFC 1347, June 1992.

[1-14] Ford, Peter S., et al. "TUBA: CLNP as IPng." *ConneXions* (May 1994): 28–33.

[1-15] Bay Networks, Inc. *The Case for IPv6*. Available at http://www.baynetworks.com/Products/Routers/Protocols/2789.html.

[1-16] Britton, E.G., et al. "TCP/IP: The next generation." *IBM Systems Journal* (Volume 34, number 3, 1995): 452–471.

[1-17] Harrington, Daniel T., et al. "Internet Protocol Version 6 and the Digital UNIX Implementation Experience." *Digital Technical Journal* (Volume 8, Number 3, 1996): 5–22.

[1-18] Stark, Thom. "IPv6: New Master of the Net." *LAN Times* (June 16, 1996): 28.

[1-19] Cini, Al. "Dead End on the Superhighway." *Internetwork* (September 1996): 31–35.

[1-20] Miller, Mark A. "Finding Your Way Through the New IP." *Network World* (December 16, 1996): 43–45.

[1-21] Melford, Bob. "TCP/IP Limitations Undone." *SunWorld Online* (January 1997), http://sunsite.icm.edu.pl:80/sunworldonline/swol-01-1997/swol-01-ipv6.html.

[1-22] Rogers, Amy. "Mobile Computing in the 'Net." *Communications Week* (January 6, 1997).

[1-23] Arcuri, Gerald. "IP Version 6 Rolls Along." *ENT, The Independent Newspaper for Windows NT Enterprise Computing* (January 15, 1997).

[1-24] Miller, Mark A. "Making the Move—The Path for an Orderly Transition from IPv4 to IPv6." *Network World* (January 20, 1997): 37–42.

[1-25] Aubrey, David. "Bandwidth Blues." *Computer Shopper* (February 1997).

[1-26] McLean, Michelle Rae. "Tempting IP Upgrade Sparks Migration Issue." *LAN Times* (March 31, 1997): 1, 28.

[1-27] Surkan, Michael. "DEC Tunnels Toward IPv6." *PC Week* (May 26, 1997): 99, 122.

[1-28] Higgins, Kelly Jackson. "Waiting in the Wings." *Communications Week* (June 9, 1997): 31–38.

[1-29] Duffy, Jim. "IPv6 Will Change Apps, Servers." *Network World* (June 23, 1997): 26.

[1-30] Held, Gilbert. "IP for the Next Generation." *Network Magazine* (July 1997): 65–70.

The IPv6 Specification

As we studied in Chapter 1, IPv6 provides capabilities that go beyond larger addresses. These include a streamlined packet format, support for source routing, integrated authentication and encryption for enhanced security, and others. Also of importance is a key difference between the IPv4 and IPv6 architectures; IPv4 is 32-bit aligned, whereas IPv6 is 64-bit aligned. As a result, when 64-bit processors are used, IPv6 packets can be processed much faster than IPv4 packets.

In this chapter, we will study the IPv6 Specification, drawing from the key reference document, RFC 1883. But before we describe the capabilities of IPv6, let's review the existing standard, IPv4.

2.1 The Benchmark: IPv4

The Internet Protocol (IP) was developed to "provide the functions necessary to deliver a package of bits (an internet datagram) from a source to a destination over an interconnected system of networks" [2-1], and has faithfully provided that function for almost two decades. IP is primarily concerned with delivery of the datagram. Equally important, however, are the issues that IP does not address, such as the end-to-end reliable delivery of data or the sequential delivery of data. IP leaves those issues for the Host-to-Host Layer and the implementations of the Transmission Control Protocol (TCP) and the User Datagram protocol (UDP) that reside there.

The term *datagram* refers to a package of data transmitted over a connectionless network. *Connectionless* means that no connection between source and destination is established prior to data transmission. Datagram transmission is analogous to mailing a letter. With both a letter and a datagram, you write a Source and Destination address on the envelope, place the information inside, and drop the package into a mailbox for pickup. But while the post office uses blue or red mailboxes, the Internet uses your network node as the pickup point.

Another type of data transmission is a virtual circuit connection, which uses a connection-oriented network. A virtual circuit is analogous to a telephone call, where the Destination address is contacted and a path defined through the network prior to transmitting data. IP is an example of a datagram-based protocol, TCP of a virtual circuit–based protocol.

In the process of delivering datagrams, IP must deal with addressing and fragmentation. The address assures that the datagram arrives at the correct destination, whether it's across town or across the world. Fragmentation is necessary because the LANs and WANs that any datagram may traverse can have differing frame sizes, and the IP datagram must always fit within the frame, as shown in Figure 2-1. (For example, an Ethernet frame can accommodate 46–1,500 octets of data, while FDDI carries up to 4,470 octets.) Specific fields within the IP header handle the addressing and fragmentation functions (see Figure 2-2). Note from the figure that each horizontal group of bits (called a word) is 32 bits wide. (As a historical note, the 32-bit word was used with IPv4 because the original processors that implemented that protocol had 32-bit word lengths. In contrast, IPv6 is built assuming a 64-bit word, which accounts for some of the protocol processing improvements that IPv6 implementers are discovering.)

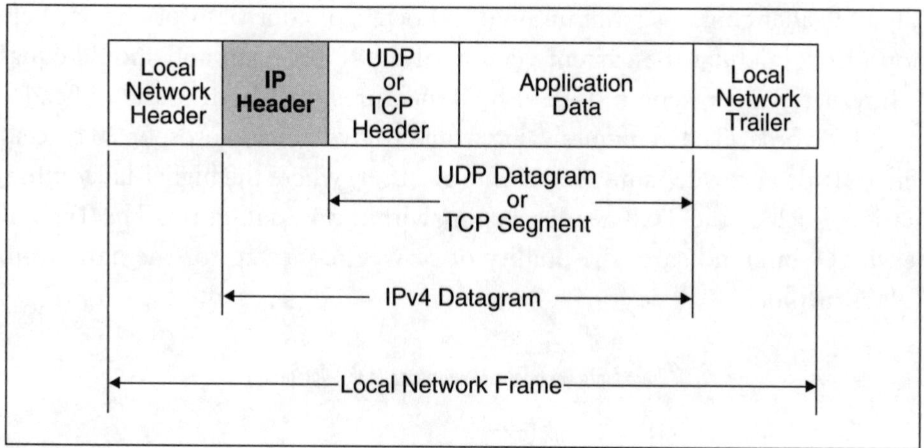

Figure 2-1. Internet transmission frame with IPv4

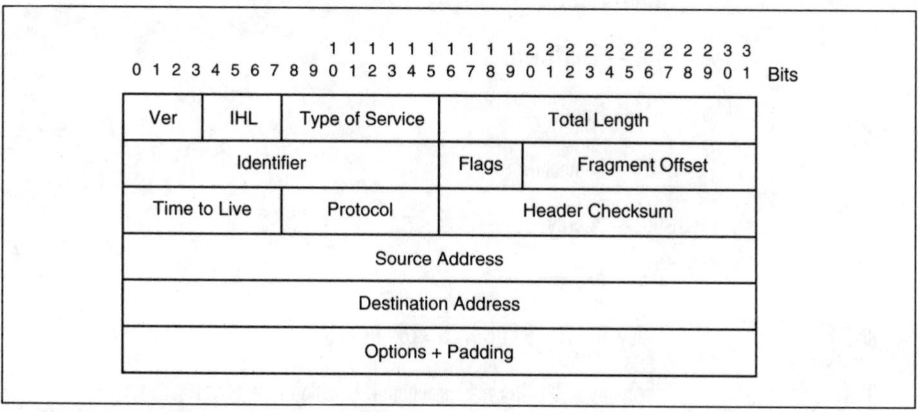

Figure 2-2. IPv4 header format

The IP header contains a minimum of 20 octets of control information. Version (4 bits) defines the current version of the IP protocol and should equal 4. Internet Header Length (IHL–4 bits) measures the length of the IP header in 32-bit words. (The minimum value would be five 32-bit words, or 20 octets.) The IHL also provides a measurement (or offset) where the higher-layer information, such as the TCP header, begins within that datagram. The Type of Service (8 bits) indicates the quality of service requested for the datagram. Values include:

Bits 0–2:	Precedence (or relative importance of this datagram)
	111—Network Control
	110—Internetwork Control
	101—CRITIC/ECP
	100—Flash Override
	011—Flash
	010—Immediate
	001—Priority
	000—Routine
Bit 3:	Delay, 0 = Normal Delay, 1 = Low Delay
Bit 4:	Throughput, 0 = Normal Throughput, 1 = High Throughput
Bit 5:	Reliability, 0 = Normal Reliability, 1 = High Reliability
Bits 6–7:	Reserved for future use (set to 0)

The Total Length field (16 bits) measures the length, in octets, of the IP datagram (IP header plus higher-layer information). The 16-bit field allows for a datagram of up to 65,535 octets, although all hosts must be able to handle datagrams of at least 576 octets.

The next 32-bit word contains three fields that deal with datagram fragmentation/reassembly. Recall that the IP datagram may be up to 65,535 octets long. What happens if the endpoint of a WAN that handles such a datagram is attached to an IEEE 802.3 LAN with a maximum data field size of 1,500 octets? IP fragments the large IP datagram into smaller pieces (i.e., fragments) that will fit. The Destination node reassembles all the fragments (sort of the antithesis of Humpty Dumpty). The sender assigns the Identification field (16 bits) to help reassemble the fragments into the datagram. Three flags indicate how the fragmentation process will be handled:

Bit 0:	Reserved (set to 0)
Bit 1:	(DF) 0 = May fragment, 1 = Don't fragment
Bit 2:	(MF) 0 = Last fragment, 1 = More fragments

The last field in this word is a 13-bit fragment offset, which indicates where a fragment belongs in the complete message. This offset is measured in 64-bit units.

The next word in the IP header contains a Time-to-Live (TTL) measurement, which is the maximum amount of time the datagram can live within the internet. When TTL = 0, the datagram is destroyed. This field is a failsafe measure, preventing misaddressed datagrams from wandering the internet forever. TTL may be measured in either router hops or seconds. If the measurement is in seconds, the maximum is 255 seconds, or 4.25 minutes (a long time to be lost in today's high-speed internetworks). The Assigned Numbers document (currently RFC 1700) specifies a default TTL = 64.

The Protocol field (8 bits) following the IP header identifies the higher-layer protocol in use. Examples include:

Decimal	Keyword	Description
1	ICMP	Internet Control Message Protocol
6	TCP	Transmission Control Protocol
17	UDP	User Datagram Protocol

The "Assigned Numbers" document (currently RFC 1700) [3-4] and Appendix G provide a more detailed listing of the protocols defined. A 16-bit header checksum completes the third 32-bit word.

The fourth and fifth words of the IP header contain the Source and Destination addresses, respectively. Recall that we discussed hardware addresses for the ARPA Network Interface Layer (or OSI Data Link Layer). The addresses within the IP header are the Internet Layer (or OSI Network Layer) addresses. The Internet address is a Logical address that gets the IP datagram through the internet to the correct host and network (LAN, MAN, or WAN). Chapter 3 will discuss both the IPv4 and IPv6 address structures in detail.

2.2 The IPv6 Specification

The IPv6 specification is defined in RFC 1883 [2-2], with additional work that documents proposed enhancements to these efforts [2-3]. RFC 1883 summarizes the following changes from IPv4 to IPv6:

- Expanded Addressing Capabilities—Increasing the address size from 32 bits to 128 bits, supporting more levels of address hierarchy, many more addressable nodes, scalable multicast addresses, plus the "anycast" address, which is used to send a packet to any one of a group of nodes.
- Header Format Simplification—Eliminating or making optional some of the header fields, thus reducing the protocol processing overhead of the IPv6 header.

- Improved Support for Extensions and Options—Including more efficient forwarding, less stringent limits on the length of options, and greater flexibility for future options.
- Flow Labeling Capability—A new function which enables packets that belong to a particular traffic "flow" to be labeled for special handling.
- Authentication and Privacy—Extensions to support authentication, data integrity, and optional data confidentiality.

In order to support these design changes, the structure of the IPv6 packet varies somewhat from its predecessor, IPv4. First of all, fields that were seldom used have been eliminated. Second, fields that provide a specific function have been removed from the base header and placed in optional extension headers. In this way, the extension header or headers are only added when required by a specific protocol function, such as fragmentation or packet routing. There is also a recommended order for these extension headers, such that headers that are only germane to the end-to-end host process need not be examined by every router along the way. The next section will explore the IPv6 base header and all of the extension headers in detail.

2.3 IPv6 Terminology

RFC 1883, section 2, defines some terms that will be relevant to our discussion of the IPv6 architecture. These definitions are paraphrased below:

Node: A device that implements IPv6.

Router: A node that forwards IPv6 packets not explicitly addressed to itself [see next page].

Host: Any node that is not a router [see next page].

Upper layer: A protocol layer immediately above IPv6, such as ICMP, OSPF, TCP, UDP, etc.

Link: A communication facility or medium over which nodes can communicate at the Data Link Layer, such as Ethernet, token ring, frame relay, PPP, etc.

Neighbors: Nodes attached to the same link.

Interface: A node's attachment to a link.

Address: An IPv6-layer identifier for an interface or a set of interfaces.

Packet: An IPv6 header plus payload.

Link MTU: The maximum transmission unit, or packet size, given in octets, that can be conveyed in one piece over a link.

Path MTU: The minimum link MTU of all the links in a path between a source node and a destination node.

Note: It is possible, though unusual, for a device with multiple interfaces to be configured to forward non-self-destined packets arriving from some set (fewer than all) of its interfaces, and to discard non-self-destined packets arriving from its other interfaces. Such a device must obey the protocol requirements for routers when receiving packets from, and interacting with neighbors over, the former (forwarding) interfaces. It must obey the protocol requirements for hosts when receiving packets from, and interacting with neighbors over, the latter (nonforwarding) interfaces.

From the definitions above, notice that an IPv6 *node* may deploy router, host, or both router and host functions. Secondly, the term *upper layer* has a slightly different meaning in the context of IPv6. When used here, it means the next highest protocol layer. Examples cited in the specification (such as the Internet Control Message Protocol—ICMP or the Open Shortest Path First—OSPF protocol) are both routing (OSI Network Layer) protocols. In more traditional networking parlance, the term upper layer might be construed to mean an Application Layer Protocol, such as the File Transfer Protocol (FTP) or the Simple Network Management Protocol (SNMP). Finally, the distinction between the *link MTU* and the *path MTU* implies that there are mechanisms that keep track of these values. As we will discover in subsequent chapters, routers can assign a link MTU to a workstation on that link, and hosts can discover the path MTU prior to sending a packet to the desired destination.

2.4 The IPv6 Header

The IPv6 packet is carried within a local network frame much like the IPv4 case; however, the IPv6 header consists of two parts: the IPv6 base header, plus optional extension headers (Figure 2-3). With or without any optional extension headers, a fixed size constraint on the local network frame must be respected. For example, the maximum amount of data that can be carried in an Ethernet frame is 1,500 octets. If extension headers are added to the IPv6 packet, less application data can be sent. The host and/or its operating system should have a mechanism to manage this.

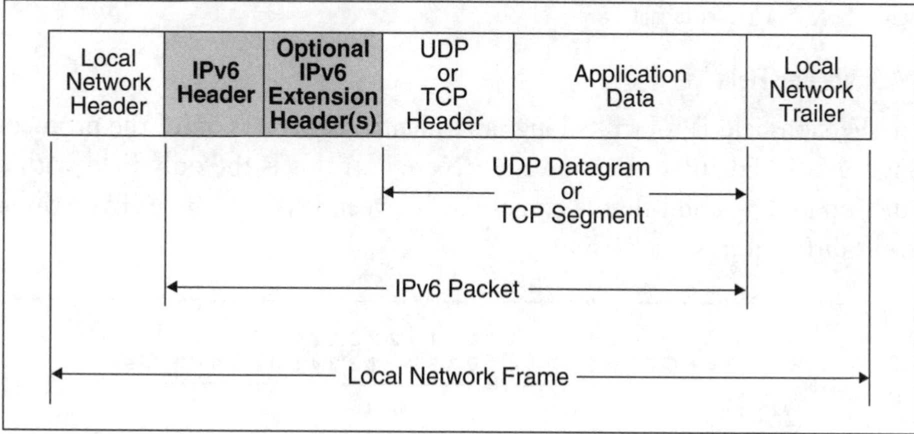

Figure 2-3. Internet transmission frame with IPv6

The IPv6 header is 40 octets long, with eight fields and two addresses (Figure 2-4). Compare this with the IPv4 header, which is 20 octets long, has ten fields, two addresses, and options.

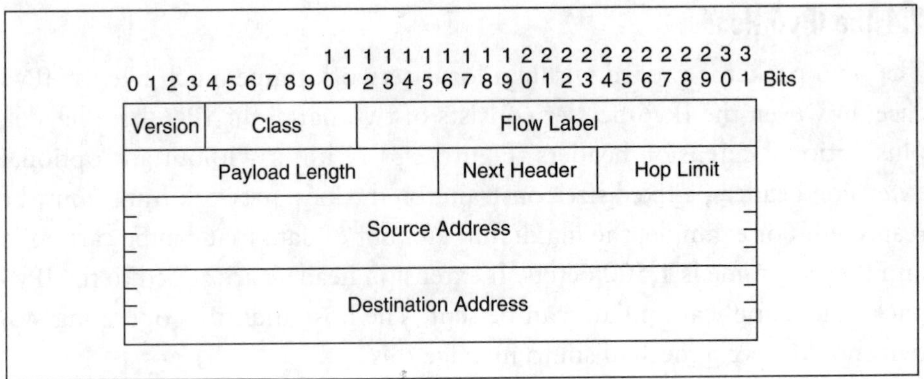

Figure 2-4. IPv6 header format

2.4.1 Version Field

The Version field is four bits long, and identifies the version of the protocol (Figure 2-5). For IPv6, Version = 6. (Note that this is the only field with a function and position that is consistent between IPv4 and IPv6. Everything else is different in some fashion.)

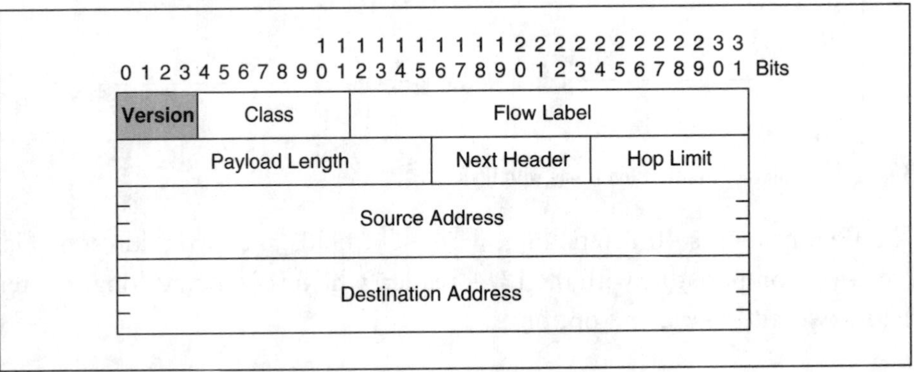

Figure 2-5. Version field

2.4.2 Class Field

The Class field (Figure 2-6) is eight bits long, and is intended for originating nodes and/or forwarding routers to identify and distinguish between different classes or priorities of IPv6 packets. (In the first publication of the IPv6 Specification RFC 1883 [2-2], this field was called the *Priority* field, reflecting this function. Enhancements to this work [2-3] renamed it the *Class* field, with a length of four bits. Futher work at the IPng Meeting at the Munich IETF plenary in August 1997 expanded the Class field to eight bits, and reduced the Flow Label field to 20 bits (from the previous 24) [2-4]). This field replaces the functions that were provided by the IPv4 Type of Service field, allowing differentiation between different categories of packet transfer service. At the time of this writing, all eight bits of the Class field have been reserved pending further definition. As such, they are set to zero on transmission and ignored on reception.

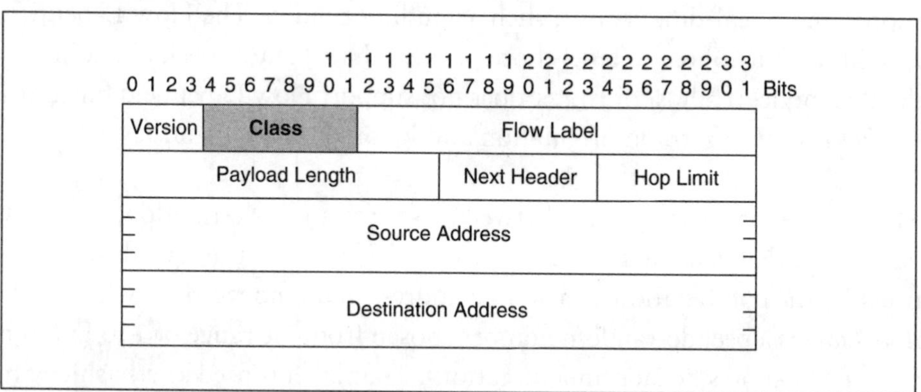

Figure 2-6. Proposed Class field

2.4.3 Flow Label Field

The Flow Label field (Figure 2-7) is 20 bits long, and may be used by a host to request special handling for certain packets, such as those with a nondefault quality of service or real-time quality of service. In the first version of the IPv6 Specification, RFC 1883, this field was 24 bits long but four of these bits have now been allocated to the Class field, as discussed in the previous section.

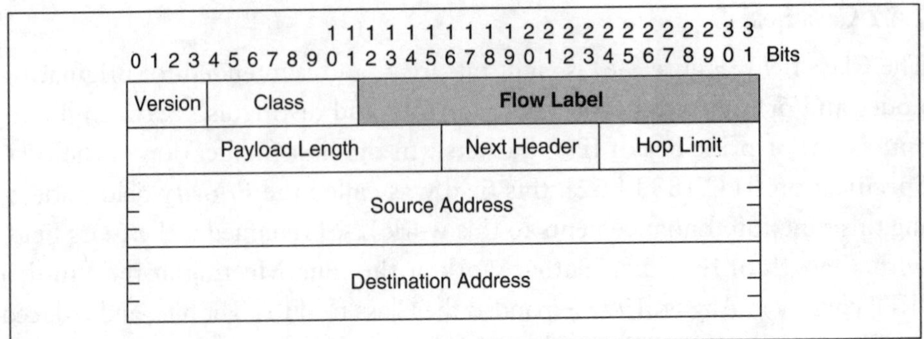

Figure 2-7. Flow Label field

A *flow* is a sequence of packets sent either to a unicast or a multicast destination that need special handling by the intervening IPv6 routers. All packets belonging to the same flow must be sent with the same source address, destination address, and flow label. An example of a flow would be packets supporting a real-time service, such as audio or video. The Flow Label field is used by that source to label those packets that require special handling by the IPv6 node. If a host or router does not support Flow Label field functions, the field is set to zero on origination and ignored on reception.

Multiple data flows may exist between a source and a destination, as well as data traffic that is not associated with a particular flow. A unique flow is identified by the combination of a source address and a nonzero flow label. The *flow label* is a pseudo-random number chosen from the range of 1 to FFFFFH (where H denotes hexadecimal notation). That label is used as a hash key by routers to look up the state associated with that flow.

RFC 1809, "Using the Flow Label Field in IPv6" [2-5] describes some of the earlier research on the subject. Like the Class field, the Flow Label field is the subject of current research and may change as industry experience matures.

2.4.4 Payload Length Field

The Payload Length field (Figure 2-8) is a 16-bit unsigned integer which measures the length, given in octets, of the payload (i.e. the balance of the IPv6 packet that follows the base IPv6 header). Note that optional extension headers are considered part of the payload, along with any upper-layer protocols, such as TCP, FTP, etc.

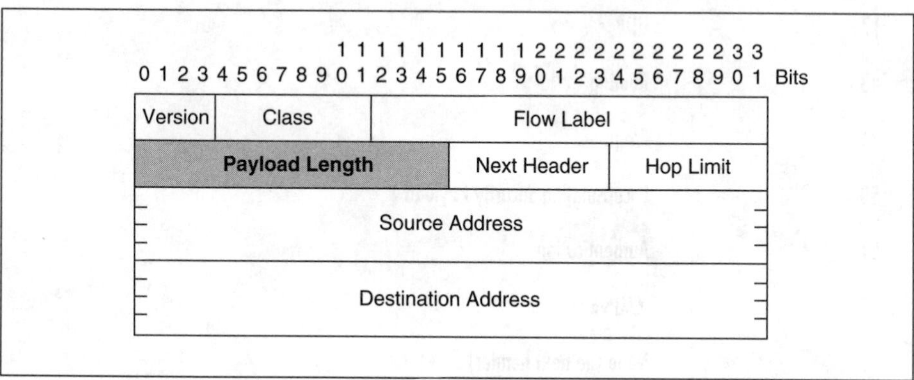

Figure 2-8. Payload Length field

The Payload Length field is similar to the IPv4 Total Length field, except that the two measurements operate on different fields. The Payload Length (IPv6) measures the data *after* the header, while the Total Length (IPv4) measures the data *and* the header.

Payloads greater than 65,535 are allowed and are called *jumbo payloads*. To indicate a jumbo payload, the value of the Payload Length is set to zero and the actual payload length is specified within an option that is carried in a Hop-by-Hop extension header. We will consider the format of this option in a following section.

2.4.5 Next Header Field

The Next Header field (Figure 2-9) is eight bits long, and identifies the header immediately following the IPv6 header. This field uses the same values as the IPv4 Protocol field. Examples are:

Value	Header
0	Hop-by-Hop Options
1	ICMPv4
4	IP in IP (encapsulation)
6	TCP
17	UDP
43	Routing
44	Fragment
50	Encapsulating Security Payload
51	Authentication
58	ICMPv6
59	None (no next header)
60	Destination Options

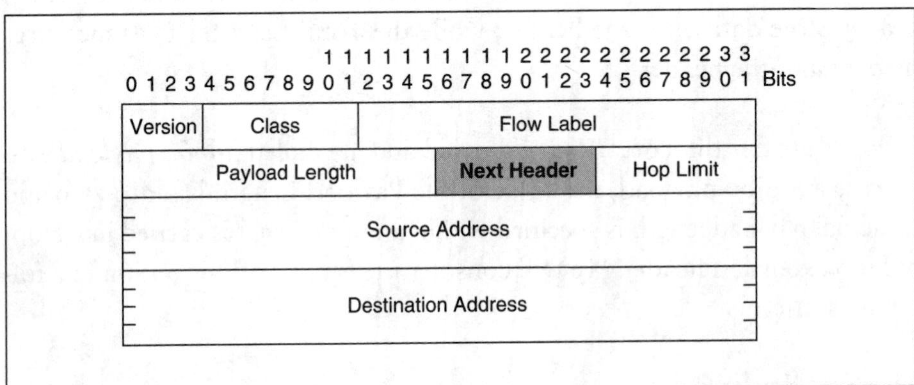

Figure 2-9. Next Header field

An IPv6 packet, which consists of an IPv6 packet header plus its payload, may consist of zero, one, or more extension headers, as shown in Figure 2-10. Many of the extension headers also employ a Next Header field. Note the values of the Next Header fields in each example shown in the figure. In the first case, no extension headers are required, the Next Header = TCP, and the TCP header and any upper-layer protocol data follows. In the second case, a Routing header is required. Therefore, the IPv6 Next Header = Routing; in the Routing header, Next Header = TCP, and the TCP header and any upper-layer protocol data follows. In the third case, both the Routing and Fragment headers are required, with the Next Header fields identified accordingly.

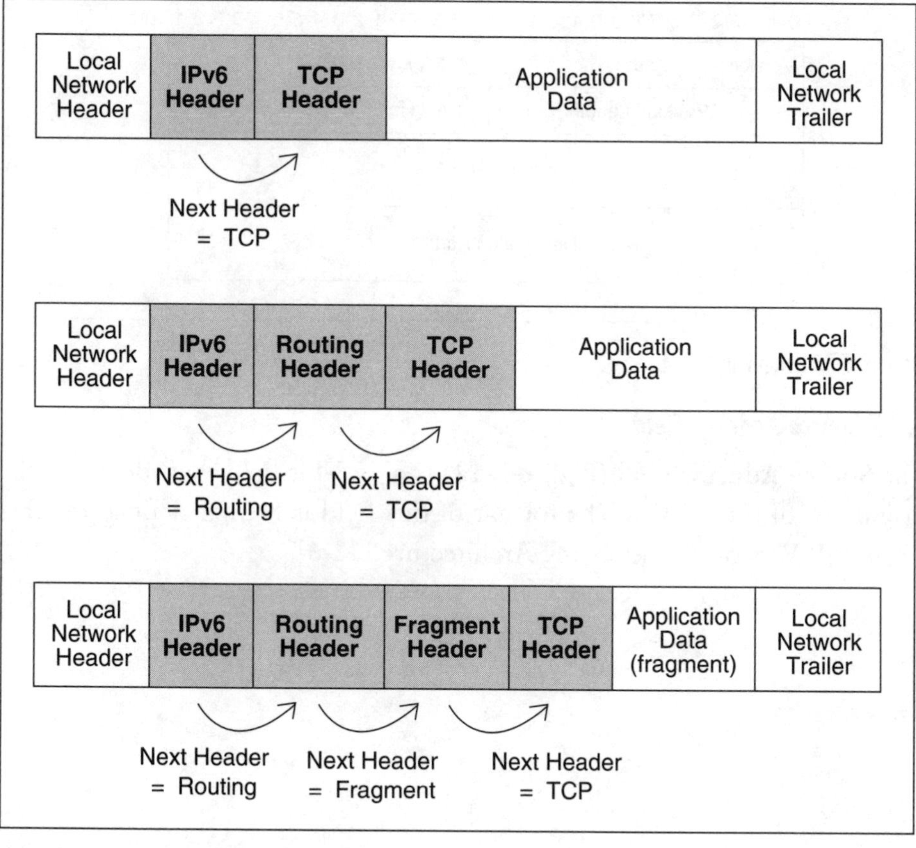

Figure 2-10. Next Header field operation

2.4.6 Hop Limit Field

The Hop Limit field (Figure 2-11) is eight bits long, and is decremented by one by each node that forwards the packet. When the Hop Limit equals zero, the packet is discarded and an error message is returned. This field is similar to the Time to Live (TTL) field found in IPv4, with one key exception. The Hop Limit field (IPv6) measures the maximum number of hops that can occur as the packet is forwarded by various nodes. The TTL field (IPv4) can be measured in either hops or seconds. Note that with the Hop Limit used in IPv6, the time basis is no longer available.

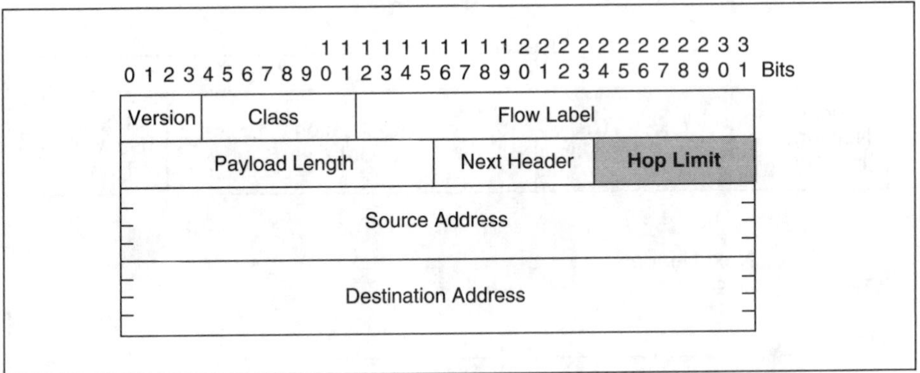

Figure 2-11. Hop Limit field

2.4.7 Source Address Field

The Source Address field (Figure 2-12) is a 128-bit field that identifies the originator of the packet. The format of this field is further defined in RFC 1884, "IP Version 6 Addressing Architecture" [2-6].

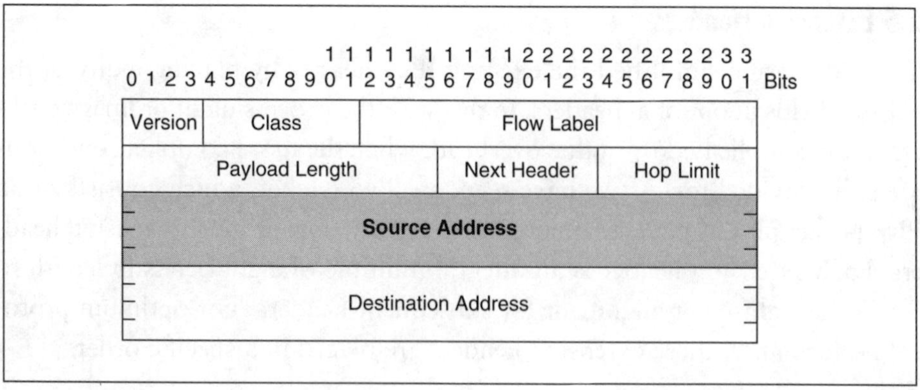

1 1 1 1 1 1 1 1 1 1 2 2 2 2 2 2 2 2 2 2 3 3
0 1 2 3 4 5 6 7 8 9 0 1 2 3 4 5 6 7 8 9 0 1 2 3 4 5 6 7 8 9 0 1 Bits
Version
Class
Flow Label
Payload Length
Next Header
Hop Limit
Source Address
Destination Address

Figure 2-12. Source Address field

2.4.8 Destination Address Field

The Destination Address field (Figure 2-13) is a 128-bit field that identifies the intended recipient of the packet. An important distinction is that the *intended* recipient may not be the *ultimate* recipient, as a Routing header may be employed to specify the path that the packet takes from its source, through intermediate destination(s), and on to its final destination.

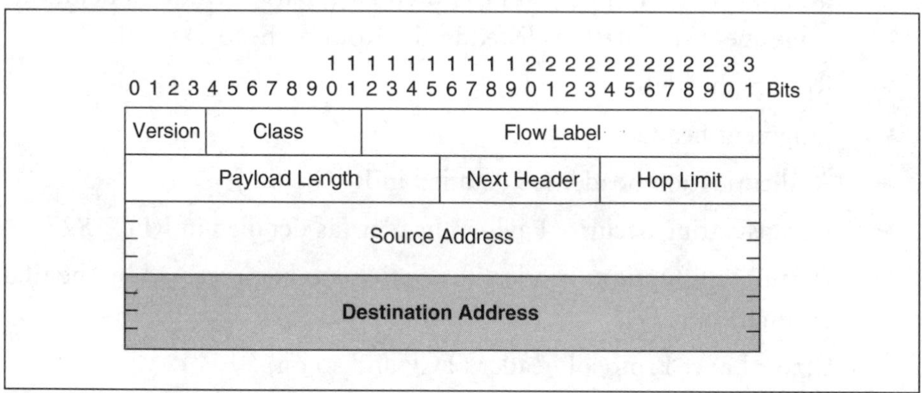

Figure 2-13. Destination Address field

2.5 Extension Headers

The IPv6 design simplified the existing IPv4 header by placing many of the existing fields in optional headers. In this way, the processing of ordinary packets is not complicated by undue overhead, while the more complex conditions are still provided for. As we have seen, an IPv6 packet, which consists of an IPv6 packet plus its payload, may consist of zero, one, or more extension headers. Each extension header is an integral multiple of eight octets in length to retain the eight-octet alignment for subsequent headers. For optimum protocol performance, these extension headers are placed in a specific order.

2.5.1 Extension Header Order

RFC 1883 recommends that the extension headers be placed in the IPv6 packet in a particular order:

- IPv6 header
- Hop-by-Hop Options header
- Destination Options header (for options to be processed by the first destination that appears in the IPv6 Destination Address field, plus subsequent destinations listed in the Routing header)
- Routing header
- Fragment header
- Authentication header (as detailed in RFC 1826)
- Encapsulating Security Payload header (as detailed in RFC 1827)
- Destination Options header (for options to be processed by the final destination only)
- Upper Layer Protocol header (TCP and so on)

Figure 2-14 illustrates the IPv6 and optional headers, with their suggested order.

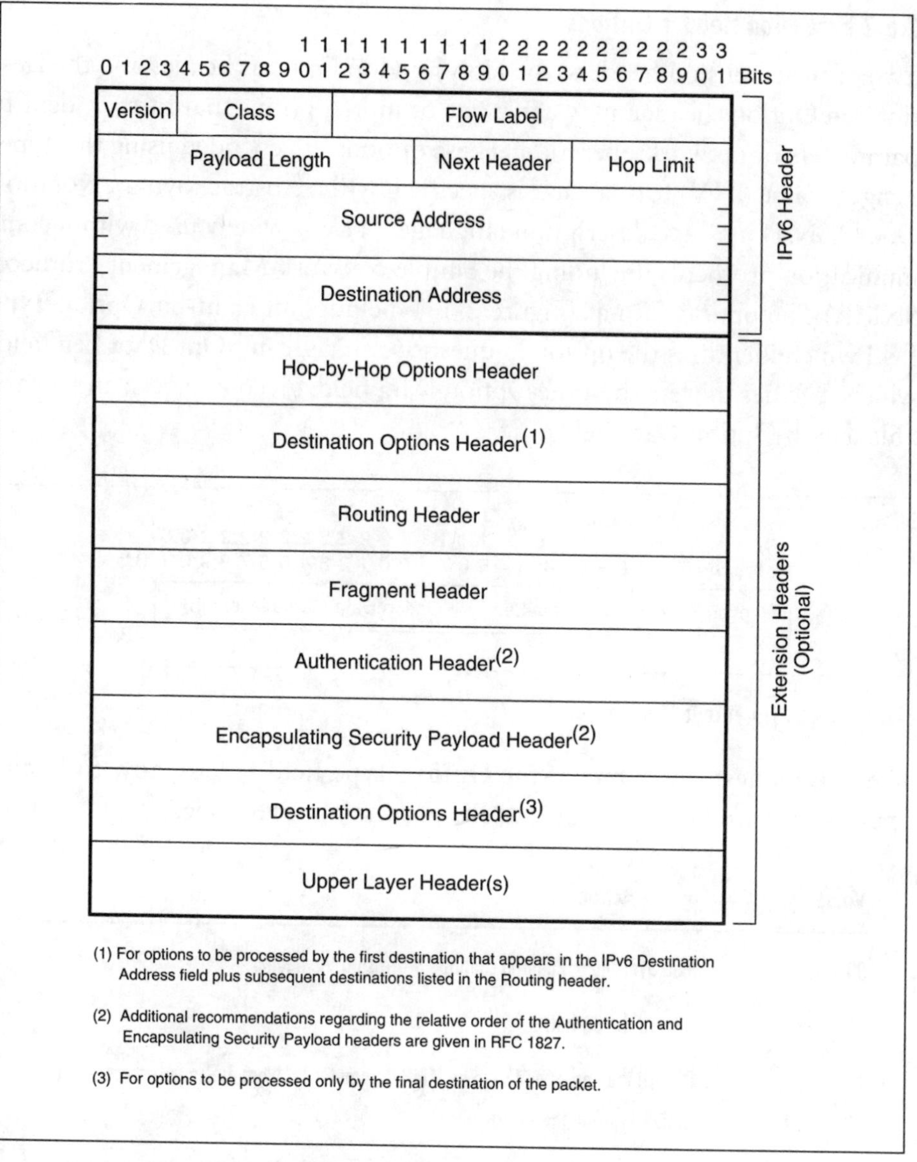
1 1 1 1 1 1 1 1 1 1 2 2 2 2 2 2 2 2 2 2 3 3
0 1 2 3 4 5 6 7 8 9 0 1 2 3 4 5 6 7 8 9 0 1 2 3 4 5 6 7 8 9 0 1 Bits
Version
Class
Flow Label
Payload Length
Next Header
Hop Limit
Source Address
Destination Address
IPv6 Header
Hop-by-Hop Options Header
Destination Options Header(1)
Routing Header
Fragment Header
Authentication Header(2)
Encapsulating Security Payload Header(2)
Destination Options Header(3)
Upper Layer Header(s)
Extension Headers (Optional)
(1) For options to be processed by the first destination that appears in the IPv6 Destination Address field plus subsequent destinations listed in the Routing header.
(2) Additional recommendations regarding the relative order of the Authentication and Encapsulating Security Payload headers are given in RFC 1827.
(3) For options to be processed only by the final destination of the packet.

Figure 2-14. IPv6 packet format with optional extension headers

2.5.2 Extension Header Options

Two of the extension headers, the Hop-by-Hop Options header and the Destination Options header, may carry one or more options that further identify parameters or network operation. These options are encoded using the Type-Length-Value (TLV) format that is specified by the Abstract Syntax Notation One (ASN.1) message description language. (TLV is widely used within communication protocols, including the Simple Network Management Protocol, SNMP.) The option format (Figure 2-15) includes an eight-bit Option Type field which identifies the option in question; an eight-bit Opt Data Len field, which specifies the length of the Option Data field, given in octets; and a variable length Option Data field.

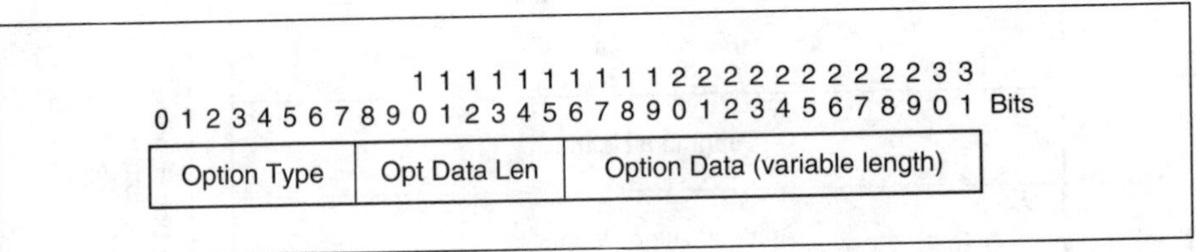

Figure 2-15. TLV encoded options format

The two highest-order bits of the Option Type field specify how to handle options that are unrecognizable at the processing IPv6 node:

Value	Action
00	Skip over the option and continue processing the header.
01	Discard the packet.
10	Discard the packet and send an ICMP Parameter Problem message (unrecognized Option Type) to the source.
11	Discard the packet and send an ICMP Parameter Problem message (unrecognized Option Type) to the source (only if destination was not multicast).

The third-highest-order bit of the Option Type field specifies whether or not the Option Data of that option can change en route to the packet's final destination:

Value	Action
0	Option data does not change en route.
1	Option data may change en route.

In addition, there are two options that are used, as necessary, to pad the options such that the extension header contains a multiple of eight octets. The Pad1 Option (Figure 2-16) is used to insert one octet of padding into the Options area of a header. Note that this option is a special case (noted by Type = 0) that does not have Opt Data Len or Option Data fields.

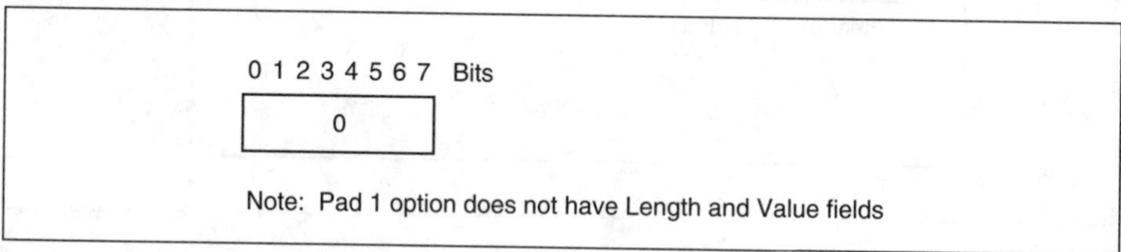

Figure 2-16. Pad1 Option format

The PadN Option (Figure 2-17) is used to insert two or more octets of padding into the Options area of a header. Note that this option has a Type field = 1. If the padding desired was N octets, the Opt Data Len field would contain the value of N-2, and the Option Data field would contain N-2 zero-valued octets.

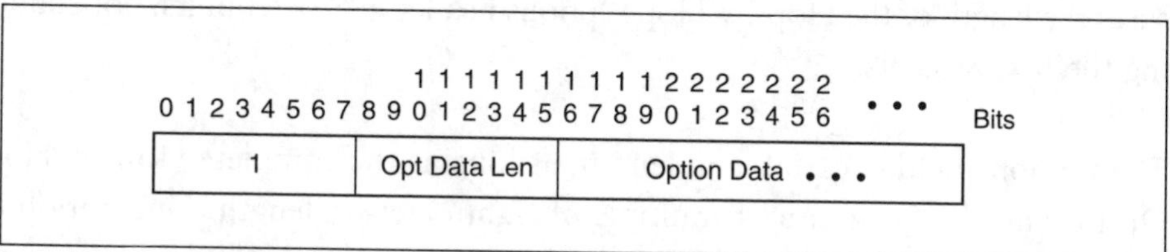

Figure 2-17. PadN Option format

Guidelines for designing new options are presented in Appendix A of RFC 1883.

2.5.3 Hop-by-Hop Options Header

The Hop-by-Hop Options header carries optional information that must be examined by every node along a packet's delivery path (see Figure 2-18). As a result, the Hop-by-Hop Options header, when present, must immediately follow the IPv6 header. (The other extension headers are not examined or processed by any node along a packet's delivery path until the packet reaches its intended destination(s).) The presence of the Hop-by-Hop Options header is identified by a value of 0 in the Next Header field of the IPv6 header. This header contains two fields, plus options.

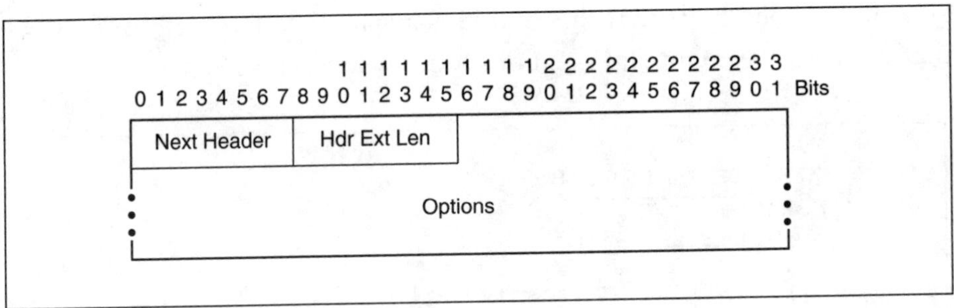

Figure 2-18. Hop-by-Hop Options header format

The Next Header field is eight bits long, and identifies the header immediately following the Hop-by-Hop Options header. This field uses the same values as the IPv4 Protocol field.

The Header Extension Length (Hdr Ext Len) field is eight bits long, and measures the length of the Hop-by-Hop Options header in 8-octet units, not counting the first 8 octets.

The Options field is variable in length, as long as the complete Hop-by-Hop Options header is an integer multiple of eight octets in length. One option is defined in RFC 1883, the Jumbo Payload option, which is used to send IPv6 packets that are longer than 65,535 octets (Figure 2-19). This option is defined by Option Type = 194, Opt Data Len = 4 (octets), and a four-octet field which carries the length of the jumbo packet in octets (excluding the IPv6 base header, but including the Hop-by-Hop Options header and any other headers). Note that the Jumbo Payload Length must be greater than 65,535. In addition, the Payload Length field = 0 (to indicate a special condition) when the Jumbo Payload is used.

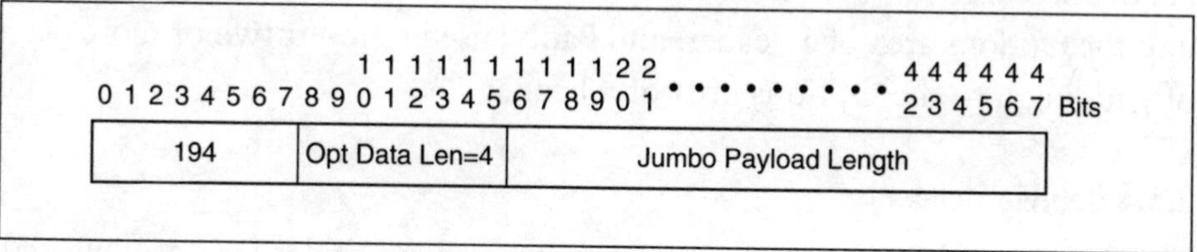

Figure 2-19. Jumbo Payload option format

2.5.4 Destination Options Header

The Destination Options header carries optional information that need be examined only by a packet's destination node(s), as shown in Figure 2-20. The presence of the Destination Options header is identified by a value of 60 in the preceding header's Next Header field. This header contains two fields plus options.

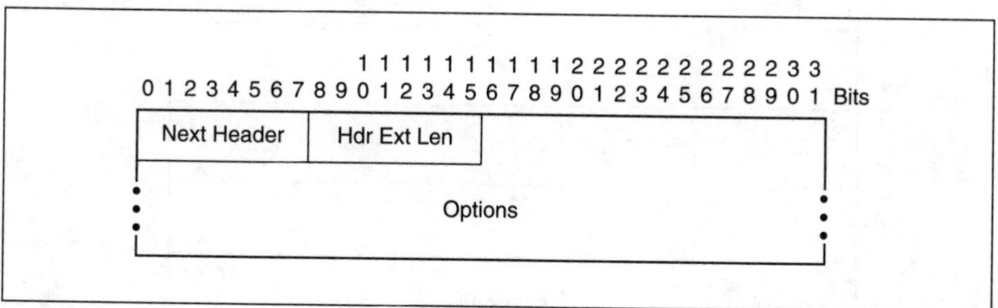

Figure 2-20. Destination Options header format

The Next Header field is eight bits long, and identifies the header immediately following the Destination Options header. This field uses the same values as the IPv4 Protocol field.

The Header Extension Length (Hdr Ext Len) field is eight bits long, and measures the length of the Destination Options header in 8-octet units, not counting the first 8 octets.

The Options field is variable in length, such that the complete Destination Options header is an integer multiple of eight octets in length. Only two options are defined in RFC 1883: the Pad1 option, used to insert one octet of padding into the Options area of a header; and PadN, used to insert two or more octets of padding into the Options area of a header.

2.5.5 Routing Header

The Routing header lists one or more intermediate nodes that are "visited" on the path from the source to the destination (see Figure 2-21). The presence of the Routing header is identified by a value of 43 in the preceding header's Next Header field. This header contains four fields, plus type-specific data.

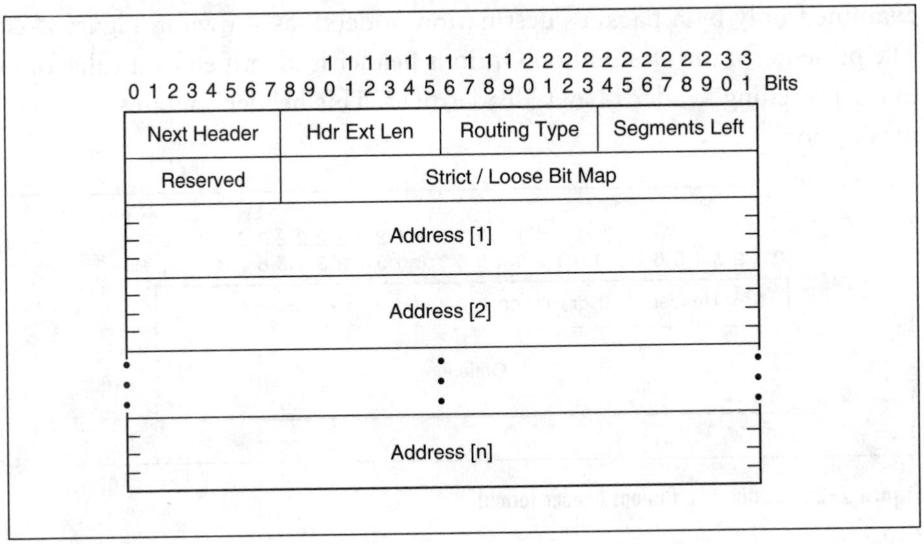

Figure 2-21. Routing header format (Type 0)

The Next Header field is eight bitslong, and identifies the header immediately following the Routing header. This field uses the same values as the IPv4 Protocol field.

The Header Extension Length (Hdr Ext Len) field is eight bits long, and measures the length of the Routing header in 8-octet units, not counting the first 8 octets. (For the Type 0 Routing header, as described below, this number is equal to two times the number of addresses in the header, and must be an even number less than or equal to 46.)

The Routing Type field is eight bits long and identifies a particular Routing header variant. (RFC 1883 defines one variant, Routing Type 0.)

The Segments Left field is eight bits long, and indicates the number of route segments remaining, or, in other words, the number of explicitly listed intermediate nodes still to be visited, before reaching the final destination.

The Type-Specific field is variable in length, with a format defined by the particular Routing Type variant. (For example, RFC 1883 defines the format for the Routing Type 0 header, as mentioned above.) This variant of the Routing header includes a Strict/Loose Bit Map field which is 24 bits long. This bit map indicates for each segment of the route whether the next destination must be a neighbor of the preceding address (S/L = 1) or whether it need not be a neighbor (S/L = 0). A list of 128-bit addresses would complete the Routing Header.

RFC 1883 gives an example of the usage of the Routing header, which is shown pictorially in Figure 2-22. In this example, note that three intermediate nodes (and four segments) separate the Source node (S) from the Destination node (D).

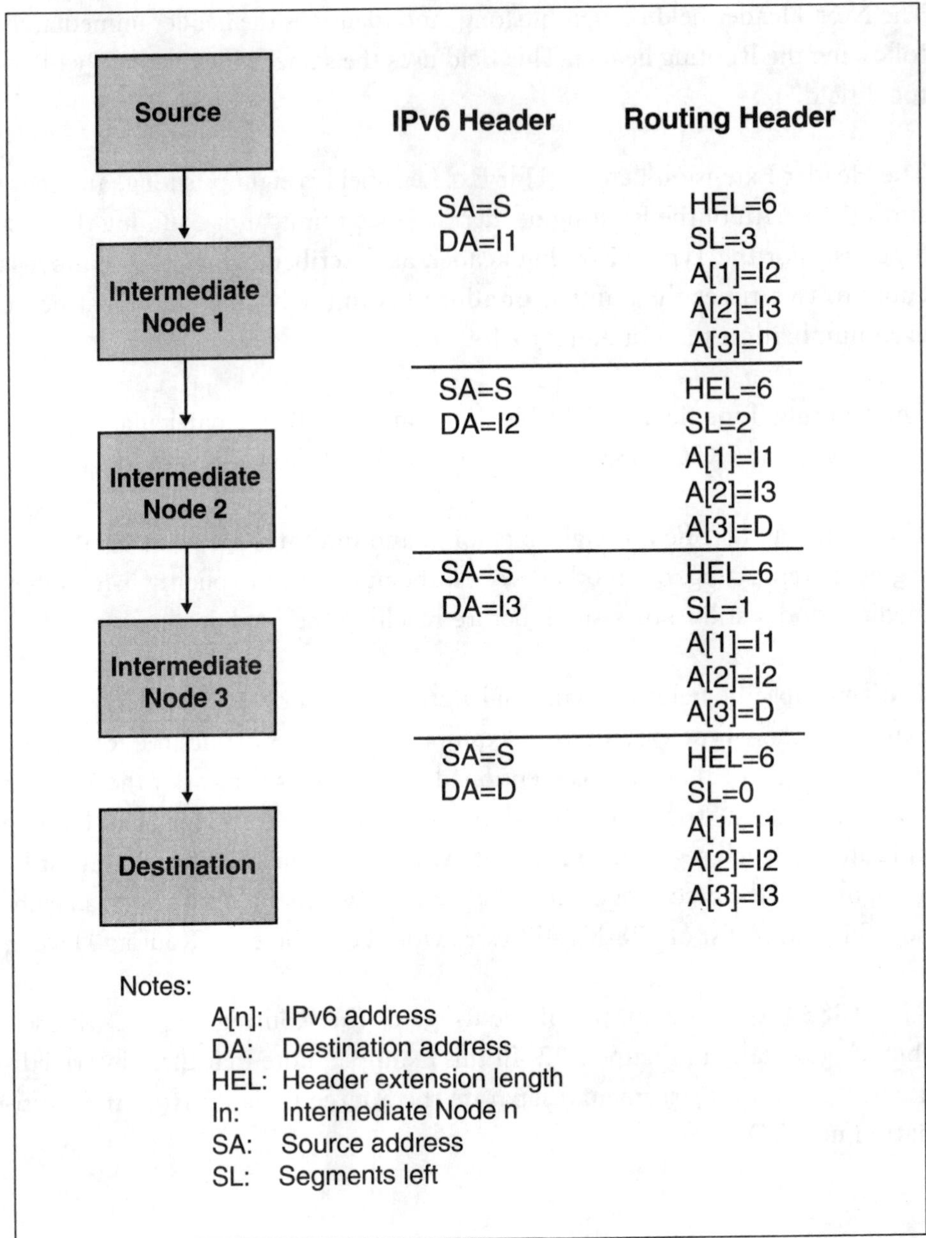

Figure 2-22. Routing header usage

To travel from the Source node to Intermediate Node 1, the IPv6 base header uses Source Address (SA) = S, and Destination Address (DA) = Intermediate Node 1 (I1). The Routing header specifies a Header Extension Length = 6, Segments Left = 3, and the addresses of the three remaining nodes along the path: Intermediate Node 2 (I2), Intermediate Node 3 (I3), and the Destination node (D).

To travel from I1 to I2, the routing algorithm exchanges the IPv6 Destination Address with the first address in the address list (I2). Note that the Source Address (SA = S) will be consistent for all segments.

To travel from I2 to I3, the routing algorithm exchanges the IPv6 Destination Address with the second address in the address list (I3).

To travel from I3 to the final destination (D), the routing algorithm exchanges the IPv6 Destination Address with the third address in the address list (D). Note that the final state of the IPv6 header addresses is now SA = S and DA = D, and the Routing header addresses list the intermediate nodes, I1, I2, and I3, in the order that they were visited.

2.5.6 Fragment Header

The Fragment header (see Figure 2-23) is used by an IPv6 source to send packets that are larger than would fit in the path maximum transmission unit (MTU) to their destinations. The presence of the Fragment header is identified by a value of 44 in the preceding header's Next Header field. Note that fragmentation for IPv6 is only done at the source node, not at intermediate routers along the packet's delivery path; this is a procedural change from IPv4.

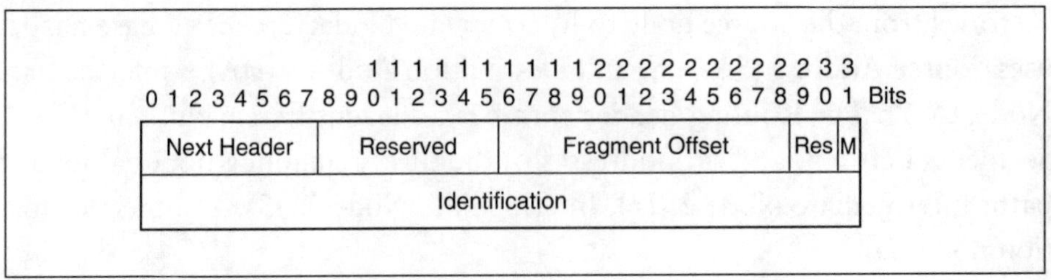

Figure 2-23. Fragment header format

The Fragment header contains six fields. The Next Header field is eight bits long, and identifies the header immediately following the Fragment header. This field uses the same values as the IPv4 Protocol field.

The Reserved field is eight bits long, and is reserved for future use. This field is initialized to zero for transmission and is ignored on reception.

The Fragment Offset field is a 13-bit unsigned integer which measures the offset, in 8-octet units, of the data following this header, relative to the start of the fragmentable part of the original packet.

The Reserved field is two bits long, and is reserved for future use. This field is initialized to zero for transmission and is ignored on reception.

The M flag is one bit long and determines whether more fragments are coming (M = 1) or whether this is the last fragment (M = 0).

The Identification field is 32 bits long and uniquely identifies the fragmented packet(s) during the reassembly process. This field is generated by the source node.

A packet requiring fragmentation is considered to consist of two parts: an unfragmentable part and a fragmentable part (Figure 2-24a). The unfragmentable part includes the IPv6 header, plus any extension headers that must be processed en route to the destination; these may include a Hop-by-Hop header and a Routing header. The fragmentable part is the balance of the packet, which may include any extension headers that are processed at the final destination node(s), the upper layer headers, and application data.

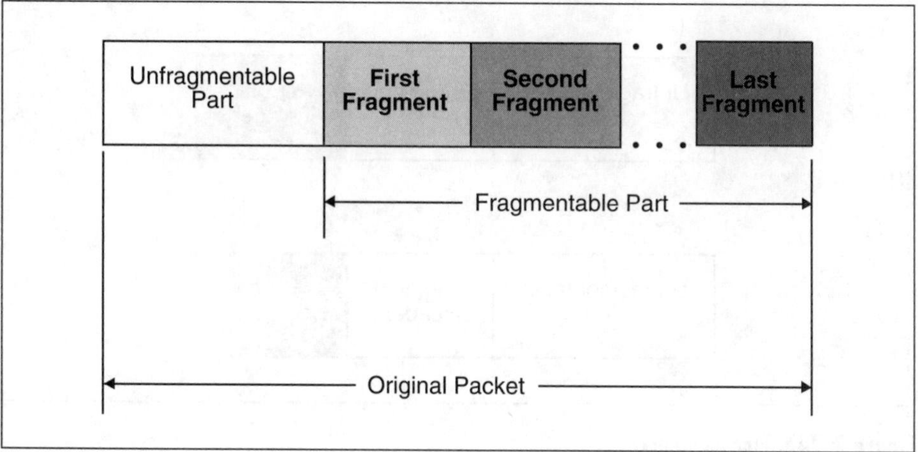

Figure 2-24a. Original packet requiring fragmentation

The fragmentable part of the original packet is divided into fragments that are an integral multiple of eight octets (except perhaps for the last fragment, which may not be an integral multiple of eight octets), as shown in Figure 2-24b. Each fragment packet consists of three parts: the unfragmentable part of the original packet, a Fragment header, and a data fragment. The unfragmentable part of each fragment contains a revised Payload Length field (within the IPv6 header portion) that matches the length of this fragment, and a Next Header field = 44 (indicating that a Fragment header comes next). The lengths of the fragments are chosen such that the resulting fragment packets fit within the MTU of the path to the packets' destination(s). (A related process, called Path MTU Discovery, will be explored in Chapter 4.) At the destination node(s), a process called reassembly is used to reconstruct the original packet from the fragment packets. The reassembly process is also described in RFC 1883.

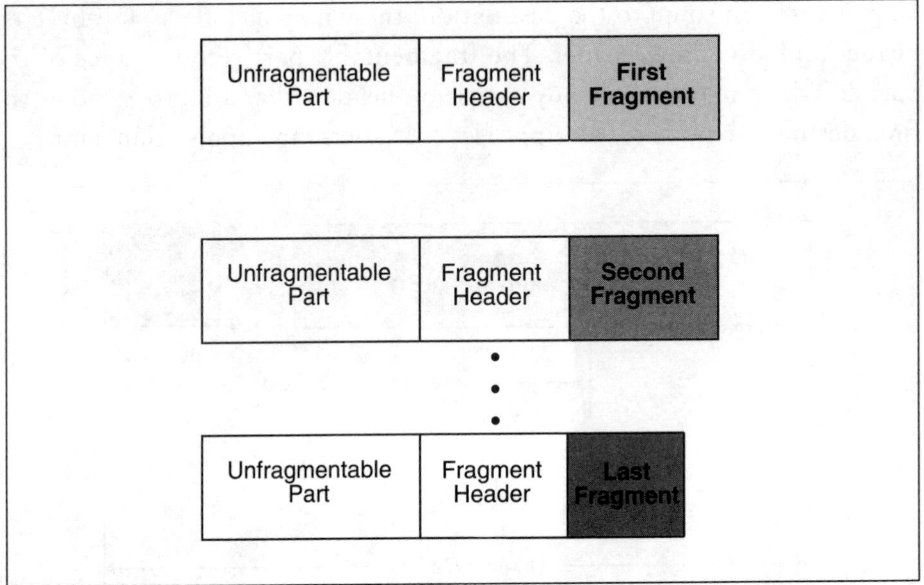

Figure 2-24b. Fragment packets

2.5.7 Authentication Header

Assuring secure data transmissions has become an increasingly important issue for network managers. The Internet community has addressed these issues in RFC 1825, "Security Architecture for the Internet Protocol" [2-7], with additional work that documents many proposed enhancements to these efforts [2-8]. Chapter 7 will discuss this architecture in detail.

Two headers are discussed in RFC 1825 that provide the IP security mechanisms. The Authentication header is defined in RFC 1826 [2-9] with additional work that documents many proposed enhancements to these efforts [2-10]. The IP Encapsulating Security Payload (ESP) is defined in RFC 1827 [2-11] with additional work that documents many proposed enhancements to these efforts [2-12]. These two mechanisms may be used separately, or jointly, as security needs dictate.

The proposed Authentication header (Figure 2-25) provides connectionless integrity and data origin authentication for IP datagrams, and also provides protection against replays. The presence of the Authentication header is identified by a value of 51 in the preceding header's Next Header field. This header contains six fields.

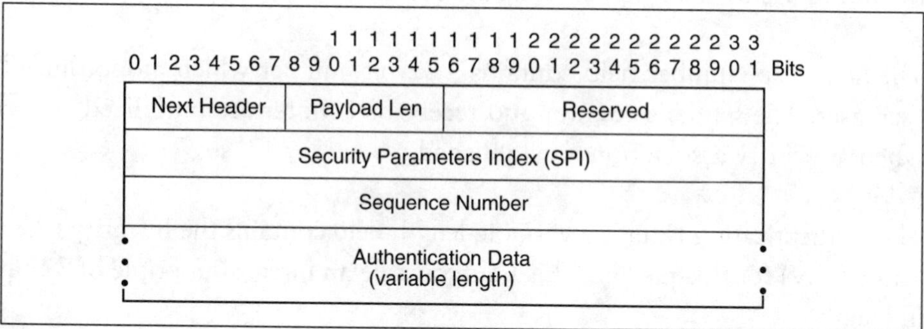

Figure 2-25. Proposed Authentication header format

The Next Header field is eight bits long, and identifies the header immediately following the Authentication header. This field uses the same values as the IPv4 Protocol field.

The Payload Len field is eight bits long, and provides the length of the Authentication field in 32-bit words, minus two (i.e. the first eight octets of the Authentication header are not counted). The minimum value is one, which consists of the 96-bit authentication value (three 32-bit words), less the value two (3 - 2 = 1). This minimum is only used in the case of a "null" authentication algorithm, employed for debugging purposes.

The Reserved field is sixteen bits long, and is reserved for future use. This field is initialized to zero for transmission. It is included in the Authentication Data calculation, but is otherwise ignored on reception.

The Security Parameters Index (SPI) field is an arbitrary 32-bit value that identifies the security association for this datagram, relative to the destination IP address contained in the IP header with which this security header is associated, and relative to the security protocol employed. The security association, as defined in RFC 1825, may include the Authentication algorithm, authentication algorithm keys, the Encryption algorithm, encryption algorithm keys, plus other security-related parameters. The value of SPI = 0 may be used for local debugging purposes. Other values, in the range of 1–255, are reserved for future use by the Internet Assigned Numbers Authority (IANA).

The Sequence Number field contains a 32-bit number which monotonically increases. The sender's counter and receiver's counter are initialized to zero when a security association is established.

The Authentication Data is a variable-length field contains the Integrity Check Value (ICV) for this packet. This field must be an integral multiple of 32 bits in length.

2.5.8 Encapsulating Security Payload Header

The proposed Encapsulating Security Payload (ESP) header (Figure 2-26) is designed to provide confidentiality, data origin authentication, connectionless integrity, an anti-replay service, and limited traffic flow confidentiality. The service or services provided depend on the security association and its implementation. The presence of the ESP header is identified by a value of 50 in the preceding header's Next Header field. This header contains seven fields, some of which are mandatory, and some of which are optional depending on the security association.

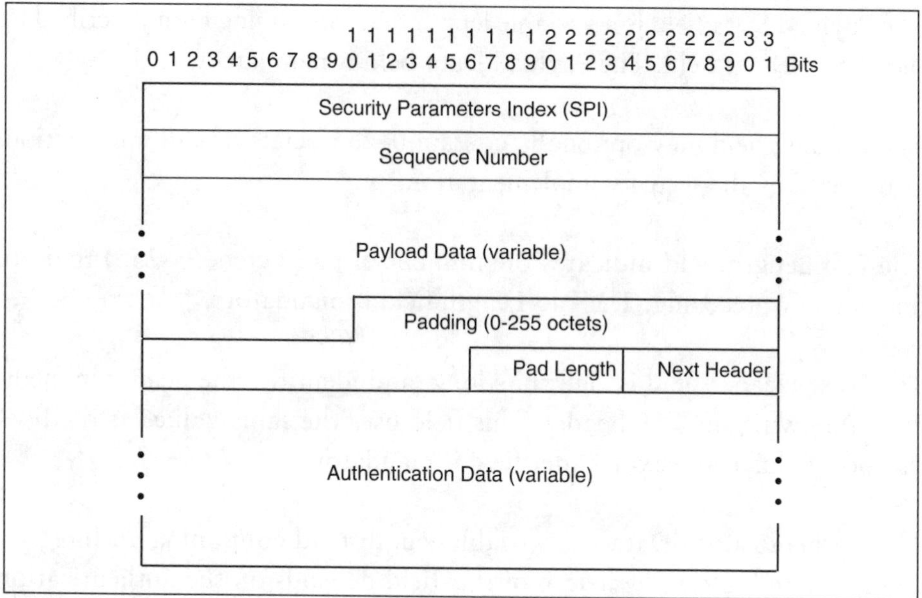

Figure 2-26. Proposed Encapsulating Security Payload header format

The Security Parameters Index (SPI) field is an arbitrary 32-bit value that identifies the security association for this datagram, relative to the destination IP address contained in the IP header with which this security header is associated, and relative to the security protocol employed. The SPI field is mandatory.

The Sequence Number field contains a 32-bit number which monotonically increases. The sender's counter and receiver's counter are initialized to zero when a security association is established. The Sequence Number field is mandatory.

The Payload Data field is a variable length field containing data described by the Next Header field. The Payload Data field is mandatory.

The Padding field may optionally contain 0–255 octets of pad information, as required by the security implementation.

The Pad Length field indicates the number of pad octets (0–255) that are immediately preceding. The Pad Length field is mandatory.

The Next Header field is eight bits long, and identifies the header immediately following the ESP header. This field uses the same values as the IPv4 Protocol field. The Next Header field is mandatory.

The Authentication Data is a variable-length field containing an Integrity Check Value (ICV). The length of this field depends on the authentication function that is selected. The Authentication Data field is optional, and is included only if that Security Association has selected authentication service.

We will study the aspects of IPv6 security in greater detail in Chapter 7.

2.5.9 No Next Header

The value of 59 in the Next Header field of an IPv6 packet or any of the extension headers indicates that nothing follows that header (Figure 2-27). As such, this is called a "No Next Header."

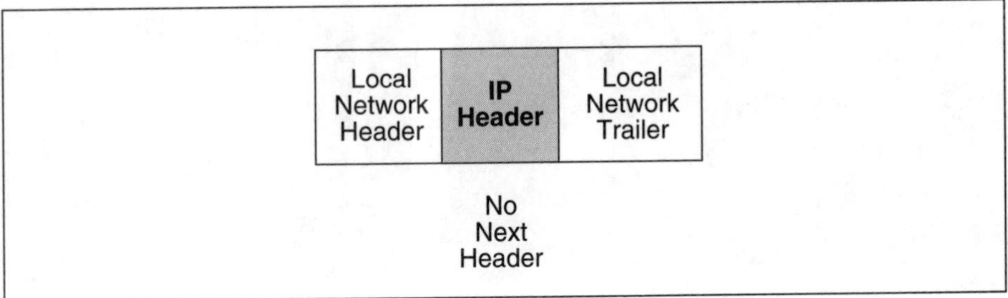

Figure 2-27. No Next Header format

2.6 Packet Size Issues

The design of IPv6 defines constraints on both the minimum and maximum packet sizes.

For the minimum size, every link in the internet is required to have an MTU of 576 octets or greater. If a link, such as ARCNET or ATM, does not have an MTU of 576 octets or greater, that link must provide the fragmentation and reassembly process at a layer below IPv6.

For the maximum size, the IPv6 header contains a Payload Length field (16 bits), which identifies payloads up to 65,535 octets in length. When the IPv6 header (40 octets) is included, the complete packet is therefore 65,575 octets.

For payloads greater than 65,535, the Jumbo Payload option within the Hop-by-Hop Options header is used. In this case, the Payload Length field in the IPv6 header is set to zero. The actual payload length (excluding the IPv6 header, but including the Hop-by-Hop Options header) is contained in the Jumbo Payload Length field within the Jumbo Payload option. Note that this number must be greater than 65,535.

2.7 Case Study

It has been said that *a picture is worth a thousand words.* To network managers, *a decoded trace from a protocol analyzer is worth considerably more.* To demonstrate this, we will be looking at a number of case studies that illustrate how the IPv6 and related protocols operate under real-time conditions. All of the experiments were generated on a twisted pair Ethernet network, using workstations running FTP Software Inc.'s Secure Client 3.0 and Network Access Suite 3.0 software, plus Bay Networks Inc.'s Access Stack Node and Digital Equipment Corp.'s RouteAbout routers. All networking devices are configured for both IPv4 and IPv6, enabling us to compare the operation of both protocols as we proceed. The case studies will be illustrated using output from Wandel & Goltermann Inc.'s Domino™ internetwork analyzer, shown in Figure 2-28.

Figure 2-28. Domino internetwork analyzer
(Courtesy of Wandel & Goltermann, Inc.)

The WG Domino Family of Internetwork Analyzers offers power, flexibility, and customization in a lightweight field analysis tool. The compact Domino employs multiple, independent processors, just like Wandel & Goltermann's world class laboratory instrument, the DA-30C Internetwork Analyzer. This approach allows wire speed filtering and capture of data, while off-loading the host PC as much as possible. In addition, the WG Examine™ decode engine offers one of the most complete sets of decodes available anywhere, with over 250 protocols currently available at all layers.

The flexible, graphical user interface provides a comfortable cockpit for such a high performance system. Default values are carefully chosen to assist in quick setups in the field. Even the protocol filters are automatically loaded with parameters (such as IP address) when filters are selected. All of this is contained in a smooth, intuitive Microsoft Windows-based Graphical User Interface which makes learning and refresh curves minimal. Extensive, context-sensitive help screens are always available to guide the user through unfamiliar activities.

Perhaps the most important component of the WG Domino is the user. The modular product family offers the user the ability to customize his analysis solution by selecting the appropriate Dominos to add to the stack. The software is also customizable, from the user-defined toolbox of applications on the opening screen, to the user-defined desktops which restore personal preferences at the touch of a key. With this level of customization, the Domino analyzers and software allow the user to work in his own way, without being forced into rigid procedures.

In our first example, we will look at a very routine scenario, the establishment of a file transfer using TCP and FTP, as shown in Figure 2-29. (For readers not familiar with the operation of TCP, consult the companion volume in this series, *Troubleshooting TCP/IP, Second Edition* (M&T Books, Inc., 1996).) The only thing that makes this scenario unique is that IPv6 provides the ARPA Internet Layer service (or OSI Network Layer service), so some of the underlying assumptions and parameters regarding the other protocol layers will change as well. In this case, the FTP Client is on one IPv6 segment, and the FTP Server is on another. A router running IPv6 connects the two segments.

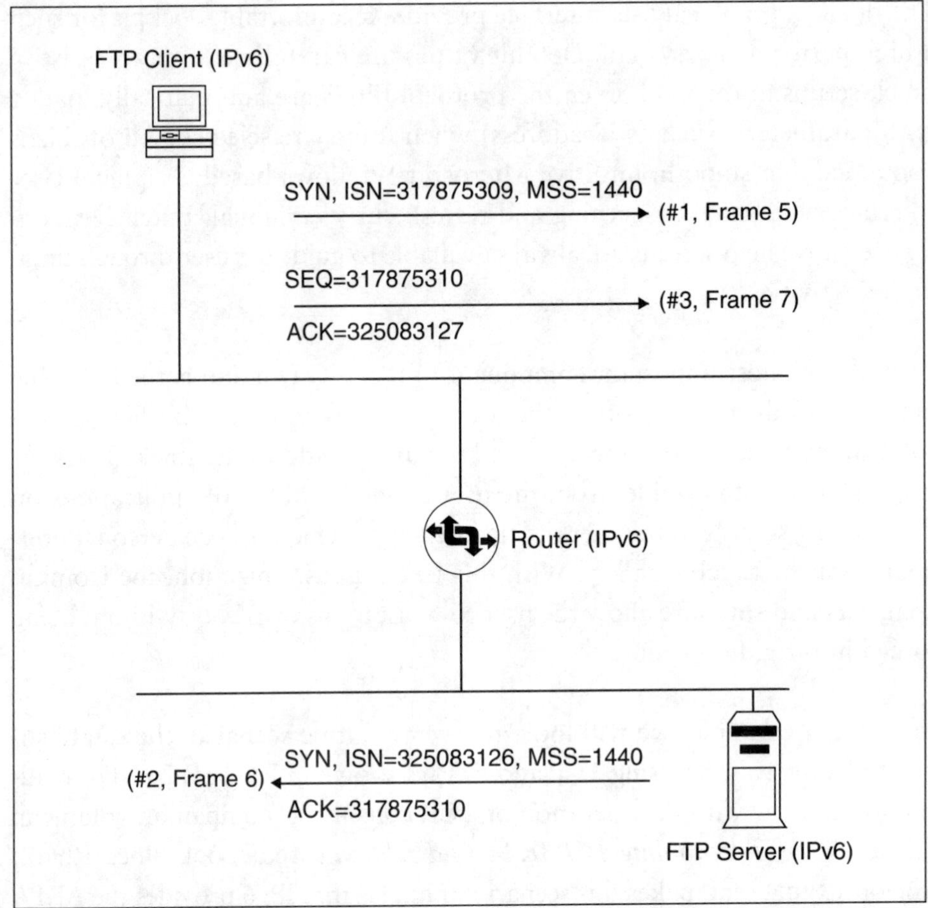

Figure 2-29. TCP connection setup over IPv6

Frame 5 is issued by the workstation that wishes to initiate an FTP file transfer from the server. Note that the frame format is set for Ethernet framing (not IEEE 802.3) because of the presence of the Ethertype field. Also note that a new Ethertype has been assigned for IPv6: 86DDH. (For reference, the Domino Analyzer represents hexadecimal characters using the 0x notation. For example, 0x86DD.)

The IPv6 header comes next, indicating Class = 0, no Flow Label, Payload Length = 40 octets, Next Header = 6 (indicating TCP), Hop Limit = 63, plus the two IPv6 addresses. (Note that portions of the IPv6 address field have been disguised to protect the anonymity of the source. These disguised portions are noted with an upper case X.) In this case, the addresses begin with a 5FH, indicating the test address format (more on this in Chapter 3).

The TCP header and data completes Frame 5. Note that Destination Port = 21 specifies an FTP connection, and that the TCP header has a length of 40 octets. The workstation has chosen an Initial Sequence Number (ISN) of 317875309 and turns on the Synchronize (SYN) flag, indicating its desire to establish a connection with the destination station. At the end of the TCP header you see something that doesn't occur very often: the Maximum Segment Size (MSS) option, with a value of 1,440 octets. Since this is an Ethernet frame, it can handle 1,500 octets at a time. The IPv6 header consumes 20 octets, and the TCP header and options consume 40 octets. Mathematically, 1,500 – 20 – 40 = 1,440, which is the maximum segment size allowed. Also note that by specifying the MSS, the workstation did not have to worry about any fragmentation issues—by definition, each segment would fit inside its own Ethernet frame.

Frame 6 is the confirmation from the server. Note that the server also sets the SYN flag, sends its own Initial Sequence Number (ISN = 325083126), and acknowledges the workstation's sequence number, ACK = 317875310 (the next expected sequence number from the workstation). The server also sets MSS = 1,440, such that fragmentation will not be required.

Frame 7 is the third part of the three-way handshake. It provides the workstation's confirmation that it has received the server's initialization parameters and is ready to proceed. Note that the Sequence Number increments to SEQ = 317875310, and the acknowledgment number increments to ACK = 325083127. The MSS option is only carried in segments that have the SYN bit set (see RFC 793, section 3.1, page 19) and is therefore not included in the TCP header in Frame 7. As a result, the header length is only 32 octets. The connection is now confirmed from both ends, and the desired file transfer may proceed.

Trace 2.7. TCP Connection Setup over IPv6

```
-------------- Frame 5  Size 98  Absolute Time  5:50:06.37341  -------------
                            Protocol Detail - ftp1.cap 8/14


IEEE 802.3/Ethernet DIX V2 Header


         Decode Status : -
          Frame Length : 98
   Destination Address : 00-00-A2-0A-1F-B8, Router
        Source Address : 00-80-C7-5F-9F-3D, FTP Client
          Frame Format : Ethernet DIX V2
             Ethertype : 0x86DD (IPv6)
        Frame Checksum : Good, Frame Check Sequence : 00 00 00 00


IPv6 - Internet Protocol (Version 6)


         Decode Status : -
        Version Number : 6 (IP Version 6)
                 Class : 0x0
            Flow Label : 0x0
        Payload Length : 40
           Next Header : 6 (Transmission Control (TCP))
             Hop Limit : 63
        Source Address : 3FFE:1XXX:0:0:0:80:C75F:9F3D
   Destination Address : 3FFE:2XXX:0:0:0:0:C0A9:82B2
```

```
TCP - Transport Control Protocol


           Decode Status : -
             Source Port : 1556 (Unknown)
        Destination Port : 21 (FTP)
         Sequence Number : 317875309
 Acknowledgement Number  : 0
             Data Offset : 0xA0
                           1010 .... = Header length = 40
                   Flags : 0x02
                           ..0. .... = No Urgent pointer
                           ...0 .... = No Acknowledgement
                           .... 0... = No Push
                           .... .0.. = No Reset
                           .... ..1. = Synchronize Sequence numbers
                           .... ...0 = No End of data flow from sender
                  Window : 8192
                Checksum : 0x30DA (Checksum Good)
          Urgent pointer : 0
                    Kind : 2 (Maximum Segment Size)
           Option length : 4
    Maximum segment size : 1440
                    Kind : 1 (No-Operation)
                    Kind : 3 (Unknown option)
                 Padding : 03 00 04 02 08 0A 00 00 11 3C 00 00 00 00


-------------- Frame 6  Size 98  Absolute Time  5:50:06.37907  -------------
                     Protocol Detail - ftp1.cap 8/14


IEEE 802.3/Ethernet DIX V2 Header


           Decode Status : -
            Frame Length : 98
     Destination Address : 00-80-C7-5F-9F-3D, Router
          Source Address : 00-00-A2-0A-1F-B8, FTP Client
            Frame Format : Ethernet DIX V2
               Ethertype : 0x86DD (IPv6)
          Frame Checksum : Good, Frame Check Sequence : 00 00 00 00
```

```
IPv6 - Internet Protocol (Version 6)


          Decode Status : -
         Version Number : 6 (IP Version 6)
                  Class : 0x0
             Flow Label : 0x0
         Payload Length : 40
            Next Header : 6 (Transmission Control (TCP))
              Hop Limit : 61
         Source Address : 3FFE:2XXX:0:0:0:0:C0A9:82B2
    Destination Address : 3FFE:1XXX:0:0:0:80:C75F:9F3D



TCP - Transport Control Protocol


              Decode Status : -
                Source Port : 21 (FTP)
           Destination Port : 1556 (Unknown)
            Sequence Number : 325083126
      Acknowledgement Number : 317875310
                Data Offset : 0xA0
                              1010 .... = Header length = 40
                      Flags : 0x12
                              ..0. .... = No Urgent pointer
                              ...1 .... = Acknowledgement
                              .... 0... = No Push
                              .... .0.. = No Reset
                              .... ..1. = Synchronize Sequence numbers
                              .... ...0 = No End of data flow from sender
                     Window : 21420
                   Checksum : 0x7823 (Checksum Good)
             Urgent pointer : 0
                       Kind : 2 (Maximum Segment Size)
              Option length : 4
        Maximum segment size : 1440
                       Kind : 1 (No-Operation)
                       Kind : 3 (Unknown option)
                    Padding : 03 00 04 02 08 0A 00 00 11 A3 00 00 11 3C
```

```
-------------- Frame 7  Size 90  Absolute Time  5:50:06.38074  -------------
                        Protocol Detail - ftp1.cap 8/14


IEEE 802.3/Ethernet DIX V2 Header


          Decode Status : -
           Frame Length : 90
    Destination Address : 00-00-A2-0A-1F-B8, Router
         Source Address : 00-80-C7-5F-9F-3D, FTP Client
           Frame Format : Ethernet DIX V2
              Ethertype : 0x86DD (IPv6)
         Frame Checksum : Good, Frame Check Sequence : 00 00 00 00


IPv6 - Internet Protocol (Version 6)


          Decode Status : -
         Version Number : 6 (IP Version 6)
                  Class : 0x0
             Flow Label : 0x0
         Payload Length : 32
            Next Header : 6 (Transmission Control (TCP))
              Hop Limit : 63
         Source Address : 3FFE:1XXX:0:0:0:80:C75F:9F3D
    Destination Address : 3FFE:2XXX:0:0:0:0:C0A9:82B2


TCP - Transport Control Protocol


          Decode Status : -
            Source Port : 1556 (Unknown)
       Destination Port : 21 (FTP)
        Sequence Number : 317875310
 Acknowledgement Number : 325083127
            Data Offset : 0x80
                          1000 .... = Header length = 32
                  Flags : 0x10
```

```
                         ..0. .... = No Urgent pointer
                         ...1 .... = Acknowledgement
                         .... 0... = No Push
                         .... .0.. = No Reset
                         .... ..0. = No Synchronize Sequence numbers
                         .... ...0 = No End of data flow from sender
          Window : 8568
        Checksum : 0xD908 (Checksum Good)
  Urgent pointer : 0
            Kind : 1 (No-Operation)
            Kind : 1 (No-Operation)
            Kind : 8 (Unknown option)
         Padding : 0A 00 00 11 3C 00 00 11 A3
```

This completes our study of the underlying IPv6 architecture. In the next chapter we will look at one of the key elements of this architecture: the structure of the IPv6 addresses.

2.8 References

[2-1] Postel, J. "Internet Protocol." RFC 791. September 1981.

[2-2] Deering, S., and R. Hinden. "Internet Protocol, Version 6 (IPv6) Specification." RFC 1883, December 1995.

[2-3] Deering, S. and R. Hinden. "Internet Protocol, Version 6 (IPv6) Specification." Work in progress, July 30, 1997.

[2-4] Minutes of the IPng Working Group Meetings are available at: http://playground.sun.com/pub/ipng/html/meetings.html.

[2-5] Partridge, C. "Using the Flow Label Field in IPv6." RFC 1809, June 1995.

[2-6] Hinden, R., and S. Deering. "IP Version 6 Addressing Architecture." RFC 1884, December 1995.

[2-7] Kent, S., and R. Atkinson. "Security Architecture for the Internet Protocol." RFC 1825.

[2-8] Kent, Stephen and Randall Atkinson. "Security Architecture for the Internet Protocol." Work in progress, July 30, 1997.

[2-9] Kent, S., and R. Atkinson. "IP Authentication Header." RFC 1826.

[2-10] Kent, Stephen and Randall Atkinson. "IP Authentication Header." Work in progress, October 2, 1997.

[2-11] Kent, S., and R. Atkinson. "IP Encapsulating Security Payload." RFC 1827.

[2-12] Kent, Stephen and Randall Atkinson. "IP Encapsulating Security Payload (ESP)." Work in progress, October 2, 1997.

3 The IPv6 Addressing Architecture

Without question, the most dramatic enhancement provided by IPv6 is the increase in address field size—from 32 bits to 128 bits per address. While IPv4's 32-bit field produces 4,294,967,296 distinct addresses, IPv6's 128-bit field has considerably more: 340,282,366,920,938,463,463,374,607,431,768,211,456 in total. It has been estimated that this equates to about 32 addresses per square inch of dry land on the Earth's surface [3-1]. (For most of us, this should be adequate!)

But before we dive into this addressing structure and all of its rigors, let's briefly consider the IPv4 addressing formats for comparison.

3.1 The Addressing Benchmark: IPv4

The IPv4 definition, RFC 791 [3-2], also specified that protocol's address structure. Each of the 32-bit IP addresses are divided into Host ID and Network ID sections, and may take one of five formats (Figure 3-1). The formats differ in the number of bits that are allocated to the Host and Network IDs and are identified by the first three bits. Class A addresses are identified by Bit 0 = 0. Bits 1 through 7 identify the network, and Bits 8 through 31 identify the specific host on that network. Class A addresses are designed for very large networks having many hosts. With a seven bit Network ID, only 128 class A addresses are available. Of these, addresses 0 and 127 are reserved.

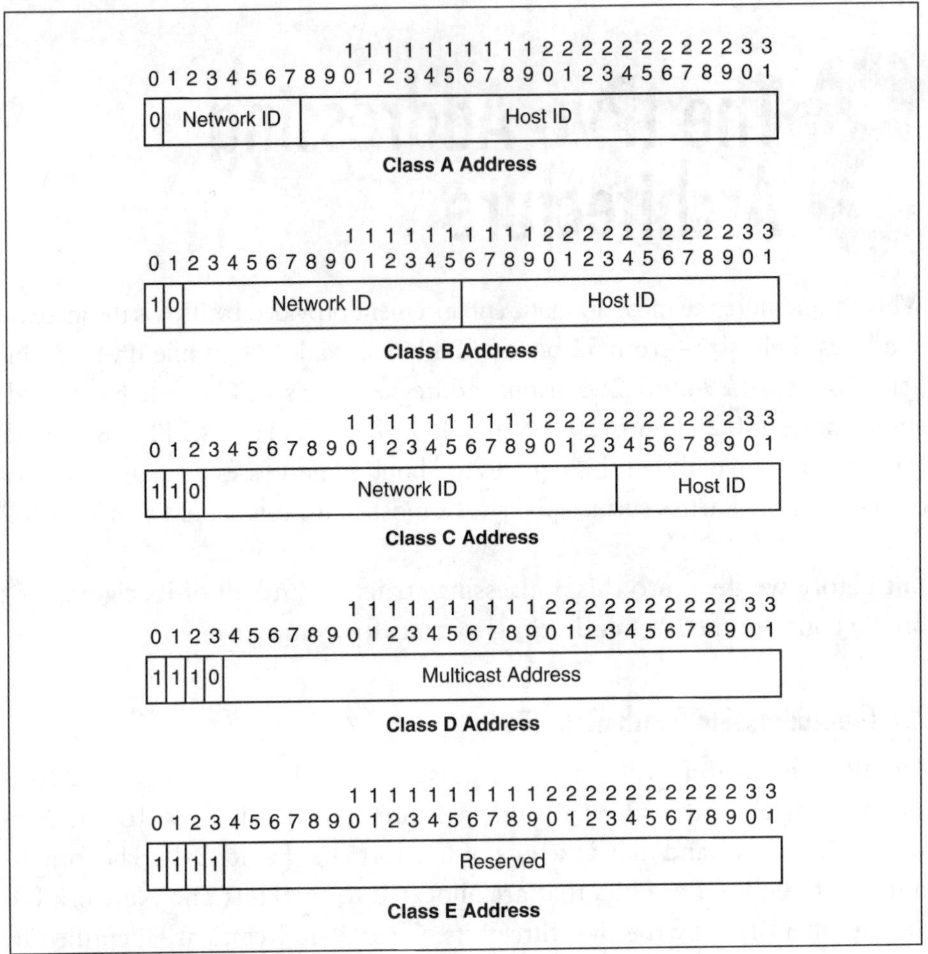

Figure 3-1. IPv4 address formats

Class B addresses are identified by the first two bits having a value of 10 (binary). The next 14 bits identify the Network and the remaining 16 bits identify the Host. 16,384 Class B addresses are possible, with addresses 0 and 16,383 reserved.

Class C addresses begin with a binary 110. The next 21 bits identify the Network, and the remaining 8 bits identify the Host. A total of 2,097,152 Class C addresses are possible, with addresses 0 and 2,097,151 reserved. Class C addresses are generally used for smaller networks such as LANs.

Class D addresses begin with a binary 1110 and are intended for multicasting purposes. Class E addresses begin with a binary 1111 and are reserved for future use.

3.1.1 Reserved Addresses

Several addresses are reserved to identify special purposes [3-3, page 4], [3-4, sections 4.2.2.11 and 4.2.3.1]:

Address	Interpretation
[Net = 0, Host = 0]	This host on this network
[Net = 0, Host = H]	Specific Host H on this network (Source address only)
[Net = all ones, Host = all ones]	Limited broadcast (within the source's subnetwork)
[Net = N, Host = all ones]	Directed broadcast to network (Destination address only)
[Net = N, Sub = all ones, Host = all ones]	Directed broadcast to all subnets on Network N (Destination address only)
[Net = N, Sub = S, Host = all ones]	Directed broadcast to all hosts on Subnet S, Network N (Destination address only)
[Net = 127, Host = any]	Internal host loopback address
The following two numbers are used for network numbers, but not IP addresses:	
[Net = N, Host = 0]	Network N, No Host
[Net = N, Sub = S, Host = 0]	Subnet S, No Host

Abbreviations:

Net = Network ID
Sub = Subnet ID
Host = Host ID

RFC 1118 [3-5] issues two cautions about IP addresses. First, it notes that BSD 4.2 UNIX systems require additional software for subnetting; BSD 4.3 systems do not. Second, some machines use an IP address of all zeros to specify a broadcast, instead of the more common all ones. BSD 4.3 requires the system administrator to choose the broadcast address. Use caution, since many problems, such as broadcast storms, can result when the broadcast address is not implemented consistently over the network. RFC 1812 [3-4] also discusses cautions in this area.

3.1.2 Dotted Decimal Notation

All IP addresses are written in what is known as *dotted decimal notation*, in which each octet is given a decimal number from 0 to 255. For example, network [10.55.31.84] is represented in binary as 00001010 00110111 00011111 01010100. The first bit (0) indicates a Class A address; the next seven bits (0001010) represent the Network ID (decimal 10); and the last 24 bits (00110111 0001111101010100) represent the Host ID.

Class A addresses begin with 1–127, Class B with 128–191, Class C with 192–223, and Class D with 224–254. Thus, an address of [150.100.200.5] is easily identified as a Class B address.

3.1.3 Subnetting

IP addresses are divided into two fields that identify a Network and a Host. A central authority assigns the Network ID and the administrator of that network assigns the Host ID. Routers send a packet to a particular network (using the Network ID), and then that Network completes the delivery to the particular Host.

The popularity of LANs in the mid-1980s inspired the Internet community to revise the IP address structure to allow for an additional field that would identify a subnetwork within an assigned Network ID. Thus the [Network, Host] address is replaced with [Network, Subnetwork, Host]. The space required for the Subnetwork field is taken by reducing the Host field. The central authority assigns the Network ID, and the individual organization assigns the Subnetwork IDs, plus the Host IDs on each subnetwork.

To differentiate between the various subnetworks, an address Mask is used. A Subnet Mask is a 32-bit number that has ONEs in the Network ID and Subnetwork ID fields, and ZEROs in the Host ID field. A logical AND function is performed between the Mask and a particular IP address to determine whether that datagram can be delivered on that subnet, i.e. directly, or whether it must go via an IP router to another subnet.

A device that needs to make a routing decision requires the Subnet Mask for assistance and uses the logical AND function to arrive at its conclusion. For example, let's suppose that the ID Destination address is D, and my address is M. Let's further suppose that the Subnet Mask is [255.255.255.0]. Two calculations are made: Subnet Mask AND Address D, plus Subnet Mask AND Address M. The result of the AND function strips off the Host portion of the address, leaving only the Network and Subnet portions. From the calculations, we have two results, each representing a Network ID and a Subnet ID. These two results are then compared, and from that, a routing decision can be made. If the two results are identical, Addresses M and D are on the same Subnetwork, and the datagram can be sent directly. If Addresses M and D are not equal, the two addresses are not on the same subnetwork, and the datagram should be sent to a router for delivery.

If the Host does not know the correct Subnet Mask, it uses the Internet Control Message Protocol—ICMP (for IPv4) to discover it. An ICMP Address Mask Request message is broadcast, awaiting an ICMP Address Mask Reply from a neighboring router.

3.2 Classless Interdomain Routing

Class A addresses are available to a few networks (126 maximum), but each network may have a very large number of hosts (16,777,214 maximum). Class B networks are available to a moderate number of networks (16,382 maximum), each with a moderate number of hosts (65,534 maximum). Class C networks are available to a large number of networks (2,097,152 maximum) that have only a few hosts (254 maximum). (In the figures above, note that the theoretical maximum numbers have been reduced by two to account for the reserved values, all zeros and all ones. Thus the maximum number of Class A networks is theoretically 128 (2^7), while the actual limit is 128 – 2 = 126.) Of these three categories, Class B networks fit the requirements of most organizations.

By the early 1990s, the IETF became concerned that the available supply of Class B addresses would be exhausted. Since a redesign of the Internet Protocol was a long term objective, a short term solution was required.

The short term solution, published in September 1993 and documented in RFCs 1466, 1467, 1517, 1518, 1519, and others, is known as Classless Interdomain Routing, or CIDR for short. According to RFC 1519 [3-6], the objective of CIDR is to allocate contiguous blocks of Class C addresses to organizations or service providers, thus providing for networks that need more than 254 hosts (traditional Class C), but not 65,534 hosts (traditional Class B). The contiguous Class C addresses would accommodate the following number of hosts:

Contiguous Class C Addresses	Maximum Hosts (Theoretical)
1	256
2	512
4	1,024
8	2,048
16	4,096

As before, note that the theoretical maximum number of contiguous host addresses (e.g. 1,024) is reduced by two upon implementation to accommodate the special addressing conditions.

The example given in RFC 1519 and shown in Figure 3-2 illustrates how a block of eight such Class C addresses could be used to provide up to 2,048 contiguous host addresses.

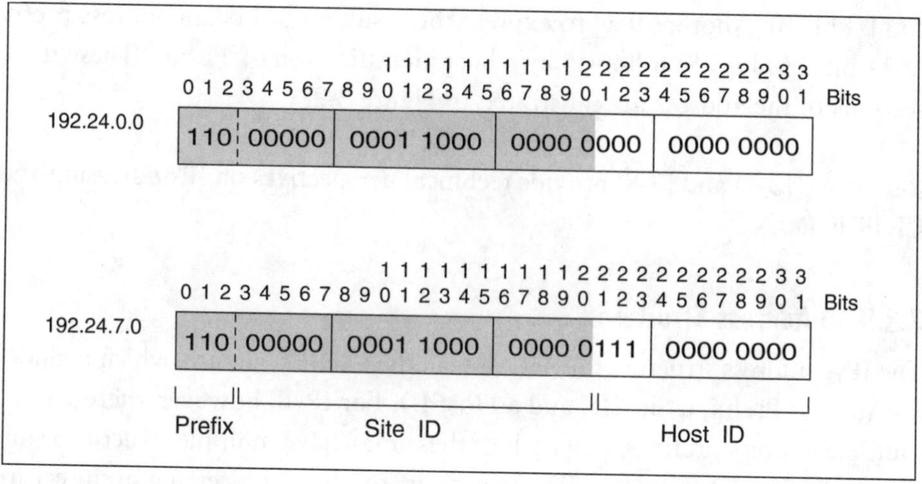

Figure 3-2. CIDR addressing

Assume that a block of 2,048 contiguous Class C addresses is allocated to an Internet Service Provider. Further suppose that this block of addresses has the range from 192.24.0.0 through 192.31.255.0. The first address has value 192.24.0.0, or C0 18 00 00H, or 11000000 00011000 00000000 00000000B. The last address has value 192.31.255.0, or C0 1F FF 00H, or 11000000 00011111 11111111 00000000B.

Further assume that one of the provider's customers needed 2,048 host addresses, the equivalent of eight Class C addresses (256 * 8 = 2,048).

This client would be assigned addresses from 192.24.0.0 or C0 18 00 00H or 11000000 000110000 00000000 00000000B, to 192.24.7.255 or C0 18 07 FF or 11000000 00011000 00000111 11111111B. An address mask of 255.255.248.0 or FF FF F8 00H or 11111111 11111111 11111000 00000000B would be used to distinguish all of the addresses assigned to this client.

Thus, this block of eight Class C network addresses could be represented as a prefix of 010B (three bits, the Class C network address prefix), followed by a site (or client) identification (18 bits, from 192.24.0 through 192.24.7), followed by the host identification (11 bits, from 000 0000 0000 through 111

1111 1111B). Another way to express the result would be an address prefix of 21 bits (3 plus 18) followed by a host identification of 11 bits. These three sections of the address are illustrated in Figure 3-2.

References [3-7] and [3-8] provide technical perspectives on IP addressing and CIDR issues.

3.3 IPv6 Address Structure

The IPv6 address structure finds it roots in the CIDR structure, which includes an Address Prefix, a Site ID, and a Host ID. For IPv6, however, there will be multiple address prefixes, and each of these may have multiple structures similar to the Site ID and Host ID. As a basis, the IPv6 addressing architecture document, RFC 1884 [3-9], defines three different types of IPv6 addresses:

- Unicast—An identifier to a single interface. A packet sent to a unicast address is delivered to the interface identified by that address, as shown in Figure 3-3. RFC 1887 [3-10] describes IPv6 unicast addresses in greater detail.
- Anycast—An identifier for a set of interfaces (typically belonging to different nodes). A packet sent to an anycast address is delivered to one of the interfaces identified by that address (the nearest one, according to the routing protocol's measure of distance), as shown in Figure 3-4. RFC 1546 [3-11] describes the concepts of anycast service in greater detail.
- Multicast—An identifier for a set of interfaces (typically belonging to different nodes). A packet sent to a multicast address is delivered to all interfaces identified by that address, as shown in Figure 3-5.

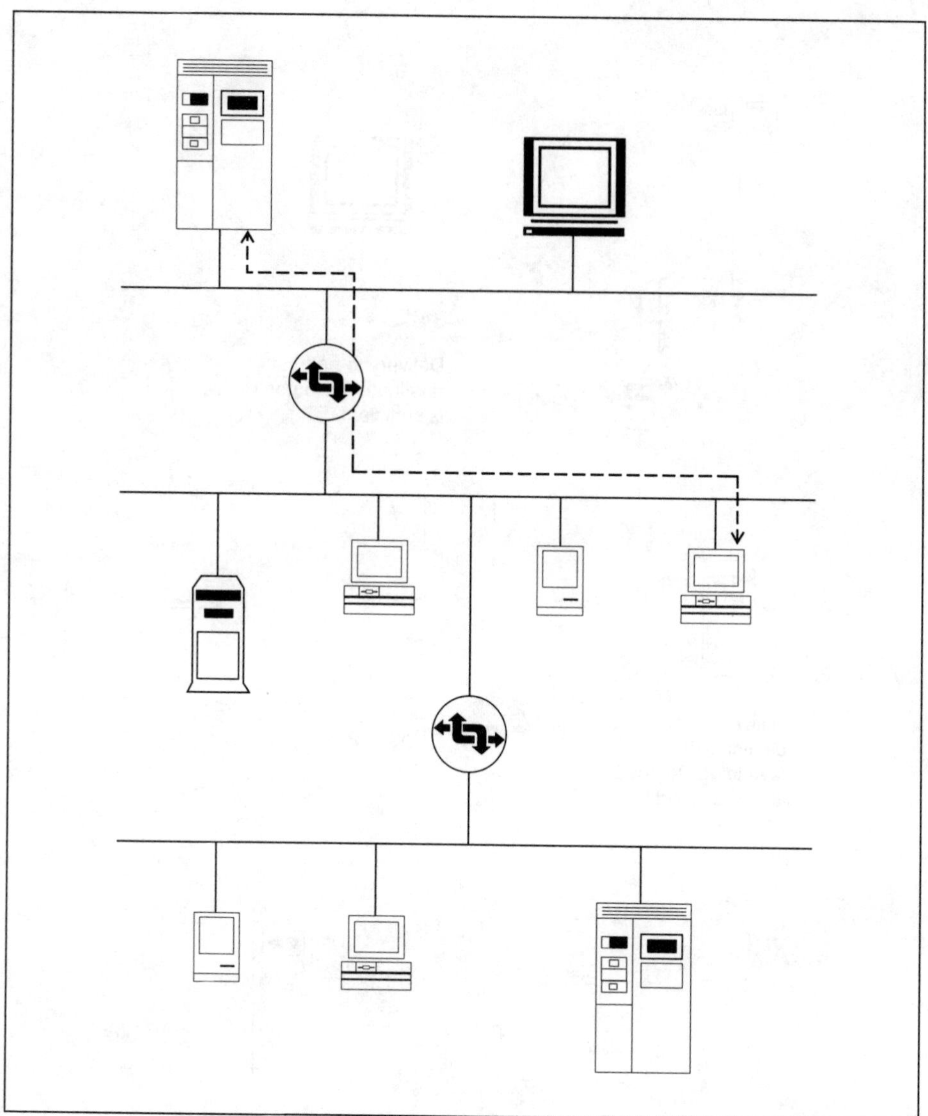

Figure 3-3. Unicast addressing

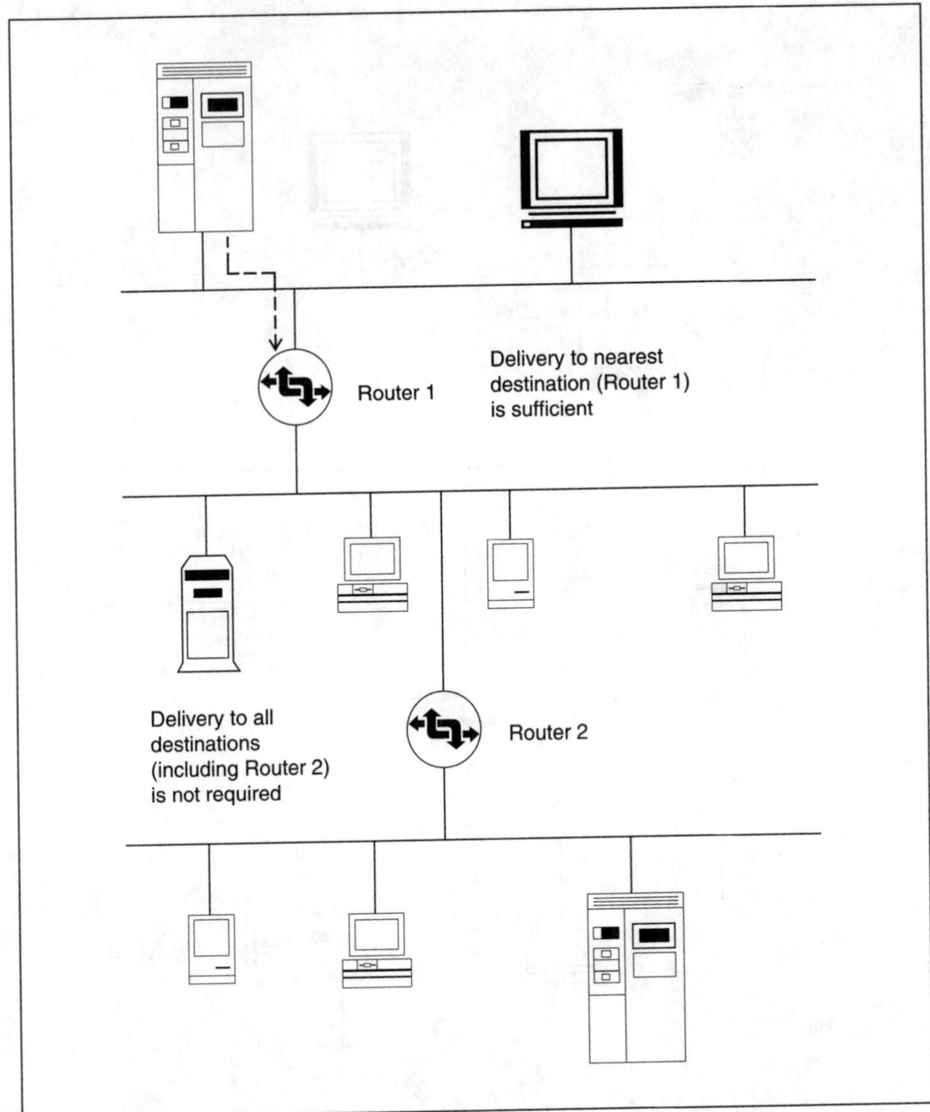

Figure 3-4. Anycast addressing

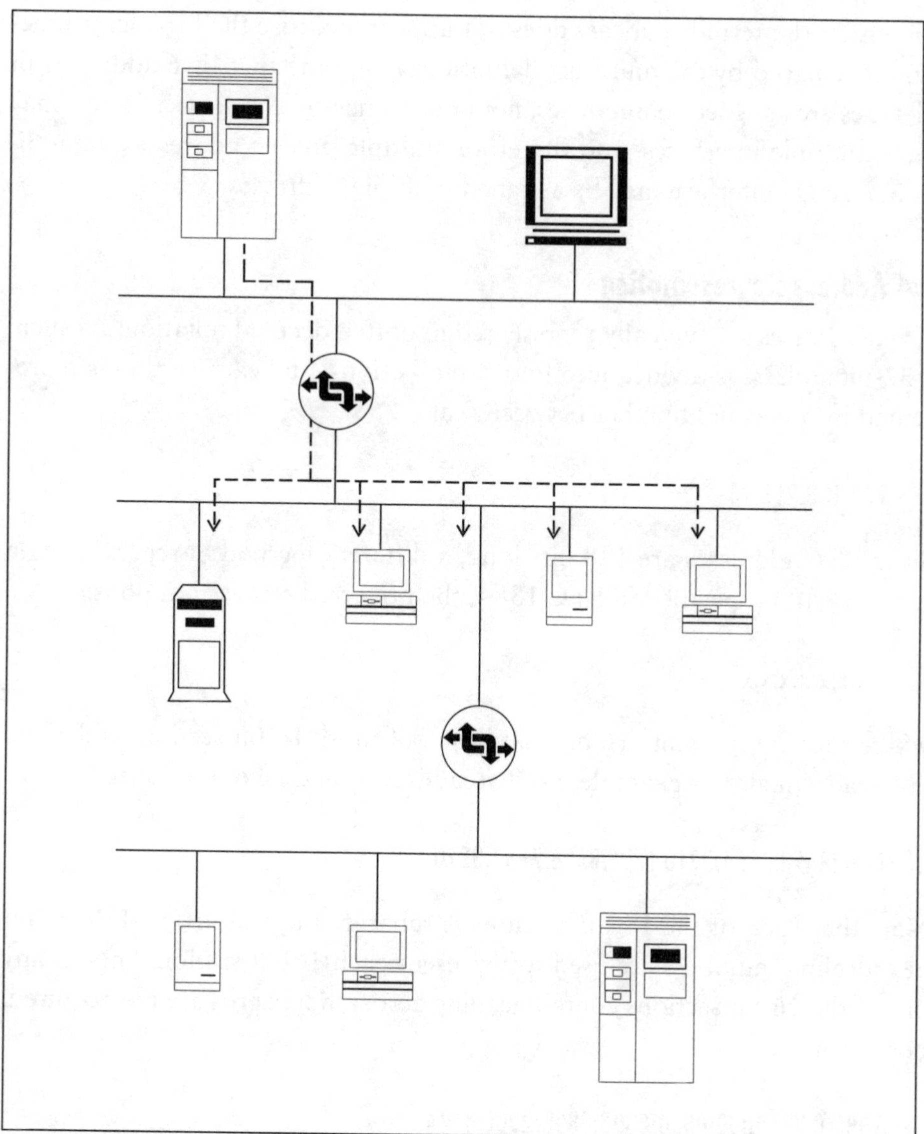

Figure 3-5. Multicast addressing

Note that the term broadcast does not appear, because the broadcast function is replaced by the multicast definition. Also note that IPv6 addresses of all types are assigned to interfaces, not nodes; one node (such as a router) may have multiple interfaces, and therefore multiple unicast addresses. In addition, a single interface may be assigned multiple addresses.

3.4 Address Representation

IPv4 addresses are typically represented in dotted decimal notation. As such, a 32-bit address is divided into four 8-bit sections, and each section is represented by a decimal number between 0 and 255:

```
128.138.213.13
```

Since IPv6 addresses are 128 bits long, a different method of representation is required. As specified in RFC 1884, the preferred representation is:

```
x:x:x:x:x:x:x:x
```

where each x represents 16 bits, and each of those 16-bit sections is defined in hexadecimal. For example, an IPv6 address could be of the form:

```
FEDC:BA98:7654:3210:FEDC:BA98:7654:3210
```

Note that each of the 16-bit sections is separated by colons, and that four hexadecimal numbers are used to represent each 16-bit section. Should any one of the 16-bit sections contain leading zeros, those zeros are not required. For example:

```
1080:0000:0000:0000:0008:0800:200C:417A
```

may be simplified to:

```
1080:0:0:0:8:800:200C:417A
```

If long strings of zeros appear in an address, a double colon (::) may be used to indicate multiple groups of 16 bits of zeros, which further simplifies the example shown above:

1080::8:800:200C:417A

The use of the double colon is restricted to appearing only once in an address, although it may be used to compress either the leading or trailing zeros in an address. For example, a loopback address of:

0:0:0:0:0:0:0:1

could be simplified as:

::1

When IPv6 addresses are expressed in text, it is common to delineate them by address and prefix length:

ipv6-address/prefix-length

where the IPv6 address is expressed in one of the notations listed above, and the prefix length is a decimal value that specifies the number of the leftmost bits of the address comprising the prefix. For example:

12AB:0000:0000:CD30:0000:0000:0000:0000/60

indicates that the 60-bit prefix (in hexadecimal) is:

12AB00000000CD3

3.5 Addressing Architecture

The 128-bit IPv6 address may be divided into a number of subfields to provide maximum flexibility for both current and future address representations. The leading bits, called the Format Prefix, define the specific type of IPv6 address. RFC 1884 defines a number of these prefixes, as shown in Figure 3-6. Additional work which documents many proposed enhancements to the IPv6 Addressing Architecture is defined in references [3-12] through [3-16].

Note that address space has been allocated for NSAP, IPX, global unicast, multicast, and other types of addresses. At the time of this writing, fifteen percent of the address space has been allocated, and the remaining 85% has been reserved for future use.

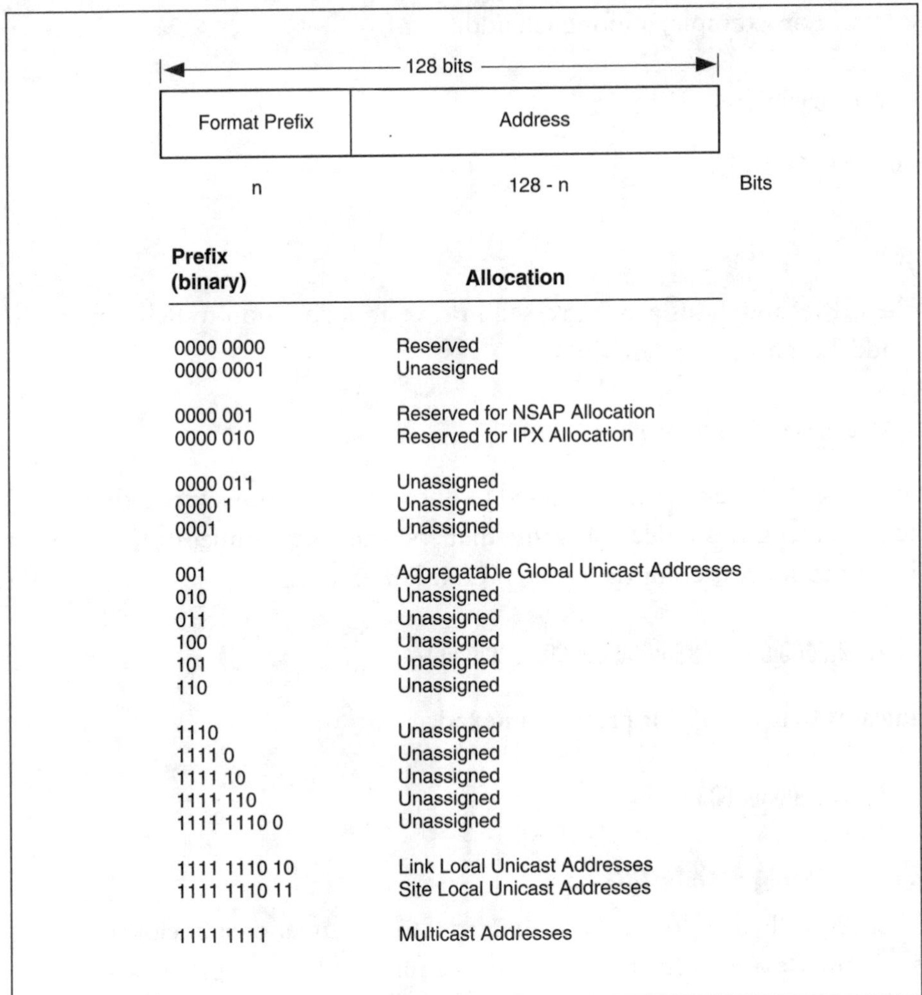

Prefix (binary)	Allocation
0000 0000	Reserved
0000 0001	Unassigned
0000 001	Reserved for NSAP Allocation
0000 010	Reserved for IPX Allocation
0000 011	Unassigned
0000 1	Unassigned
0001	Unassigned
001	Aggregatable Global Unicast Addresses
010	Unassigned
011	Unassigned
100	Unassigned
101	Unassigned
110	Unassigned
1110	Unassigned
1111 0	Unassigned
1111 10	Unassigned
1111 110	Unassigned
1111 1110 0	Unassigned
1111 1110 10	Link Local Unicast Addresses
1111 1110 11	Site Local Unicast Addresses
1111 1111	Multicast Addresses

Figure 3-6. Addressing architecture with proposed Aggregatable Global Unicast address prefix

A multicast address begins with the binary value 11111111; any other prefix identifies a unicast address. Anycast addresses are part of the allocation for unicast addresses and are not given a unique identifier.

3.5.1 Unicast Addresses

A number of forms for unicast addresses have been defined for IPv6, some with more complex structures that provide for hierarchical address assignments. The most simple form is a unicast address with no internal structure, in other words, with no address-defined hierarchy (Figure 3-7).

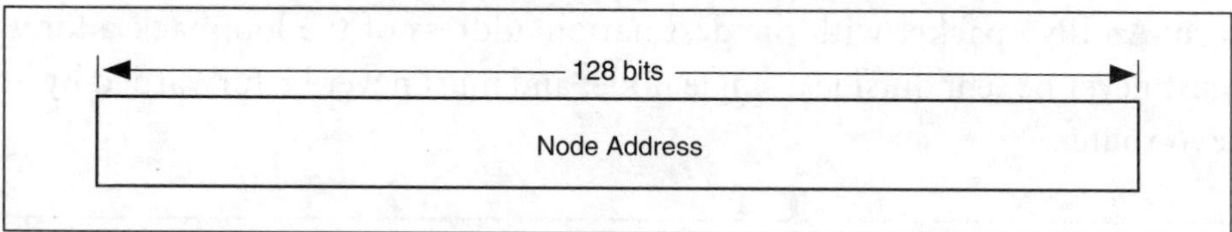

Figure 3-7. Unicast address without internal structure

The next possibility would be to specify a Subnet Prefix within the 128-bit address, thus dividing the address into a Subnet Prefix (with n bits) and an Interface ID (with 128-n bits), as shown in Figure 3-8.

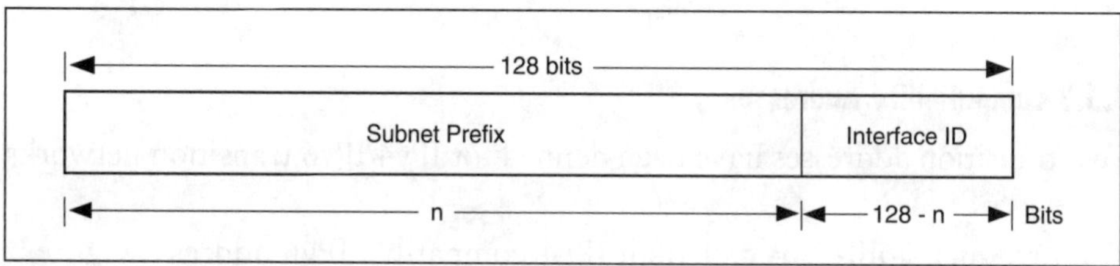

Figure 3-8. Unicast address with subnet

Some special addresses are also defined in RFC 1884.

The address 0:0:0:0:0:0:0:0 (also represented as 0::0, or simply ::) is defined as the unspecified address, which indicates the absence of an address (Figure 3-9). This address might be used on startup when a node has not yet had an address assigned. The unspecified address may never be assigned to any node.

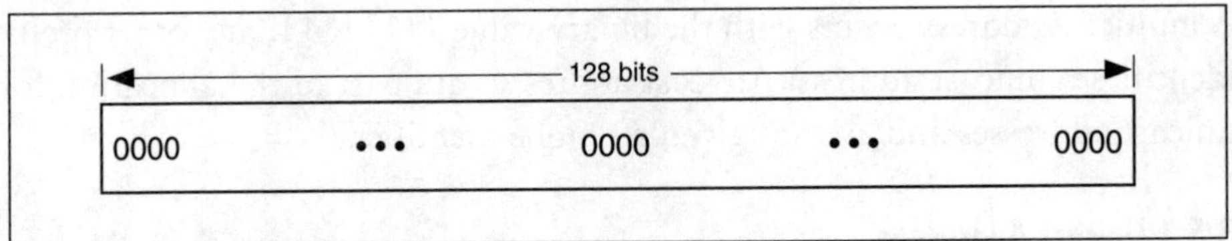

Figure 3-9. Unspecified address

The address 0:0:0:0:0:0:0:1 (also represented as 0::1, or simply ::1) is defined as the loopback address (Figure 3-10). This address is used by a node to send a packet to itself. The loopback address may never be assigned to any interface. An IPv6 packet with the destination address of the loopback address must never be sent outside a single node, and must never be forwarded by an IPv6 router.

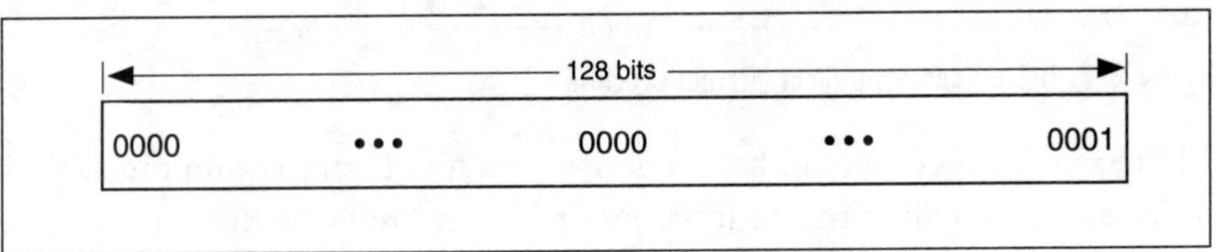

Figure 3-10. Loopback address

3.5.2 Compatibility Addresses

Two transition addresses have been defined for IPv4/IPv6 transition networks.

The first such address is called an IPv4-compatible IPv6 address (Figure 3-11). It is used when two IPv6 devices (such as hosts or routers) need to communicate via an IPv4 routing infrastructure. The devices at the edge of the IPv4 would use this special unicast address which carries an IPv4 address in the low-order 32 bits. This process is called *automatic tunneling*. Note that the prefix is 96 bits of all zeros.

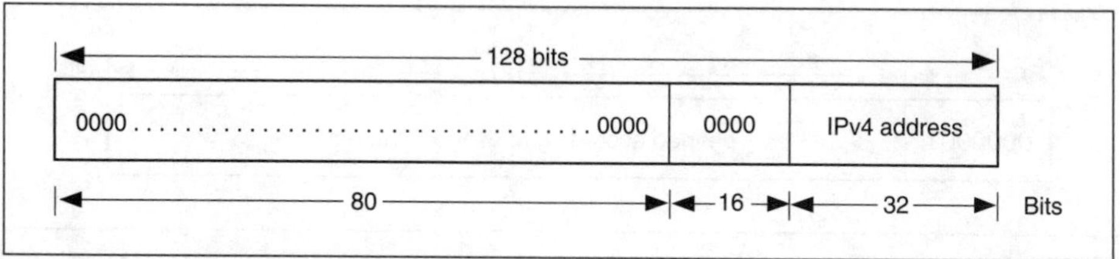

Figure 3-11. IPv4-compatible IPv6 address

The second type of transition address is called an IPv4-mapped IPv6 address (Figure 3-12). This address is used by IPv4-only nodes that do not support IPv6. For example, an IPv6 host would use an IPv4-mapped IPv6 address to communicate with another host which only supports IPv4. Note that the prefix is 80 bits of zeros, followed by 16 bits of ones.

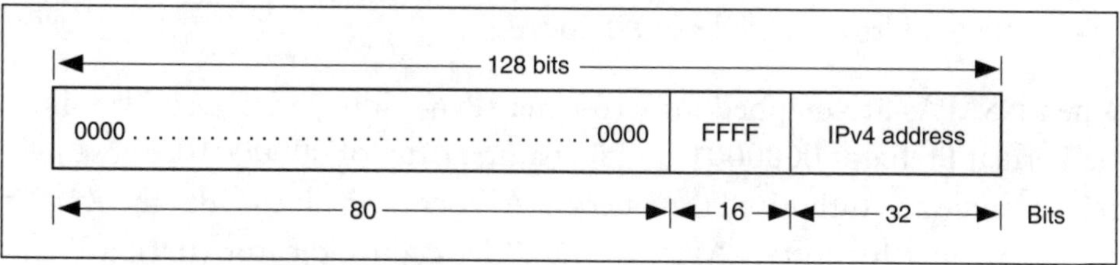

Figure 3-12. IPv4-mapped IPv6 address

3.5.3 Addresses Supporting OSI Architectures

Many networks incorporate elements derived from Open Systems Interconnection (OSI) protocols into their addressing and routing architectures. One example is the OSI Connectionless Network Protocol, ISO 8473, and its addressing scheme, which uses the Network Service Access Point (NSAP) addresses. Other examples are the OSI routing protocols, End System to Intermediate System (ES-IS), defined in ISO 9542, or the Intermediate System to Intermediate System (IS-IS), defined in ISO 10589. Since NSAP addresses (called NSAPAs) are typically 20 octets in length, mechanisms must be provided to adapt this format to the 16-octet IPv6 addressing structure. Addresses supporting NSAPAs have a seven-bit Format Prefix of 0000001 (Figure 3-13) and are defined in RFC 1888 [3-17].

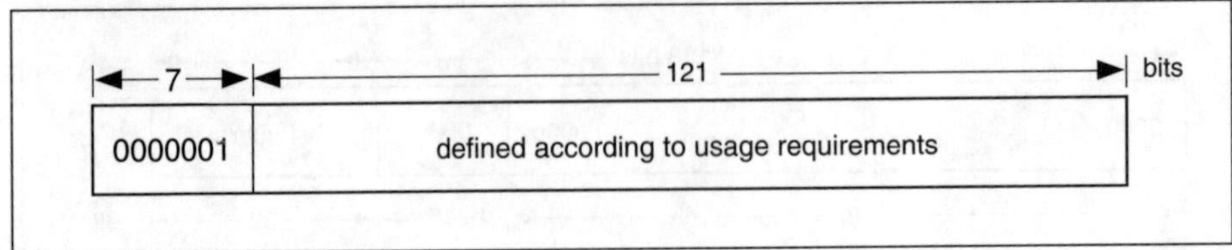

Figure 3-13. NSAP address

RFC 1888 defines four mechanisms for the support of OSI NSAP addressing in an IPv6 network:

- Restricted NSAPA mapping into 16-octet IPv6 addresses
- Truncated NSAPA for routing, full NSAPA in IPv6 option
- Normal IPv6 address, full NSAPA in IPv6 option
- IPv6 address carried as OSI address

When NSAPAs are mapped into 16-octet IPv6 addresses, a zero bit follows the Format Prefix of 0000001, yielding a first octet of 00000010. Subsequent fields include an Authority Format code (AFcode), which encodes the Authority and Format Identifier (AFI), an Initial Domain Indicator (IDI), a Prefix, an Area, and an End System ID (Figure 3-14).

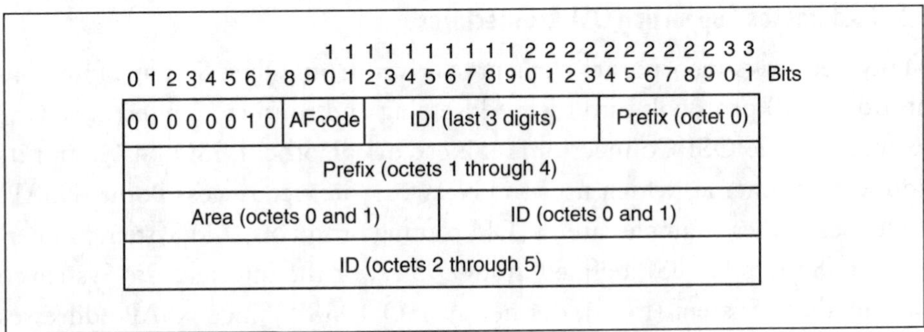

Figure 3-14. Restricted NSAPA address

A truncated NSAPA used as an IPv6 address takes the high-order octets of the NSAP address, which include the routing information consisting of the

Routing Domain and the Area identifiers, and then truncates other NSAP fields that are not required (Figure 3-15).

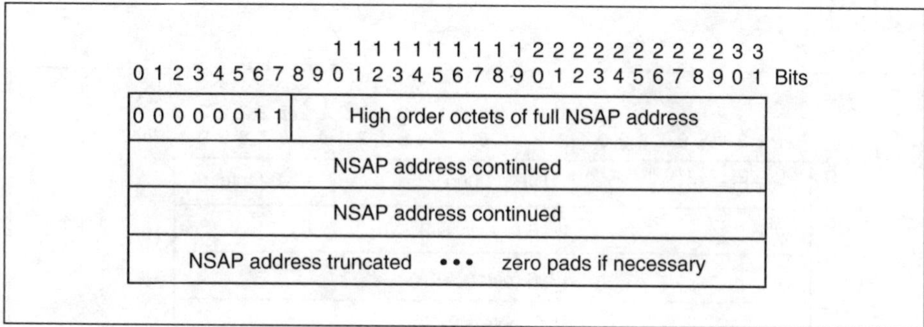

Figure 3-15. Truncated NSAPA address

A third alternative is to carry full NSAPAs as an option within the Destination Options header (Figure 3-16). Note that the Option Type = 195 (decimal), and that the full (20 octet) NSAPAs are then included in the destination option.

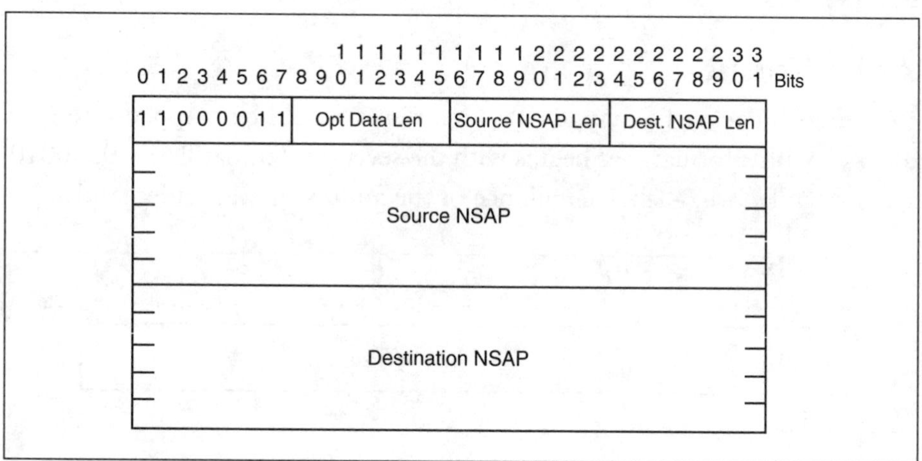

Figure 3-16. Carriage of full NSAPAs in IPv6 destination option

The final alternative allows an IPv6 address to be embedded inside a 20-octet NSAP address (Figure 3-17). The first octet is an Authority and Format Indicator, and the next two octets are known as the Internet Code Point (ICP). Taken together, these three octets comprise the Initial Domain Part (IDP) of the NSAPA. The next 16 octets contain the IPv6 address; the final octet, called a selector, is set to zero.

1 1 1 1 1 1 1 1 1 1 2 2 2 2 2 2 2 2 2 2 3 3
0 1 2 3 4 5 6 7 8 9 0 1 2 3 4 5 6 7 8 9 0 1 2 3 4 5 6 7 8 9 0 1 Bits

AFI = 35	ICP = 0000	IPv6 (octet 0)
IPv6 (octets 1-4)		
IPv6 (octets 5-8)		
IPv6 (octets 9-12)		
IPv6 (octets 13-15)		00000000

Figure 3-17. IPv6 address carried as OSI address

Details concerning NSAP address implementations are also provided in RFC 1888.

3.5.4 IPX Addresses

Internetwork Packet Exchange (IPX) addresses would be mapped into IPv6 addresses with a format that begins with the seven-bit Format Prefix 0000010, as shown in Figure 3-18. The balance of the address is still under study.

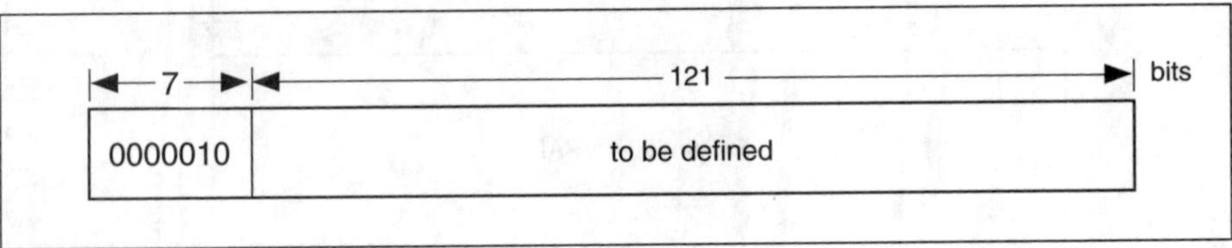

Figure 3-18. IPX address

3.5.5 Aggregatable Global Unicast Addresses

Many communication networks, such as the global telephone network, are based on a hierarchical addressing scheme. A hierarchy facilitates easier scaling and routing. For example, calls within North America require the North American Zone Code (1), the Area Code (e.g. 303), the Central Office Code (e.g. 555), and the Line Number (1212). Calls from North America to London require the International Access Code (011), the Country Code (44 for the United Kingdom), a City Code (71 for London), and then the local telephone number. If the network grows, you can add another Area Code or Country Code, which facilitates the scaling challenge. If you are calling within the country, there is no need to dial the International Access Code or the Country Code, which facilitates the routing challenge.

For IPv6, the hierarchy for the aggregatable addresses is organized into three levels: a public topology, a site topology, and an interface identifier, as proposed in Reference [3-13]. The *public topology* is the collection of providers and exchanges that provide public Internet transit service. The *site topology* is local to a specific site or organization, but does not provide public transit service to nodes outside its site. *Interface identifiers* provide unique identification for interfaces on a specific link.

Thus, an aggregation-based architecture would include the long-haul providers, the exchanges, and subscribers (Figure 3-19). In some cases, subscribers would connect directly to an exchange. This would provide access to multiple long-haul providers and allow a change of providers to be made without having to renumber their organization.

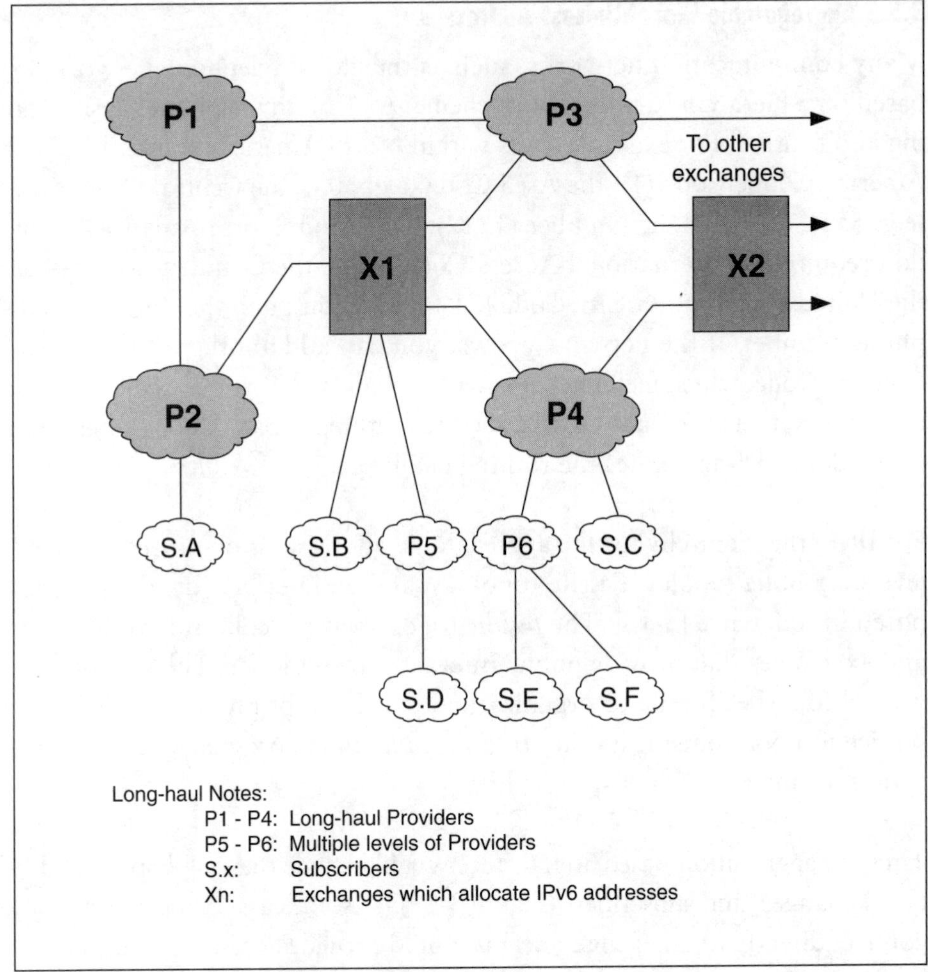

Figure 3-19. Proposed Aggregation hierarchy

The aggregatable global unicast address begins with a Format Prefix of 001, and includes four other fields that specify various levels of the hierarchy (Figure 3-20). The Top-Level Aggregation Identifier (TLA) is the top level of the hierarchy and is a 13-bit field. Thus 8,192 (2^{13}) TLAs can be assigned for each Format Prefix value defined. The TLA is proposed for organizations that provide "public native IPv6 service," according to Reference [3-14]. These organizations must also have a track record of providing public Internet transit service, and must have a plan to allocate the next level of aggregation (called the NLA).

The Next-Level Aggregation Identifier (NLA) is used by organizations to create an addressing hierarchy and to identify sites. The NLA is a 32-bit field, and its usage is also proposed in Reference [3-14]. As illustrated in Figure 3-20, the 32-bit NLA ID space may be allocated among several levels of sites. The organization responsible for the TLA defines the bit layout of the NLA space. The bit layout of the next level NLA (such as NLA2, shown in Figure 3-21) is the responsibility of the previous level NLA ID (such as NLA1). Taken together, the combination of the Format Prefix, TLA ID, and NLA ID constitute the Public Topology (48 bits total).

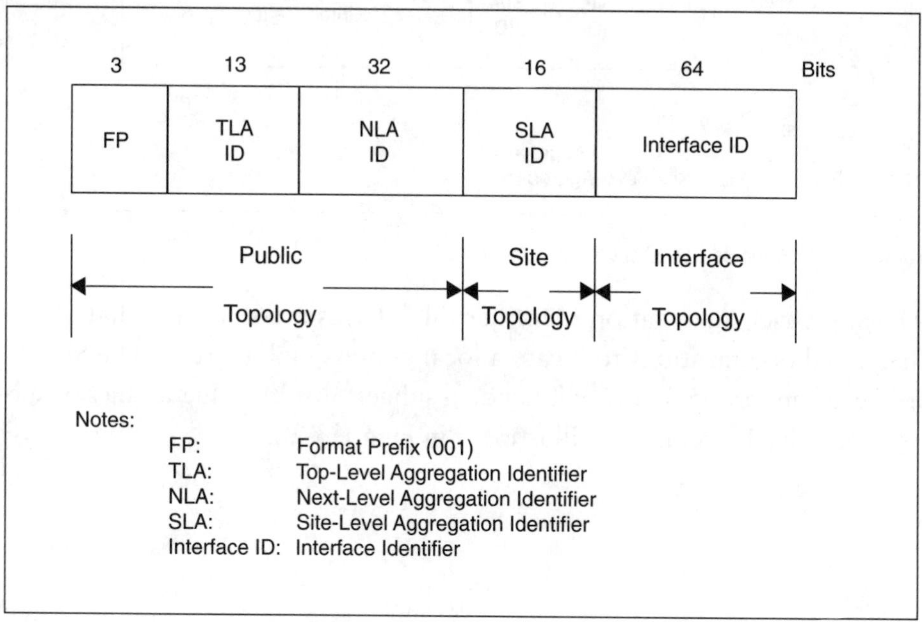

Figure 3-20. Proposed Aggregatable global unicast address

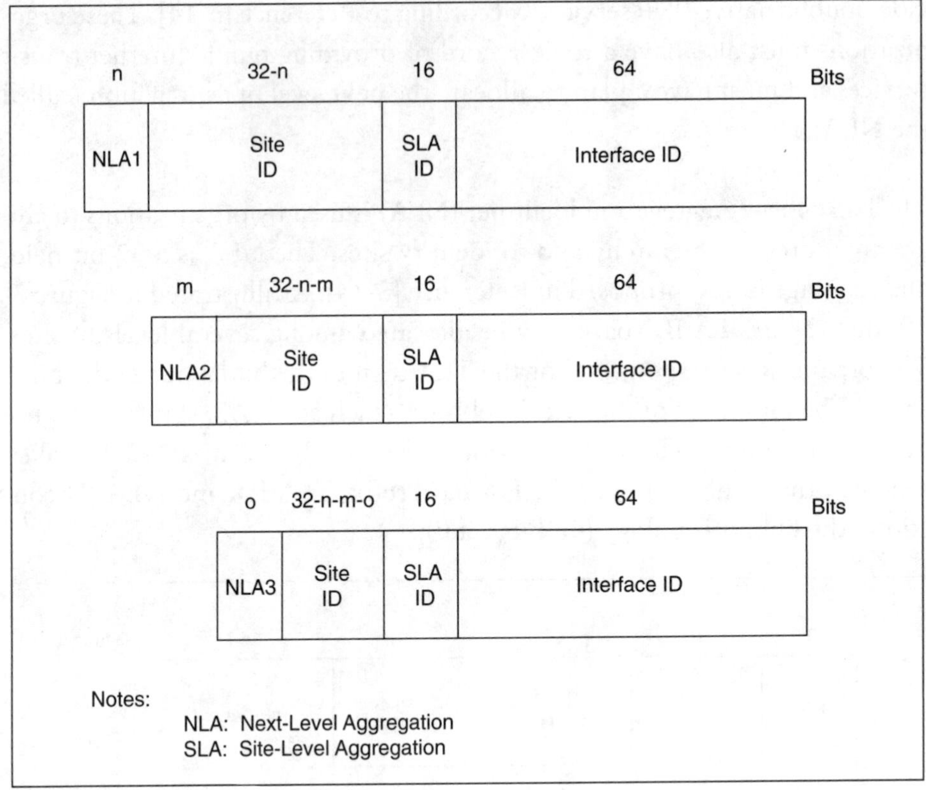

Figure 3-21. Proposed NLA ID space assignment

The Site-Level Aggregation Identifier (SLA ID) is a 16-bit field that allows individual organizations to create a local addressing hierarchy. The SLA ID field can support 65,535 (2^{16}) individual subnets. Multiple hierarchies of subnets may also be defined, as illustrated in Figure 3-22.

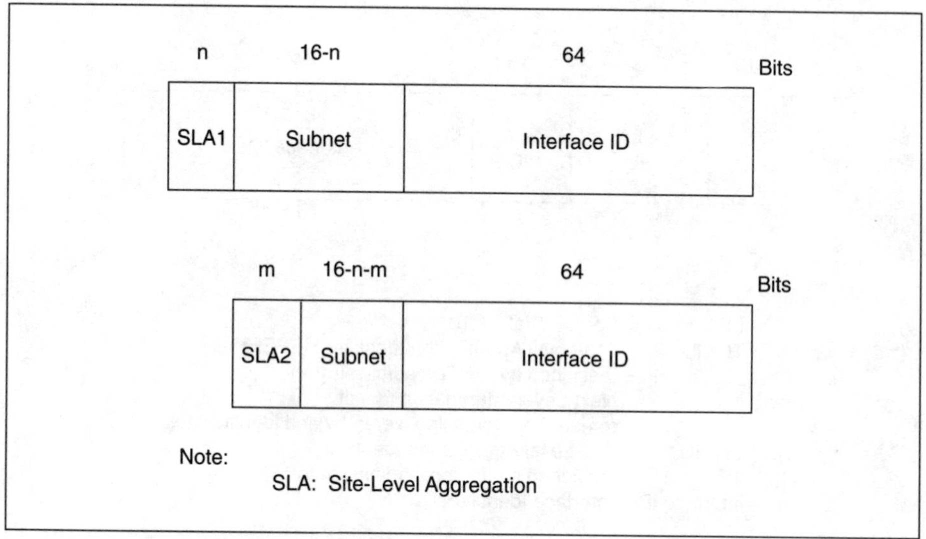

Figure 3-22. Proposed SLA ID field hierarchy

The last field is the Interface Identifier, which identifies interfaces on a link. Each Interface ID is 64 bits long, and is structured according to the IEEE EUI-64 format, which will be discussed in a following section.

3.5.6 Testing Addresses

A special allocation of addresses has been proposed for the purposes of testing IPv6 software and is described in Reference [3-15]. (This allocation of testing addresses is intended to replace the previously-assigned testing allocation defined in RFC 1897.) These addresses are only to be used for IPv6 testing and are not routable in the Internet. The testing address format is based on the Aggregatable Global Unicast Address, with the various fields assigned as follows (Figure 3-23):

FP:	001
TLA ID:	1FFE H (assigned for 6bone testing)
NLA ID:	Assigned by the TLA administrator
SLA ID:	Assigned by the individual organization
Interface ID:	An interface identifier for that link (Ethernet, token ring, etc.)

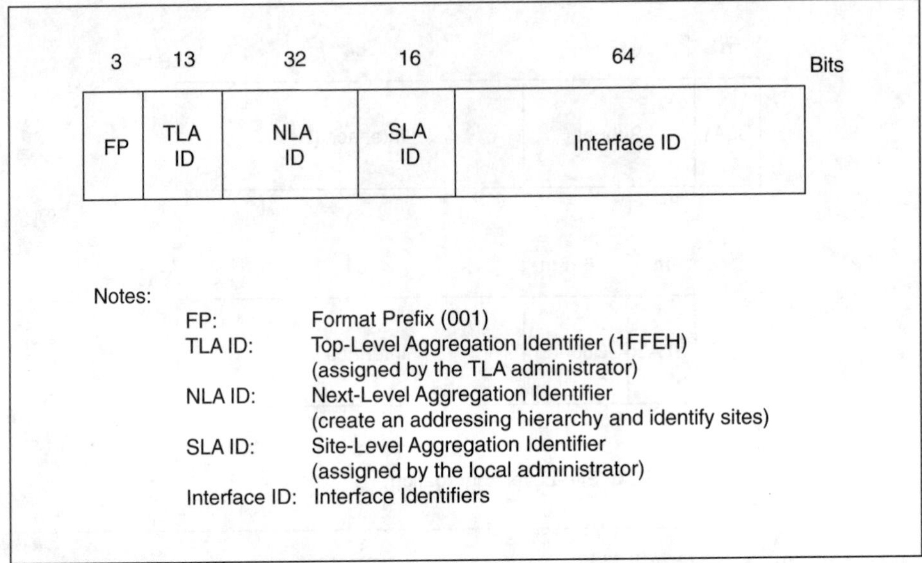

Figure 3-23. Proposed Testing address

3.5.7 Local Use Addresses

Two addresses are defined for local use only. The Link-Local address is used for a single link and is intended for auto-address configuration, neighbor discovery, or when no routers are present. The Link-Local address (Figure 3-24) begins with the Format Prefix 1111111010 and includes a 64-bit Interface ID field. Routers never forward packets with Link-Local source or destination addresses to other links.

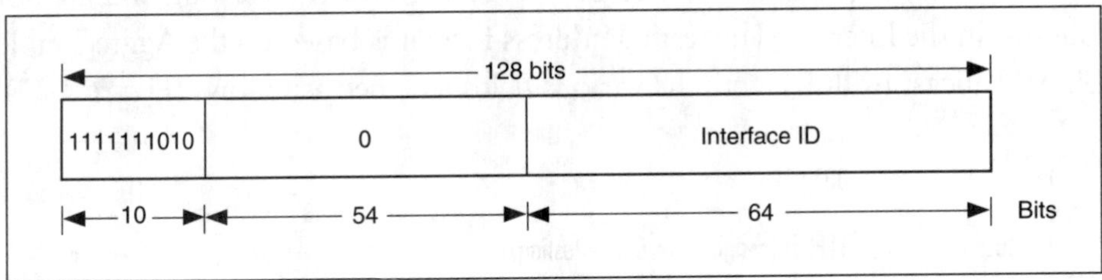

Figure 3-24. Unicast Link-Local address

The Site-Local address is used by organizations that have not yet connected to the Internet. Instead of fabricating an IPv6 address, they may use the Site-Local address. Routers never forward packets with Site-Local source addresses outside of that site. This address (Figure 3-25) begins with the Format Prefix 1111111011 and includes both a 16-bit Subnet ID field and a 64-bit Interface ID field.

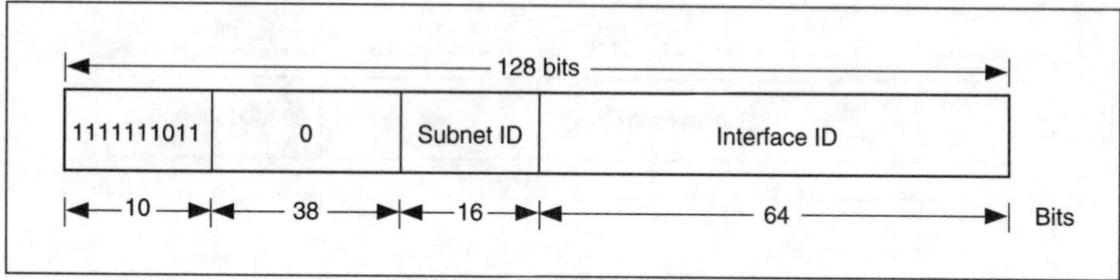

Figure 3-25. Unicast Site-Local address

3.6 Anycast Addresses

An anycast address is one that is assigned to multiple interfaces, typically on different nodes. A packet with an anycast destination address is routed to the nearest interface having that address, as measured by the routing protocol's definition of distance.

RFC 1884 notes several possible uses for the anycast address:

- Identifying a set of routers belonging to an Internet Service Provider (ISP).
- Identifying the set of routers attached to a particular subnet.
- Identifying the set of routers that provide entry to a particular routing domain.

Two restrictions are placed on anycast addresses. First, they must not be used as a source address for an IPv6 packet. Second, an anycast address may only be assigned to routers, not hosts.

One anycast address is predefined and required: the Subnet-Router anycast address (Figure 3-26). This address begins with a variable-length subnet prefix, and concludes with zeros for filler. All routers on that subnet must support this anycast address. It is intended to be used for applications where a node needs to communicate with one member of a group of routers on a remote subnet.

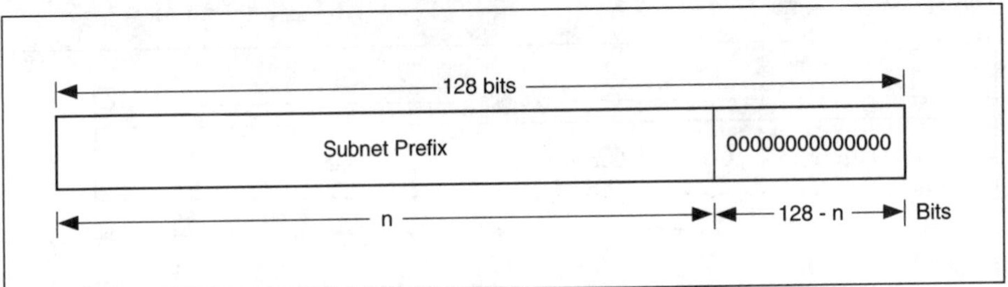

Figure 3-26. Subnet-Router anycast address (required)

3.7 Multicast Addresses

The multicast address identifies a group of nodes, and each of these nodes may belong to multiple multicast groups. The multicast address (Figure 3-27) begins with the Format Prefix 11111111 and includes three additional fields. The Flags field contains four one-bit flags. The three most significant flag bits are reserved for future use and are initialized to zero. The fourth flag is called the T, or transient, bit. When T = 0, the multicast address is a permanently assigned (or well-known) multicast address, assigned by the global Internet numbering authority. When T = 1, a transient (or non-permanently assigned) multicast address is indicated.

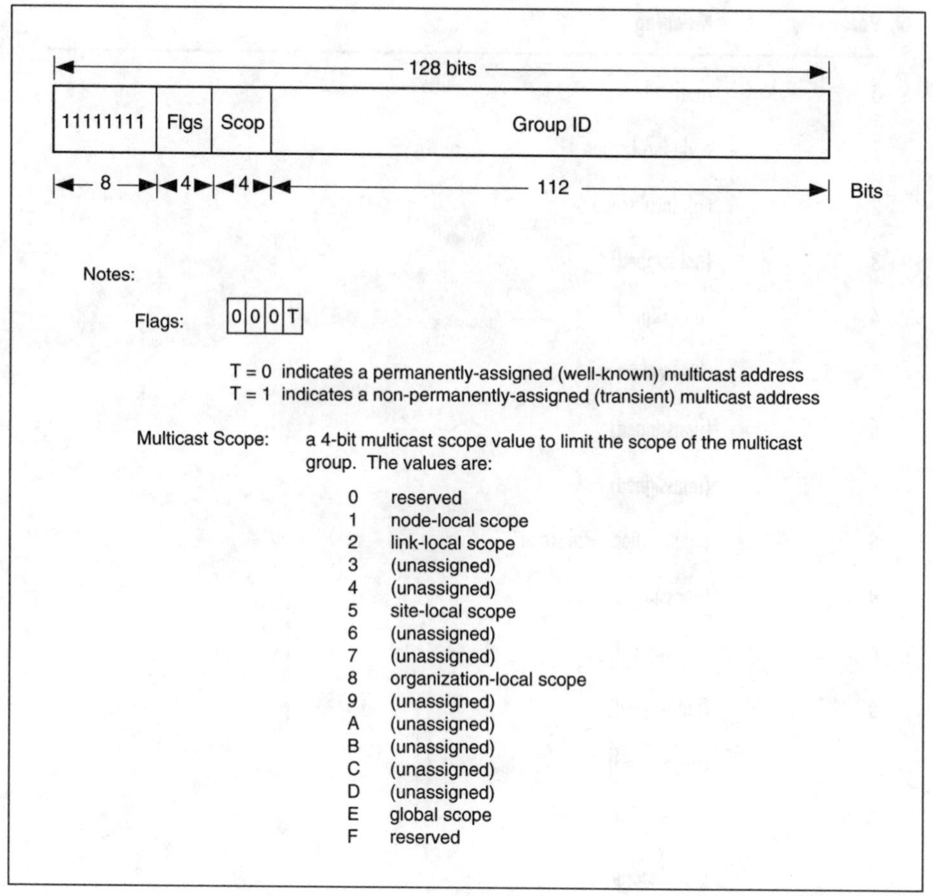

Figure 3-27. Multicast address

The Scop field is a four-bit field that is used to limit the scope of the multicast group. Scop field values are:

Value	Meaning
0	reserved
1	node-local scope
2	link-local scope
3	(unassigned)
4	(unassigned)
5	site-local scope
6	(unassigned)
7	(unassigned)
8	organization-local scope
9	(unassigned)
A	(unassigned)
B	(unassigned)
C	(unassigned)
D	(unassigned)
E	global scope
F	reserved

The Group ID field identifies the multicast group, either permanent or transient, within the given scope.

Multicast addresses may not be used as source addresses in IPv6 datagrams or appear in any routing header.

Additional work that documents many proposed enhancements to RFC 1884 is defined in Reference [3-16]. These two documents define the following well-known multicast addresses.

Reserved Multicast Addresses:

FF00:0:0:0:0:0:0:0

FF01:0:0:0:0:0:0:0

FF02:0:0:0:0:0:0:0

FF03:0:0:0:0:0:0:0

FF04:0:0:0:0:0:0:0

FF05:0:0:0:0:0:0:0

FF06:0:0:0:0:0:0:0

FF07:0:0:0:0:0:0:0

FF08:0:0:0:0:0:0:0

FF09:0:0:0:0:0:0:0

FF0A:0:0:0:0:0:0:0

FF0B:0:0:0:0:0:0:0

FF0C:0:0:0:0:0:0:0

FF0D:0:0:0:0:0:0:0

FF0E:0:0:0:0:0:0:0

FF0F:0:0:0:0:0:0:0

The above multicast addresses are reserved and shall never be assigned to any multicast group.

All Nodes Addresses:

FF01:0:0:0:0:0:0:1

FF02:0:0:0:0:0:0:1

The above multicast addresses identify the group of all IPv6 nodes within scope 1 (node-local) or 2 (link-local). For example, the address FF02:0:0:0:0:0:0:1 (or FF02::1) has the meaning "all nodes on this link."

All Routers Addresses:

FF01:0:0:0:0:0:0:2

FF02:0:0:0:0:0:0:2

FF05:0:0:0:0:0:0:2

The above multicast addresses identify the group of all IPv6 routers within scope 1 (node-local), 2 (link-local), or 5 (site-local). For example, the address FF02:0:0:0:0:0:0:2 (or FF02::2) has the meaning "all routers on this link."

Solicited-Node Address:

FF02:0:0:0:0:1:FFXX:XXXX

The above multicast address is computed as a function of a node's unicast and anycast addresses. The solicited-node multicast address is formed by taking the low-order 24 bits of the address (unicast or anycast) and appending those bits to the 104-bit prefix FF02:0:0:0:0:1:FF00::/104.

This results in a multicast address in the range

FF02:0:0:0:0:1:FF00:0000

to

FF02:0:0:0:0:1:FFFF:FFFF

For example, the solicited-node multicast address corresponding to the IPv6 address

4037::01:800:200E:8C6C

is

FF02::1:FF0E:8C6C.

IPv6 addresses that differ only in the high-order bits, e.g., due to multiple high-order prefixes associated with different aggregations (providers), will map to the same solicited-node address. This reduces the number of multicast addresses a node must join.

A node is required to compute and support a solicited-node multicast address for every unicast and anycast address it is assigned.

3.8 IEEE EUI-64 Addresses

The Institute of Electrical and Electronics Engineers (IEEE) administers the addressing scheme for all local networks that adhere to the IEEE Project 802 series of standards. These include Carrier Sense Multiple Access with Collision Detection (CSMA/CD) networks, such as IEEE 802.3 10BASE-T or IEEE 802.5 token ring.

An IEEE 802 address consists of two parts: a Company ID and an Extension ID. The IEEE assigns Company IDs (sometimes called a manufacturer's ID) to organizations manufacturing network interface hardware. The company, in turn, assigns the Extension ID (sometimes called the Board ID). Taken together, the Company ID and Extension ID become a unique identifier (or serial number) for this network hardware; it is typically embedded in an address read only memory (ROM) on that network board.

In the past, the IEEE has allocated 24 bits each to the Company ID and the Extension ID, yielding a 48-bit address. The IEEE has recently enhanced this addressing scheme to expand the Extension ID field to 40 bits, thus accommodating more hardware interfaces (approximately 1 trillion – 10^{12}) per manufacturer. This new scheme, which provides for addresses that are 64 bits long, is called EUI-64 ™ and is shown in Figure 3-28 [3-18].

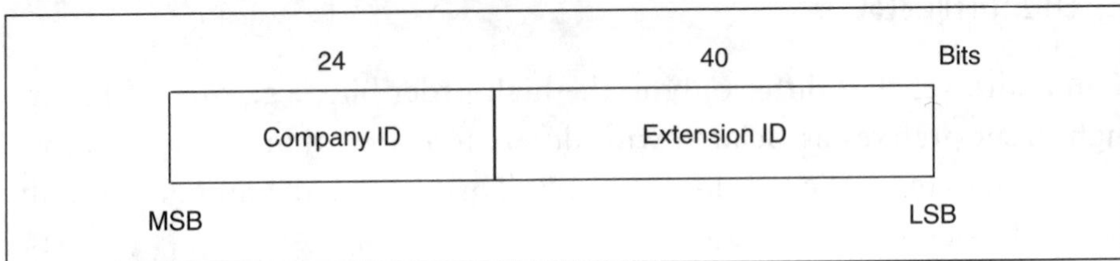

Figure 3-28. IEEE EUI-64 address

Within the IEEE addressing scheme (both 48-bit and EUI-64), there are two flag bits: the Individual/Group (I/G) bit and the Universal/Local (U/L) bit. These flag bits identify whether the address is an Individual Address (I/G = 0), a Group Address (I/G = 1), Universally (or globally) administered (U/L = 0), or Locally administered (U/L = 1).

Many of the IPv6 addresses incorporate an Interface ID field, which is defined using the EUI-64 format. The EUI-64 address with universal (or global) significance is illustrated in Figure 3-29 (note the seventh bit of the first octet: U/L = 0). The EUI-64 address with a local significance (used for interface identifiers on links or nodes with IPv6) is illustrated in Figure 3-30. Note that, in this case, the seventh bit of the first octet has been inverted (U/L = 1).

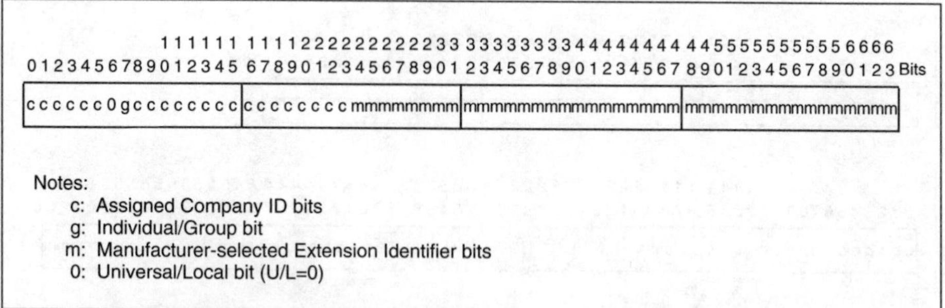

Figure 3-29. IEEE EUI-64 address (universal)

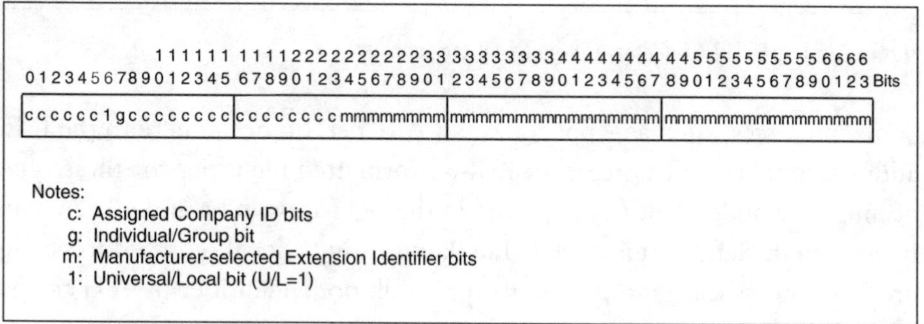

Figure 3-30. IEEE EUI-64 address (local)

To convert from the 48-bit address to the EUI-64 address, 16 bits are inserted between the Company ID and the Extension ID, as shown in Figure 3-31. These 16 bits are represented by the hexadecimal characters FFFE, or 1111 1111 1111 1110 in binary, which are shown in the lower portion of Figure 3-31 between the Company ID (c bits) and the manufacturer-defined Extension ID (m bits).

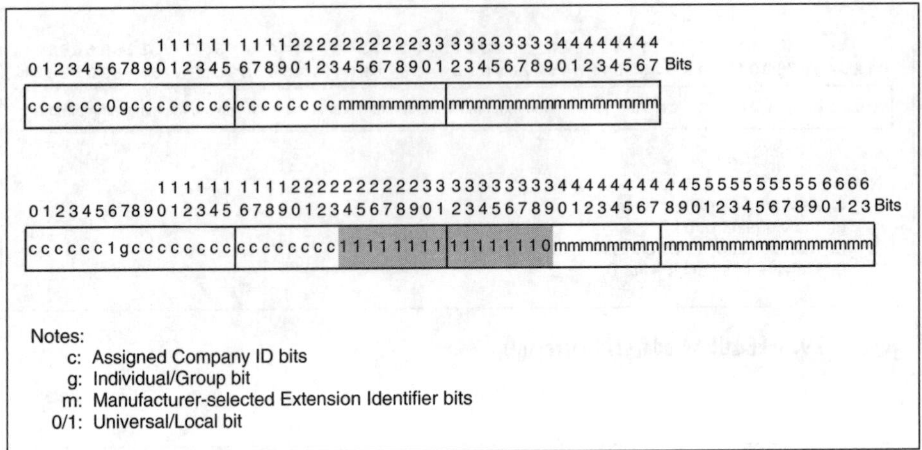

Figure 3-31. IEEE EUI-64 address (48- to 64-bit compatibility)

Some interfaces, such as AppleTalk and ARCnet, do not adhere to the IEEE addressing scheme. To create an EUI-64 formatted identifier for these types of links, the node identifier is placed in the right-most bits, and all zeros are filled in to the left. In this case, U/L = 0, indicating a local scope address. Figure 3-32 shows the example of an AppleTalk node identifier of 4FH carried in the EUI-64 format.

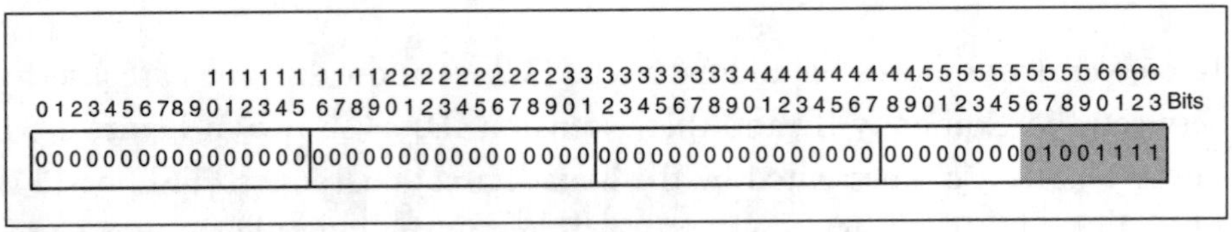

111111 1111222222222233 3333333344444444 4455555555556666
0123456789012345 6789012345678901 2345678901234567 8901234567890123 Bits
0000000000000000 0000000000000000 0000000000000000 0000000001001111

Figure 3-32. IEEE EUI-64 address (with nonglobal identifiers)

3.9 Required Addresses for Nodes

RFC 1884 [3-9], plus the proposed enhancements [3-12] summarize the following requirements for nodes and their addresses:

A host is required to recognize the following addresses as identifying itself:

- Its Link-Local Address for each interface
- Assigned Unicast Addresses
- Loopback Address
- All-Nodes Multicast Address
- Solicited-Node Multicast Address for each of its assigned unicast and anycast addresses
- Multicast Addresses of all other groups to which the host belongs

A router is required to recognize the following addresses as identifying itself:

- The Subnet-Router Anycast Addresses for the interfaces it is configured to act as a router on
- All other Anycast Addresses with which the router has been configured
- All-Routers Multicast Address
- Solicited-Node Multicast Address for each of its assigned unicast and anycast addresses
- Multicast Addresses of all other groups to which the router belongs

The only address prefixes which should be predefined in an implementation are the following:

- Unspecified Address
- Loopback Address
- Multicast Prefix (FF)
- Local-Use Prefixes (Link-Local and Site-Local)
- Predefined Multicast Addresses
- IPv4-Compatible Prefixes

Implementations should assume all other addresses are unicast unless specifically configured (e.g., anycast addresses).

3.10 Case Study

As an example of IPv4 and IPv6 addresses in operation, consider the network shown in Figure 3-33. This network consists of two segments connected via a router. Subnet 242 (at the top of Figure 3-33) has stations running both IPv4 and IPv6, while Subnet 243 runs only IPv4. The router between the two segments runs IPv6 on the upper interface (connecting to Network 242) and IPv4 on the lower interface (connecting to Network 243). The analyzer is set to capture all of the data on Network 242, and then the router and workstation are booted. The workstation has three different client packages installed: IPv6, Novell Inc.'s NetWare, and Microsoft Corp.'s Windows 95.

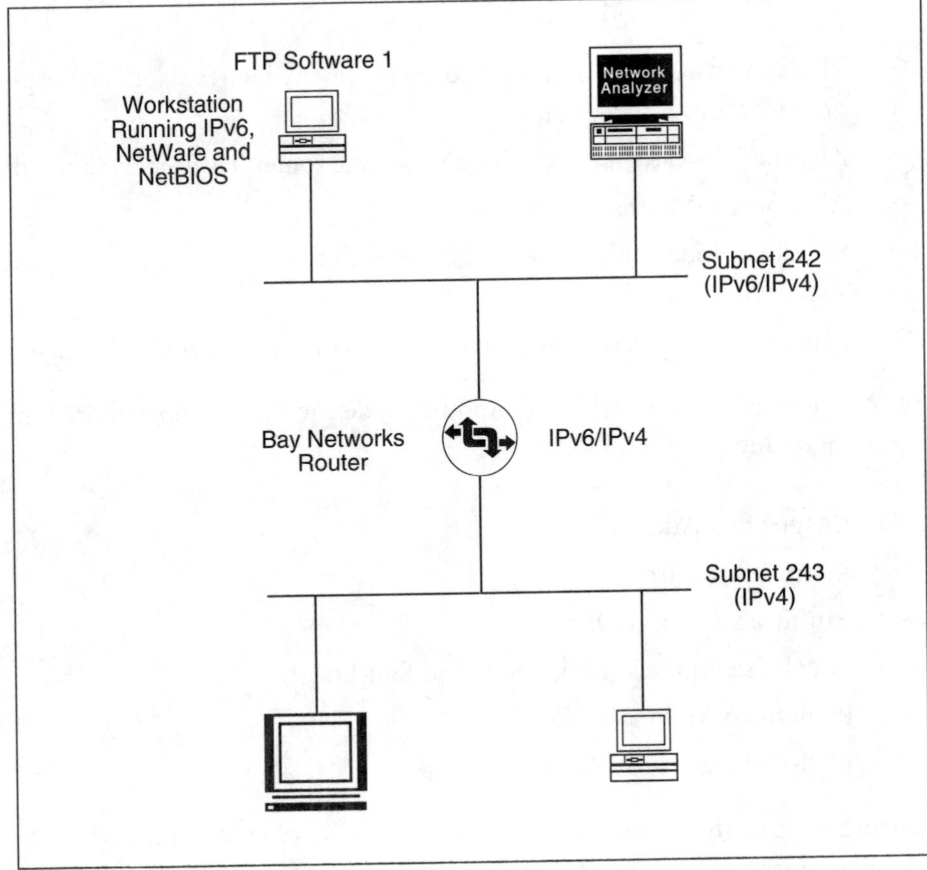

Figure 3-33. Workstation initialization

A summary of the captured data is shown in Trace 3.10a. The five columns in the trace show the frame number, time between frames (called DeltaTime), the Destination hardware address, the Source hardware address, and a brief interpretation of the frame contents and intended operation.

A number of different protocol processes are illustrated in this startup sequence. In Frame 1, we see the first Breath of Live (BOFL) packet which is transmitted from the Bay Networks router port (labeled Bay IPv6 P1) on a periodic basis. We can also observe the Address Resolution Protocol (ARP), communication between the various devices using Internet Control Message Protocol (ICMPv6), the Routing Information Protocol (RIP), Novell's Service Advertising Protocol (SAP), the Network Basic Input/Output System (NetBIOS) protocol, which is used with Windows 95, and several others. Note that the first transmission from the workstation (labeled FTP Software 1) occurs in Frame 35 with the start of the NetWare client initialization process. The workstation's TCP/IP protocol stack initializes beginning in Frame 51, and the Windows 95 client initializes beginning in Frame 54. These initialization processes are complete in Frame 112, as the workstation is able to send an ICMPv6 Echo Request message as a test of its readiness to process IPv6 packets.

Trace 3.10a. IPv6 Workstation Initialization Summary

```
-------------        Protocol Summary - bootast2.cap 8/22       --------------

 Frame DeltaTime    Destination        Source       Interpretation

  1                  Bay IPv6 P1      Bay IPv6 P1   BOFL(WF) Seq=1
  2 151.4 ms           Broadcast      Bay IPv6 P1   ARP REQUEST
  3 239.9 ms 33-33-A2-0A-1F-B8        Bay IPv6 P1   ICMPv6 Neighbor Solicitation
  4 119.6 ms 33-33-00-00-00-09        Bay IPv6 P1   RPC FRAME TOO SHORT
  5   2.6 sec          Broadcast      Bay IPv6 P1   ARP REQUEST
  6   1.1 sec 33-33-A2-0A-1F-B8       Bay IPv6 P1   ICMPv6 Neighbor Solicitation
  7 702.8 ms         Bay IPv6 P1      Bay IPv6 P1   BOFL(WF) Seq=2
  8 407.3 ms           Broadcast      Bay IPv6 P1   RIP (TCP/IP)
  9 890.2 ms 33-33-00-00-00-01        Bay IPv6 P1   ICMPv6 Router Advertisement
 10   3.7 sec        Bay IPv6 P1      Bay IPv6 P1   BOFL(WF) Seq=3
 11   1.1 sec          Broadcast      Bay IPv6 P1   RPC FRAME TOO SHORT
```

```
12   3.9 sec        Bay IPv6 P1     Bay IPv6 P1   BOFL(WF) Seq=4
13   5.0 sec        Bay IPv6 P1     Bay IPv6 P1   BOFL(WF) Seq=5
14   2.1 sec  33-33-00-00-00-01     Bay IPv6 P1   ICMPv6 Router Advertisement
15   2.9 sec        Bay IPv6 P1     Bay IPv6 P1   BOFL(WF) Seq=6
16   5.0 sec        Bay IPv6 P1     Bay IPv6 P1   BOFL(WF) Seq=7
17  48.0 ms   33-33-00-00-00-09     Bay IPv6 P1   UDP D=521 S=521 Len=72
18   5.0 sec        Bay IPv6 P1     Bay IPv6 P1   BOFL(WF) Seq=8
19  34.5 ms           Broadcast     Bay IPv6 P1   RIP (TCP/IP)
20   2.8 sec  33-33-00-00-00-01     Bay IPv6 P1   ICMPv6 Router Advertisement
21   2.1 sec        Bay IPv6 P1     Bay IPv6 P1   BOFL(WF) Seq=9
22   5.0 sec        Bay IPv6 P1     Bay IPv6 P1   BOFL(WF) Seq=10
23   5.0 sec        Bay IPv6 P1     Bay IPv6 P1   BOFL(WF) Seq=11
24   5.0 sec        Bay IPv6 P1     Bay IPv6 P1   BOFL(WF) Seq=12
25   3.7 sec  33-33-00-00-00-09     Bay IPv6 P1   UDP D=521 S=521 Len=72
26   1.3 sec        Bay IPv6 P1     Bay IPv6 P1   BOFL(WF) Seq=13
27   4.7 sec          Broadcast     Bay IPv6 P1   RIP (TCP/IP)
28 342.8 ms         Bay IPv6 P1     Bay IPv6 P1   BOFL(WF) Seq=14
29   5.0 sec        Bay IPv6 P1     Bay IPv6 P1   BOFL(WF) Seq=15
30   5.0 sec        Bay IPv6 P1     Bay IPv6 P1   BOFL(WF) Seq=16
31   5.0 sec        Bay IPv6 P1     Bay IPv6 P1   BOFL(WF) Seq=17
32   5.0 sec        Bay IPv6 P1     Bay IPv6 P1   BOFL(WF) Seq=18
33   2.3 sec  33-33-00-00-00-09     Bay IPv6 P1   UDP D=521 S=521 Len=72
34   2.7 sec        Bay IPv6 P1     Bay IPv6 P1   BOFL(WF) Seq=19
35   1.1 sec          Broadcast  FTP Software 1   RIP (Novell)
36    290 us          Broadcast  FTP Software 1   RIP (Novell)
37    160 us          Broadcast  FTP Software 1   RIP (Novell)
38    130 us          Broadcast  FTP Software 1   RIP (Novell)
39    130 us          Broadcast  FTP Software 1   RIP (Novell)
40    130 us          Broadcast  FTP Software 1   RIP (Novell)
41    130 us          Broadcast  FTP Software 1   SAP General Service Query
42    1.8 ms          Broadcast  FTP Software 1   RIP (Novell)
43   3.1 sec          Broadcast     Bay IPv6 P1   RIP (TCP/IP)
44 717.8 ms         Bay IPv6 P1     Bay IPv6 P1   BOFL(WF) Seq=20
45   5.0 sec        Bay IPv6 P1     Bay IPv6 P1   BOFL(WF) Seq=21
46   5.0 sec        Bay IPv6 P1     Bay IPv6 P1   BOFL(WF) Seq=22
47   5.0 sec        Bay IPv6 P1     Bay IPv6 P1   BOFL(WF) Seq=23
48   5.0 sec        Bay IPv6 P1     Bay IPv6 P1   BOFL(WF) Seq=24
49 985.4 ms   33-33-00-00-00-09     Bay IPv6 P1   UDP D=521 S=521 Len=72
50   4.0 sec        Bay IPv6 P1     Bay IPv6 P1   BOFL(WF) Seq=25
51   1.1 sec          Broadcast  FTP Software 1   ARP REQUEST
52 377.2 ms   01-00-5E-00-00-02  FTP Software 1   ICMP Router Solicitation
53 508.1 ms   33-33-C7-5F-9F-3D  FTP Software 1   ICMPv6 Neighbor Solicitation
54   1.6 sec            NetBIOS  FTP Software 1   NetBIOS Add Name and Query
55    380 us            NetBIOS  FTP Software 1   NetBIOS Add Group Name
56    130 us            NetBIOS  FTP Software 1   NetBIOS Add Name and Query
57 291.2 ms           Broadcast     Bay IPv6 P1   RIP (TCP/IP)
58 818.1 ms             NetBIOS  FTP Software 1   NetBIOS Add Name and Query
59    290 us            NetBIOS  FTP Software 1   NetBIOS Add Group Name
60    160 us            NetBIOS  FTP Software 1   NetBIOS Add Name and Query
```

```
 61 274.2 ms        Bay IPv6 P1      Bay IPv6 P1   BOFL(WF) Seq=26
 62 535.4 ms            NetBIOS  FTP Software 1   NetBIOS Add Name and Query
 63   290 us            NetBIOS  FTP Software 1   NetBIOS Add Group Name
 64   160 us            NetBIOS  FTP Software 1   NetBIOS Add Name and Query
 65 397.7 ms 33-33-00-00-00-02  FTP Software 1   ICMPv6 Router Solicitation
 66 863.5 ms 33-33-00-00-00-01     Bay IPv6 P1   ICMPv6 Router Advertisement
 67   3.2 sec       Bay IPv6 P1     Bay IPv6 P1   BOFL(WF) Seq=27
 68   1.8 sec         Broadcast  FTP Software 1   NetBIOS-NS (TCP/IP)
 69   510 us          Broadcast  FTP Software 1   NetBIOS-NS (TCP/IP)
 70   290 us          Broadcast  FTP Software 1   NetBIOS-NS (TCP/IP)
 71 509.3 ms          Broadcast  FTP Software 1   NetBIOS-NS (TCP/IP)
 72   450 us          Broadcast  FTP Software 1   NetBIOS-NS (TCP/IP)
 73   260 us          Broadcast  FTP Software 1   NetBIOS-NS (TCP/IP)
 74 771.1 ms          Broadcast  FTP Software 1   SAP Nearest Service Query
 75  47.5 ms          Broadcast  FTP Software 1   NetBIOS-NS (TCP/IP)
 76   480 us          Broadcast  FTP Software 1   NetBIOS-NS (TCP/IP)
 77   260 us          Broadcast  FTP Software 1   NetBIOS-NS (TCP/IP)
 78   1.8 sec       Bay IPv6 P1     Bay IPv6 P1   BOFL(WF) Seq=28
 79   5.0 sec       Bay IPv6 P1     Bay IPv6 P1   BOFL(WF) Seq=29
 80   4.6 sec 33-33-00-00-00-09     Bay IPv6 P1   UDP D=521 S=521 Len=72
 81 389.5 ms        Bay IPv6 P1     Bay IPv6 P1   BOFL(WF) Seq=30
 82   5.0 sec       Bay IPv6 P1     Bay IPv6 P1   BOFL(WF) Seq=31
 83   3.5 sec         Broadcast     Bay IPv6 P1   RIP (TCP/IP)
 84 806.9 ms          Broadcast  FTP Software 1   SAP General Service Query
 85  73.9 ms          Broadcast  FTP Software 1   SAP Nearest Service Query
 86 586.8 ms        Bay IPv6 P1     Bay IPv6 P1   BOFL(WF) Seq=32
 87   3.9 sec         Broadcast  FTP Software 1   SAP General Service Query
 88  10.0 ms          Broadcast  FTP Software 1   SAP Nearest Service Query
 89  55.7 ms            NetBIOS  FTP Software 1   NetBIOS Add Name and Query
 90   420 us          Broadcast  FTP Software 1   NetBIOS-NS (TCP/IP)
 91 358.1 ms          Broadcast  FTP Software 1   NetBIOS-NS (TCP/IP)
 92 439.1 ms            NetBIOS  FTP Software 1   NetBIOS Add Name and Query
 93  83.4 ms          Broadcast  FTP Software 1   NetBIOS-NS (TCP/IP)
 94 191.6 ms        Bay IPv6 P1     Bay IPv6 P1   BOFL(WF) Seq=33
 95 589.9 ms            NetBIOS  FTP Software 1   NetBIOS Add Name and Query
 96   4.4 sec       Bay IPv6 P1     Bay IPv6 P1   BOFL(WF) Seq=34
 97   5.0 sec       Bay IPv6 P1     Bay IPv6 P1   BOFL(WF) Seq=35
 98   3.2 sec 33-33-00-00-00-09     Bay IPv6 P1   UDP D=521 S=521 Len=72
 99   1.7 sec       Bay IPv6 P1     Bay IPv6 P1   BOFL(WF) Seq=36
100 191.7 ms          Broadcast  FTP Software 1   SAP General Service Query
101  10.0 ms          Broadcast  FTP Software 1   SAP Nearest Service Query
102   4.8 sec       Bay IPv6 P1     Bay IPv6 P1   BOFL(WF) Seq=37
103   3.2 sec         Broadcast     Bay IPv6 P1   RIP (TCP/IP)
104   1.8 sec       Bay IPv6 P1     Bay IPv6 P1   BOFL(WF) Seq=38
105   5.0 sec       Bay IPv6 P1     Bay IPv6 P1   BOFL(WF) Seq=39
106   2.4 sec         Broadcast  FTP Software 1   SAP General Service Query
107   2.6 sec       Bay IPv6 P1     Bay IPv6 P1   BOFL(WF) Seq=40
108   5.0 sec       Bay IPv6 P1     Bay IPv6 P1   BOFL(WF) Seq=41
109   1.9 sec 33-33-00-00-00-09     Bay IPv6 P1   UDP D=521 S=521 Len=72
```

```
110   3.1 sec        Bay IPv6 P1    Bay IPv6 P1   BOFL(WF) Seq=42
111   5.0 sec        Bay IPv6 P1    Bay IPv6 P1   BOFL(WF) Seq=43
112   1.7 sec        Bay IPv6 P1 FTP Software 1   ICMPv6 Echo Request
113     8.3 ms 33-33-C7-5F-9F-3D    Bay IPv6 P1   ICMPv6 Neighbor Solicitation
114     1.4 ms       Bay IPv6 P1 FTP Software 1   ICMPv6 Neighbor Advertisement
115     7.6 ms    FTP Software 1    Bay IPv6 P1   ICMPv6 Echo Reply
116   1.0 sec        Bay IPv6 P1 FTP Software 1   ICMPv6 Echo Request
117     5.0 ms    FTP Software 1    Bay IPv6 P1   ICMPv6 Echo Reply
118    64.2 ms         Broadcast    Bay IPv6 P1   RIP (TCP/IP)
119  974.3 ms        Bay IPv6 P1 FTP Software 1   ICMPv6 Echo Request
120     5.0 ms    FTP Software 1    Bay IPv6 P1   ICMPv6 Echo Reply
```

With all of these protocols in operation, a number of different addresses are also utilized.

The first address of interest is an ICMPv6 address sent from the router in an ICMPv6 Router Advertisement message, shown in Frame 9 (Trace 3.10b). The Destination Hardware address is 33-33-00-00-00-01H (a group address), and Source Hardware address is 00-00-A2-0A-1F-B8H (the Bay IPv6 router, port 1). The Ethernet frame specifies an EtherType of 86DDH, indicating that IPv6 data is contained within this frame. Within the IPv6 packet, the IPv6 Source address is FE80::A20A:1FB8 (a link-local address), and the IPv6 Destination address is FF02::1 (a multicast address identifying all nodes on this link).

Trace 3.10b. ICMPv6 Router Advertisement Packet Addressing

```
------------- Frame 9  Size 122  Absolute Time  13:24:22.56659  ------------
                  Protocol Detail - bootast2.cap 8/22



IEEE 802.3/Ethernet DIX V2 Header


            Decode Status : -
             Frame Length : 122
      Destination Address : 33-33-00-00-00-01 ( Group, Locally Administered Addr
           Source Address : 00-00-A2-0A-1F-B8, Bay IPv6 P1 ( OUI = WELLFLEET, U
             Frame Format : Ethernet DIX V2
                Ethertype : 0x86DD (IPv6)
           Frame Checksum : Good, Frame Check Sequence : 00 00 00 00
```

```
IPv6 - Internet Protocol (Version 6)


         Decode Status : -
        Version Number : 6 (IP Version 6)
                 Class : 0x0
            Flow Label : 0x0
        Payload Length : 64
           Next Header : 58 (ICMPv6)
             Hop Limit : 255
        Source Address : FE80:0:0:0:0:0:A20A:1FB8
   Destination Address : FF02:0:0:0:0:0:0:1


ICMPv6 - Internet Control Message Protocol (Version 6)


              Decode Status : -
                  ICMP Type : 134 (Router Advertisement)
 Router Advertisement Code : 0
                   Checksum : 47173
          Current Hop Limit : 64
                      Flags : 0x00
                              0... .... = Administered Protocol is not Used for Ad
                              .0.. .... = Administered Protocol is not Used for Au
            Router Lifetime : 1800 Seconds(s)
             Reachable Time : 0 Milliseconds(s)
       Retransmission Time : 0 Milliseconds(s)

                              ----- Options -----

                     Option : 1 (Source Link Layer Address)
              Option Length : 1
 Source Link Layer Address : 00-00-A2-0A-1F-B8, Bay IPv6 P1

                     Option : 5 (Maximum Transmission Unit)
              Option Length : 1
Maximum Transmission Unit : 1500
```

```
              Option : 3 (Prefix Information)
       Option Length : 4
       Prefix Length : 80
               Flags : 0xC0
                       1... .... = Prefix Length Can be Used for On-Link Determi
                       .1.. .... = Prefix Length Can be Used for Auton Addr Conf
      Valid Lifetime : 4294967295 (Infinity)
  Preferred Lifetime : 604800 Seconds(s)
              Prefix : 3FFE:1XXX:0:0:0:0:0:0
```

In Frame 19, the Bay router sends a Routing Information Protocol (RIP) packet identifying all of the routes that it is aware of (Trace 3.10c). This message is sent to a broadcast Destination Hardware address (FF-FF-FF-FF-FF-FF-FF H), and also to a broadcast Destination IPv4 address for all stations on that subnet (192.32.242.255). (Also note that this RIP message is sent using IPv4, not IPv6, as identified by the different EtherType field (0800 H).) The User Datagram Protocol (UDP) header identifies Port 520 (the RIP address) as the logical Source and Destination address. Finally, the RIP packet carries information on the routing distance to other subnets.

Trace 3.10c. RIP Message Addressing

```
------------- Frame 19  Size 130  Absolute Time  13:24:51.67789 -------------
                   Protocol Detail - bootast2.cap 8/22


IEEE 802.3/Ethernet DIX V2 Header


        Decode Status : -
         Frame Length : 130
  Destination Address : FF-FF-FF-FF-FF-FF, Broadcast ( Group, Locally Admin
       Source Address : 00-00-A2-0A-1F-B8, Bay IPv6 P1 ( OUI = WELLFLEET, U
         Frame Format : Ethernet DIX V2
            Ethertype : 0x800 (IP)
       Frame Checksum : Good, Frame Check Sequence : 00 00 00 00
```

```
IP - Internet Protocol


          Decode Status : -
                Version : 4, Header length : 20
        Type of Service : 0x00
                          000. .... = Routine Precedence
                          ...0 .... = Normal Delay
                          .... 0... = Normal Throughput
                          .... .0.. = Normal Reliability
                          .... ..00 = Reserved
           Total length : 112 bytes
         Identification : 7
       Fragment Control : 0x00
                          0... .... .... .... = Reserved
                          .0.. .... .... .... = May Fragment
                          ..0. .... .... .... = Last Fragment
                          ...0 0000 0000 0000 = Fragment Offset = 0 bytes
           Time to Live : 1 seconds/hops
               Protocol : 17 (UDP)
               Checksum : 0x533B (Checksum Good)
         Source Address : 192.32.242.250
    Destination Address : 192.32.242.255
 No IP options


UDP - User Datagram Protocol


          Decode Status : -
            Source Port : 520 (RIP (TCP/IP))
       Destination Port : 520 (RIP (TCP/IP))
             UDP Length : 92
               Checksum : 0xC453 (Checksum Good)
```

```
RIP (TCP/IP) - Routing Information Protocol


          Decode Status : -
                Command : 2 (Response)
                Version : 1
                 Unused : 0x00

                Entry 1
      Address Family ID : 0x02 (IP)
              Route Tag : 0x00
             IP Address : 192.32.242.0
            Subnet Mask : 0.0.0.0
               Next Hop : 0.0.0.0
                 Metric : 0x1

                Entry 2
      Address Family ID : 0x02 (IP)
              Route Tag : 0x00
             IP Address : 192.32.243.0
            Subnet Mask : 0.0.0.0
               Next Hop : 0.0.0.0
                 Metric : 0x1

                Entry 3
      Address Family ID : 0x02 (IP)
              Route Tag : 0x00
             IP Address : 192.32.244.0
            Subnet Mask : 0.0.0.0
               Next Hop : 0.0.0.0
                 Metric : 0x2

                Entry 4
      Address Family ID : 0x02 (IP)
              Route Tag : 0x00
             IP Address : 192.32.245.0
            Subnet Mask : 0.0.0.0
               Next Hop : 0.0.0.0
                 Metric : 0x3
```

Since the workstation is also a NetWare client, the NetWare driver must also be initialized. This process begins in Frame 35 (Trace 3.10d) and uses Novell's Internetwork Packet Exchange (IPX) protocol to carry a NetWare Routing Information Protocol (RIP) packet. (Note that the TCP/IP RIP packet sent by the router in Frame 19 and the IPX RIP Request packet sent by the workstation are two different protocols that just happen to have the same name.

Also notice that the NetWare client sends IEEE 802.3 frames, in contrast to the Ethernet frames sent by the router. Both frames have the same length, but a slightly different frame format.) The NetWare RIP Request packet is sent to Destination Hardware address FF-FF-FF-FF-FF-FF-FF H, and is also broadcast to NetWare Destination Node address FF-FF-FF-FF-FF-FF H.

Trace 3.10d. NetWare RIP Packet Addresses

```
-------------  Frame 35  Size 122  Absolute Time  13:25:48.50787  ----------
                     Protocol Detail - bootast2.cap 8/22


IEEE 802.3/Ethernet DIX V2 Header


          Decode Status : -
           Frame Length : 64
    Destination Address : FF-FF-FF-FF-FF-FF, Broadcast ( Group, Locally Admin
         Source Address : 00-80-C7-5F-9F-3D, FTP Software 1 ( OUI = XIRCOM
           Frame Format : IEEE 802.3
      IEEE 802.3 Length : 40
         Frame Checksum : Good, Frame Check Sequence : 00 00 00 00



IPX - Novell Internet Packet Exchange Protocol



          Decode Status : -
               Checksum : 0xFFFF (Not Verified)
                 Length : 40
      Transport Control : 0x00
                          0000 .... = Reserved
                          .... 0000 = Hop count = 0
            Packet Type : 0x01 (RIP)
    Destination Address : 00000000.FFFFFFFFFFFF
                          Destination Network : 00 00 00 00
                          Destination Node    : FF-FF-FF-FF-FF-FF, Broadcast
                          Destination Socket  : 0x453 (RIP)
         Source Address : 00000000.0080C75F9F3D
                          Source Network   : 00 00 00 00
                          Source Node      : 00-80-C7-5F-9F-3D, FTP Software 1
                          Source Socket    : 0x4000 (Dynamic)
```

```
RIP (Novell) - Novell Routing Information Protocol


          Decode Status : -
              Operation : 0x01 (Request)
                Network : FF FF FF FF, Hops : 9441, Ticks : 1217
```

The next communication from the workstation identifies the beginning of the IPv6 client startup procedure with the transmission of an ARP Request (Frame 51), an ICMP Router Solicitation (Frame 52), and ICMPv6 Neighbor Solicitation message in Frame 53 (Trace 3.10e). The Neighbor Solicitation message uses an IPv6 Source address of the unspecified address (0::0), which indicates that it is initializing and has not yet learned its address. The IPv6 Destination address is a special type of a multicast called the solicited node multicast address (FF02:0:0:0:0:1:FF5F:9F3D).

Trace 3.10e. ICMPv6 Neighbor Solicitation Message Addressing

```
-------------- Frame 53  Size 90  Absolute Time  13:26:19.69059  ------------
                     Protocol Detail - bootast2.cap 8/22


IEEE 802.3/Ethernet DIX V2 Header


              Decode Status : -
               Frame Length : 90
        Destination Address : 33-33-C7-5F-9F-3D ( Group, Locally Administered Addr
             Source Address : 00-80-C7-5F-9F-3D, FTP Software 1 ( OUI = XIRCOM, U
               Frame Format : Ethernet DIX V2
                  Ethertype : 0x86DD (IPv6)
             Frame Checksum : Good, Frame Check Sequence : 00 00 00 00
```

```
IPv6 - Internet Protocol (Version 6)


           Decode Status : -
          Version Number : 6 (IP Version 6)
                   Class : 0x0
              Flow Label : 0x0
          Payload Length : 32
             Next Header : 58 (ICMPv6)
               Hop Limit : 255
          Source Address : ::0.0.0.0
     Destination Address : FF02:0:0:0:0:1:FF5F:9F3D


ICMPv6 - Internet Control Message Protocol (Version 6)


           Decode Status : -
               ICMP Type : 135 (Neighbor Solicitation)
Neighbor Solicitation Code : 0
                Checksum : 17735
          Target Address : FE80:0:0:0:0:80:C75F:9F3D

             ----- Options -----
                  Option : 1 (Source Link Layer Address)
           Option Length : 1
 Source Link Layer Address : 00-80-C7-5F-9F-3D, FTP Software 1
```

The final initialization event occurs when the NetBIOS driver within the workstation starts up in Frame 54 (Trace 3.10f). This NetBIOS message is sent to a special NetBIOS group Hardware address (03-00-00-00-00-01 H). This communication uses an IEEE 802.3 frame format, and includes the IEEE 802.2 Logical Link Control (LLC) header. The LLC header includes the Destination Service Access Point (DSAP) address of F0H, which identifies a NetBIOS application. The NetBIOS message contains an Add Name and Query command, which contains the name to be added (Mark A. Miller).

Trace 3.10f. NetBIOS Message Addressing

```
-------------- Frame 54  Size 65  Absolute Time  13:26:21.38154  ------------
                    Protocol Detail - bootast2.cap 8/22


IEEE 802.3/Ethernet DIX V2 Header


          Decode Status : -
           Frame Length : 65
    Destination Address : 03-00-00-00-00-01, NetBIOS ( Group, Locally Adminis
         Source Address : 00-80-C7-5F-9F-3D, FTP Software 1 ( OUI = XIRCOM, N
           Frame Format : IEEE 802.3
      IEEE 802.3 Length : 47
         Frame Checksum : Good, Frame Check Sequence : 00 00 00 00


LLC - IEEE 802.2 Logical Link Control Protocol


        Decode Status : -
                 DSAP : 0xF0 (NetBIOS) (Individual), SSAP : 0xF0 (NetBIOS) (Command)
                        Unnumbered frame, UI


NetBIOS - Network Basic Input/Output System Protocol


          Decode Status : -
                 Length : 44
              Delimiter : 0xEFFF
                Command : 0x01 (Add Name and Query)
   Response Correlator : 0x01
NetBIOS Name To Be Added : MARK A. MILLER
```

In this chapter, we have studied the addressing architecture that is used with IPv6. In our case study, we saw a number of these addresses in use, many of which were employed under special conditions. In the next chapter, we will explore some of these special cases, many of which are required for communication within the IPv6 internetwork, and use the Internet Control Message Protocol (ICMPv6).

3.11 References

[3-1] Miller, Mark. "Finding Your Way Through the New IP." *Network World* (December 16, 1996): 43–45.

[3-2] Postel, J. "Internet Protocol." RFC 791, September 1981.

[3-3] Reynolds, J., and J. Postel. "Assigned Numbers." RFC 1700, October 1994.

[3-4] Baker, F., editor. "Requirements for IP Version 4 Routers." RFC 1812, June 1995.

[3-5] Krol, E. "The Hitchhikers Guide to the Internet." RFC 1118, September 1989.

[3-6] Fuller, V., T. Li, J. Yu, and K. Varadhan, "Classless Inter-Domain Routing (CIDR): An Address Assignment and Aggregation Strategy." RFC 1519, September 1993.

[3-7] Solensky, Frank. "CIDR Effects: Getting More out of IPv4." *ConneXions, The Interoperability Report* (May 1994): 14–17.

[3-8] Hudgins-Bonafield, Christine. "The Prospect of IP Renumbering." *Network Computing* (June 1, 1996): 84–92.

[3-9] Hinden, R., and S. Deering. "IP Version 6 Addressing Architecture." RFC 1884, December 1995.

[3-10] Rekhter, Y., and T. Li. "An Architecture for IPv6 Unicast Address Allocation." RFC 1887, December 1995.

[3-11] Partridge, C., T. Mendez, and W. Milliken. "Host Anycasting Service." RFC 1546, November 1993.

[3-12] Hinden, R., and S. Deering. "IP Version 6 Addressing Architecture." Work in progress, November 4, 1997.

[3-13] Hinden, R., S. Deering, and M. O'Dell. "An IPv6 Aggregatable Global Unicast Address Format." Work in progress, July 16, 1997.

[3-14] Hinden, R., and M. O'Dell. "TLA and NLA Assignment Rules." Work in progress, November 10, 1997.

[3-15] Hinden, R., R. Fink, and J. Postel. "IPv6 Testing Address Allocation." Work in progress, July 16, 1997.

[3-16] Hinden, R., and S. Deering. "IPv6 Multicast Address Assignments." Work in progress, July 16, 1997.

[3-17] Bound, J., B. Carpenter, D. Harrington, J. Houldsworth, A. Lloyd. "OSI NSAPs and IPv6." RFC 1888, August 1996.

[3-18] IEEE, Guidelines for 64-bit Global Identifier (EUI-64) Registration Authority, http://standards.ieee.org/db/oui/tutorials/EUI64.html, March 1997.

4 Intranetwork Communication in IPv6

If networks were flawless, you wouldn't have to read this chapter. But hosts lose communication with distant endpoints, routers send packets to the wrong destination, and other problems occur. A mechanism is therefore necessary for communication *within* the internetwork to describe (and hopefully remedy) these types of failures. That is the purpose of the *intra*network communication facilities that are built into IPv6.

These include the Internet Control Message Protocol for IPv6 (ICMPv6), plus other messages that support group membership, router communication, and neighbor communication.

As in the last two chapters, we will begin by quickly reviewing the benchmark: ICMP for IPv4.

4.1 The Intranetwork Communications Benchmark: ICMPv4

If we lived in Networking Utopia, datagrams would always be routed to their intended destination with no errors, excessive delays, or retransmissions required. Since this doesn't always happen, an adjunct module to IP, known as the Internet Control Message Protocol (ICMP), reports any errors that may have occurred in processing. Examples of errors would be datagrams that cannot be delivered or routes that are incorrect. ICMP is considered to be an integral part of IP, and is required to be implemented in IP modules contained in both hosts and routers. ICMP messages are contained within IP datagrams, with the IP header preceding the ICMP message and ICMP data. The specific purpose and format of the ICMP message is further identified by a Type field within the ICMP header.

Thirteen different formats of ICMP messages are defined, each with a specific ICMPv4 header format. Several of these share a common message structure, resulting in six unique message formats, shown in Figure 4-1. The first three fields are common to all headers, however. The Type field (1 octet) identifies one of the thirteen unique ICMP messages:

Type Code	ICMPv4 Messages
0	Echo Reply
3	Destination Unreachable
4	Source Quench
5	Redirect
8	Echo
11	Time Exceeded
12	Parameter Problem
13	Timestamp
14	Timestamp Reply
15	Information Request (obsolete)
16	Information Reply (obsolete)
17	Address Mask Request
18	Address Mask Reply

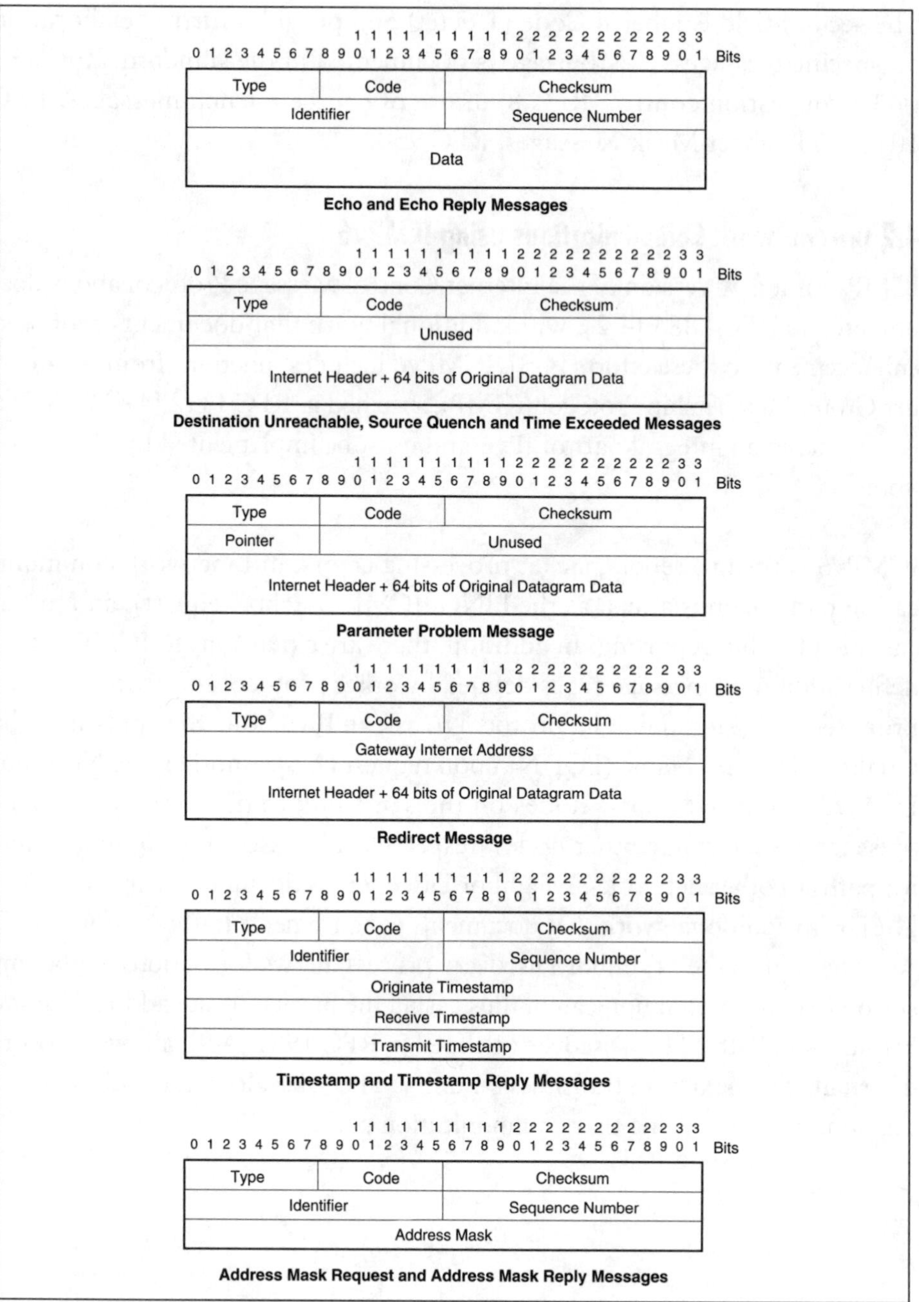

Figure 4-1. ICMPv4 messages

The second field is labeled Code (1 octet) and provides further elaboration on specific messages. ICMP usage is documented in the standard, RFC 792 [4-1]; congestion control, RFC 896; use of source quench messages, RFC 1016; and Subnet Mask Messages, RFC 950.

4.2 Intranetwork Communications using ICMPv6

ICMPv6 is a new version of the Internet Control Message Protocol and is documented in RFC 1885 [4-2], with additional work that documents proposed enhancements to these efforts [4-3]. ICMPv6 includes functions from the Internet Group Membership Protocol (IGMP), specified in RFC 1112 [4-4]. ICMPv6 is considered an integral part of IPv6 and must be implemented by every IPv6 node.

ICMPv6 is used to report packet processing errors, intranetwork communication path diagnosis such as the PING (ICMPv6 Echo Request), and multicast membership reporting. In addition, there are extensions to ICMPv6 that define additional message types defined by other protocols or processes. One proposed extension defines a protocol to ask an IPv6 node to supply its Fully Qualified Domain Name (FQDN) upon request [4-5]. Another, the Neighbor Discovery process, allows nodes on the same link to discover each other's presence, to determine other nodes' respective addresses, and to find routers for paths to other networks. Neighbor Discovery is documented in RFC 1970 [4-6], with additional work that documents enhancements to these efforts [4-7]. An extension to the Neighbor Discovery process allows for options containing site prefixes to be communicated, thus easing the burden of site address renumbering [4-8]. Path MTU Discovery, defined in RFC 1981 [4-9], allows a host to determine the maximum transmission unit (MTU) size along the path to a destination, thus optimizing that communication path.

Thus, all of these processes provide communication *within* the IPv6 internetwork. We will begin by looking at the fundamental messages defined for ICMPv6.

4.3 ICMPv6 Error Messages

With respect to IPv6, an ICMPv6 message would be considered an upper-layer protocol. As such, the ICMPv6 message is preceded by an IPv6 header, and zero or more IPv6 extension headers (review Figure 2-14). The header preceding the ICMPv6 header will have a Next Header field value of 58.

ICMPv6 messages have three fields that are common to all messages, plus a variable length message body whose contents depend on the type of message being transmitted (Figure 4-2). The common fields are:

Type, eight bits long, which indicates the type of message.

Code, eight bits long, which creates an additional level of message granularity and depends on the message type being sent.

Checksum, 16 bits long, which is used to detect data corruption in the ICMPv6 message and parts of the IPv6 header.

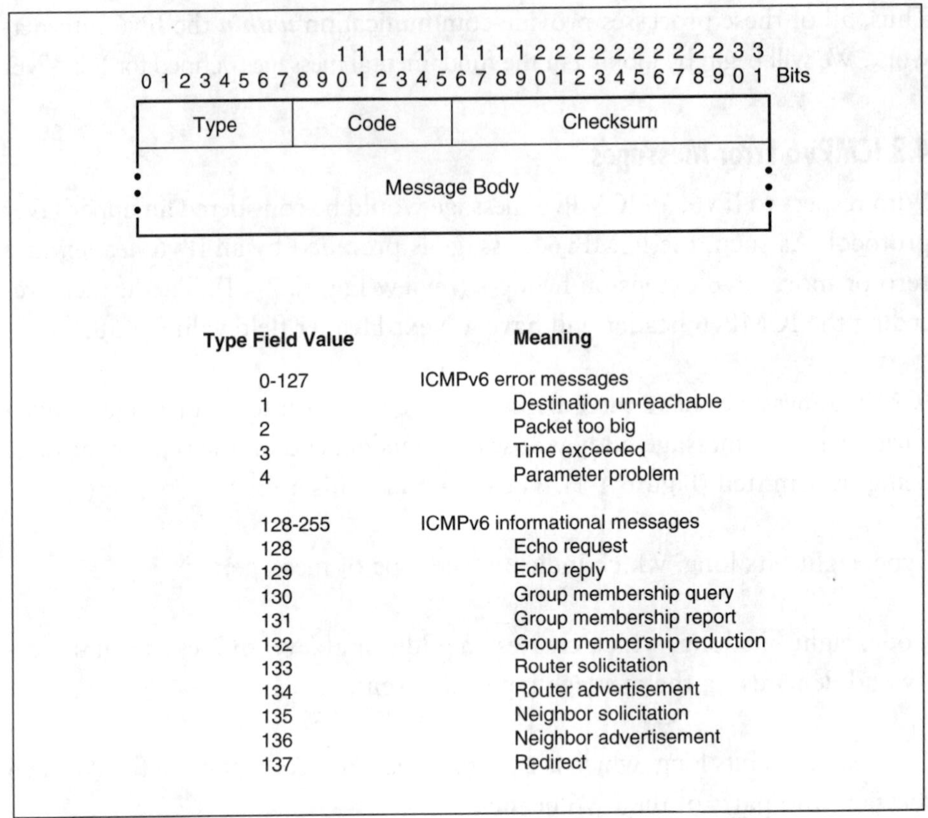

Figure 4-2. ICMPv6 messages

ICMPv6 messages are grouped into two categories: error messages and informational messages. These two categories are readily identified by the high-order bit of the message Type field.

IPv6 nodes that discard a packet may send an ICMPv6 error message to the original destination. There are four cases in which this may occur, and each of these circumstances produces a different error message: the destination was not reachable, the packet was too big, the packet exceeded its allowable time to live, or a parameter problem occurred. Each error message format is similar, with an 8-octet section that contains the Type, Code, Checksum and a parameter field, plus a copy (or partial copy) of the originally transmitted packet.

Error messages have a zero in the high-order bit, and therefore have message types from 0–127:

Type	Message
1	Destination Unreachable
2	Packet Too Big
3	Time Exceeded
4	Parameter Problem

Informational messages have a one in the high-order bit, and therefore have message types 128–255:

Type	Message
128	Echo Request
129	Echo Reply
130	Group Membership Query
131	Group Membership Report
132	Group Membership Reduction
133	Router Solicitation
134	Router Advertisement
135	Neighbor Solicitation
136	Neighbor Advertisement
137	Redirect

Note that message types 133–137 are defined by the Neighbor Discovery protocol and are examples of extensions to the ICMPv6 message set.

4.3.1 Destination Unreachable Message

The Destination Unreachable message is defined by ICMPv6 Type = 1 (Figure 4-3). The Code field may take on one of five values:

Code	Meaning
0	No route to destination
1	Communication with destination administratively prohibited
2	Not a neighbor
3	Address unreachable
4	Port unreachable

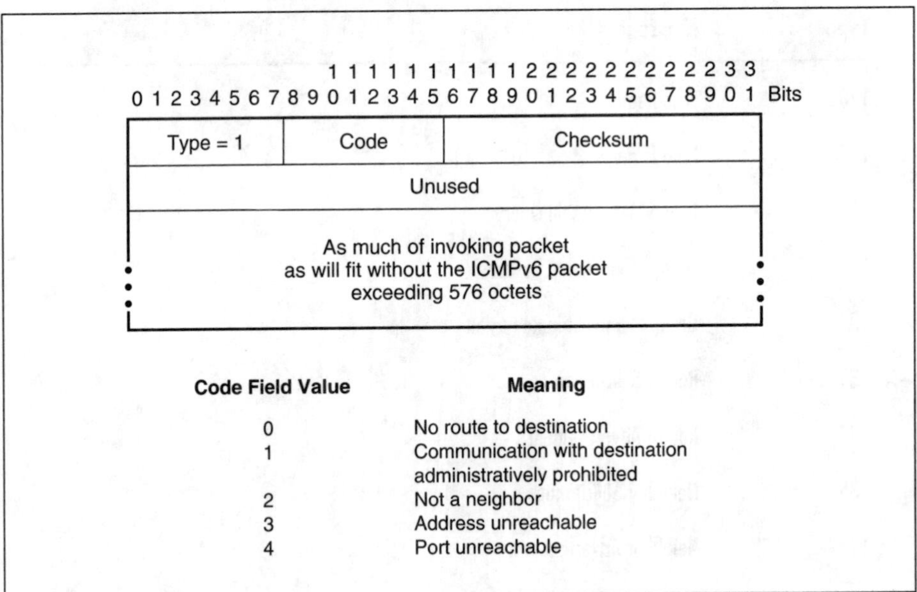

Figure 4-3. Destination Unreachable message

The Unused field should be initialized to all zeros by the sender and ignored by the receiver.

When a packet cannot be delivered to its destination address for reasons other than congestion, a Destination Unreachable message should be generated by a router, or by the IPv6 layer in the originating node.

Code = 0 (no route to destination) is used when the failure to deliver is caused by a forwarding node that does not have a matching entry in its routing table; as a result, the router does not know of any path to that destination. Code = 1 (communication prohibited) is used when the failure to deliver is caused by some administrative procedure, such as a firewall filter that prohibits the packet's transmission. Code = 2 (not a neighbor) is used when the delivery fails because the next destination address in the Routing header is not a neighbor of the processing node, but the "strict" bit (in the Routing header) was set. Code = 3 (address unreachable) is set when the failure to deliver is caused by an unresolvable Data Link Layer address, or when there is some failure of the Data Link Layer hardware. Lastly, Code = 4 (port unreachable) is used when the destination node's Transport Layer does not have an active listener process.

A node receiving the ICMPv6 Destination Unreachable message must notify the upper-layer protocol.

4.3.2 Packet Too Big Message

The Packet Too Big message is defined by ICMPv6 Type = 2 (Figure 4-4). The Code = 0, and the MTU field contains the maximum transmission unit (MTU) of the next-hop link.

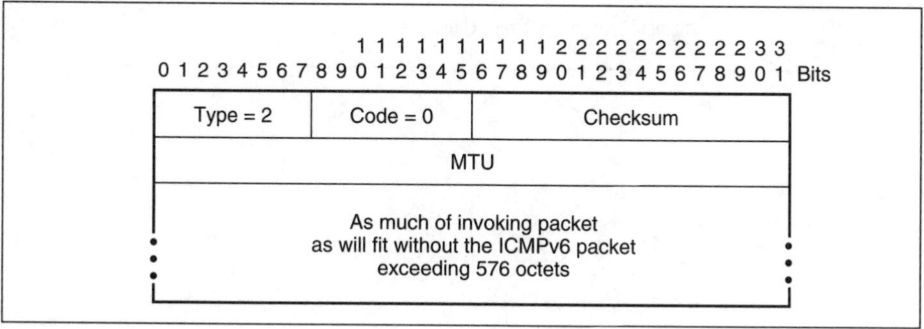

Figure 4-4. Packet Too Big message

This message is used in conjunction with the Path MTU Discovery process, defined in RFC 1981. In this process, a host sends its maximum size packet to see whether that size packet can be transmitted to the final destination. If any intermediate link cannot accommodate that packet, the Packet Too Big message is returned, along with the MTU of the smaller link. A second attempt is then made with this smaller size packet. If that second attempt is not successful, another Packet Too Big message will be returned (this time from a further link downstream), along with another (smaller) MTU. This process continues until the test packet successfully reaches its destination without an error message being returned.

The Packet Too Big message is also sent in response to a packet sent to a multicast destination address. This allows the MTU Discovery process to operate for IPv6 multicast configurations.

An incoming Packet Too Big message must be passed to the upper-layer protocol process.

4.3.3 Time Exceeded Message

The Time Exceeded message is defined by ICMPv6 Type = 3 (Figure 4-5). The Code field may take on one of two values:

Code	Meaning
0	Hop limit exceeded in transit
1	Fragment reassembly time exceeded

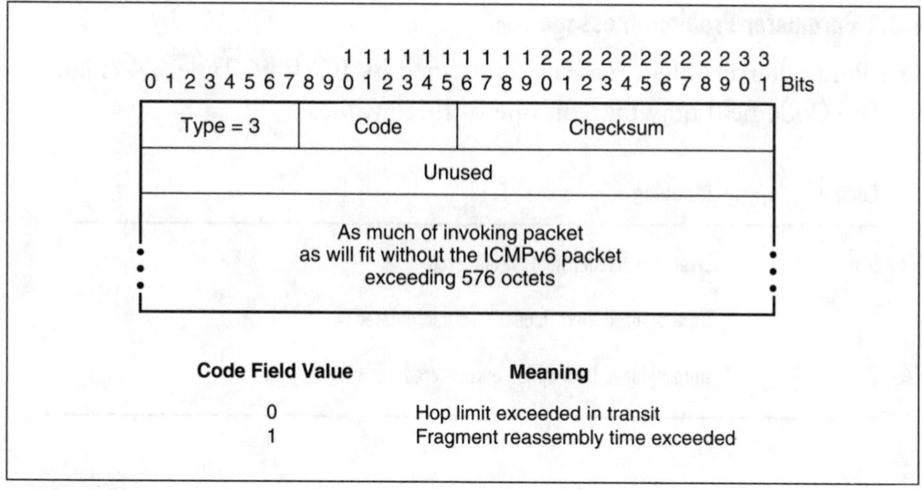

Figure 4-5. Time Exceeded message

The Unused field should be initialized to all zeros by the sender and ignored by the receiver.

If a router receives a packet with a Hop Limit of zero, or a router decrements a packet's Hop Limit to zero, it will discard the packet and send a Time Exceeded message with Code = 0 to the source of the packet. In this case, either the Hop Limit was set too low initially, or a routing loop exists.

If a router is not able to reassemble all of the fragments of a message within a reasonable time (typically on the order of a few minutes), it is likely that a fragment has been lost; therefore, complete reassembly of that message will not be possible. When this occurs, a Time Exceeded message with Code = 1 is sent.

An incoming Time Exceeded message must be passed to the upper layer protocol process.

4.3.4 Parameter Problem Message

The Parameter Problem message is defined by ICMPv6 Type = 4 (Figure 4-6). The Code field may take on one of three values:

Code	Meaning
0	Erroneous header field encountered
1	Unrecognized Next Header type encountered
2	Unrecognized IPv6 option encountered

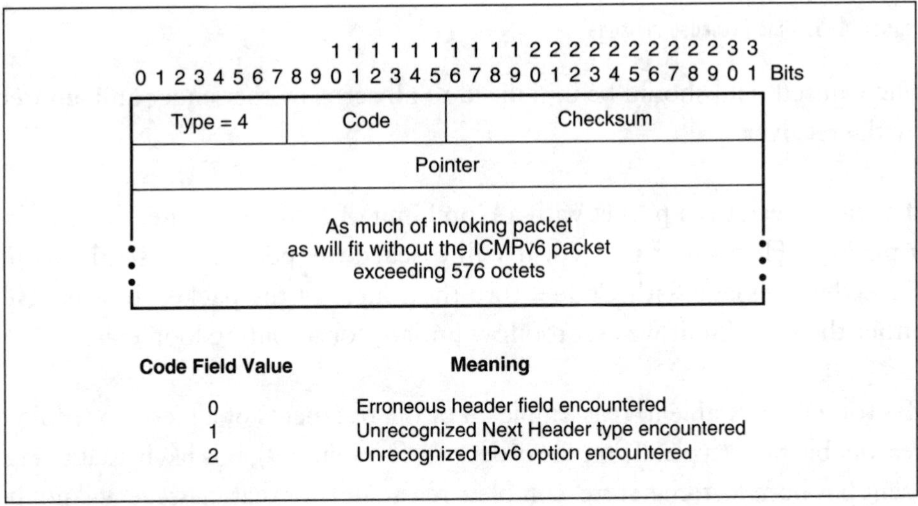

Figure 4-6. Parameter Problem message

The Pointer field contains a pointer that identifies the offset, in octets, within the invoking packet where the error was detected. The pointer will point beyond the end of the ICMPv6 packet if the field in error is beyond what can fit in the 576-octet limit of an ICMPv6 error message.

The Parameter Problem message is used when an IPv6 node finds a field in the IPv6 header or extension headers that prevent the processing of the packet. When this occurs, the packet is discarded and the Parameter Problem message is sent to the packet's source, indicating the type and location of the problem. The Pointer field indicates the octet of the original packet's header where the error was detected.

A node receiving the Parameter Problem message must notify the upper-layer protocol process.

4.4 Echo Request/Reply Messages

The Echo Request message is defined by ICMPv6 Type = 128, with Code = 0 (Figure 4-7). Two additional 16-bit fields are added: an Identifier and a Sequence Number. Both of these fields are used to match Echo Replies to this Echo Request. The Data field contains zero or more octets of arbitrary data.

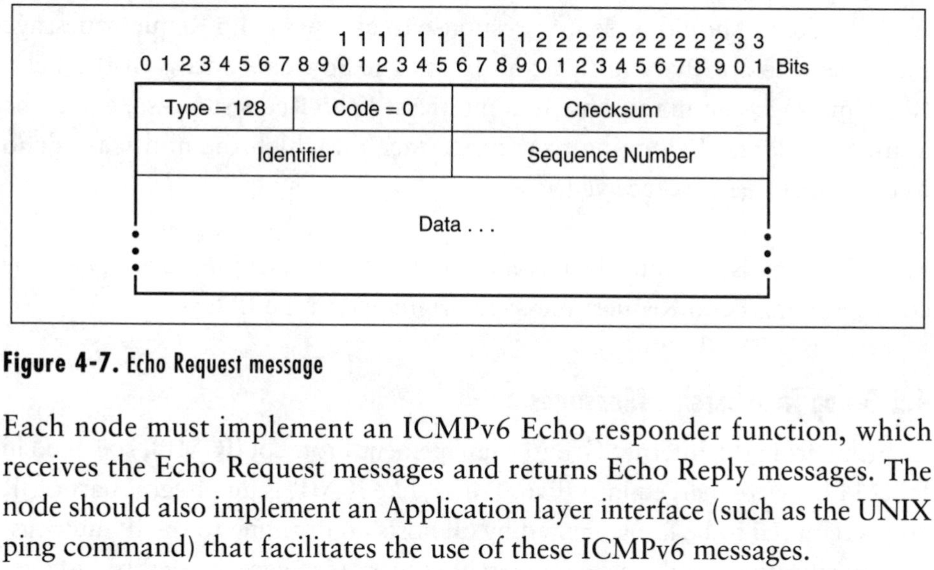

Bits 0–31 (0 1 2 3 4 5 6 7 8 9 1 0 1 1 1 2 1 3 1 4 1 5 1 6 1 7 1 8 1 9 2 0 2 1 2 2 2 3 2 4 2 5 2 6 2 7 2 8 2 9 3 0 3 1)

Bits 0–7	Bits 8–15	Bits 16–31
Type = 128	Code = 0	Checksum
Identifier		Sequence Number
Data . . .		

Figure 4-7. Echo Request message

Each node must implement an ICMPv6 Echo responder function, which receives the Echo Request messages and returns Echo Reply messages. The node should also implement an Application layer interface (such as the UNIX ping command) that facilitates the use of these ICMPv6 messages.

A node receiving an Echo Request message may notify the upper-layer protocol process.

The Echo Reply message is defined by ICMPv6 Type = 129, with Code = 0 (Figure 4-8). The Identifier, Sequence Number, and Data field values are taken from the Echo Request message that is being responded to.

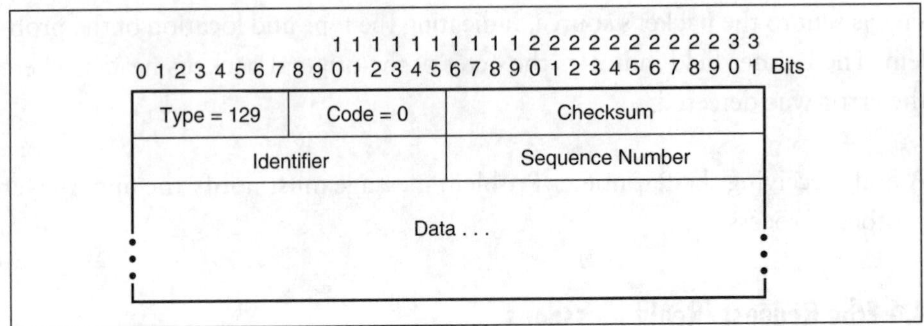

Figure 4-8. Echo Reply message

The Source Address of the Echo Reply message sent in response to a unicast Echo Request message must be the same as the Destination Address of that Echo Request message.

An Echo Reply should be sent in response to an IPv6 Echo Request message that is sent to an IPv6 multicast address. The Source Address of the Echo Reply message sent in response to a multicast Echo Request message must be a unicast address belonging to the interface on which the multicast Echo Request message was received.

Echo Reply messages must be passed to the ICMPv6 user interface, unless the corresponding Echo Request message originated in the IP layer.

4.5 Group Membership Messages

Elements from the Internet Group Management Protocol (IGMP), specified in RFC 1112, were merged into IPv6. IGMP, like ICMP, is an integral part of IP, and is required to be implemented by all hosts conforming to the IP multicasting specification. Multicast Membership Query messages are sent to discover which host groups have members on their attached local networks. Hosts respond to a Query by generating a Membership Report message. Hosts terminating their membership in a group issue a Membership Reduction message.

The Group Membership messages are defined by ICMPv6 Type = 130 (Group Membership Query, Figure 4-9), Type = 131 (Group Membership Report, Figure 4-10), and Type = 132 (Group Membership Reduction, Figure 4-11). All of these messages use Code = 0.

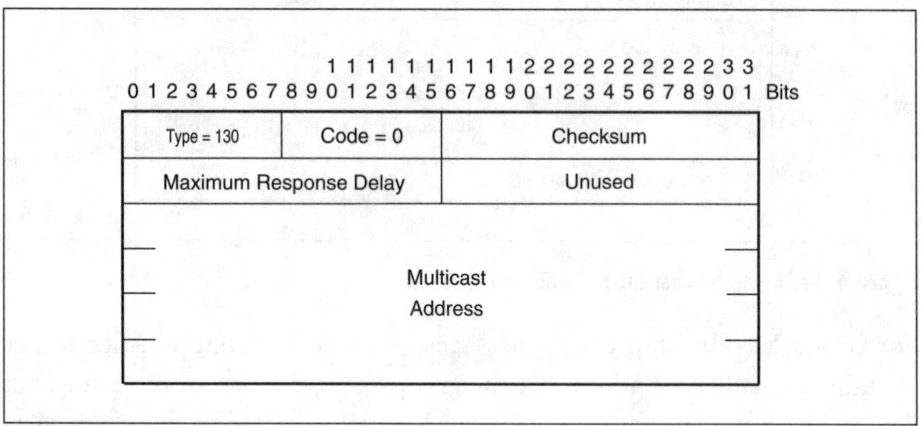

Figure 4-9. Group Membership Query message

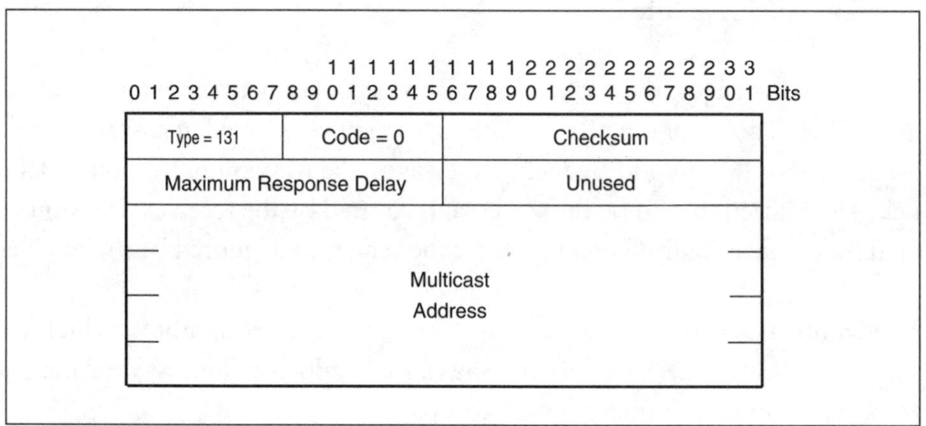

Figure 4-10. Group Membership Report message

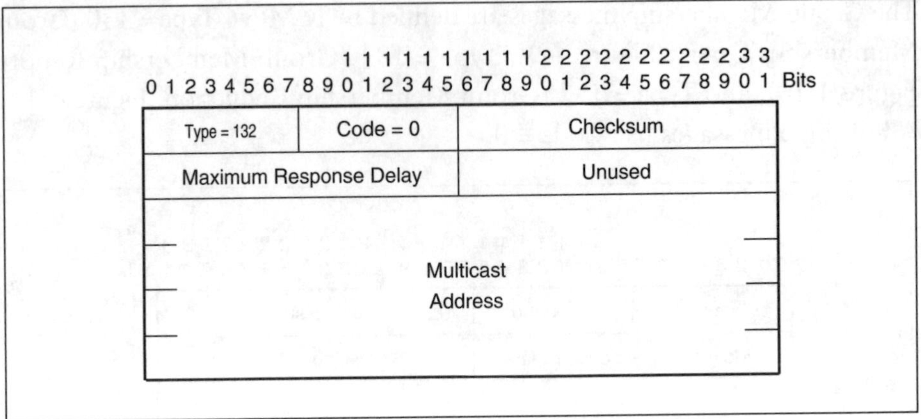

Figure 4-11. Group Membership Reduction message

For Group Membership Query messages, the IPv6 Destination Address field contains the multicast address of the group being queried or the Link-Local All-Nodes multicast address. For Group Membership Report or Group Membership Reduction messages, the IPv6 Destination Address field contains the multicast address of the group being reported or terminated. In all cases, the Hop Limit field is set to one.

For Query messages, the Maximum Response Delay field contains the maximum time that responding Report messages may be delayed, measured in milliseconds. For Report and Reduction messages, the Maximum Response Delay field is initialized to zero by the sender and ignored by the receiver. The Unused field should be initialized to all zeros by the sender and ignored by the receiver.

The Multicast Address field contains the multicast group about which the message is being sent. In Query messages, the Multicast Address field may be zero, which implies a query for all groups.

4.6 Neighbor Discovery Protocol

The Neighbor Discovery Protocol, defined in RFC 1970 [4-6], and further documented in reference [4-7], combines the functions of three IPv4 mechanisms: the Address Resolution Protocol (ARP), from RFC 826; ICMP Router Discovery messages, from RFC 1256; and the ICMP Redirect message, from RFC 792.

Nodes (hosts or routers) use Neighbor Discovery to determine the Data Link Layer addresses for their neighbors on attached links, and also to purge cached values that are no longer valid. Nodes also use this protocol to actively track which neighbors are reachable and which are not, and also to detect Data Link Layer addresses that have changed. Hosts use Neighbor Discovery to find neighboring routers that are willing to forward packets on their behalf.

According to RFC 1970, the Neighbor Discovery protocol defines mechanisms for solving the following problems:

- Router Discovery: How hosts locate routers that reside on an attached link.
- Prefix Discovery: How hosts discover the set of address prefixes that define which destinations are on-link for an attached link. (Nodes use prefixes to distinguish destinations that reside on-link from those only reachable through a router.)
- Parameter Discovery: How a node learns such link parameters as the link MTU or such Internet parameters as the hop limit value to place in outgoing packets.
- Address Autoconfiguration: How nodes automatically configure an address for an interface.
- Address Resolution: How nodes determine the Link Layer address of an on-link destination (such as a neighbor) given only the destination's IP address.
- Next-hop Determination: The algorithm for mapping an IP destination address into the IP address of the neighbor to which traffic for the destination should be sent. The next-hop can be a router or the destination itself.

- Neighbor Unreachability Detection: How nodes determine that a neighbor is no longer reachable. For neighbors used as routers, alternate default routers can be tried. For both routers and hosts, address resolution can be performed again.
- Duplicate Address Detection: How a node determines that an address it wishes to use is not already in use by another node.
- Redirect: How a router informs a host of a better first-hop node to reach a particular destination.

Combining the IPv4 ARP, Router Discovery, and Redirect functions into the IPv6 Neighbor Discovery process allows for an efficient and consistent way of disseminating information. Five ICMPv6 messages facilitate the Neighbor Discovery information: Router Solicitation, Router Advertisement, Neighbor Solicitation, Neighbor Advertisement, and Redirect. These will be studied individually in the following subsections. In addition, many of these five messages include options, which will be considered at the end of this section.

4.6.1 Router Solicitation Message

The Router Solicitation Message is transmitted by a host to prompt routers to generate Router Advertisement messages quickly.

In the IPv6 header, the Source Address field identifies the sending interface (or an unspecified address if no sending address has been assigned), and the Destination Address field typically identifies the all-routers multicast address.

An Authentication header is included if a security association exists between the sender and the destination address.

In the ICMPv6 message, the Type = 133, the Code = 0, and the Reserved field should be initialized to all zeros by the sender and ignored by the receiver (Figure 4-12).

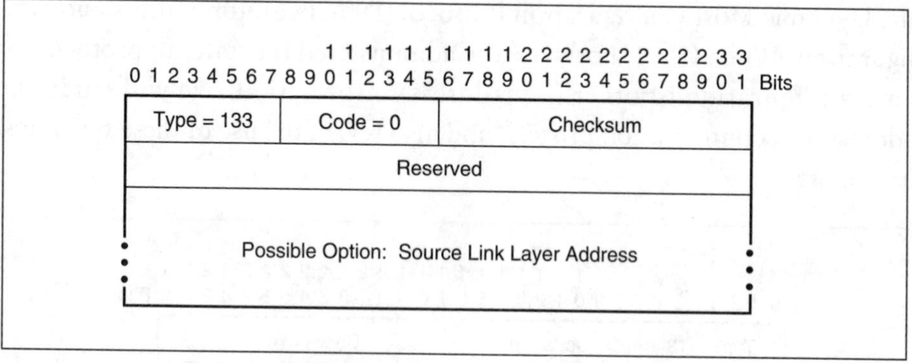

Figure 4-12. Router Solicitation message

A possible option is the Source Data Link Layer Address, if known.

4.6.2 Router Advertisement Message

Routers transmit Router Advertisement messages on a periodic basis, or in response to a host's Router Solicitation message.

In the IPv6 header, the Source Address field is the link-local address assigned to the interface from which this message was sent, and the Destination Address field is typically the Source Address of an invoking Router Solicitation, or the all-nodes multicast address.

An Authentication header is included if a security association exists between the sender and the destination address.

In the ICMPv6 message, the Type = 134 and the Code = 0 (Figure 4-13). The Current Hop Limit field is the default value that should be placed in the Hop Count field of the IPv6 header for outgoing IPv6 packets. A value of zero means unspecified by this router. Two single-bit flags identify the Managed Address Configuration (M flag) and the Other Stateful Configuration (O flag). When M = 1, hosts use the administered (or stateful) protocol, such as the Dynamic Host Configuration Protocol (DHCPv6), for address autoconfiguration. When O = 1, hosts use the administered (or stateful) protocol for autoconfiguration of other (nonaddress) information. We will study the address autoconfiguration process, and also revisit the use of these two flags, in Chapter 5.

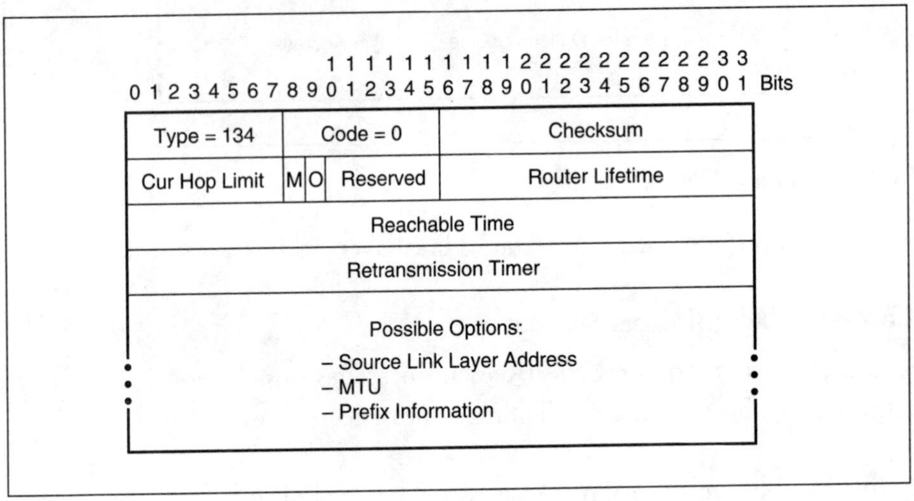

```
                      1 1 1 1 1 1 1 1 1 1 2 2 2 2 2 2 2 2 2 2 3 3
  0 1 2 3 4 5 6 7 8 9 0 1 2 3 4 5 6 7 8 9 0 1 2 3 4 5 6 7 8 9 0 1  Bits
```

Type = 134	Code = 0			Checksum
Cur Hop Limit	M	O	Reserved	Router Lifetime
Reachable Time				
Retransmission Timer				
Possible Options: – Source Link Layer Address – MTU – Prefix Information				

Figure 4-13. Router Advertisement message

The Reserved field should be initialized to all zeros by the sender and ignored by the receiver. The Router Lifetime field specifies the lifetime associated with the default router in units of seconds. The Reachable Time specifies the time, in milliseconds, that a node assumes a neighbor is reachable after having received a reachability confirmation. The Retransmission Timer specifies the time, in milliseconds, between retransmitted Neighbor Solicitation messages.

Possible options include the Source Data Link Layer Address, the MTU, and Prefix Information.

4.6.3 Neighbor Solicitation Message

Neighbor Solicitation messages are sent by nodes to request the Data Link Layer address of a target node, while also providing their own Data Link

Layer address to that target. Neighbor Solicitations are multicast when the node needs to resolve an address, and unicast when the node seeks to verify the reachability of a neighbor.

In the IPv6 header, the Priority = 15, the Hop Limit = 255, the Source Address field is either an address assigned to the interface from which this message is sent or the unspecified address, and the Destination Address field is either the solicited-node multicast address corresponding to the target address, or the target address.

An Authentication header is included if a security association exists between the sender and the destination address.

In the ICMPv6 message, the Type = 135 and the Code = 0 (Figure 4-14). The Reserved field should be initialized to all zeros by the sender and ignored by the receiver. The Target Address field is the IPv6 address of the target of the solicitation (which must not be a multicast address).

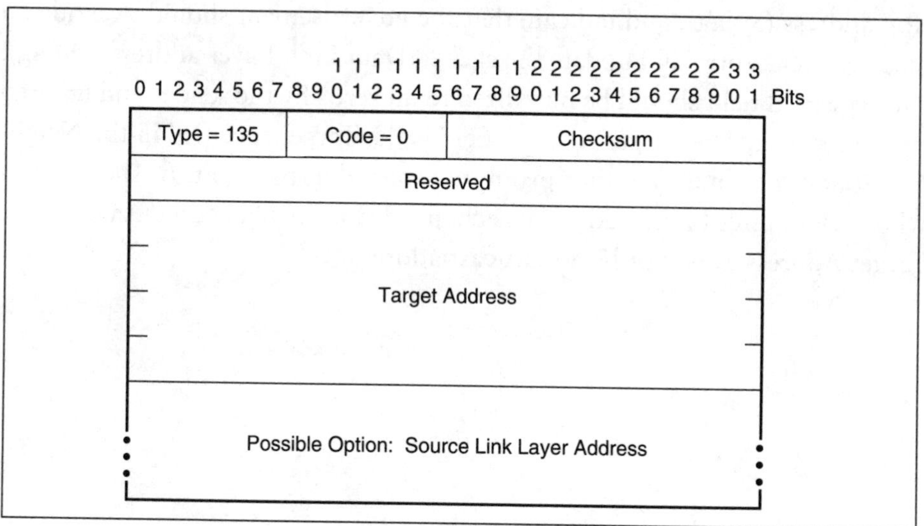

Figure 4-14. Neighbor Solicitation message

A possible option is the Source Data Link Layer Address.

4.6.4 Neighbor Advertisement Message

Neighbor Advertisement messages are sent by nodes in response to Neighbor Solicitation messages, or are sent unsolicited to propagate new information quickly.

In the IPv6 header, the Priority = 15, the Hop Limit = 255, the Source Address field is an address assigned to the interface from which this advertisement is sent, and the Destination Address field is either the Source Address of an invoking Neighbor Solicitation or the unspecified address (if the solicitation's Source Address is the unspecified address).

An Authentication header is included if a security association exists between the sender and the destination address.

In the ICMPv6 message, the Type = 136 and the Code = 0 (Figure 4-15). Three single-bit flags identify the sender as a Router (R flag), indicate that the advertisement was sent in response to a Neighbor Solicitation from the Destination address (S flag), and indicate that the advertisement should override an existing cache entry and update the cached Data Link Layer address (O flag). The Reserved field should be initialized to all zeros by the sender and ignored by the receiver. The Target Address field is the Target specified in the Neighbor Solicitation message that prompted this advertisement, or the address whose Data Link Layer address has changed (for unsolicited messages). The Target Address must not be a multicast address.

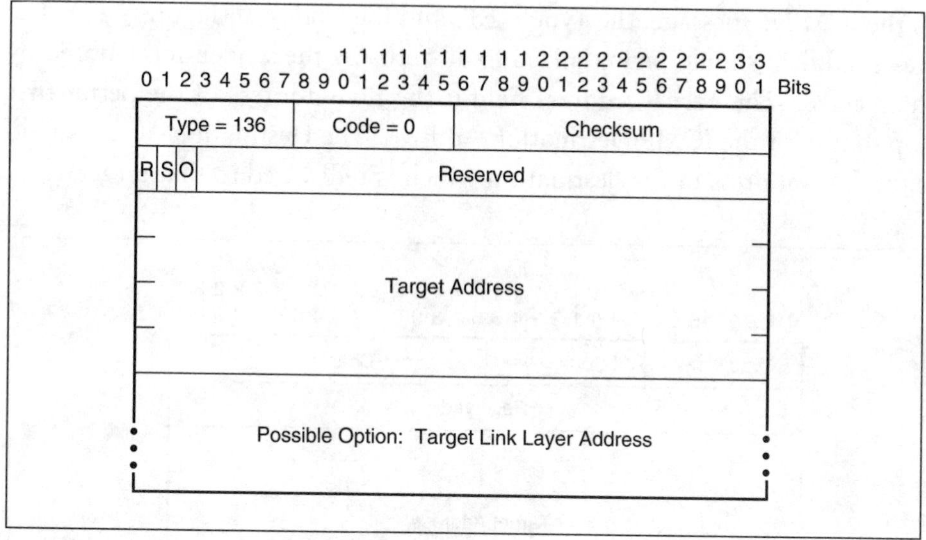

Figure 4-15. Neighbor Advertisement message

A possible option is the Target Data Link Layer Address, identifying the Data Link Layer address for the target (the sender of the advertisement).

4.6.5 Redirect Message

Redirect messages are sent by routers to inform a host of a better first-hop node on the path to a destination.

In the IPv6 header, the Priority = 15, the Hop Limit = 255, the Source Address field must be the link-local address assigned to the interface from which this message is sent, and the Destination Address field is the Source Address of the message that triggered the redirect.

An Authentication header is included if a security association exists between the sender and the destination address.

In the ICMPv6 message, the Type = 137 and the Code = 0 (Figure 4-16). The Reserved field should be initialized to all zeros by the sender and ignored by the receiver. The Target Address field is the IPv6 address of the better first hop to use for the ICMP Destination Address. The Destination Address field is the IPv6 address of the destination which is redirected to that target.

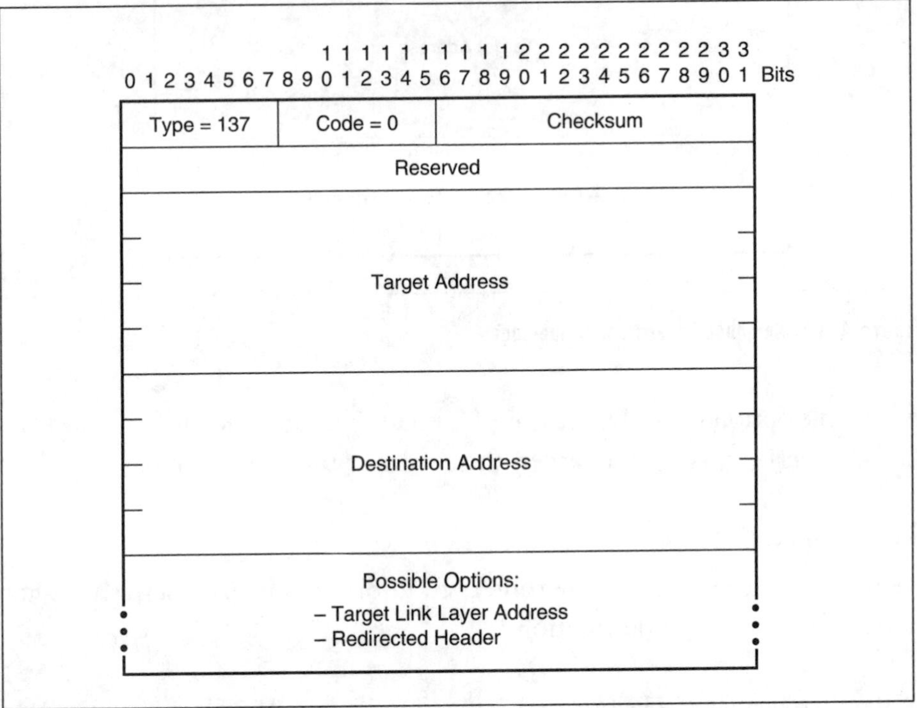

Figure 4-16. Redirect message

Possible options are the Target Data Link Layer Address and the Redirected Header.

4.6.6 Neighbor Discovery Message Options

Neighbor Discovery messages include zero or more options, some of which may appear multiple times in the same message. Five options are currently defined and are illustrated in Figures 4-17 through 4-21.

The Source Link Layer Address option (Figure 4-17) contains the Data Link Layer address of the sender of the packet. It is used in the Neighbor Solicitation, Router Solicitation, and Router Advertisement messages, and must be silently ignored for other Neighbor Discovery messages.

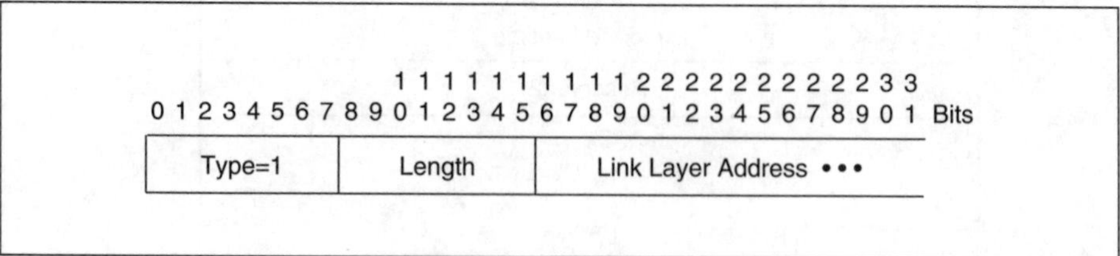

Figure 4-17. Source Link Layer Address option

This option is identified by Type = 1. The Length measures the length of the option in 8-octet units. For example, IEEE 802 addresses would use Length = 1. The Data Link Layer Address would complete the option.

The Target Link Layer Address option (Figure 4-18) contains the Data Link Layer address of the target. It is used in Neighbor Advertisement and Redirect messages, and must be silently ignored for other Neighbor Discovery messages.

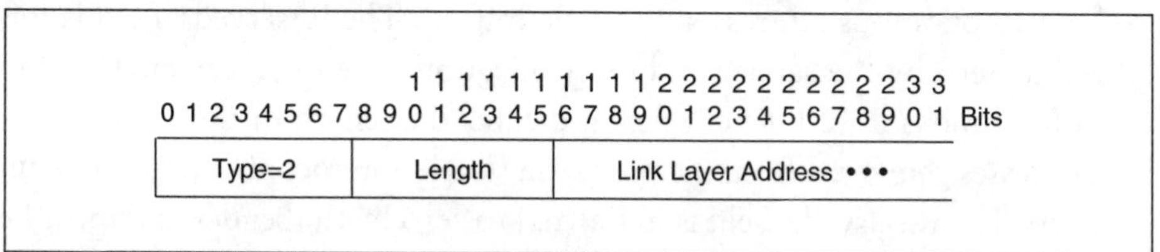

Figure 4-18. Target Link Layer Address option

This option is identified by Type = 2. The Length measures the length of the option in 8-octet units. For example, IEEE 802 addresses would use Length = 1. The Data Link Layer Address would complete the option.

The Prefix Information option (Figure 4-19) provides hosts with on-link prefixes and prefixes for Address Autoconfiguration. The Prefix Information option appears in Router Advertisement messages and must be silently ignored for other messages.

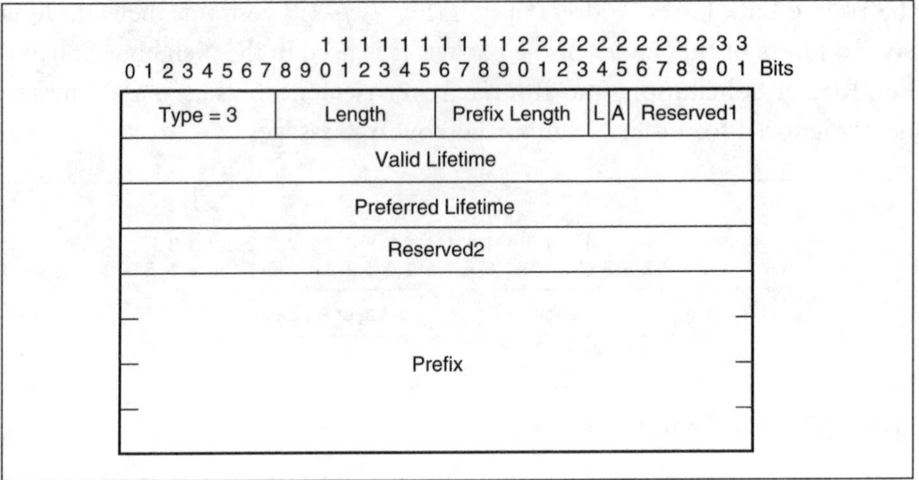

Figure 4-19. Prefix Information option

This option is identified by Type = 3 and Length = 4. The Prefix Length is an 8-bit field that indicates the number of leading bits in the Prefix that are valid, and may take on the range of 0 to 128. The single-bit L flag (on-link) indicates that this prefix may be used for on-link determination. The single-bit A flag (autonomous address autoconfiguration) indicates that the prefix may be used for autonomous address autoconfiguration. The Reserved1 field is initialized to zero by the sender and must be ignored by the receiver. The Preferred Lifetime is a 32-bit field that indicates the length of time in seconds that addresses generated from the prefix via stateless autoconfiguration remain preferred. The Reserved2 field is initialized to zero by the sender and must be ignored by the receiver. The Prefix is a 128-bit field which contains an IPv6 address or a prefix for an IPv6 address.

The Redirected Header option (Figure 4-20) is used in Redirect messages; it contains all or part of the packet that is being redirected. This option must be silently ignored for other Neighbor Discovery messages.

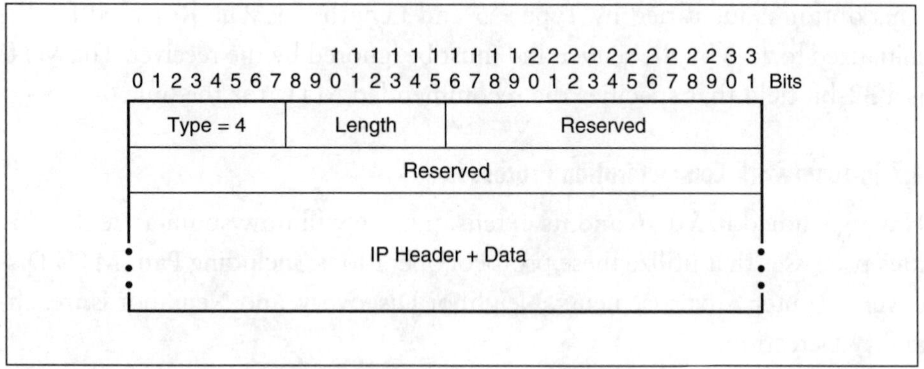

Figure 4-20. Redirected Header option

This option is identified by Type = 4. The Length field measures the length of the option in units of 8 octets. The Reserved fields are initialized to zero by the sender and must be ignored by the receiver. The IP Header + Data field contains the original packet truncated to ensure that the size of the Redirect message does not exceed 576 octets.

The MTU option (Figure 4-21) is used in Router Advertisement messages to insure that all nodes on a link use the same MTU value in those cases where the link MTU is not well known. This option MUST be silently ignored for other Neighbor Discovery messages.

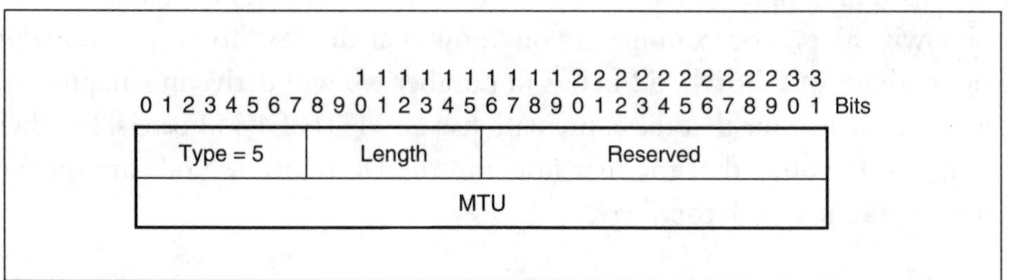

Figure 4-21. MTU option

This option is identified by Type = 5 and Length = 1. The Reserved field is initialized to zero by the sender and must be ignored by the receiver. The MTU is a 32-bit field that specifies the recommended MTU for the link.

4.7 Intranetwork Communication Processes

Having studied ICMPv6 and its extensions, we will now summarize the various processes that utilize these protocol operations, including Path MTU Discovery, Router Advertisements, Neighbor Discovery, and Neighbor Unreachability Detection.

4.7.1 Path MTU Discovery Process

The Path MTU Discovery Process is documented in RFC 1981 [4-9]. Recall that a link's MTU is the maximum transmission unit size, given in octets, that can be conveyed in one piece over that link. For example, the MTU of an Ethernet is 1,500 octets. Also recall that fragmentation is a host (not a router) responsibility, which implies that the host must have some knowledge of the network topology. (Otherwise, it would not know if fragmentation were required or not.) Path MTU Discovery answers these topology questions for the host.

The Path MTU Process is illustrated in Figure 4-22; it begins with the Source Node assuming that the Path MTU (PMTU) is also the MTU of the first hop (a known value). For example, if you know that the first hop is on an FDDI ring, with an MTU of 4,352 octets (a number we will derive in Chapter 5), then you will assume that the entire path has an MTU of 4,352 octets. In other words, you assume that the first hop and the Destination Node are on the same type of network topology.

The Source Node then transmits a packet and checks to see whether an ICMPv6 Packet Too Big message is received. If no message is received, then the entire path has an MTU of 4,352 octets and the Source Node can continue transmitting. If a Packet Too Big Message is received, then the PMTU must be reduced by the MTU that is returned in that message (review Figure 4-4). A packet is transmitted again, this time with a smaller MTU, and a similar test is made. This process continues until no Packet Too Big Messages are returned, at which time the PMTU has been discovered and transmission may proceed. On a periodic basis, the PMTU is retested to see if its value can be increased.

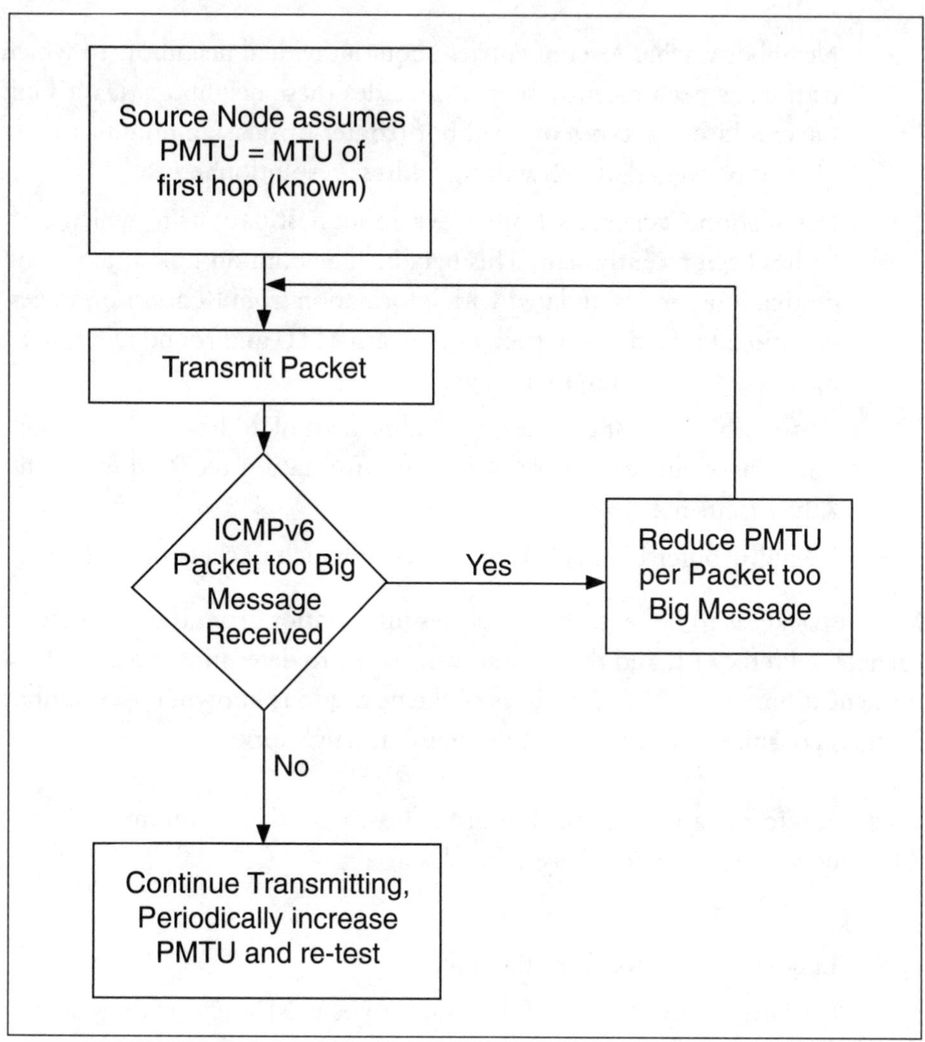

Figure 4-22. Path MTU Discovery

4.7.2 The Model of a Host

The Neighbor Discovery documents, RFC 1970 [4-5] and Reference [4-7], define a conceptual model of a host, which includes the various data structures that are maintained in order to facilitate interaction with neighboring nodes. The information to be maintained includes the following:

- Neighbor Cache: A set of entries about individual neighbors to which traffic has been recently sent. It includes these neighbors' Data Link Layer addresses, types of neighbor (router or host), a pointer to any queued packets that are waiting address resolution, etc.
- Destination Cache: A set of entries about destinations to which traffic has been recently sent. This may include both on-link and off-link destinations, and is updated with information from Redirect messages. Additional information, such as the Path MTU and round trip timers, may also be stored in this cache.
- Prefix List: A list of prefixes that define a set of addresses that are on-link. These entries are created from information received in Router Advertisements.
- Default Router List: A list of routers to which packets may be sent.

When a packet is to be sent, the node uses information from the Destination Cache, the Prefix List, and the Default Router list to determine the IP address of the next hop. Once the IP address of the next hop is known, the Neighbor Cache is consulted for information about that neighbor.

In addition to the above information, the host maintains a number of variables. Suggested names for these variables are:

- LinkMTU: The MTU of the link.
- CurHopLimit: The default hop limit to be used when sending unicast IPv6 packets.
- BaseReachableTime: A base value used for computing the random ReachableTime value.

- ReachableTime: The time a neighbor is considered reachable after receiving a reachability confirmation.
- RetransTimer: The time between retransmissions of Neighbor Solicitation messages to a neighbor when resolving the address or when probing the reachability of a neighbor.

Note that specific Neighbor Discovery implementations may use different variable names, but their external behavior must be consistent with the Neighbor Discovery specification.

4.7.3 Router and Prefix Discovery

Router Discovery is defined in RFC 1970 as the process used to locate neighboring routers, and also to learn prefixes and configuration parameters that relate to address autoconfiguration. Prefix Discovery is defined as the process through which hosts learn the ranges of IP addresses that reside on-link, and are therefore reachable directly without going through a router. When routers transmit Router Advertisement messages, which contain both router and prefix information, both the Router Discovery and Prefix Discovery processes are satisfied. Review Figure 4-13 for further details on the Router Advertisement message contents.

4.7.4 Address Resolution and Neighbor Unreachability Detection

Similar to the manner in which Router Solicitation/Router Advertisement messages are used to convey routing information through the internetwork, Neighbor Solicitation/Advertisement messages convey information regarding the addresses and reachability of neighbors. In addition, the Neighbor Solicitation/Advertisement messages are used in the duplicate address detection process which is part of the address autoconfiguration algorithm that we will study in Chapter 5.

Address Resolution is the process through which a node determines the Data Link Layer address of a neighbor when given only its IPv6 address. (In IPv4 environments, the Address Resolution Protocol—ARP—would handle these functions.) Address Resolution is performed only for addresses that are determined to be on-link, and for which Data Link Layer communication is required.

Neighbor Unreachability Detection is the process through which a communication path failure is identified and (hopefully) corrected. The specific recovery procedure will vary depending on the network element failing, and may require further Address Resolution, the switch to another router, etc.

The Neighbor Cache information, which is part of the host's conceptual data structure, is consulted during the Address Resolution and Neighbor Unreachability processes. To support the Neighbor Unreachability Detection algorithm, additional information is maintained. The neighbor's reachability state may take on one of five possible values. In addition, transitions between some of these states are dependent on the expiration of timers that are part of the process implementation. The five states are:

- INCOMPLETE: Address resolution is in progress, and the Data Link Layer address of the neighbor has not yet been determined.
- REACHABLE: The neighbor is known to have been recently reachable (i.e. within tens of seconds), as determined by the value of the variable ReachableTime.
- STALE: The neighbor is no longer known to be reachable, as determined by the value of the variable ReachableTime, but until traffic is sent to that neighbor, no attempt should be made to verify its reachability.
- DELAY: The neighbor is no longer known to be reachable, as determined by the value of the variable ReachableTime, although traffic has been recently sent to that neighbor. Delay sending probes until the upper-layer protocols have had a chance to confirm reachability.
- PROBE: The neighbor is no longer known to be reachable, and unicast Neighbor Solicitation probes are being sent every RetransTimer milliseconds to verify reachability.

When a packet is to be sent, the transmitting node consults its Neighbor Cache for information regarding that neighbor. If no entry exists, Address Resolution will be required. Address Resolution consists of creating a Neighbor Cache entry in the INCOMPLETE state and sending a Neighbor Solicitation message targeted at the neighbor. The solicitation is sent to the solicited-node multicast address that corresponds to the target address. While waiting for a response, the sender retransmits Neighbor Solicitation messages at an interval equal to the RetransTimer value (approximately every 1,000 milliseconds). When a Neighbor Advertisement response is received, the Data Link Layer address is entered into the Neighbor Cache entry, and the packet can then be transmitted.

Digital Equipment Corp.'s UNIX IPv6 implementation of the Neighbor Reachability process is illustrated in Figure 4-23, taken from Reference [4-10]. (Note that RFC 1970 specifies the various state transitions that occur, but it allows specific vendor implementations to vary from that model as long as external behavior is consistent with the RFC's specifications.) This implementation illustrates the five values of the Neighbor Reachability state, along with a sixth state NONE. (NONE indicates that timeouts have occured, and that the Neighbor Unreachability Detection is giving up on neighbor discovery.) The various transitions that occur between these states are also shown. Note that the INCOMPLETE and PROBE states trigger the transmission of Neighbor Solicitation messages, and the receipt of a Neighbor Advertisement causes the process to enter the REACHABLE state.

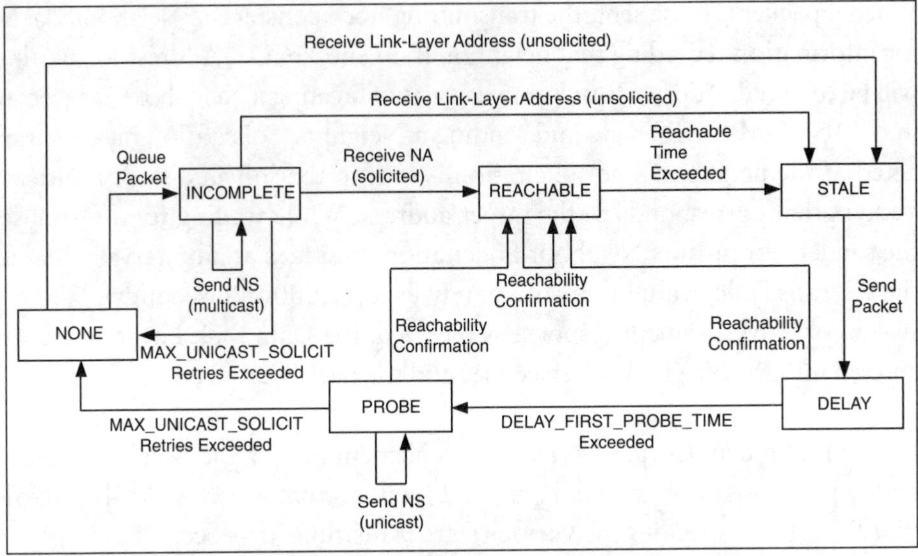

Figure 4-23. Digital's UNIX Neighbor Reachability implementation state diagram
(This figure is reprinted with permission from the Digital Technical Journal of Digital Equipment Corporation, volume 8, number 3, copyright 1996.)

4.8 Case Studies

To illustrate the various intranetwork communication protocols and processes that we have studied in this chapter, we will take a look at some rather routine conditions that occur on an IPv6 network segment: Router Advertisement messages, Neighbor Advertisement messages, ICMPv6 Echo Request and Reply messages, and others.

4.8.1 Router Advertisement Messages

Routers, in contrast with their IPv4 operation, have expanded roles in IPv6. In addition to their key function of packet routing, routers now disseminate a variety of address- and routing-related information to the other nodes on link. This information is communicated on a periodic basis using ICMPv6 Router Advertisement messages. In the example shown in Figure 4-24a, a router running both IPv6 and IPv4 (called a dual router) connects an IPv4 segment with another segment running both protocols. The router's port 1 (IPv4) connects to subnet 244 (in the upper portion of Figure 4-24a), while router port 2 (IPv6/IPv4) connects to subnet 245 (in the lower portion of the figure).

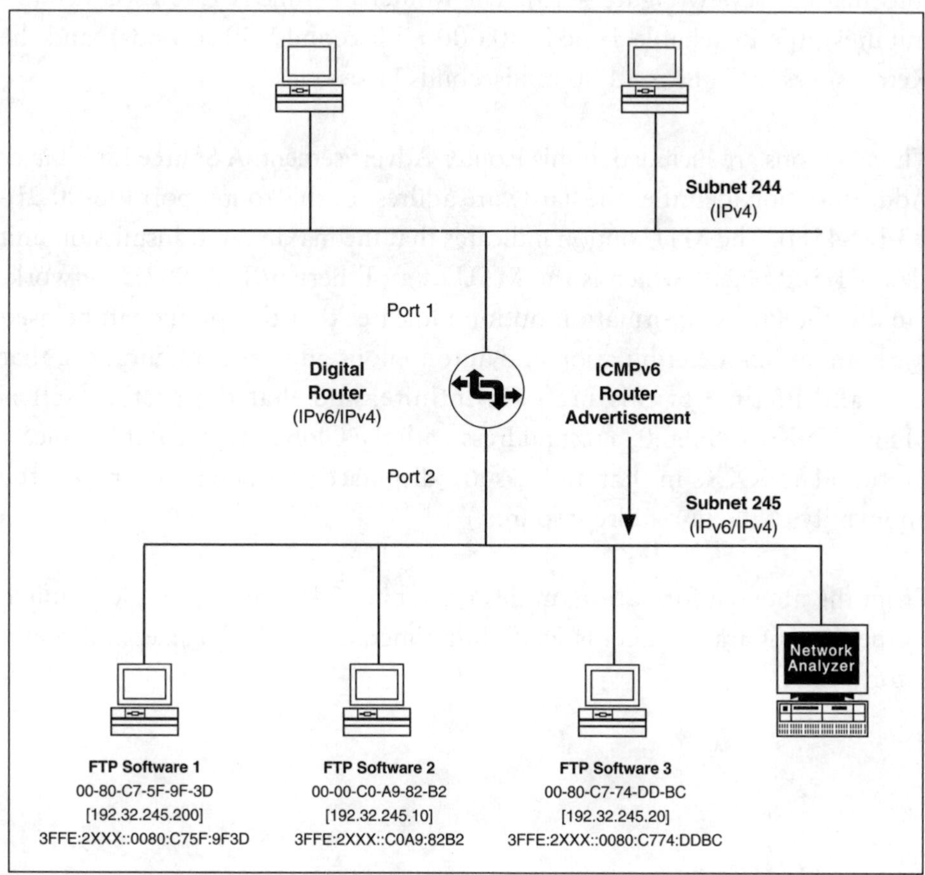

Figure 4-24a. Router Advertisement message communication

The Router Advertisement message is broadcast periodically from port 2 (IPv6-enabled) to all stations on subnet 245; Frame 4 illustrates one of these broadcasts (Trace 4.8.1). Notice that this message is sent to a Group hardware address. In the IPv6 header, the Source Address = FE80:0:0:0:0:800:2BB3:FD45, which is a Link Local address for port 2 of the router. The IPv6 Destination Address = FF02:0:0:0:0:0:1 is a defined multicast address meaning "all nodes on this link."

The ICMPv6 message is Type 134 (Router Advertisement), with both the M and O flags indicating that the administered protocol (such as DHCPv6) should be used for both address autoconfiguration and the autoconfiguration of other information (review Figure 4-13). The Router Lifetime is 1,800 seconds (30 minutes), the Reachable Time is 30,000 milliseconds (30 seconds), and the Retransmission Time is 1,000 milliseconds (1 second).

Three options are included in this Router Advertisement. A Source Link Layer Address option identifies the hardware address of this router port (08-00-2B-B3-FD-45H). The MTU option indicates that the maximum transmission unit size is 1,500 octets, which is the MTU of an Ethernet/IEEE 802.3 network. Finally, the Prefix Information option indicates that this prefix can be used for both on-link determination and autonomous address configuration, that the valid lifetime of this prefix is infinite, and that the prefix itself is 3FFE:2XXX:0:0:0:0:0:0, a test address with the Global Aggregatable Unicast prefix. (The XXXs in that address are disguised characters to protect the anonymity of the test address source.)

From the above information, nodes on subnet 245 are able to glean much of their configuration details, including timer values, MTU size, and prefix information.

Trace 4.8.1. Router Advertisement

```
-------------- Frame 4  Size 122  Absolute Time  11:31:41.29130 --------------
                    Protocol Detail - xpiboot.cap 8/26


IEEE 802.3/Ethernet DIX V2 Header


       Decode Status : -
        Frame Length : 122
 Destination Address : 33-33-00-00-00-01 ( Group, Locally Administered )
      Source Address : 08-00-2B-B3-FD-45, Digital P2 ( OUI = DEC, Universally
        Frame Format : Ethernet DIX V2
           Ethertype : 0x86DD (IPv6)
      Frame Checksum : Good, Frame Check Sequence : 00 00 00 00


IPv6 - Internet Protocol (Version 6)


       Decode Status : -
      Version Number : 6 (IP Version 6)
               Class : 0x0
          Flow Label : 0x0
      Payload Length : 64
         Next Header : 58 (ICMPv6)
           Hop Limit : 255
      Source Address : FE80:0:0:0:0:800:2BB3:FD45
 Destination Address : FF02:0:0:0:0:0:0:1
```

```
ICMPv6 - Internet Control Message Protocol (Version 6)


            Decode Status : -
                ICMP Type : 134 (Router Advertisement)
  Router Advertisement Code : 0
                 Checksum : 24575
        Current Hop Limit : 64
                    Flags : 0xC0
                            1... .... = Use Admin Proto for Addr Autoconfiguration
                            .1.. .... = Use Admin Proto for Autocon of Non-Addr Info
          Router Lifetime : 1800 Seconds(s)
           Reachable Time : 30000 Milliseconds(s)
      Retransmission Time : 1000 Milliseconds(s)

                  ----- Options -----

                   Option : 1 (Source Link Layer Address)
            Option Length : 1
  Source Link Layer Address : 08-00-2B-B3-FD-45, Digital P2

                   Option : 5 (Maximum Transmission Unit)
            Option Length : 1
  Maximum Transmission Unit : 1500

                   Option : 3 (Prefix Information)
            Option Length : 4
            Prefix Length : 80
                    Flags : 0xC0
                            1... .... = Prefix Len Can be Used for On-Link Determin
                            .1.. .... = Prefix Len Can be Used for Auto Addr Config
           Valid Lifetime : 4294967295 (Infinity)
       Preferred Lifetime : 604800 Seconds(s)
                   Prefix : 3FFE:2XXX:0:0:0:0:0:0
```

4.8.2 Successful ICMPv6 Communication: Stations 1 and 3

The ICMPv6 Echo Request and Echo Reply messages (PINGs) are frequently used to test IP-level connectivity between workstations. In this example, the Address Resolution procedure must be used first to identify the Data Link Layer address of the node in question. Two stations are involved in this exchange: FTP Software 1 and FTP Software 3 (Figure 4-24b and Trace 4.8.2).

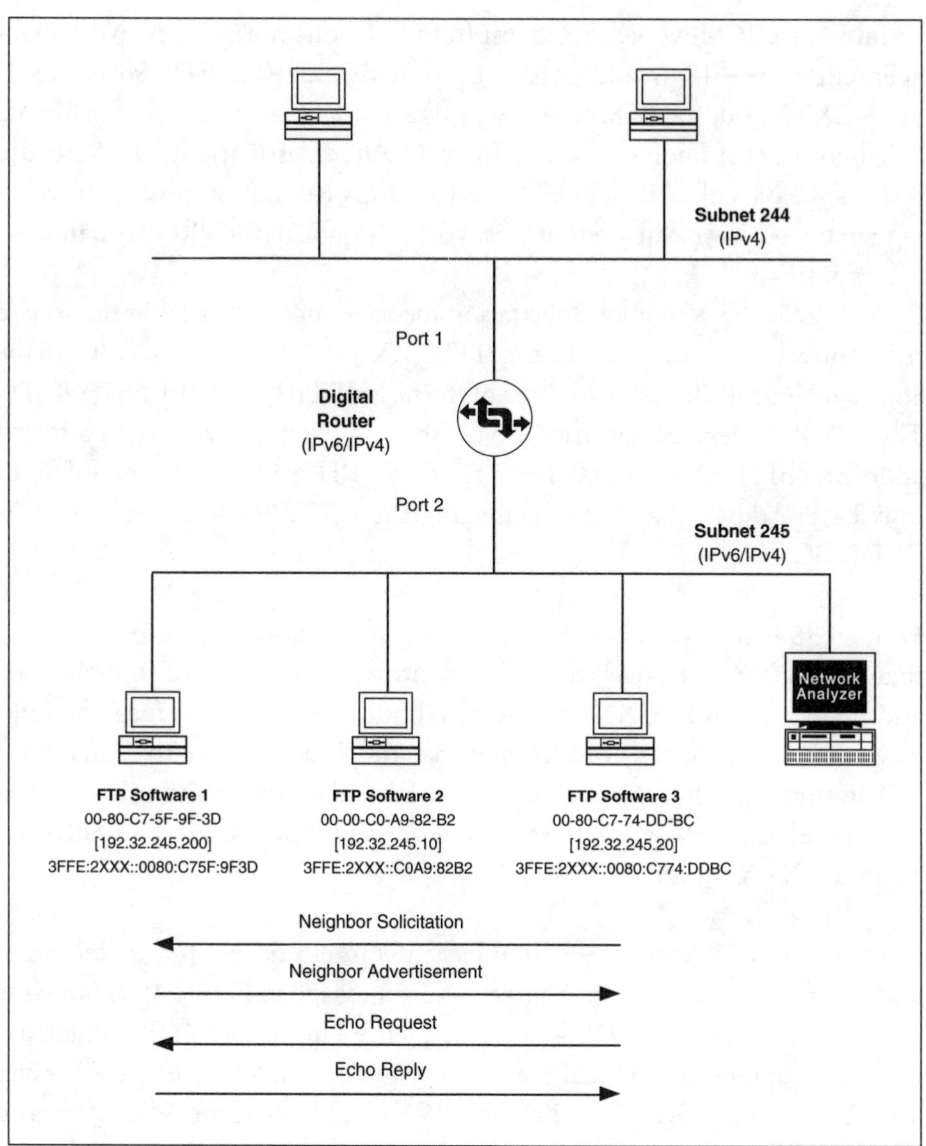

Figure 4-24b. Successful communication: Stations 1 and 3

To initiate the ICMPv6 Echo Request from FTP Software 3, the network manager enters the IPv6 address of desired destination FTP Software 1: 3FFE:2XXX::0080:C75F:9F3D. Workstation FTP Software 3 consults its Neighbor Cache; finding no entry for the desired destination, FTP Software 3 starts the Neighbor Reachability and Address Resolution process (reviewing Figure 4-23, we can see that this workstation is in the PROBE state).

Frame 197 is the Neighbor Solicitation message that is sent from the source (FTP Software 3, with IPv6 address 3FFE:2XXX:0:0:0:80:C774:DDBC) to the Solicited Node Multicast Addresses of the target (FF02:0:0:0:0:1:FF5F:9F3D). The ICMPv6 message specifies a Neighbor Solicitation type, with a target address of 3FFE:2XXX:0:0:0:80:C75F:9F3D (FTP Software 1) and a Source Link Layer Address that identifies the originator (FTP Software 3): 00-80-C7-74-DD-BC.

Frame 198 is the Neighbor Advertisement message sent in response. Note that the IPv6 Source and Destination addresses have changed to the testing address prefix (3FFE:2XXX). The Neighbor Advertisement message indicates that the sender is not a router, that this is a response to a Neighbor Solicitation, and that the current Data Link Layer address should be overridden with this new entry, the target address of workstation FTP Software 1 (3FFE:2XXX:0:0:0:80:C75F:9F3D).

Workstation FTP Software 3 now has the target address that it required, and it can send the ICMPv6 Echo Request message in Frame 199. Note the message Identifier of 62920 and the Sequence Number of 4608, which are used to distinguish individual messages. Workstation FTP Software 1 issues an ICMPv6 Echo Reply in Frame 199, using that same Identifier and Sequence Number.

Trace 4.8.2. Address Resolution and Reachability Confirmation: Stations 1 and 3

```
-------------- Frame 197  Size 90  Absolute Time  11:36:23.25510  --------------
                    Protocol Detail - xpiboot.cap 8/26


IEEE 802.3/Ethernet DIX V2 Header


          Decode Status : -
           Frame Length : 90
    Destination Address : 33-33-C7-5F-9F-3D ( Group, Locally Administered Addr
         Source Address : 00-80-C7-74-DD-BC, FTP Software 3 ( OUI = XIRCOM, U
           Frame Format : Ethernet DIX V2
              Ethertype : 0x86DD (IPv6)
         Frame Checksum : Good, Frame Check Sequence : 00 00 00 00


IPv6 - Internet Protocol (Version 6)


          Decode Status : -
         Version Number : 6 (IP Version 6)
                  Class : 0x0
             Flow Label : 0x0
         Payload Length : 32
            Next Header : 58 (ICMPv6)
              Hop Limit : 255
         Source Address : 3FFE:2XXX:0:0:0:80:C774:DDBC
    Destination Address : FF02:0:0:0:0:1:FF5F:9F3D


ICMPv6 - Internet Control Message Protocol (Version 6)


             Decode Status : -
                 ICMP Type : 135 (Neighbor Solicitation)
 Neighbor Solicitation Code : 0
                  Checksum : 41341
            Target Address : 3FFE:2XXX:0:0:0:80:C75F:9F3D
```

```
                  ----- Options -----

                Option : 1 (Source Link Layer Address)
         Option Length : 1
Source Link Layer Address : 00-80-C7-74-DD-BC, FTP Software 3


-------------- Frame 198  Size 90  Absolute Time  11:36:23.25680 --------------
                    Protocol Detail - xpiboot.cap 8/26


IEEE 802.3/Ethernet DIX V2 Header


         Decode Status : -
          Frame Length : 90
   Destination Address : 00-80-C7-74-DD-BC, FTP Software 3 ( OUI = XIRCOM, I
        Source Address : 00-80-C7-5F-9F-3D, FTP Software 1 ( OUI = XIRCOM, U
          Frame Format : Ethernet DIX V2
             Ethertype : 0x86DD (IPv6)
        Frame Checksum : Good, Frame Check Sequence : 00 00 00 00


IPv6 - Internet Protocol (Version 6)


         Decode Status : -
        Version Number : 6 (IP Version 6)
                 Class : 0x0
            Flow Label : 0x0
        Payload Length : 32
           Next Header : 58 (ICMPv6)
             Hop Limit : 64
        Source Address : 3FFE:2XXX:0:0:0:80:C75F:9F3D
   Destination Address : 3FFE:2XXX:0:0:0:80:C774:DDBC
```

```
ICMPv6 - Internet Control Message Protocol (Version 6)


            Decode Status : -
                ICMP Type : 136 (Neighbor Advertisement)
Neighbor Advertisement Code : 0
                 Checksum : 7571
                    Flags : 0x60
                            0... .... = Sender is Not a Router
                            .1.. .... = Response to a Neighbor Solicitation
                            ..1. .... = Override Link-Layer Entry
           Target Address : 3FFE:2XXX:0:0:0:80:C75F:9F3D

                    ----- Options -----

                   Option : 2 (Target Link Layer Address)
            Option Length : 1
  Target Link Layer Address : 00-80-C7-5F-9F-3D, FTP Software 1


------------- Frame 199  Size 122  Absolute Time  11:36:23.25744 -------------
                   Protocol Detail - xpiboot.cap 8/26


IEEE 802.3/Ethernet DIX V2 Header


           Decode Status : -
            Frame Length : 122
     Destination Address : 00-80-C7-5F-9F-3D, FTP Software 1 ( OUI = XIRCOM, I
          Source Address : 00-80-C7-74-DD-BC, FTP Software 3 ( OUI = XIRCOM, U
            Frame Format : Ethernet DIX V2
               Ethertype : 0x86DD (IPv6)
          Frame Checksum : Good, Frame Check Sequence : 00 00 00 00
```

```
IPv6 - Internet Protocol (Version 6)


            Decode Status : -
           Version Number : 6 (IP Version 6)
                    Class : 0x0
               Flow Label : 0x0
           Payload Length : 64
              Next Header : 58 (ICMPv6)
                Hop Limit : 63
           Source Address : 3FFE:2XXX:0:0:0:80:C774:DDBC
      Destination Address : 3FFE:2XXX:0:0:0:80:C75F:9F3D


ICMPv6 - Internet Control Message Protocol (Version 6)


            Decode Status : -
                ICMP Type : 128 (Echo Request)
                Echo Code : 0
                 Checksum : 18372
               Identifier : 62920
          Sequence Number : 4608
                ICMP Data : [56 byte(s) of data]


-------------- Frame 200  Size 122  Absolute Time  11:36:23.25878 --------------
                    Protocol Detail - xpiboot.cap 8/26


IEEE 802.3/Ethernet DIX V2 Header


            Decode Status : -
             Frame Length : 122
      Destination Address : 00-80-C7-74-DD-BC, FTP Software 3 ( OUI = XIRCOM, I
           Source Address : 00-80-C7-5F-9F-3D, FTP Software 1 ( OUI = XIRCOM, U
             Frame Format : Ethernet DIX V2
                Ethertype : 0x86DD (IPv6)
           Frame Checksum : Good, Frame Check Sequence : 00 00 00 00
```

```
IPv6 - Internet Protocol (Version 6)


             Decode Status : -
            Version Number : 6 (IP Version 6)
                     Class : 0x0
                Flow Label : 0x0
            Payload Length : 64
               Next Header : 58 (ICMPv6)
                 Hop Limit : 63
            Source Address : 3FFE:2XXX:0:0:0:80:C75F:9F3D
       Destination Address : 3FFE:2XXX:0:0:0:80:C774:DDBC


ICMPv6 - Internet Control Message Protocol (Version 6)


             Decode Status : -
                 ICMP Type : 129 (Echo Reply)
                 Echo Code : 0
                  Checksum : 18116
                Identifier : 62920
           Sequence Number : 4608
                 ICMP Data : [56 byte(s) of data]
```

4.8.3 Successful ICMPv6 Communication: Stations 2 and 3

To further verify the connectivity between another pair of workstations, FTP Software 3 now issues an ICMP Echo Request for FTP Software 2 (Figure 4-24c and Trace 4.8.3). As in the previous example, the Address Resolution process occurs with a Neighbor Solicitation (Frame 238), a Neighbor Advertisement (Frame 239), an ICMPv6 Echo Request (Frame 240), and an ICMP Echo Reply (Frame 241). Note that the ICMPv6 Echo Request/Reply Identifier is the same (62920), but a different Sequence Number is used (5632). The results are comparable to those in the previous example, indicating that workstation FTP Software 3 still had not yet fully populated its Neighbor Cache at this time. The reader is invited to verify all the addresses employed as an exercise.

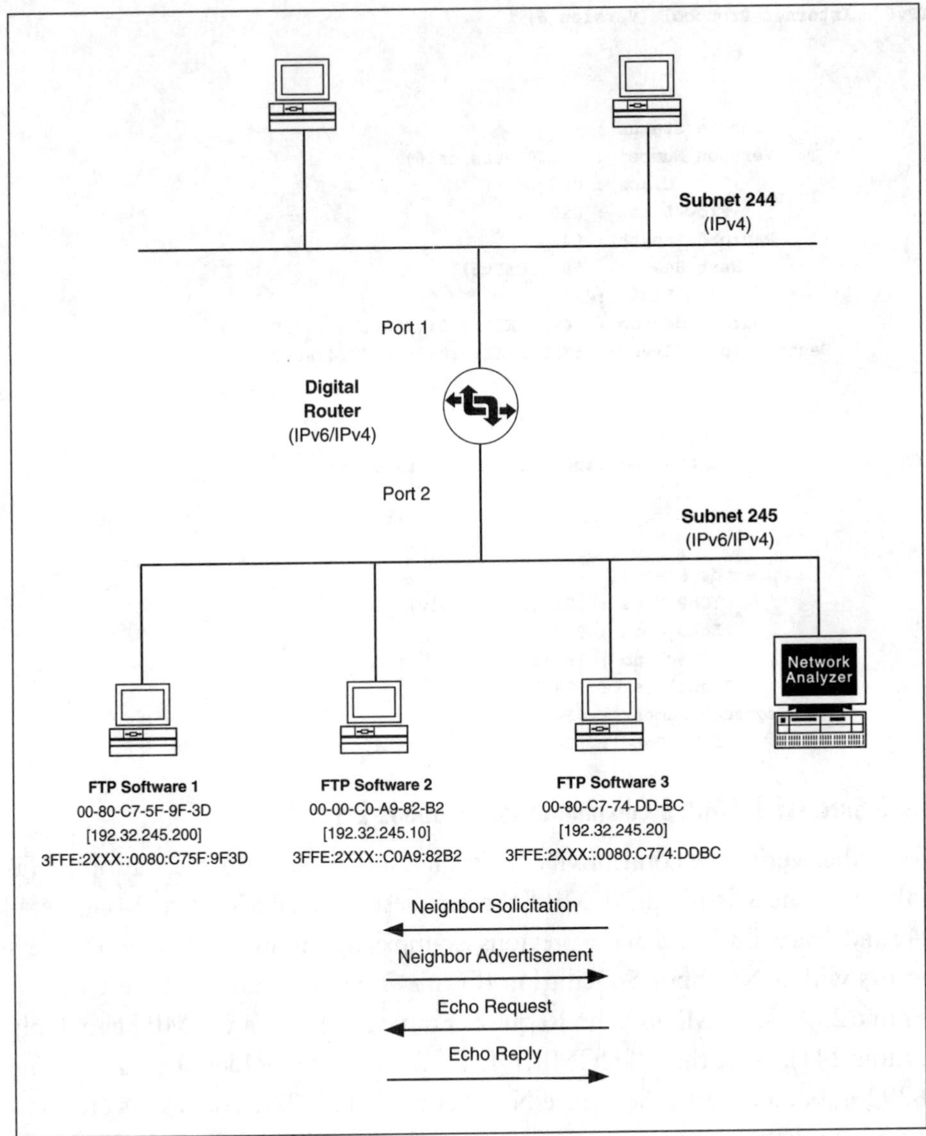

Figure 4-24c. Successful communication: Stations 2 and 3

Trace 4.8.3. Address Resolution and Reachability Confirmation: Stations 2 and 3

```
------------- Frame 238  Size 90  Absolute Time  11:37:31.80499 -------------
                     Protocol Detail - xpiboot.cap 8/26


IEEE 802.3/Ethernet DIX V2 Header


             Decode Status : -
              Frame Length : 90
       Destination Address : 33-33-C0-A9-82-B2 ( Group, Locally Administered
Addr
            Source Address : 00-80-C7-74-DD-BC, FTP Software 3 ( OUI = XIRCOM, U
              Frame Format : Ethernet DIX V2
                 Ethertype : 0x86DD (IPv6)
            Frame Checksum : Good, Frame Check Sequence : 00 00 00 00


IPv6 - Internet Protocol (Version 6)


             Decode Status : -
            Version Number : 6 (IP Version 6)
                     Class : 0x0
                Flow Label : 0x0
            Payload Length : 32
               Next Header : 58 (ICMPv6)
                 Hop Limit : 255
            Source Address : 3FFE:2XXX:0:0:0:80:C774:DDBC
       Destination Address : FF02:0:0:0:0:1:FFA9:82B2


ICMPv6 - Internet Control Message Protocol (Version 6)


             Decode Status : -
                 ICMP Type : 135 (Neighbor Solicitation)
  Neighbor Solicitation Code : 0
                  Checksum : 59519
            Target Address : 5F00:2:0:0:0:0:C0A9:82B2
```

```
                 ----- Options -----

                 Option : 1 (Source Link Layer Address)
          Option Length : 1
 Source Link Layer Address : 00-80-C7-74-DD-BC, FTP Software 3


-------------- Frame 239  Size 90  Absolute Time  11:37:31.80656  --------------
                 Protocol Detail - xpiboot.cap 8/26


IEEE 802.3/Ethernet DIX V2 Header


          Decode Status : -
           Frame Length : 90
    Destination Address : 00-80-C7-74-DD-BC, FTP Software 3 ( OUI = XIRCOM, I
         Source Address : 00-00-C0-A9-82-B2, FTP Software 2 ( OUI = WESTERN D
           Frame Format : Ethernet DIX V2
              Ethertype : 0x86DD (IPv6)
         Frame Checksum : Good, Frame Check Sequence : 00 00 00 00


IPv6 - Internet Protocol (Version 6)


          Decode Status : -
         Version Number : 6 (IP Version 6)
                  Class : 0x0
             Flow Label : 0x0
         Payload Length : 32
            Next Header : 58 (ICMPv6)
              Hop Limit : 64
         Source Address : 3FFE:2XXX:0:0:0:0:C0A9:82B2
    Destination Address : 3FFE:2XXX:0:0:0:80:C774:DDBC
```

```
ICMPv6 - Internet Control Message Protocol (Version 6)


             Decode Status : -
                 ICMP Type : 136 (Neighbor Advertisement)
  Neighbor Advertisement Code : 0
                  Checksum : 35030
                     Flags : 0x60
                             0... .... = Sender is Not a Router
                             .1.. .... = Response to a Neighbor Solicitation
                             ..1. .... = Override Link-Layer Entry
            Target Address : 3FFE:2XXX:0:0:0:0:C0A9:82B2

                 ----- Options -----

                    Option : 2 (Target Link Layer Address)
             Option Length : 1
   Target Link Layer Address : 00-00-C0-A9-82-B2, FTP Software 2



-------------- Frame 240  Size 122  Absolute Time  11:37:31.80720  --------------
                    Protocol Detail - xpiboot.cap 8/26


IEEE 802.3/Ethernet DIX V2 Header


             Decode Status : -
              Frame Length : 122
       Destination Address : 00-00-C0-A9-82-B2, FTP Software 2 ( OUI = WESTERN D
            Source Address : 00-80-C7-74-DD-BC, FTP Software 3 ( OUI = XIRCOM, U
              Frame Format : Ethernet DIX V2
                 Ethertype : 0x86DD (IPv6)
            Frame Checksum : Good, Frame Check Sequence : 00 00 00 00
```

```
IPv6 - Internet Protocol (Version 6)

               Decode Status : -
              Version Number : 6 (IP Version 6)
                       Class : 0x0
                  Flow Label : 0x0
              Payload Length : 64
                 Next Header : 58 (ICMPv6)
                   Hop Limit : 63
              Source Address : 3FFE:2XXX:0:0:0:80:C774:DDBC
         Destination Address : 3FFE:2XXX:0:0:0:0:C0A9:82B2

ICMPv6 - Internet Control Message Protocol (Version 6)

               Decode Status : -
                   ICMP Type : 128 (Echo Request)
                   Echo Code : 0
                    Checksum : 35705
                  Identifier : 62920
             Sequence Number : 5632
                   ICMP Data : [56 byte(s) of data]

-------------  Frame 241  Size 122  Absolute Time  11:37:31.80848  -------------
                   Protocol Detail - xpiboot.cap 8/26

IEEE 802.3/Ethernet DIX V2 Header

               Decode Status : -
                Frame Length : 122
         Destination Address : 00-80-C7-74-DD-BC, FTP Software 3 ( OUI = XIRCOM, I
              Source Address : 00-00-C0-A9-82-B2, FTP Software 2 ( OUI = WESTERN D
                Frame Format : Ethernet DIX V2
                   Ethertype : 0x86DD (IPv6)
              Frame Checksum : Good, Frame Check Sequence : 00 00 00 00
```

```
IPv6 - Internet Protocol (Version 6)


            Decode Status : -
           Version Number : 6 (IP Version 6)
                    Class : 0x0
               Flow Label : 0x0
           Payload Length : 64
              Next Header : 58 (ICMPv6)
                Hop Limit : 63
           Source Address : 3FFE:2XXX:0:0:0:0:C0A9:82B2
      Destination Address : 3FFE:2XXX:0:0:0:80:C774:DDBC


ICMPv6 - Internet Control Message Protocol (Version 6)


            Decode Status : -
                ICMP Type : 129 (Echo Reply)
                Echo Code : 0
                 Checksum : 35449
               Identifier : 62920
          Sequence Number : 5632
                ICMP Data : [56 byte(s) of data]
```

4.8.4 Unsuccessful ICMPv6 Communication

As a final example of intranetwork communication, workstation FTP Software 1 is shut down, and an attempt is made to send it an ICMPv6 Echo Request from workstation FTP Software 3 (Figure 4-24d and Trace 4.8.4). The results illustrate the Neighbor Unreachability Detection process in operation.

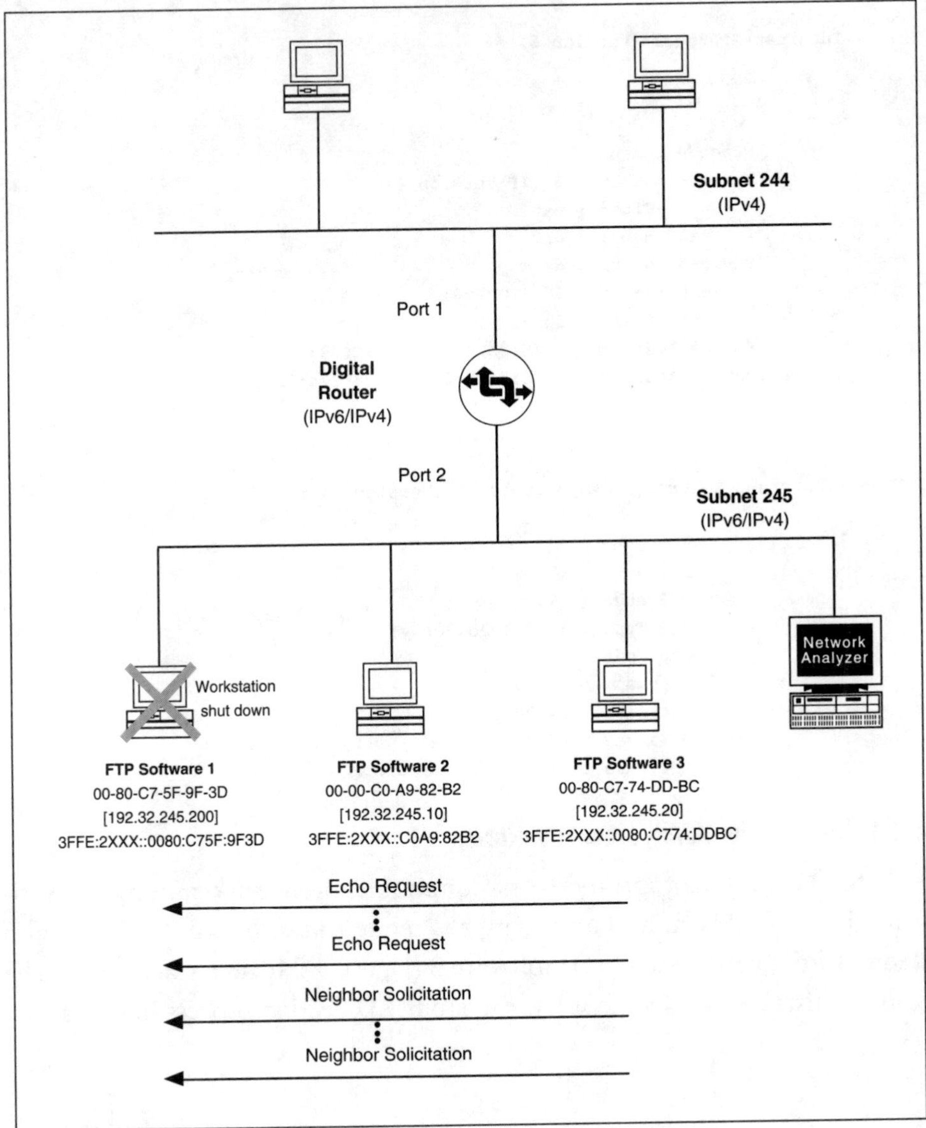

Figure 4-24d. Neighbor Unreachability Detection in operation

Note from the trace that five ICMPv6 Echo Request messages are sent in Frames numbered 407–412 at one second intervals (not all frames are shown in this example, as non-ICMPv6 frames have been filtered out). Neighbor Solicitation messages start in Frame 414 and are transmitted approximately every 1.0

second (or 1,000 milliseconds, the value of the RETRANS_TIMER constant) as the workstation moves through the REACHABLE, STALE, and DELAY states (review Figure 4-23). Beginning in Frame 422, the only transmissions are Neighbor Solicitations, indicating that the workstation has moved from the DELAY to the PROBE state, and is attempting to confirm reachability.

Trace 4.8.4. Neighbor Unreachability Detection in Operation

```
--------------------- Protocol Detail  xpiboot.cap  8/22  --------------------

Frame Delta Time   Destination       Source          Interpretation

407    3.4 sec   FTP Software 1   FTP Software 3 ICMPv6 Echo Request
                                                    Identifier=62920 Seq=9728
408    1.0 sec   FTP Software 1   FTP Software 3 ICMPv6 Echo Request
                                                    Identifier=62920 Seq=9984
410    1.0 sec   FTP Software 1   FTP Software 3 ICMPv6 Echo Request
                                                    Identifier=62920 Seq=10240
411    1.0 sec   FTP Software 1   FTP Software 3 ICMPv6 Echo Request
                                                    Identifier=62920 Seq=10496
412    1.0 sec   FTP Software 1   FTP Software 3 ICMPv6 Echo Request
                                                    Identifier=62920 Seq=10752
414  849.7 ms 33-33-C7-5F-9F-3D   FTP Software 3 ICMPv6 Neighbor Solicitation
                                                    Target_Address=
                                                    3FFE:2XXX:0:0:0:80:C75F:9F3D
                                                    Opt = Src Link Layer Addr
416   152.8 ms   FTP Software 1   FTP Software 3 ICMPv6 Echo Request
                                                    Identifier=62920 Seq=11008
417  849.6 ms 33-33-C7-5F-9F-3D   FTP Software 3 ICMPv6 Neighbor Solicitation
                                                    Target_Address=
                                                    3FFE:2XXX:0:0:0:80:C75F:9F3D
                                                    Opt = Src Link Layer Addr
418  1193.9 ms   FTP Software 1   FTP Software 3 ICMPv6 Echo Request
                                                    Identifier=62920 Seq=11264
419 1808.4 ms 33-33-C7-5F-9F-3D   FTP Software 3 ICMPv6 Neighbor Solicitation
                                                    Target_Address=
                                                    3FFE:2XXX:0:0:0:80:C75F:9F3D
                                                    Opt = Src Link Layer Addr
420   235.0 ms   FTP Software 1   FTP Software 3 ICMPv6 Echo Request
                                                    Identifier=62920 Seq=11520
422    1.0 sec 33-33-C7-5F-9F-3D  FTP Software 3 ICMPv6 Neighbor Solicitation
                                                    Target_Address=
                                                    3FFE:2XXX:0:0:0:80:C75F:9F3D
                                                    Opt = Src Link Layer Addr
```

```
425    1.0 sec 33-33-C7-5F-9F-3D   FTP Software 3 ICMPv6 Neighbor Solicitation
                                                   Target_Address=
                                                   3FFE:2XXX:0:0:0:80:C75F:9F3D
                                                   Opt = Src Link Layer Addr
426    1.0 sec 33-33-C7-5F-9F-3D   FTP Software 3 ICMPv6 Neighbor Solicitation
                                                   Target_Address=
                                                   3FFE:2XXX:0:0:0:80:C75F:9F3D
                                                   Opt = Src Link Layer Addr
427    1.0 sec 33-33-C7-5F-9F-3D   FTP Software 3 ICMPv6 Neighbor Solicitation
                                                   Target_Address=
                                                   3FFE:2XXX:0:0:0:80:C75F:9F3D
                                                   Opt = Src Link Layer Addr
428    1.0 sec 33-33-C7-5F-9F-3D   FTP Software 3 ICMPv6 Neighbor Solicitation
                                                   Target_Address=
                                                   3FFE:2XXX:0:0:0:80:C75F:9F3D
                                                   Opt = Src Link Layer Addr
430    1.0 sec 33-33-C7-5F-9F-3D   FTP Software 3 ICMPv6 Neighbor Solicitation
                                                   Target_Address=
                                                   3FFE:2XXX:0:0:0:80:C75F:9F3D
                                                   Opt = Src Link Layer Addr
431    208.5 ms 33-33-00-00-00-01      Digital P2 ICMPv6 Router Advertisement
                                                   MTU=1500
                                                   Router_Lifetime=1800
                                                   Opt = Src Link Layer Addr
                                                   Prefix=
                                                   3FFE:2XXX:0:0:0:0:0:0
432  793.9 ms 33-33-C7-5F-9F-3D   FTP Software 3 ICMPv6 Neighbor Solicitation
                                                   Target_Address=
                                                   3FFE:2XXX:0:0:0:80:C75F:9F3D
                                                   Opt = Src Link Layer Addr
433    1.0 sec 33-33-C7-5F-9F-3D   FTP Software 3 ICMPv6 Neighbor Solicitation
                                                   Target_Address=
                                                   3FFE:2XXX:0:0:0:80:C75F:9F3D
                                                   Opt = Src Link Layer Addr
434    1.0 sec 33-33-C7-5F-9F-3D   FTP Software 3 ICMPv6 Neighbor Solicitation
                                                   Target_Address=
                                                   3FFE:2XXX:0:0:0:80:C75F:9F3D
                                                   Opt = Src Link Layer Addr
```

In this chapter, we have studied the many ways in which communication can occur within an IPv6 network for the purposes of disseminating configuration, parameter, and connectivity information using the ICMPv6 protocol. The processes we investigated include Router Advertisements, Neighbor Discovery, and Path MTU Discovery. In the next chapter, we will look at another complementary process, Address Autoconfiguration, which allows workstations to automatically determine their addresses upon station initialization.

4.9 References

[4-1] Postel, J. "Internet Control Message Protocol." RFC 792, September 1991.

[4-2] Conta, A., and S. Deering. "Internet Control Message Protocol (ICMPv6) for the Internet Protocol Version 6 (IPv6) Specification." RFC 1885, December 1985.

[4-3] Conta, A. and S. Deerling. "Internet Control Message Protocol (ICMPv6) for the Internet Protocol Version 6 (IPv6) Specification." Work in progress, October 22, 1997.

[4-4] Deering, S. "Host Extensions for IP Multicasting." RFC 1112, August 1989.

[4-5] Crawford, Matt. "IPv6 Name Lookups Through ICMP." Work in progress, July 24, 1997.

[4-6] Narten, Thomas, Erik Nordmark, and W. A. Simpson. "Neighbor Discovery for IP Version 6 (IPv6)." RFC 1970, August 1996.

[4-7[Narten, Thomas, Erik Nordmark, and W.A Simpson. "Neighbor discovery for IP Version 6 (IPV6). Work in progress, July 30, 1997.

[4-8] Nordmark, Erik. "Site Prefixes in Neighbor Discovery." Work in progress, July 30, 1997.

[4-9] McCann, J., et al. "Path MTU Discovery for IP version 6." RFC 1981, August 1996.

[4-10] Harrington, Daniel T., et al. "Internet Protocol Version 6 and the Digital UNIX Implementation Experience." *Digital Technical Journal* (Volume 8, Number 3, 1996): 5–22.

Autoconfiguration and Local Network Issues

As we have seen thus far, IPv6 has some capabilities (and some resulting complexities) that go beyond what IPv4 presently offers. Fortunately, the architects of IPv6 developed additional protocols and processes that ameliorate those complexities.

In this chapter, we will study one of the most important ancillary protocols, Stateless Address Autoconfiguration, which allows a workstation to automatically join an IPv6 network upon startup. The autoconfiguration process is also very useful for network managers who are migrating their existing IPv4 internetworks to IPv6, as it eliminates many of the requirements for human configuration of addresses, routing parameters, and so on. Should the autoconfiguration process fail, or be inadequate in a particular situation, the proposed Dynamic Host Configuration Protocol for IPv6 (DHCPv6) has also been defined. In addition, there are issues unique to particular LAN or WAN topologies that factor into the overall implementation issue. We will consider all of these subjects in this chapter.

5.1 Stateless Address Autoconfiguration

The word autoconfiguration is best described by its two roots: *auto*, meaning self, and *configuration*, meaning a functional arrangement. According to RFC 1971 [5-1], and the additional work that documents proposed enhancements to these efforts [5-2], the autoconfiguration process includes creating a Link-Local address and verifying its uniqueness on the link, as well as determining what information should be autoconfigured (addresses, other information, or both). Note that the autoconfiguration process specified in RFC

1971 applies to hosts only; it is assumed that routers are configured by some other means.

There are three methods for obtaining addresses: a stateless mechanism, a stateful mechanism, or both. Both stateless and stateful autoconfiguration may be used simultaneously. Which type of autoconfiguration is in use is specified by Router Advertisement messages.

In a *stateful autoconfiguration* model, hosts obtain addresses, configuration information, parameters, etc., from a server. That server maintains a database containing the necessary information and keeps tight control over the address assignments. The stateful autoconfiguration model for IPv6 is defined by the proposed Dynamic Host Configuration Protocol for IPv6 (DHCPv6), which we will consider in the next section.

In contrast, *stateless autoconfiguration* requires no manual configuration or hosts, minimal (or no) configuration of routers, and no additional servers. The stateless approach is used when a site is not concerned about the specific addresses that are used, as long as they are unique and routable.

With stateless autoconfiguration, a host generates its own address using two elements of information: locally available information (i.e. available from the host itself), plus information advertised by routers. The host part is called an interface identifier, which identifies an interface on a subnet. The router part comes from an address prefix which identifies the subnet associated with a link. The derived address is a combination of these two elements. If a router does not exist on a subnet, the host can still generate a special type of address called the Link-Local address (review Figure 3-24). The Link-Local address may only be used for communication between nodes attached to the same link.

Note that the stateless autoconfiguration process, as defined in RFC 1971, applies to hosts only, not routers. (Because hosts obtain some of their address information from routers, those routers must be configured using some other means.) The only exception to this rule is that routers can generate their own Link-Local addresses, and can verify the uniqueness of these addresses on the link, when they are booted or rebooted. (We will see an example of this in the case study in Section 5.9.1.)

IPv6 addresses are "leased" to an interface for a particular period of time, which may be infinite. Associated with the address is a lifetime indicating how long it may be bound to that interface. Upon expiration of the lifetime, both the binding and the address become invalid, and the address may be reassigned to another interface in the Internet. In support of these bindings, the assigned address may have two phases: *preferred*, meaning that the use of that address is unrestricted; and *deprecated*, indicating that the further use of the address is discouraged, in anticipation of an invalid binding.

The Link-Local address is generated by combining the Link-Local address prefix (1111 1110 10, as shown in Figure 3-24) with a 64-bit interface identifier, as shown in Figure 5-1a. The interface identifier is specific to the LAN or WAN topology in use. In most cases, it is derived from the hardware address that resides in a ROM on the network interface card. We will look at the various interface identifiers in subsequent sections of this chapter. (As a historical note, earlier RFC and Internet Draft documents used the term "interface token" instead of the currently used term "interface identifier".)

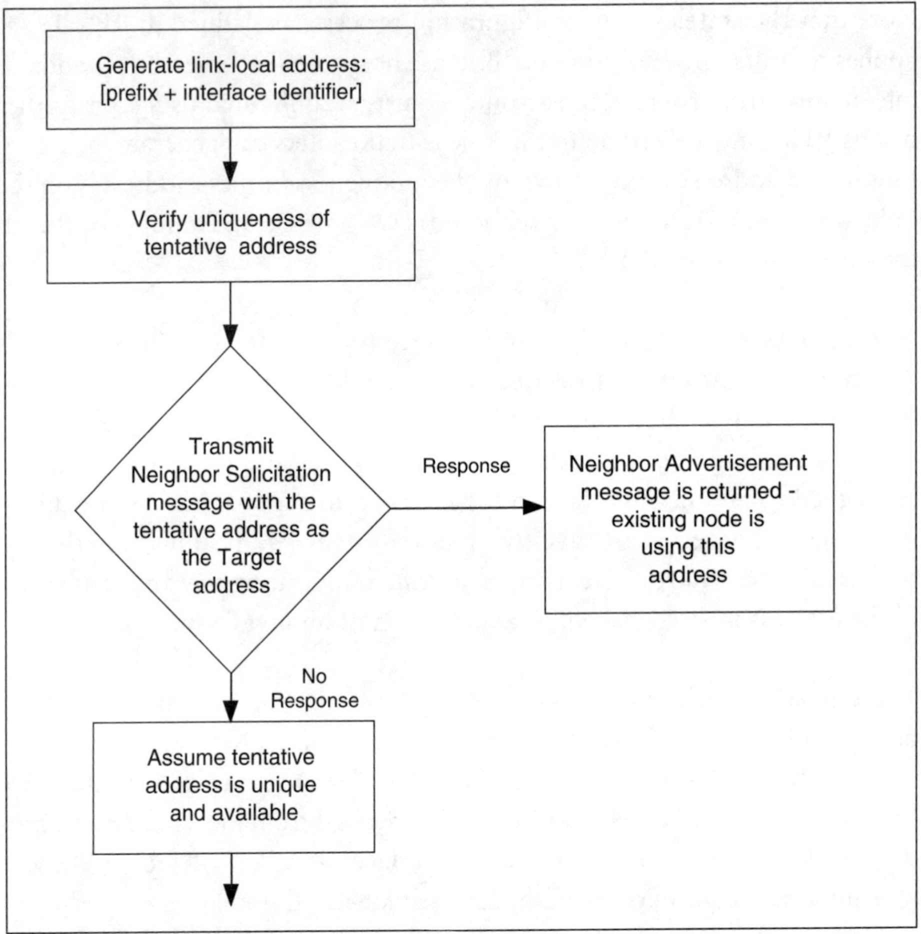

Figure 5-1a. The Stateless Autoconfiguration Process.

The next step determines the uniqueness of the tentative address that has been derived by combining the Link-Local prefix and the interface identifier. In this step, a Neighbor Solicitation message is transmitted with the tentative address as the target address. If another node is using this address, a Neighbor Advertisement message is returned. In this event, autoconfiguration stops and some manual intervention is required. If no Neighbor Advertisement responses are returned, the tentative address is considered unique and IP-level connectivity with the neighboring nodes is now possible. Note that both hosts and routers can generate Link-Local addresses using this part of the autoconfiguration process.

The next phase is performed by hosts only; it involves listening for the Router Advertisement messages that routers periodically transmit, or forcing an immediate Router Advertisement message by transmitting a Router Solicitation message (Figure 5-1b). If no Router Advertisements are received, meaning that no routers are present, a stateful method, such as DHCPv6, should be used to complete the configuration process.

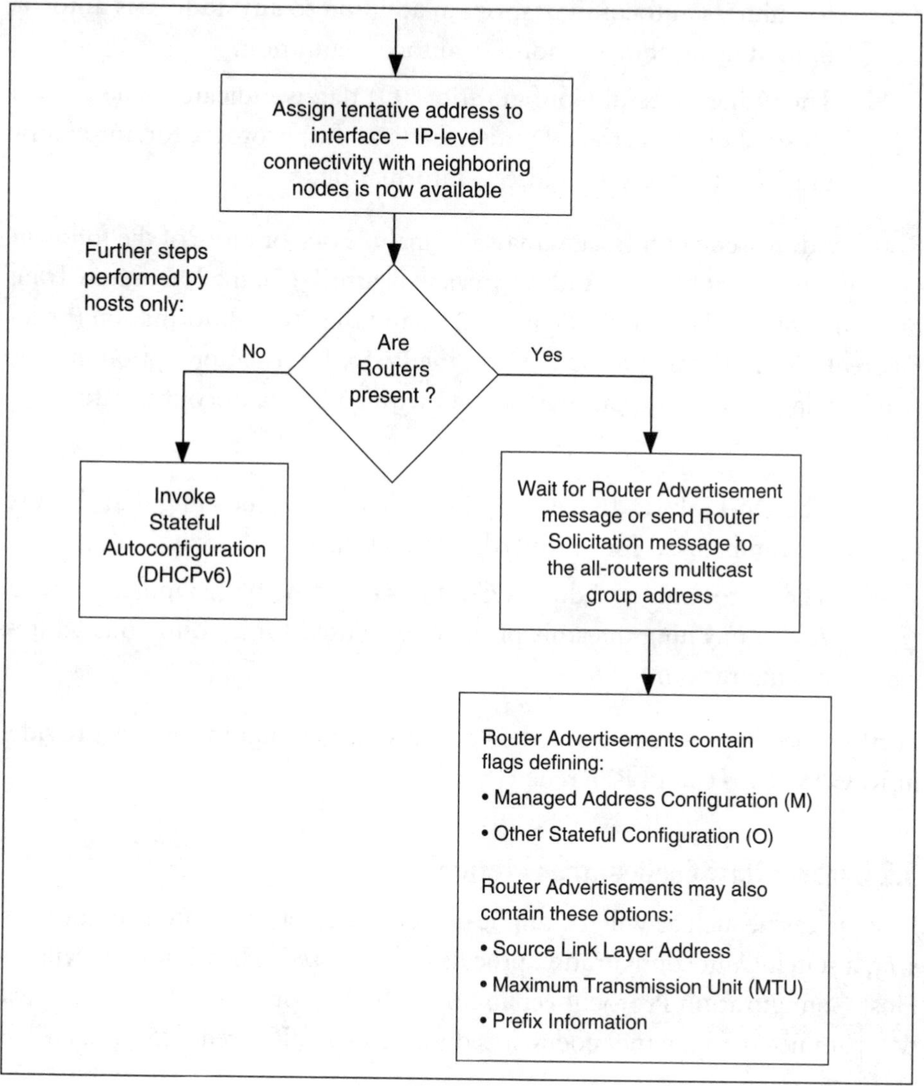

Figure 5-1b. The Stateless Autoconfiguration Process, con't.

If routers are present, Router Advertisement messages will be periodically sent. According to RFC 1970, Router Advertisements include two key flags, M and O, which are used in the autoconfiguration process (review Figure 4-13):

- The Managed Address Configuration (M) flag is indicated when M = 1. In this case, hosts should use the administered (stateful) protocol for address autoconfiguration, in addition to any addresses autoconfigured using stateless address autoconfiguration.
- The Other Stateful Configuration (O) flag is indicated when O = 1. Hosts should use the administered (stateful) protocol for autoconfiguration of other (nonaddress) information.

Router Advertisement messages may also include one or more of the following options: Source Link Layer Address (review Figure 4-17), the Maximum Transmission Unit (MTU) (review Figure 4-21), and the Prefix Information (review Figure 4-19). According to RFC 1970, the Prefix Information option includes two key flags, L and A, that may be used with address autoconfiguration:

- The On-Link (L) flag is indicated when L = 1, meaning that this prefix can be used for on-link determination.
- The Autonomous Address Configuration (A) flag is indicated when A = 1, meaning that this prefix can be used for autonomous address configuration.

Further specifics regarding stateless address autoconfiguration are provided in RFC 1971 [5-1] and Reference [5-2].

5.2 Dynamic Host Configuration Protocol

In some cases, such as when a duplicate address exists or routers are not present, a stateful autoconfiguration process must be used. The proposed Dynamic Host Configuration Protocol version 6 (DHCPv6) provides these configuration parameters to Internet nodes; it is documented in Reference [5-3]. DHCPv6 consists of two elements: a protocol that delivers node-specific configuration information from a DHCPv6 server to a client, and a mechanism for allocating network addresses and other parameters to IPv6 nodes.

DHCPv6 is built on a client/server model, which relies on a total of six Request and Reply messages for communication of these parameter details. Several types of functional DHCPv6 nodes are defined:

- DHCPv6 Client: A node that initiates requests on a link to obtain configuration parameters.
- DHCPv6 Server: A node that responds to requests from clients to provide addresses, prefix lengths, or other configuration parameters.
- DHCPv6 Relay: A node that acts as an intermediary to deliver DHCPv6 messages between clients and servers.
- DHCPv6 Agent: either a server or a relay.

Communication between DHCPv6 agents uses the following well-known multicast addresses:

- FF02:0:0:0:0:0:1:2 Link-Local All-DHCP-Agents multicast group
- FF05:0:0:0:0:0:1:2 Site Local All-DHCP-Servers multicast group
- FF05:0:0:0:0:0:1:2 Site Local All-DHCP-Relays multicast group

All of the proposed DHCPv6 messages have a common srructure, which begins with a Message Type (Msg-type) field indicating the specific function (Figure 5-2). Configuration parameters, which are called *extensions*, are included in the DHCPv6 messages. Extensions have been defined to specify an IP address, Timezones, Domain Name Server, Directory Agent, Network Time Protocol Server, Network Information Server, Transmission Control Protocol (TCP) parameters, Client-Server Authentication, and many other parameters.

A DHCPv6 Solicit message is sent by a Client (or a Relay, on behalf of a Client) to obtain one or more Server addresses, and is identified by Msg-type = 1. This message includes a C flag, which requests deallocation of Client resources at the server; an A flag, which indicates the presence of a Relay address; plus the Client's and possible Relay's addresses.

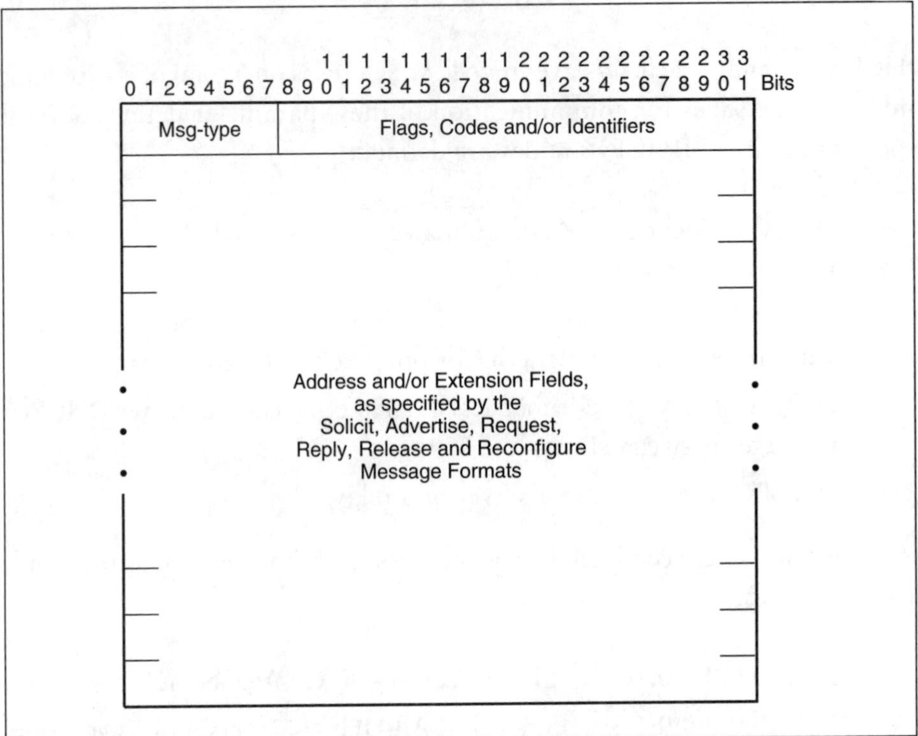

Figure 5-2. Proposed DHCPv6 Message Structure

The DHCPv6 Advertise message is sent by a DHCPv6 agent to inform a prospective Client about the IP address where Request messages can be sent; it is identified by Msg-type = 2. This message includes an S flag, indicating that the Agent address is also a Server address, plus several addresses and extensions.

The DHCPv6 Request message is sent by a Client to request parameters from a DHCPv6 Server; it is identified by Msg-type = 3. This message includes an S flag, indicating that the Server address is present; a C flag, which can request the Server to clear all existing resources and bindings associated with the Client; a Transaction identifier; plus several addresses and extensions.

The DHCPv6 Reply message is sent by a Server in response to every Request or Release message that is received; it is identified by Msg-type = 4. This message includes an L flag, indicating that a Link-Local address is present; an Error Code; a Transaction ID; plus possibly the Client's Link-Local Address and extensions.

The DHCPv6 Release message is sent from a Client to the Server (without assistance from a Relay) to request the release of particular extensions; it is identified by Msg-type = 5. This message includes a D flag, indicating that the Server should send the reply directly back to the Client; a Transaction identifier; plus several addresses and extensions.

The DHCPv6 Reconfigure message is sent from a Server to a Client Server (without assistance from a Relay) to indicate that certain parameters, which are specified in the extensions, need to be requested again by the Client; it is identified by Msg-type = 6. This message includes a Transaction identifier, a Server address, plus extensions.

In addition to its synergy with the Stateless Address Autoconfiguration protocol, DHCPv6 also collaborates with the Domain Name System, which we will study in Chapter 7.

In the following sections, we will consider specific support issues for various LANs and WANs that are used to convey IPv6 packets, and the various framing, addressing, and parameter issues that arise.

5.3 IPv6 over ARCNET

ARCNET stands for the Attached Resource Computer Network, which was developed by Datapoint Corporation and marketed by a number of firms, including Novell, Inc. ARCNET's data rate of 2.5 Mbps makes it somewhat obsolete by today's standards; however, because of the network's resilience, there are still a number of ARCNETs installed throughout the world. Reference [5-4] documents the proposal for the transmission of IPv6 packets over

ARCNETs. RFC 1201, "Transmitting IP Traffic over ARCNET Networks", is also a worthwhile reference.

Packets to be transmitted over an ARCNET can be carried in one of three different types of frame formats, as shown in Figures 5-3a, b, and c. A packet fragmentation and reassembly process, which uses the Split Flag and Sequence Number fields, allows up to 120 fragmented frames per packet. As a result, the largest packet size is 60,480 (120 * 504 octets, where 504 is the MTU of the ARCNET Long Frame Format). Since a packet size of this magnitude is not likely to occur, it is recommended that a Router Advertisement include an MTU option of the appropriate length.

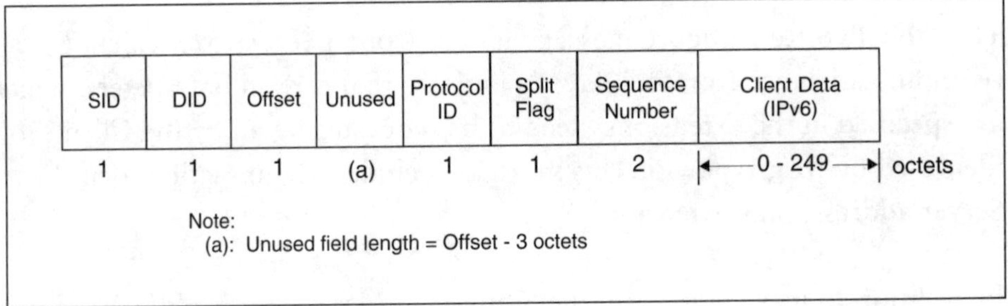

Figure 5-3a. ARCNET Short Frame Format with IPv6 Client data

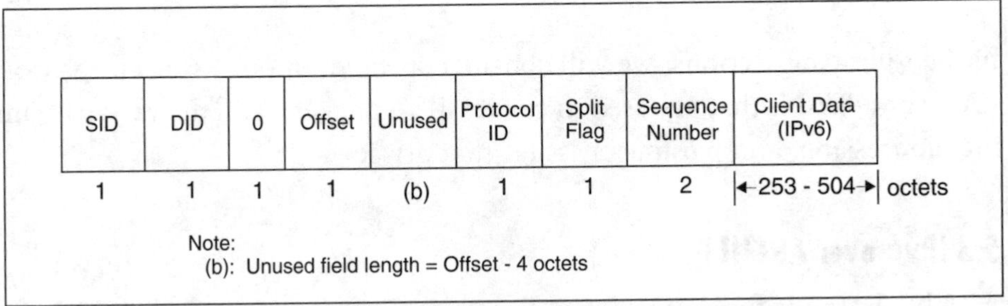

Figure 5-3b. ARCNET Long Frame Format with IPv6 Client data

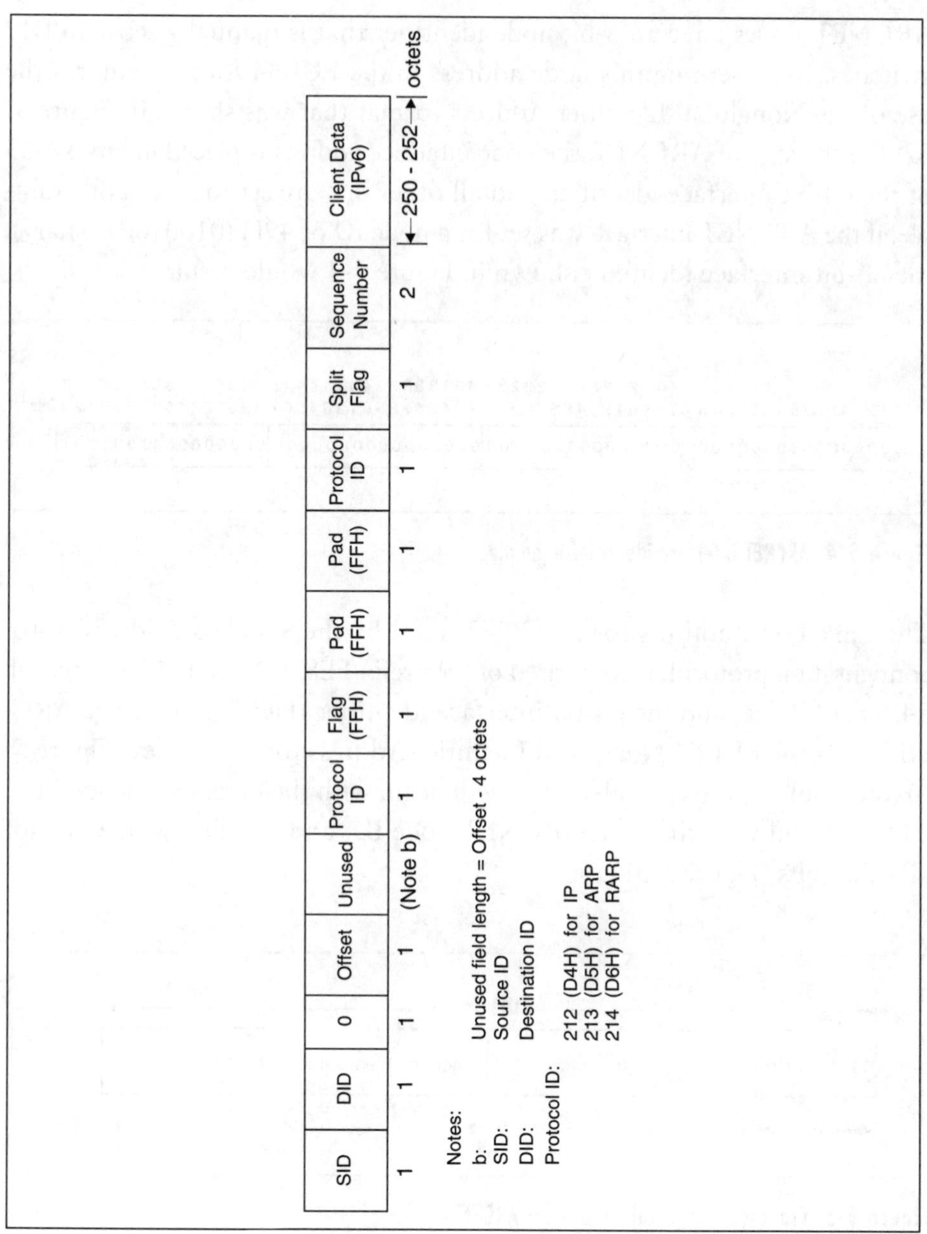

Figure 5-3c. ARCNET Exception Frame Format with IPv6 Client data

ARCNET nodes have an 8-bit node identifier that is manually set with DIP switches. Representing this node address in the EUI-64 format requires the use of the Nonglobal Identifier Address format that was shown in Figure 3-32. For the case of ARCNET, the node interface address is placed in bits 57–63 of the 64-bit interface identifier, and all other bits are set to zero. For example, if the ARCNET interface was set for a node ID of 49H (01001001 binary), the 64-bit interface identifier shown in Figure 5-4 would result.

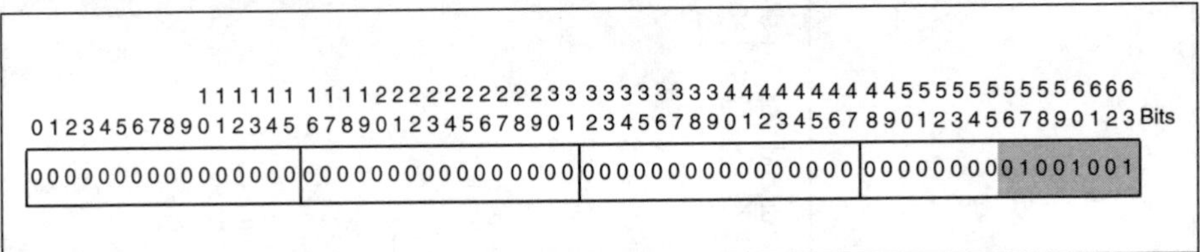

Figure 5-4. ARCNET interface identifier example

The Link-Local address for ARCNET, used by the Stateless Address Autoconfiguration protocol, is comprised of the prefix FE8H (1111 1110 10 binary), 54 bits of zeros, and the 64-bit interface identifier (Figure 5-5). Since ARCNET uses the EUI-64 Nonglobal Identifier Address format (review Figure 5-4), the resulting Link-Local address will begin with the binary sequence 1111 1110 10, end with the 8-bit ARCNET node ID, and be filled with zeros for all other bits (Figure 5-5).

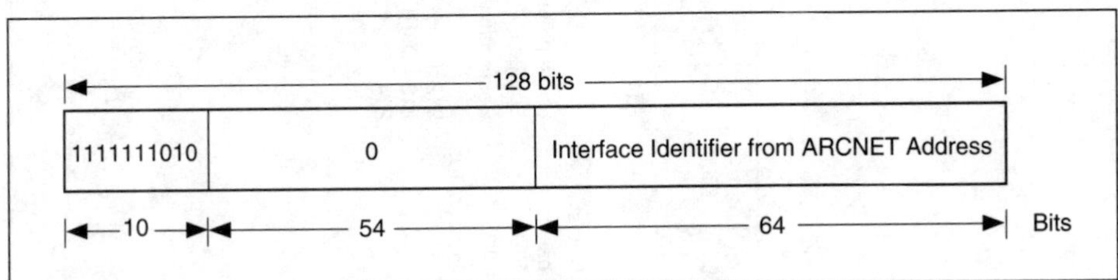

Figure 5-5. Proposed Link-Local address for ARCNET

The IPv6 Neighbor Discovery process requires a procedure to map IPv6 addresses to Source/Target Link Layer addresses, which may then be carried as an option within the Router Solicitation, Router Advertisement, Neighbor Solicitation, Neighbor Advertisement, or Redirect messages, discussed in Chapter 4. The Source/Target Link Layer Address option is carried within many of the ICMPv6 packets to convey this information. For ARCNETs, the 8-bit ARCNET node ID is placed in the first octet of the option and the remaining five octets are filled with padding (Figure 5-6).

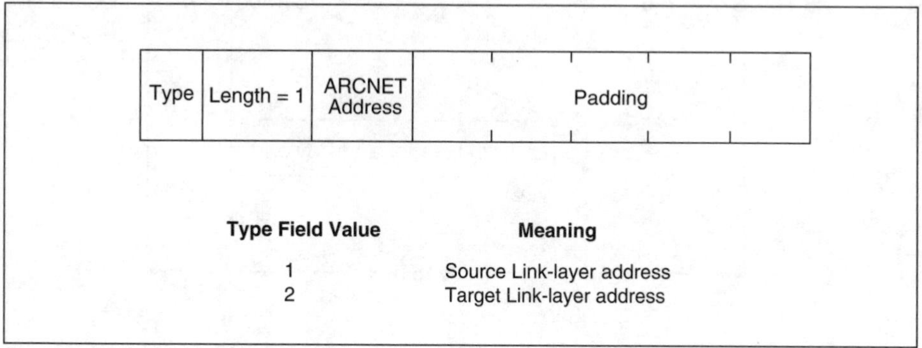

Figure 5-6. Proposed ARCNET Unicast address mapping (Source/Target Link Layer Address option)

ARCNET provides only one multicast address, 00H (00000000 binary); therefore, all IPv6 multicast addresses should be mapped to this address.

Further details on the proposed ARCNET support are found in Reference [5-4].

5.4 IPv6 over Ethernet

Ethernet, originally developed by Digital Equipment Corporation (DEC), Intel Corporation, and Xerox Corporation, has been traditionally popular with TCP/IP-based internetworks. Support for IPv6 over Ethernet networks is documented in RFC 1972 [5-5], with additionsl work that documents proposed enhancements to these efforts [5-6].

The Ethernet frame may carry as much as 1500 octets of data in the information field; therefore, we would say the maximum transmission unit (MTU) for Ethernet is 1500 octets. This size may be reduced by a Router Advertisement packet specifying a smaller MTU, as detailed in RFC 1970. The Ethernet Type (Ethertype) field contains the value 86DDH to specify IPv6 (Figure 5-7).

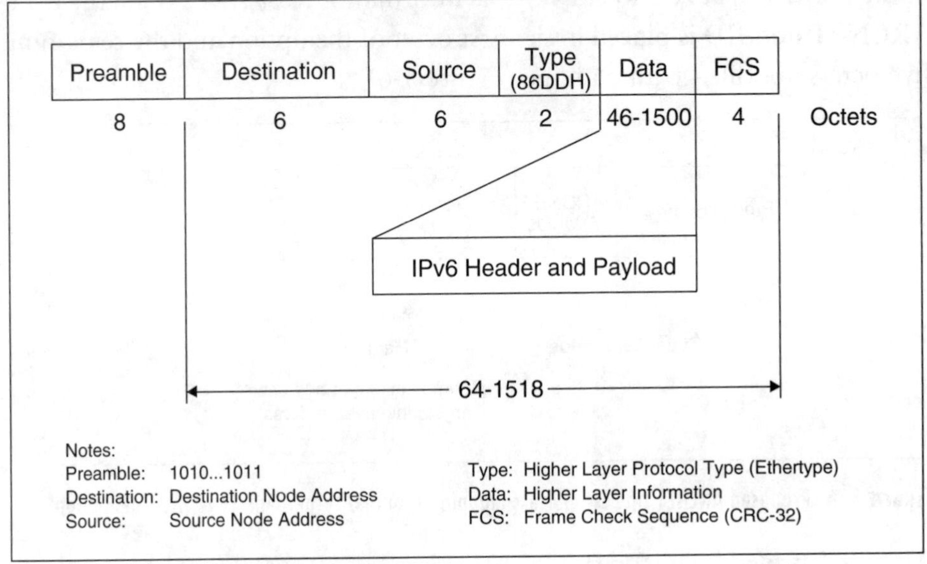

Figure 5-7. Ethernet frame with IPv6 packet
(Courtesy of Digital Equipment Corp.)

The Link-Local address is formed by prepending the Link-Local prefix (FE80::0) to the interface identifier. For Ethernet networks, the interface identifier is the 48-bit Ethernet address, expanded in the center with the hexadecimal characters FFFE (review Figure 3-31) to create an EUI-64 compatible 64-bit address (Figure 5-8).

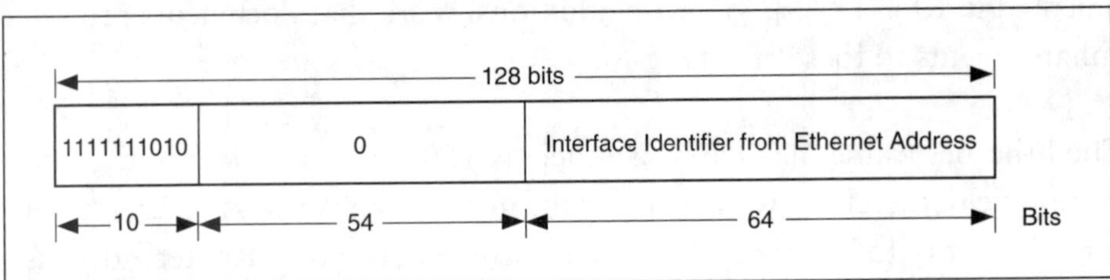

Figure 5-8. Proposed Link-Local address for Ethernet

The Source/Target Link Layer Address option for Ethernet is shown in Figure 5-9, and is similar in format to the ARCNET example shown above.

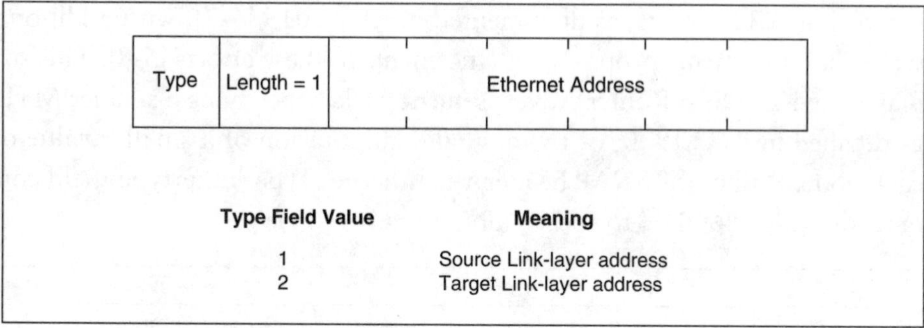

Figure 5-9. Ethernet Unicast address mapping

For multicast addresses, an IPv6 address with a multicast destination address (e.g. DST) is transmitted to the Ethernet multicast address that begins with the value 3333H and ends with the last four octets of the DST address. (Note from Figure 5-10 that the value 3333H occupies the first two octets of the Ethernet multicast address, and the last four octets of the 16-octet IPv6 address (designated DST13, DST14, DST15, and DST16) occupy the last four octets of the Ethernet address.)

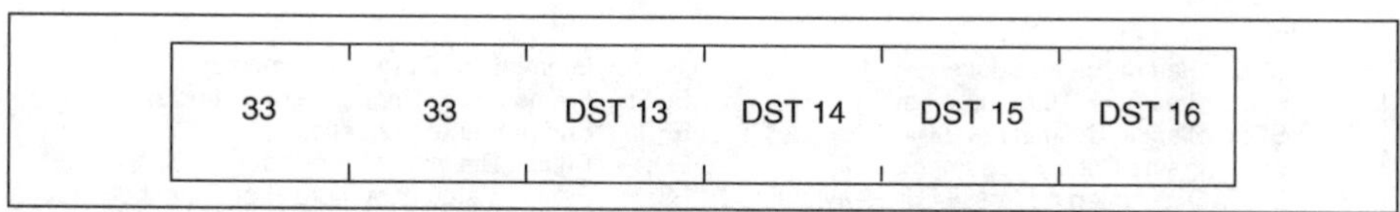

Figure 5-10. Ethernet Multicast address mapping (Source/Target Link Layer Address option)

Further details on Ethernet support are found in RFC 1972 [5-5] and Reference [5-6].

5.5 IPv6 over FDDI

The FDDI frame may carry as much as 4,500 octets of data in the information field, which includes 22 octets in the frame header and trailer. When IPv6 packets are sent over FDDI, the Logical Link Control (LLC—3 octets) and

Subnetwork Access Protocol (SNAP—5 octets) headers are also included. Therefore, the maximum IPv6 MTU would be 4,470 octets. To allow for future protocol extensions, the default MTU size for IPv6 packets on an FDDI network is 4,352 octets, as documented in RFC 2019 [5-7], with additional work that documents proposed enhancements to these efforts [5-8]. This size may be reduced by a Router Advertisement packet specifying a smaller MTU, as detailed in RFC 1970, or by manual configuration of a smaller value on each node. Within the SNAP header, the Ethernet Type (Ethertype) field contains the value 86DDH to specify IPv6 (Figure 5-11).

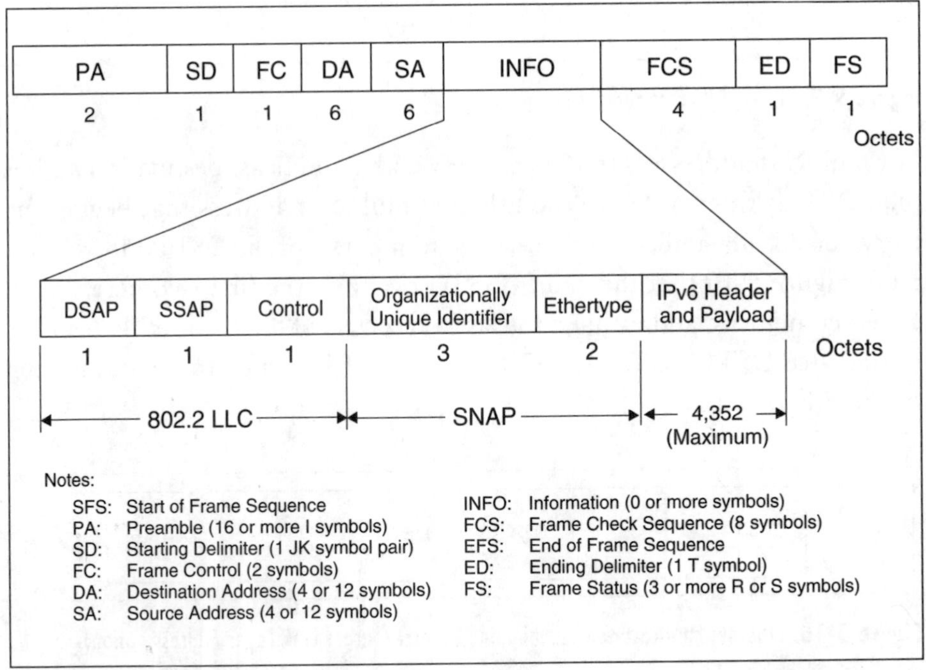

Figure 5-11. FDDI frame with IPv6 packet
(Courtesy of American National Standards Institute)

For FDDI networks, the interface identifier is the 48-bit FDDI address, expanded with the hexadecimal characters FFFE into an EUI-64 address. Therefore, the Link Local address would be an 80-bit prefix (FE80::) followed by the 64-bit FDDI interface identifier (Figure 5-12).

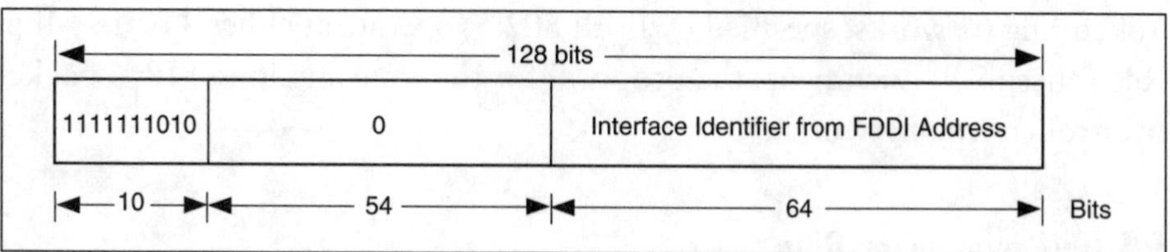

Figure 5-12. Proposed Link Local address for FDDI

Similar to the Ethernet case, the FDDI Unicast address mapping, used with the Source/Target Address option, ends with the 48-bit FDDI address (Figure 5-13).

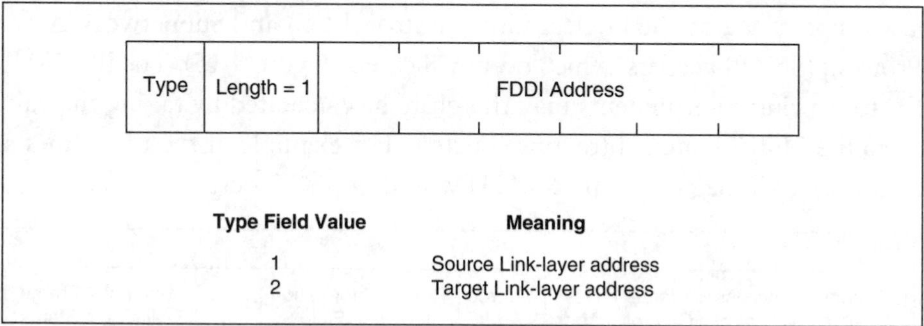

Figure 5-13. FDDI Unicast address mapping (Source/Target Link Layer Address option)

For multicast addresses, an IPv6 address with a multicast destination address (e.g. DST) is transmitted to the FDDI multicast address that begins with the value 3333H and ends with the last four octets of the DST address (Figure 5-14).

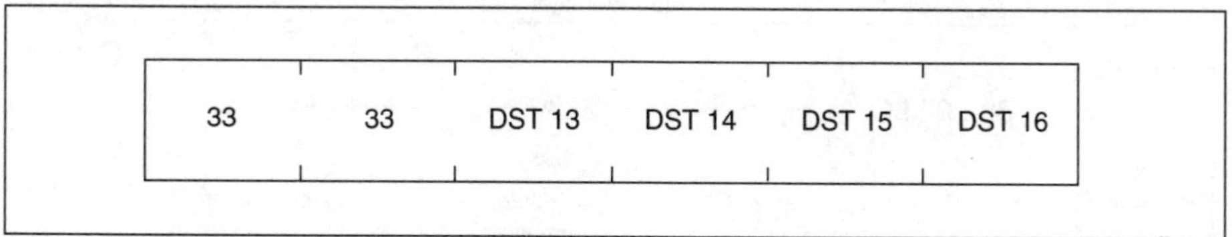

Figure 5-14. FDDI Multicast address mapping

Further details on FDDI support are found in RFC 2019 [5-7] and reference [5-8].

Token ring networks, specified by IEEE 802.5, operate at either 4 or 16 Mbps. Reference [5-9] documents the proposal for the transmission of IPv6 packets over token ring networks.

5.6 IPv6 over Token Ring

The token ring frame may carry a variable amount of data in the information field, typically 2K, 4K, or 8K octets. Since this value may vary, the actual MTU size is set using a static configuration or Router Advertisement messages. When the topology is source route bridged, the Largest Frame (LF) subfield of the Routing Information field defines the MTU. The IPv6 packet is always preceded by the Logical Link Control (LLC) and Subnetwork Access Protocol (SNAP) headers, which occupy 8 octets (Figure 5-15). The IPv6 MTU for token ring environments may therefore be calculated by taking the value from the LF field and subtracting 8 octets. For example, if the LF defines an MTU of 1,470 octets, the IPv6 MTU would be 1,462 octets.

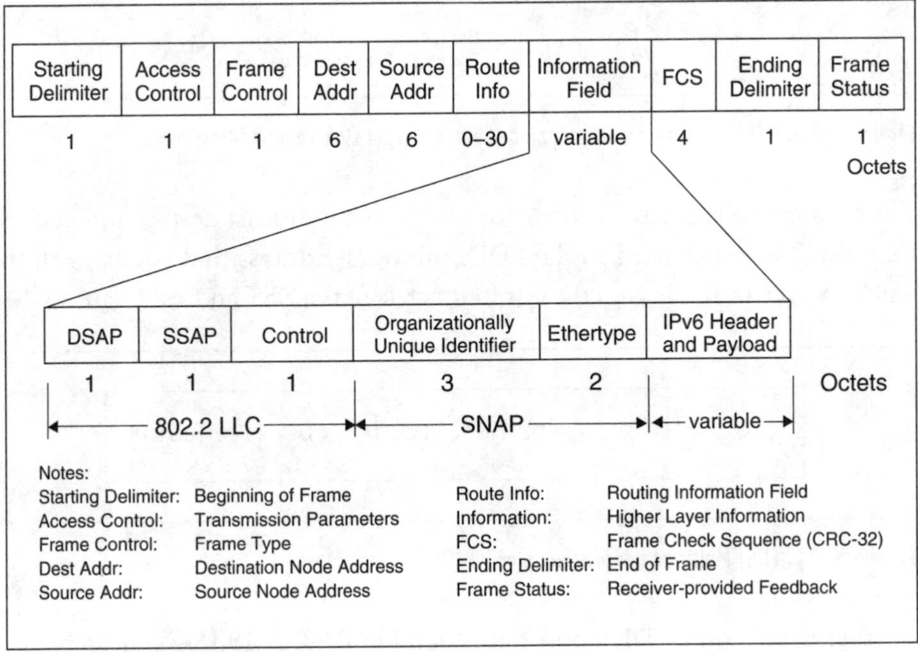

Figure 5-15. Token Ring frame with IPv6 packet *(Courtesy of IEEE)*

For token ring networks, the interface identifier is the 48-bit FDDI address, expanded with the hexadecimal characters FFFE into an EUI-64 address. Therefore, the Link Local address would be an 80-bit prefix (FE80::) followed by the 64-bit FDDI interface identifier (Figure 5-16). Note that locally assigned (non-ROM-based) token ring addresses should not be used.

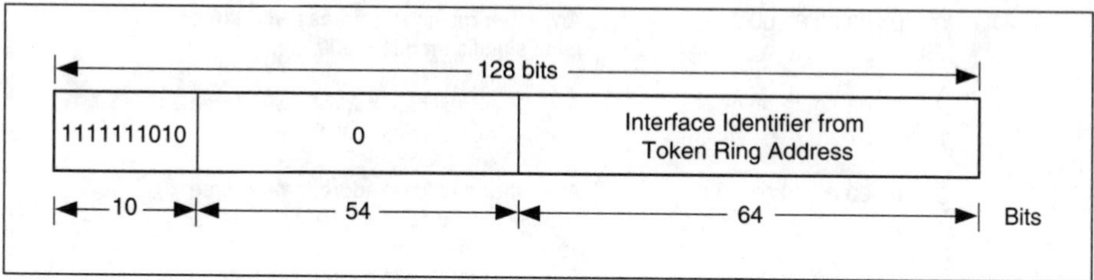

Figure 5-16. Proposed Link-Local address for Token Ring

Similar to the Ethernet and FDDI cases, the token ring Unicast address mapping, used with the Source/Target Address option, ends with the 48-bit token ring address (Figure 5-17).

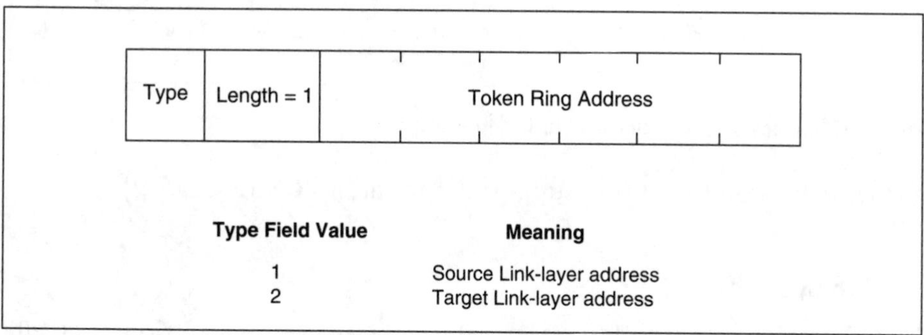

Figure 5-17. Proposed Token Ring Unicast address mapping (Source/Target Link Layer Address option)

All IPv6 packets with multicast destination addresses are transmitted to token ring functional addresses. Figure 5-18 illustrates the specific mapping between the IPv6 addresses and the token ring functional addresses.

Token Ring MAC Functional Address (canonical)	IPv6 Multicast Addresses
03 00 80 00 00 00	All nodes (FF01::1 and FF02::1) and solicited node (FF02::1:FFXX:XXXX) addresses
03 00 40 00 00 00	All routers addresses (FF0X::2)
03 00 00 80 00 00	Any other multicast address with three least significant bits = 000
03 00 00 40 00 00	Any other multicast address with three least significant bits = 001
03 00 00 20 00 00	Any other multicast address with three least significant bits = 010
03 00 00 10 00 00	Any other multicast address with three least significant bits = 011
03 00 00 08 00 00	Any other multicast address with three least significant bits = 100
03 00 00 04 00 00	Any other multicast address with three least significant bits = 101
03 00 00 02 00 00	Any other multicast address with three least significant bits = 110
03 00 00 01 00 00	Any other multicast address with three least significant bits = 111

Figure 5-18. Proposed Token Ring Multicast address mapping

Further details on token ring support are found in Reference [5-9].

5.7 IPv6 over PPP

The Point to Point Protocol (PPP) is used extensively for transmission of TCP/IP traffic over WAN links. Support for IPv6 over PPP is documented in RFC 2023 [5-10] with additional work that documents proposed enhancements to these efforts [5-11]. PPP consists of three elements: an encapsulation (or framing) format for serial links; a Link Control Protocol (LCP) for establishing, configuring, and testing the link connection; and a family of Network Control Protocols (NCPs) for establishing and configuring different Network Layer protocols. For example, the NCP for establishing and configuring IPv6 over PPP is called the IPv6 Control Protocol, or IPV6CP.

The PPP frame is shown in Figure 5-19. Note that either one IPv6 packet or one IPV6CP packet would fit inside the information field of that PPP frame. The Protocol field defines the type of packet that is carried: 0057H indicates IPv6, while 8057H indicates IPV6CP.

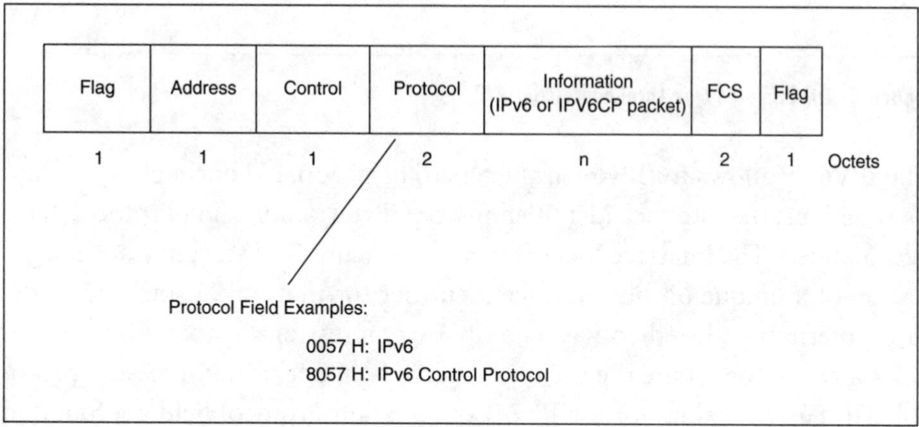

Figure 5-19. PPP frame with IPv6 or IPV6CP packet

For LANs such as Ethernet or token ring, the interface identifier used with the Stateless Address Autoconfiguration process is based on the hardware address, which is typically resident in a ROM on the network interface card. For PPP links, the interface identifier may be selected using one of the following methods (listed in the order of preference):

1. If an IEEE global identifier (either EUI-48 or EUI-64) is available anywhere on the node, then that address should be used.
2. If an IEEE global identifier is not available, then a different source of uniqueness, such as a machine serial number, should be used.
3. If a good source of uniqueness cannot be found, a random number should be generated.

The resulting Link-Local address for PPP is shown in Figure 5-20.

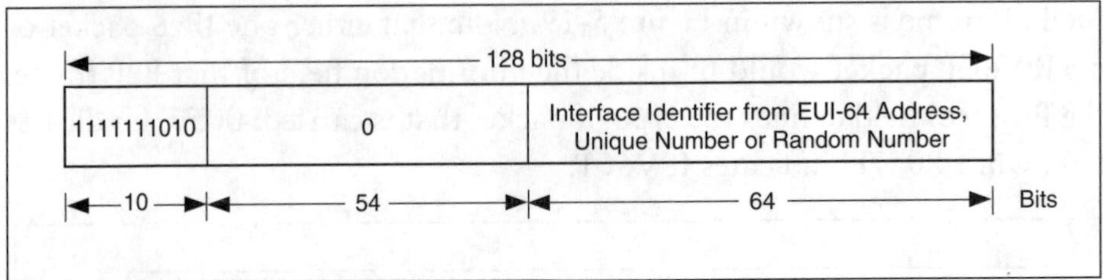

Figure 5-20. Proposed Link-Local address for PPP

The IPV6CP allows for IPv6 parameters to be negotiated during link startup. Two options, the Interface Identifier and the IPv6 Compression Protocol, have been defined. The Interface Identifier option (Figure 5-21) facilitates the negotiation of a unique 64-bit interface identifier for that link, using one of the three alternatives listed above. The IPv6-Compression-Protocol option provides a way to negotiate the use of a specific IPv6 packet compression protocol. The current values for the IPv6-Compression-Protocol field are found in the most recent "Assigned Numbers" document (currently RFC 1700).

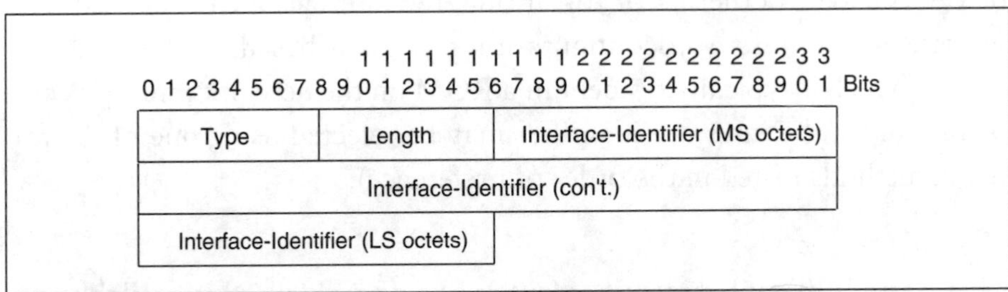

Figure 5-21. Proposed IPV6CP Interface Identifier Configuration option

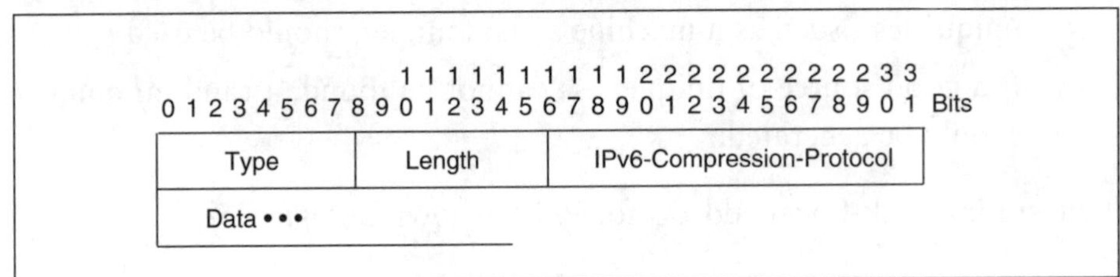

Figure 5-22. Proposed IPV6CP IPv6-Compression-Protocol Configuration option

Further details on PPP support are found in RFC 2023 [5-10] and Reference [5-11].

5.8 Mobile IPv6

In the local networks we have discussed thus far, all users are assumed to have a hardware connection to the network, and to stay that way for some period of time. Recent research deals with mobile users and the particular issues that their configuration brings [5-12]. Each mobile node is always identified by a home address, regardless of its current attachment to the Internet. When it is away from its home address, it is associated with a *care-of address*, which provides details regarding its current location. Any IPv6 packet sent to the home address would therefore be routed to the care-of address. This process is equally applicable to a user moving from one Ethernet segment to another Ethernet segment as to another user moving from an Ethernet segment to a wireless LAN cell.

The association between the home address and the care-of address is called a *binding* for the mobile node. The care-of address may be obtained using either stateless or stateful (DHCPv6) address autoconfiguration, according to the Neighbor Discovery protocol that we discussed in Chapter 4. The binding registration is accomplished by the mobile node sending an IPv6 packet containing a Binding Update destination option to the home agent, which replies with a Binding Acknowledgement to the mobile node.

5.9 Case Studies

In our previous case studies, we considered the use of various IPv6 address types and the various intranetwork communication processes that are used, such as the ICMPv6 messages supporting Neighbor Discovery and Router Advertisements. In the two case studies that follow, we will look at two related implementation issues: address autoconfiguration and the proper use of Link-Local addresses.

5.9.1 Generating a Link-Local Address for a Router

Recall from our earlier discussions that both hosts and routers may use the autoconfiguration process to obtain Link-Local addresses, but then hosts continue in the process to obtain other parameters from routers. (For obvious reasons, routers must obtain much of their configuration information through other means, such as manual configuration files, so that they can then be in a position to assist the hosts when those hosts initialize.) In this case study, we will build on the experience from Section 3.10, which discussed the various addresses that a workstation uses upon initialization. This time, however, we will concentrate on a router, and will look at the process through which a router generates its Link-Local address (Figure 5-23).

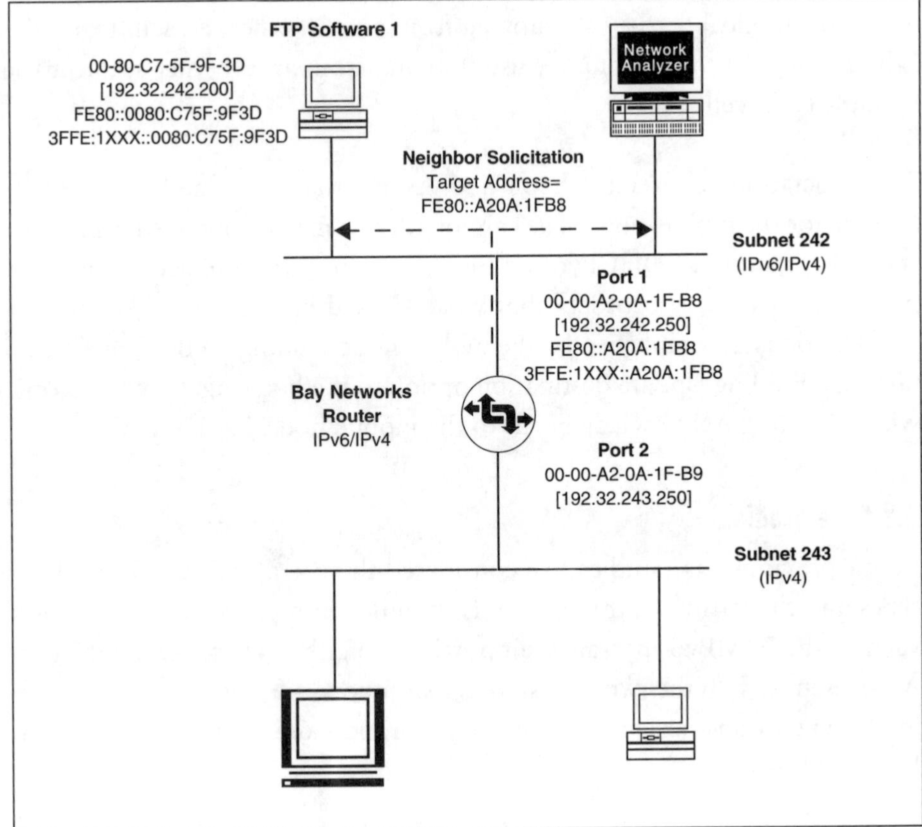

Figure 5-23. Link-Local address generation

The network analyzer is initialized to capture data on segment 242, and then the Bay Networks' router is turned on. From Trace 5.9.1a, we see the first Bay "Breath of Life" (BOFL) frame that is sent from the IPv6 Port (Port 1). The BOFL is a periodic transmission from Bay Router ports that notifies the router's upper-layer protocols (such as IPv6) that the transmission media is currently available. The default period for BOFL transmissions is every five seconds. (We see other BOFL transmissions in Frames 7 and 10.) The first ICMPv6 Neighbor Solicitation message, testing a tentative Link-Local address for the router (FE80:0:0:0:0:0:A20A:1FB8), is sent in Frame 3. Another Neighbor Solicitation message, this one with a different address prefix for the Neighbor Solicitation Target address (3FFE:1XXX), occurs in Frame 6. Once these processes complete, the first Router Advertisement, using the verified Link-Local address for the IPv6 Source address (FE80:0:0:0:0:0:A20A:1FB8), is sent in Frame 9.

Trace 5.9.1a. Router Address Autoconfiguration Summary

```
--------------        Protocol Summary - bootast2.cap 9/4       --------------


  Frame DeltaTime     Destination       Source          Interpretation

    1                  Bay IPv6 P1   Bay IPv6 P1   BOFL(WF) Seq=1
    2  151.4 ms          Broadcast   Bay IPv6 P1   ARP REQUEST
    3  239.9 ms 33-33-A2-0A-1F-B8   Bay IPv6 P1   ICMPv6 Neighbor Solicitation
    4  119.6 ms 33-33-00-00-00-09   Bay IPv6 P1   RPC FRAME TOO SHORT
    5  2.6 sec           Broadcast   Bay IPv6 P1   ARP REQUEST
    6  1.1 sec  33-33-A2-0A-1F-B8   Bay IPv6 P1   ICMPv6 Neighbor Solicitation
    7  702.8 ms        Bay IPv6 P1   Bay IPv6 P1   BOFL(WF) Seq=2
    8  407.3 ms          Broadcast   Bay IPv6 P1   RIP (TCP/IP)
    9  890.2 ms 33-33-00-00-00-01   Bay IPv6 P1   ICMPv6 Router Advertisement
   10  3.7 sec         Bay IPv6 P1   Bay IPv6 P1   BOFL(WF) Seq=3
```

From the detail trace of Frame 3 (Trace 5.9.1b), note first that the Ethernet Destination address is 33-33-A2-0A-1F-B8, which is the mapping of an Ethernet multicast address (review Figure 5-10). The IPv6 Destination address is FF02:0:0:0:0:1:FF0A:1FB8, the solicited node address for Port 1 of the Bay Networks' router. The ICMPv6 Neighbor Solicitation message follows the IPv6 header, with a Target address (the Link-Local tentative address) of

FE80:0:0:0:0:0:A20A:1FB8. If you compare this Tentative address with Figure 5-8, you will notice two subtleties. First, the Bay Networks' router has a hardware address of 00-00-A2-0A-1F-B8 (see the Source Link Layer Address option in the Neighbor Solicitation message); thus, the first 16 bits of the address (0000H) are indistinguishable from the zeros that appear in octets 11 and 12 of the Tentative address. Secondly, the hardware address is a 48-bit address, and has not been extended for compatibility with EUI-64 format. If it had been extended for compatibility, we would see the address 00-00-A2-FF-FE-0A-1F-B8 in this Tentative address (review Figure 3-31). This Link-Local address structure uses the Pre-EUI-64 format, defined in RFC 1972, which added 16 bits of zero to the beginning of a 48-bit hardware address instead of adding the FFFEH in the middle.

Trace 5.9.1b. Router Neighbor Solicitation (Tentative Link-Local Address)

```
-------------- Frame 3  Size 90  Absolute Time  13:24:16.59808  --------------
                    Protocol Detail - bootast2.cap 9/4


IEEE 802.3/Ethernet DIX V2 Header


Decode Status : -
                  Frame Length : 90
           Destination Address : 33-33-A2-0A-1F-B8 ( Group, Locally Administered Addr
                Source Address : 00-00-A2-0A-1F-B8, Bay IPv6 P1 ( OUI = WELLFLEET, U
                  Frame Format : Ethernet DIX V2
                     Ethertype : 0x86DD (IPv6)
                Frame Checksum : Good, Frame Check Sequence : 00 00 00 00
```

```
IPv6 - Internet Protocol (Version 6)


              Decode Status : -
             Version Number : 6 (IP Version 6)
                      Class : 0x0
                 Flow Label : 0x0
             Payload Length : 32
                Next Header : 58 (ICMPv6)
                  Hop Limit : 255
             Source Address : ::0.0.0.0
        Destination Address : FF02:0:0:0:0:1:FF0A:1FB8


ICMPv6 - Internet Control Message Protocol (Version 6)


              Decode Status : -
                  ICMP Type : 135 (Neighbor Solicitation)
 Neighbor Solicitation Code : 0
                   Checksum : 13527
             Target Address : FE80:0:0:0:0:0:A20A:1FB8

                ----- Options -----
                     Option : 1 (Source Link Layer Address)
              Option Length : 1
  Source Link Layer Address : 00-00-A2-0A-1F-B8, Bay IPv6 P1
```

In the next Neighbor Solicitation message, shown in Frame 6 (Trace 5.9.1c), note that the ICMPv6 Neighbor Solicitation message uses a different address (an Aggregatable Global Unicast address type with prefix 3FFE:1XXXH), which is the prefix that has been assigned by the router to Subnet 242.

Trace 5.9.1c. Router Neighbor Solicitation (Assigned Prefix Address)

```
-------------- Frame 6  Size 90  Absolute Time  13:24:20.56627  --------------
                    Protocol Detail - bootast2.cap 9/4


IEEE 802.3/Ethernet DIX V2 Header


             Decode Status : -
              Frame Length : 90
       Destination Address : 33-33-A2-0A-1F-B8 ( Group, Locally Administered Addr
            Source Address : 00-00-A2-0A-1F-B8, Bay IPv6 P1 ( OUI = WELLFLEET, U
              Frame Format : Ethernet DIX V2
                 Ethertype : 0x86DD (IPv6)
            Frame Checksum : Good, Frame Check Sequence : 00 00 00 00


IPv6 - Internet Protocol (Version 6)


             Decode Status : -
            Version Number : 6 (IP Version 6)
                     Class : 0x0
                Flow Label : 0x0
            Payload Length : 32
               Next Header : 58 (ICMPv6)
                 Hop Limit : 255
            Source Address : ::0.0.0.0
       Destination Address : FF02:0:0:0:0:1:FF0A:1FB8


ICMPv6 - Internet Control Message Protocol (Version 6)


             Decode Status : -
                 ICMP Type : 135 (Neighbor Solicitation)
Neighbor Solicitation Code : 0
                  Checksum : 54358
            Target Address : 3FFE:1XXX:0:0:0:0:A20A:1FB8
```

```
                  ----- Options -----

                 Option : 1 (Source Link Layer Address)
          Option Length : 1
 Source Link Layer Address : 00-00-A2-0A-1F-B8, Bay IPv6 P1
```

By the time the first Router Advertisement is issued in Frame 9 (Trace 5.9.1d), the tentative Link-Local address has been verified, and is now being used as the IPv6 Source Address (FE80:0:0:0:0:0:A20A:1FB8). Also note the presence of the Prefix Information option, which carries parameters that will be used by hosts on that segment as part of their autoconfiguration process.

Reviewing the trace summary (Trace 5.9.1a), we also do not see any ICMPv6 Neighbor Advertisement messages (which would have been returned had a duplicate existed). From this, we can conclude that there were no duplicate hardware addresses existing on that segment, and that the Link-Local address, as generated, can be fully employed.

Trace 5.9.1d. Router Advertisement with Link-Local Address

```
-------------- Frame 9  Size 122  Absolute Time  13:24:22.56659  -------------
                    Protocol Detail - bootast2.cap 8/22


IEEE 802.3/Ethernet DIX V2 Header


          Decode Status : -
           Frame Length : 122
    Destination Address : 33-33-00-00-00-01 ( Group, Locally Administered Addr
         Source Address : 00-00-A2-0A-1F-B8, Bay IPv6 P1 ( OUI = WELLFLEET, U
           Frame Format : Ethernet DIX V2
              Ethertype : 0x86DD (IPv6)
         Frame Checksum : Good, Frame Check Sequence : 00 00 00 00
```

```
IPv6 - Internet Protocol (Version 6)


          Decode Status : -
         Version Number : 6 (IP Version 6)
                  Class : 0x0
             Flow Label : 0x0
         Payload Length : 64
            Next Header : 58 (ICMPv6)
              Hop Limit : 255
         Source Address : FE80:0:0:0:0:0:A20A:1FB8
    Destination Address : FF02:0:0:0:0:0:0:1


ICMPv6 - Internet Control Message Protocol (Version 6)


               Decode Status : -
                   ICMP Type : 134 (Router Advertisement)
  Router Advertisement Code : 0
                    Checksum : 47173
           Current Hop Limit : 64
                       Flags : 0x00
                               0... .... = Administered Protocol is not Used for Ad
                               .0.. .... = Administered Protocol is not Used for Au
             Router Lifetime : 1800 Seconds(s)
              Reachable Time : 0 Milliseconds(s)
        Retransmission Time : 0 Milliseconds(s)
```

```
                ----- Options -----

                 Option : 1 (Source Link Layer Address)
          Option Length : 1
Source Link Layer Address : 00-00-A2-0A-1F-B8, Bay IPv6 P1

                 Option : 5 (Maximum Transmission Unit)
          Option Length : 1
Maximum Transmission Unit : 1500

                 Option : 3 (Prefix Information)
          Option Length : 4
          Prefix Length : 80
                  Flags : 0xC0
                          1... .... = Prefix Length Can be Used for On-Link Determi
                          .1.. .... = Prefix Length Can be Used for Auton Addr Conf
         Valid Lifetime : 4294967295 (Infinity)
     Preferred Lifetime : 604800 Seconds(s)
                 Prefix : 3FFE:1:0:0:0:0:0:0
```

5.9.2 Using Link-Local Addresses

Recall that the Link-Local address, by definition, must stay on the local link and not be forwarded by the router. As a second example of the use of Link-Local addresses, consider what happens when a workstation (labeled FTP Software 1) attempts to send an ICMPv6 Echo Request (PING) message to both the IPv6 side and the IPv4 side of the same router (Figure 5-24). In the summary trace (Trace 5.9.2a), note that Echo Request/Reply messages from the workstation to the router's Port 1 are successful in Frames 3 through 29. A subsequent test to router Port 2 elicits Neighbor Solicitation messages (Frames 34 and following).

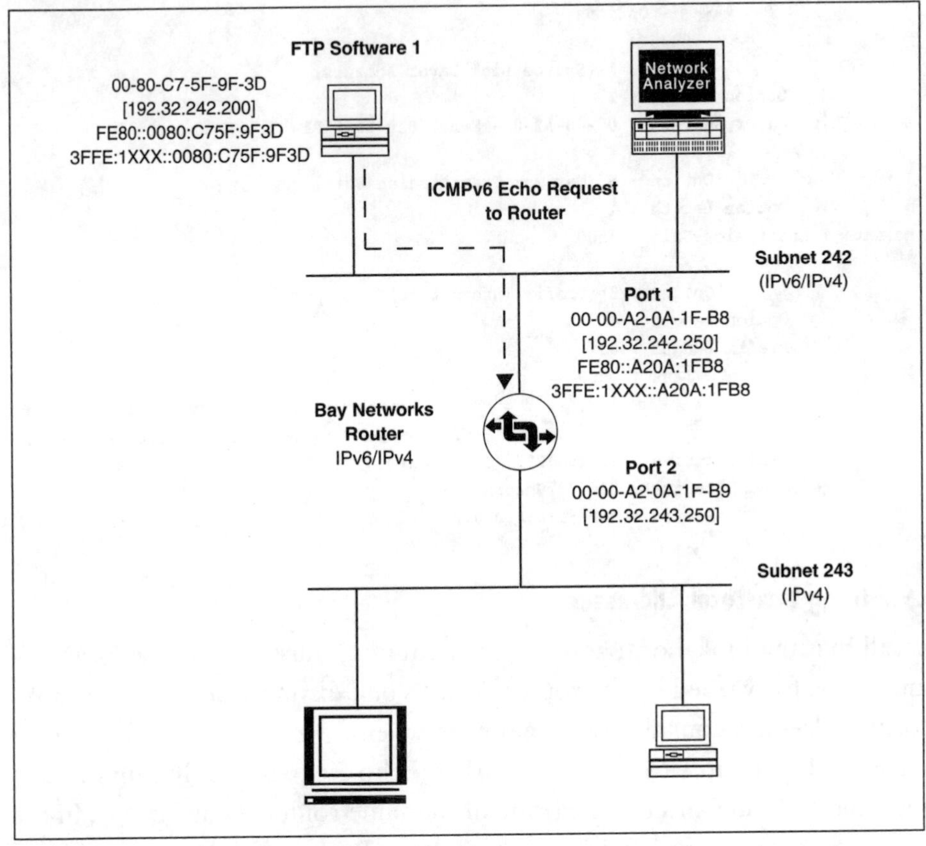

Figure 5-24. Using Link-Local addresses

Trace 5.9.2a. ICMPv6 Echo Request/Reply Summary

```
--------------        Protocol Summary - astping.cap 9/4        --------------


  Frame DeltaTime     Destination      Source            Interpretation

    1                   Bay IPv6 P1      Bay IPv6 P1 BOFL(WF) Seq=661
    2   5.0 sec         Bay IPv6 P1      Bay IPv6 P1 BOFL(WF) Seq=662
    3   5.0 sec         Bay IPv6 P1      Bay IPv6 P1 BOFL(WF) Seq=663
    4   1.9 sec         Bay IPv6 P1   FTP Software 1 ICMPv6 Echo Request
                                                      Identifier=47570 Seq=9984

    5    1.0 ms      FTP Software 1      Bay IPv6 P1 ICMPv6 Echo Reply
                                                      Identifier=47570 Seq=9984

    6   1.0 sec         Bay IPv6 P1   FTP Software 1 ICMPv6 Echo Request
                                                      Identifier=47570 Seq=10240
```

```
 7   800 us      FTP Software 1       Bay IPv6 P1 ICMPv6 Echo Reply
                                                      Identifier=47570 Seq=10240
 8  1.0 sec         Bay IPv6 P1  FTP Software 1 ICMPv6 Echo Request
                                                      Identifier=47570 Seq=10496
 9   610 us      FTP Software 1       Bay IPv6 P1 ICMPv6 Echo Reply
                                                      Identifier=47570 Seq=10496
10 999.4 ms         Bay IPv6 P1       Bay IPv6 P1 BOFL(WF) Seq=664
11  42.9 ms         Bay IPv6 P1  FTP Software 1 ICMPv6 Echo Request
                                                      Identifier=47570 Seq=10752
12   800 us      FTP Software 1       Bay IPv6 P1 ICMPv6 Echo Reply
                                                      Identifier=47570 Seq=10752
13  1.0 sec         Bay IPv6 P1  FTP Software 1 ICMPv6 Echo Request
                                                      Identifier=47570 Seq=11008
14   800 us      FTP Software 1       Bay IPv6 P1 ICMPv6 Echo Reply
                                                      Identifier=47570 Seq=11008
15 844.7 ms  33-33-A2-0A-1F-B8  FTP Software 1 ICMPv6 Neighbor Solicitation
                                                      Target_Address=
                                                      FE80:0:0:0:0:0:A20A:1FB8
                                                      Opt = Src Link Layer Addr
16   900 us      FTP Software 1       Bay IPv6 P1 ICMPv6 Neighbor Advertisement
                                                      Target_Address=
                                                      FE80:0:0:0:0:0:A20A:1FB8
                                                      Opt = Tgt Link Layer Addr
17  36.0 ms      FTP Software 1       Bay IPv6 P1 ICMPv6 Neighbor Solicitation
                                                      Target_Address=
                                                      FE80:0:0:0:0:80:C75F:9F3D
                                                      Opt = Src Link Layer Addr
18   1.3 ms         Bay IPv6 P1  FTP Software 1 ICMPv6 Neighbor Advertisement
                                                      Target_Address=
                                                      FE80:0:0:0:0:80:C75F:9F3D
                                                      Opt = Tgt Link Layer Addr
19  118.0 ms        Bay IPv6 P1  FTP Software 1 ICMPv6 Echo Request
                                                      Identifier=47570 Seq=11264
20   770 us      FTP Software 1       Bay IPv6 P1 ICMPv6 Echo Reply
                                                      Identifier=47570 Seq=11264
21  1.0 sec         Bay IPv6 P1  FTP Software 1 ICMPv6 Echo Request
                                                      Identifier=47570 Seq=11520
22   800 us      FTP Software 1       Bay IPv6 P1 ICMPv6 Echo Reply
                                                      Identifier=47570 Seq=11520
23  1.0 sec         Bay IPv6 P1  FTP Software 1 ICMPv6 Echo Request
                                                      Identifier=47570 Seq=11776
24   800 us      FTP Software 1       Bay IPv6 P1 ICMPv6 Echo Reply
                                                      Identifier=47570 Seq=11776
25 886.5 ms         Bay IPv6 P1       Bay IPv6 P1 BOFL(WF) Seq=665
26 156.1 ms         Bay IPv6 P1  FTP Software 1 ICMPv6 Echo Request
                                                      Identifier=47570 Seq=12032
27   800 us      FTP Software 1       Bay IPv6 P1 ICMPv6 Echo Reply
                                                      Identifier=47570 Seq=12032
```

```
28  1.0 sec        Bay IPv6 P1  FTP Software 1 ICMPv6 Echo Request
                                                 Identifier=47570 Seq=12288
29   800 us     FTP Software 1     Bay IPv6 P1 ICMPv6 Echo Reply
                                                 Identifier=47570 Seq=12288
30  2.7 sec 33-33-00-00-00-09      Bay IPv6 P1 UDP D=521 S=521 Len=72
31  46.7 ms     Broadcast          Bay IPv6 P1 RIP (TCP/IP) Response
                                                 ID=IP Entries=4
32  1.0 sec        Bay IPv6 P1     Bay IPv6 P1 BOFL(WF) Seq=666
33  5.0 sec        Bay IPv6 P1     Bay IPv6 P1 BOFL(WF) Seq=667
34  1.2 sec  33-33-A2-0A-1F-B9  FTP Software 1 ICMPv6 Neighbor Solicitation
                                                 Target_Address=
                                                 FE80:0:0:0:0:0:A20A:1FB9
                                                 Opt = Src Link Layer Addr
35  1.0 sec  33-33-A2-0A-1F-B9  FTP Software 1 ICMPv6 Neighbor Solicitation
                                                 Target_Address=
                                                 FE80:0:0:0:0:0:A20A:1FB9
                                                 Opt = Src Link Layer Addr
36  1.0 sec  33-33-A2-0A-1F-B9  FTP Software 1 ICMPv6 Neighbor Solicitation
                                                 Target_Address=
                                                 FE80:0:0:0:0:0:A20A:1FB9
                                                 Opt = Src Link Layer Addr
37  1.8 sec        Bay IPv6 P1     Bay IPv6 P1 BOFL(WF) Seq=668
38 195.7 ms  33-33-A2-0A-1F-B9  FTP Software 1 ICMPv6 Neighbor Solicitation
                                                 Target_Address=
                                                 FE80:0:0:0:0:0:A20A:1FB9
                                                 Opt = Src Link Layer Addr
39  1.0 sec  33-33-A2-0A-1F-B9  FTP Software 1 ICMPv6 Neighbor Solicitation
                                                 Target_Address=
                                                 FE80:0:0:0:0:0:A20A:1FB9
                                                 Opt = Src Link Layer Addr
40  989.2 ms 33-33-A2-0A-1F-B9  FTP Software 1 ICMPv6 Neighbor Solicitation
                                                 Target_Address=
                                                 FE80:0:0:0:0:0:A20A:1FB9
                                                 Opt = Src Link Layer Addr
```

The first ICMPv6 Echo Request is sent in Frame 4 from the workstation to the router's first port, which is configured for both IPv6 and IPv4. Note that within the IPv6 header, both the Source and Destination IPv6 addresses are Link-Local addresses (beginning with FE80H), as shown in Trace 5.9.2b. The expected ICMPv6 Echo Reply comes in Frame 5.

Trace 5.9.2b. ICMPv6 Echo Request/Reply with Valid Link-Local Address

```
-------------- Frame 4  Size 122  Absolute Time  5:38:00.59773  --------------
                     Protocol Detail - astping.cap 9/4


IEEE 802.3/Ethernet DIX V2 Header


            Decode Status : -
             Frame Length : 122
      Destination Address : 00-00-A2-0A-1F-B8, Bay IPv6 P1 ( OUI = WELLFLEET, I
           Source Address : 00-80-C7-5F-9F-3D, FTP Software 1 ( OUI = XIRCOM, U
             Frame Format : Ethernet DIX V2
                Ethertype : 0x86DD (IPv6)
           Frame Checksum : Good, Frame Check Sequence : 00 00 00 00


IPv6 - Internet Protocol (Version 6)


            Decode Status : -
           Version Number : 6 (IP Version 6)
                    Class : 0x0
               Flow Label : 0x0
           Payload Length : 64
              Next Header : 58 (ICMPv6)
                Hop Limit : 255
           Source Address : FE80:0:0:0:0:80:C75F:9F3D
      Destination Address : FE80:0:0:0:0:0:A20A:1FB8


ICMPv6 - Internet Control Message Protocol (Version 6)


            Decode Status : -
                ICMP Type : 128 (Echo Request)
                Echo Code : 0
                 Checksum : 62137
               Identifier : 47570
          Sequence Number : 9984
                ICMP Data : [56 byte(s) of data]
```

```
-------------- Frame 5  Size 122  Absolute Time  5:38:20.07069 --------------
                  Protocol Detail - astping.cap 9/4


IEEE 802.3/Ethernet DIX V2 Header


        Decode Status : -
         Frame Length : 122
  Destination Address : 00-80-C7-5F-9F-3D, FTP Software 1 ( OUI = XIRCOM, I
       Source Address : 00-00-A2-0A-1F-B8, Bay IPv6 P1 ( OUI = WELLFLEET, U
         Frame Format : Ethernet DIX V2
            Ethertype : 0x86DD (IPv6)
       Frame Checksum : Good, Frame Check Sequence : 00 00 00 00


IPv6 - Internet Protocol (Version 6)


        Decode Status : -
       Version Number : 6 (IP Version 6)
                Class : 0x0
           Flow Label : 0x0
       Payload Length : 64
          Next Header : 58 (ICMPv6)
            Hop Limit : 1
       Source Address : FE80:0:0:0:0:0:A20A:1FB8
  Destination Address : FE80:0:0:0:0:80:C75F:9F3D


ICMPv6 - Internet Control Message Protocol (Version 6)


        Decode Status : -
            ICMP Type : 129 (Echo Reply)
            Echo Code : 0
             Checksum : 61881
           Identifier : 47570
      Sequence Number : 9984          ICMP Data : [56 byte(s) of data]
```

In a second example, the workstation issues an Echo Request to the router's Port 2. Reviewing Figure 5-24, note that Port 2 has a valid Link-Local address assigned (FE80:0:0:0:0:0:A20A:1FB9), but that address is located on another subnet. To get to that subnet, you must pass through the router. However, the router knows not to pass a Link-Local address, so no reply is ever received. We can see in the Neighbor Solicitation message that the Target Address identifies port 2 (FE80:0:0:0:0:0:A20A:1FB9), but since Port 2 is not a neighbor on Subnet 242, no response is received.

Trace 5.9.2c. ICMPv6 Neighbor Solicitation in Response to Invalid Link-Local Address

```
-------------- Frame 34  Size 90  Absolute Time  5:38:20.07069  --------------
Protocol Detail - astping.cap 9/4


IEEE 802.3/Ethernet DIX V2 Header


               Decode Status : -
                Frame Length : 90
         Destination Address : 33-33-A2-0A-1F-B9 ( Group, Locally Administered Addr
              Source Address : 00-80-C7-5F-9F-3D, FTP Software 1 ( OUI = XIRCOM, U
                Frame Format : Ethernet DIX V2
                   Ethertype : 0x86DD (IPv6)
              Frame Checksum : Good, Frame Check Sequence : 00 00 00 00



IPv6 - Internet Protocol (Version 6)



               Decode Status : -
              Version Number : 6 (IP Version 6)
                       Class : 0x0
                  Flow Label : 0x0
              Payload Length : 32
                 Next Header : 58 (ICMPv6)
                   Hop Limit : 255
              Source Address : FE80:0:0:0:0:80:C75F:9F3D
         Destination Address : FF02:0:0:0:0:1:A20A:1FB9
```

```
ICMPv6 - Internet Control Message Protocol (Version 6)


              Decode Status : -
                  ICMP Type : 135 (Neighbor Solicitation)
 Neighbor Solicitation Code : 0
                   Checksum : 10716
             Target Address : FE80:0:0:0:0:0:A20A:1FB9

                    ----- Options -----

                     Option : 1 (Source Link Layer Address)
              Option Length : 1
  Source Link Layer Address : 00-80-C7-5F-9F-3D, FTP Software 1
```

This chapter has considered the implications for implementing IPv6 on local and wide area networks. At the time of this writing, the support for IPv6 over other LAN and WAN media, including Asynchronous Transfer Mode (ATM) and frame relay, is under development. As the IPv6 industry becomes more mature, additional media types will invariably be supported. In the next chapter, we will move from the OSI Data Link Layer to the OSI Network Layer, and will consider issues relevant to IPv6 routing processes.

5.10 References

[5-1] Thomson, Susan, and Thomas Narten. "IPv6 Stateless Address Autoconfiguration." RFC 1971, August 1996.

[5-2] Thomson, Susan, and Thomas Narten. "IPv6 Stateless Address Autoconfiguration." Work in progress, July 30, 1997.

[5-3] Bound, J., and C. Perkins. "Dynamic Host Configuration Protocol for IPv6 (DHCPv6)." Work in progress, May 26, 1997.

[5-4] Souvatzis, I. "Transmission of IPv6 Packets over ARCNET Networks." Work in progress, August 1, 1997.

[5-5] Crawford, Matt. "Transmission of IPv6 Packets over Ethernet." RFC 1972, August 1996.

[5-6] Crawford, Matt. "Transmission of IPv6 Packets over Ethernet." Work in progress, September 26, 1997.

[5-7] Crawford, Matt. "Transmission of IPv6 Packets over FDDI Networks." RFC 2019, October 1996.

[5-8] Crawford, Matt. "Transmission of IPv6 Packets over FDDI Networks." Work in progress, September 26, 1997.

[5-9] Crawford, Matt, et al. "Transmission of IPv6 Packets over Token Ring Networks." Work in progress, November 6, 1997.

[5-10] Haskin, D., and E. Allen. "IP Version 6 over PPP." RFC 2023, October 1996.

[5-11] Haskin, D., and E. Allen. "IP version 6 over PPP." Work in progress, July 1997.

[5-12] Johnson, David B., and Charles Perkins. "Mobility Support for IPv6." Work in progress, July 1997.

6 Routing Issues

In the last chapter, we considered IPv6 issues specific to local networks and covered the ARPA Network Interface Layer (or the OSI Data Link Layer). In this chapter, we move up one layer and consider issues specific to the routing processes at the ARPA Internet Layer (or the OSI Network Layer). First, let's look at some definitions.

An *autonomous system* (AS) is a network that is administered by a single entity. Routing protocols fall into two general categories: Interior Gateway Protocols, or IGPs, and Exterior Gateway Protocols, or EGPs. An IGP is used to convey routing information within an AS, while an EGP is used to convey routing information between ASs.

At the time of this writing, one IGP, the Routing Information Protocol (RIP), has been enhanced to support IPv6. In addition, IPv6 enhancements have been proposed for another IGP, the Open Shortest Path First (OSPF) protocol. IPv6 enhancements to one EGP, the Border Gateway Protocol (BGP), have also been proposed. We will begin our study by considering changes to RIP.

6.1 Routing Information Protocol for IPv6

The Routing Information Protocol is one of the most widely used Interior Gateway Protocols; it was originally defined in 1988 and documented in RFC 1058. Support for RIP with IPv6 is called RIPng and is documented in RFC 2080 [6-1].

RIP is a Distance Vector Algorithm-based protocol, with history that dates back to the early days of the ARPANet. RIP is designed for networks of moderate size, with a few limitations:

- The protocol is limited to networks whose longest path (or network diameter) is 15 hops.
- The protocol depends on a process called "counting to infinity" to resolve certain situations, such as routing loops. This process may consume a large amount of network bandwidth before resolution.
- The protocol depends on fixed metrics to compare alternative routes, without regard for real-time parameters such as delay, reliability, or load.

RIPng is the protocol that allows routers to exchange information for computing routes through an IPv6-based internetwork. Each router that implements RIPng is assumed to have a routing table that has an entry for each reachable IPv6 destination. Each entry contains the following:

- The IPv6 prefix of the destination.
- A metric that indicates the total cost of getting a datagram from the router to that destination.
- The IPv6 address of the next router along the path to the destination, called the next hop.
- A Route Change Flag that indicates whether the information about that route has recently changed.
- Various timers, such as a 30-second timer which triggers the transmission of routing table information to neighboring routers.

RIPng is a User Datagram Protocol (UDP)-based protocol which sends and receives packets on UDP port number 521. The RIPng packet (Figure 6-1) includes three fields: Command (Request or Response), Version (1), and a Route Table Entry. Each Route Table Entry (Figure 6-2) includes the IPv6 Prefix, the Route Tag (to separate internal from external routes), a Prefix Length field (to determine the number of significant bits in the Prefix), and the Metric (defining the current metric for the destination).

RIPng also provides the ability to specify the immediate next hop IPv6 address for packets. This next hop is specified by a special RTE, The Next Hop Route Table Entry (Figure 6-3). The Next Hop RTE is identified by the value of FFH in the Metric field. The Prefix field specifies the IPv6 address of the next hop; the Route Tag and the Prefix Length are set to zero on transmission and ignored on reception.

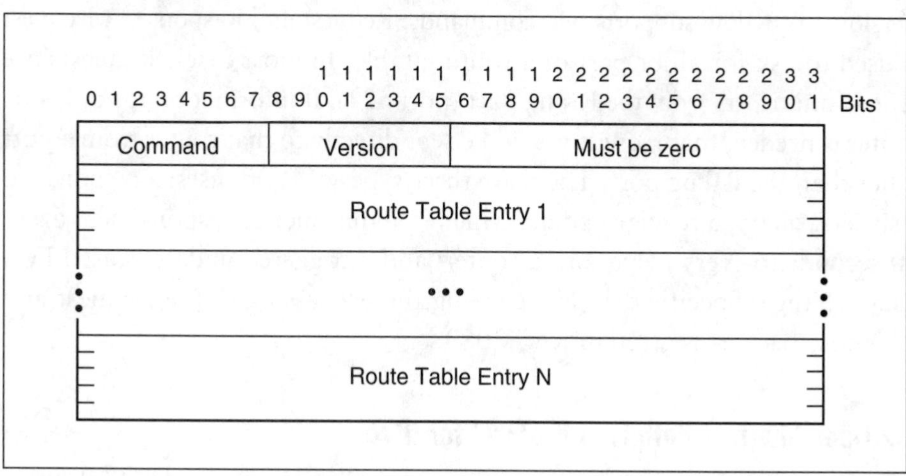

Figure 6-1. RIPng packet format

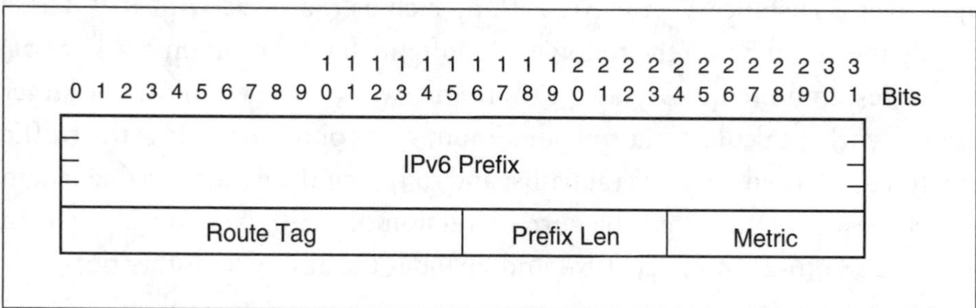

Figure 6-2. Route Table Entry format

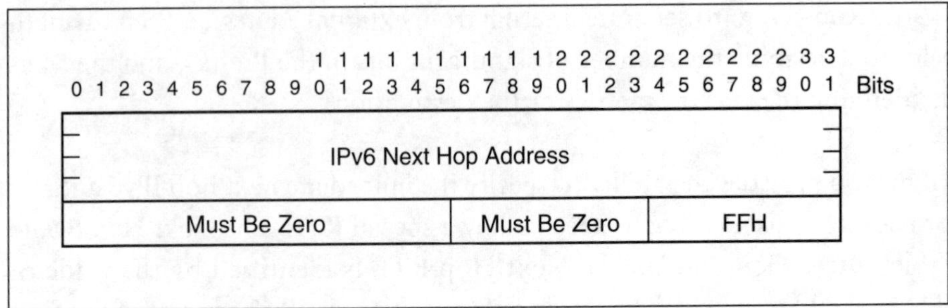

Figure 6-3. Next Hop RTE format

Version 1 of RIPng supports two commands: Request and Response. A Request is used to ask for all or part of a routing table. In most cases, Requests are sent as multicasts from the RIPng port (port 521). If information for only one router is needed, that request would be sent directly to that router from a port other than the RIPng port. There are three types of Responses: a response to a specific query; a regular update, which is an unsolicited response sent every 30 seconds to every neighboring router; and a triggered update caused by a route change. Specific details regarding the processing of the Request and Response packets is given in RFC 2080.

6.2 Open Shortest Path First Protocol for IPv6

The Open Shortest Path First (OSPF) protocol operates using a Link State Algorithm (LSA) and is defined in RFC 1583. An LSA offers several advantages over a Distance Vector Algorithm, such as that used with RIP. These include the ability to do the following: configure hierarchical (instead of flat) topologies; to more quickly adapt to internetwork changes; allow for larger internetworks; calculate multiple minimum-cost routes that allow the traffic load to be balanced over several paths; and to permit the use of variable-length subnet masks. In addition, the current version of OSPF (version 2), defined in RFC 1583 [6-2], supports IPv4 and includes the ability to authenticate the source of the data.

There are five packet types defined for OSPF: Hello, Database Description, Link State Request, Link State Update, and Link State Acknowledgment. The current proposal for OSPF for IPv6 [6-3] suggests that these packet types have a consistent header, shown in Figure 6-4. The most notable difference between this proposed header and the one currently defined for OSPF for IPv4 is the absence of the Authentication field (compare sections A.3 of References [6-2] and [6-3]). Since IPv6 has its own Authentication header available, that function is removed from the OSPF for IPv6 header field to avoid redundancy.

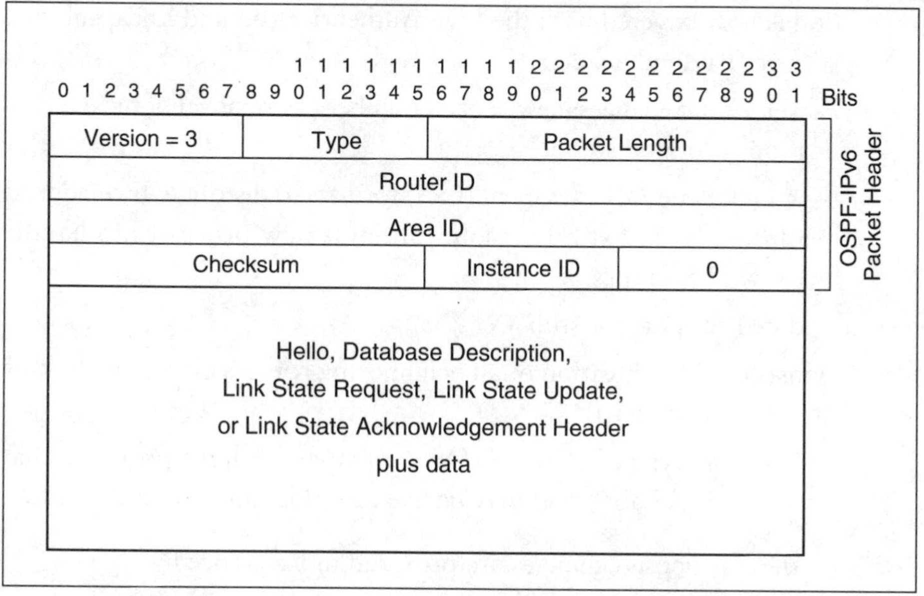

Figure 6-4. Proposed OSPF for IPv6 header

Some additional changes to OSPF have been proposed to provide support for IPv6 [6-3]. Among these changes are:

➢ Protocol processing on a per-link basis, not on a per-subnet basis, since multiple subnets can be assigned to a single link with IPv6. (Recall that RFC 1883 defines an IPv6 link as a "communication facility or medium over which nodes can communicate at the link layer.")

- Removal of addressing semantics from the OSPF packet headers, leaving a network protocol–independent core. For example, IPv6 addresses are not carried in OSPF packets, with the exception of the Link State Advertisement payloads carried in the Link State Update packets.
- New Flooding Scope for Link State Advertisements (Link-local scope).
- Support to run multiple OSPF protocol instances per link.
- Use of Link Local addresses, which are not forwarded by routers.
- Removing authentication from the OSPF packet header, as this function is now covered with the IPv6 Authentication and Encapsulating Security Payload headers.
- Packet format changes: new version number (3), removal of the Authentication field, and so on.
- New Link State Advertisement (LSA) formats to distribute IPv6 address resolution and next hop resolution, plus new processes to handle unknown LSA types.
- Updated support for stub areas.
- Consistent identification of all neighboring routers on a given link by their OSPF Router ID.
- Removal of Type of Service (TOS) semantics, with the provision that the IPv6 Flow Label field may be used for this function in the future.

Details on these proposed changes are provided in Reference [6-3].

6.3 Border Gateway Protocol

An autonomous system exchanges routing information with another autonomous system using an Exterior Gateway Protocol, or EGP. The most prevalent is the Border Gateway Protocol (BGP), which has gone through several iterations. These include BGP-1 (RFC 1105), BGP-2 (RFC 1163), BGP-3 (RFC 1267), and BGP-4 (RFCs 1771, 1772, 1773, and 1774). The primary function of a BGP system is to exchange network reachability information with other BGP systems. This information includes data on the list of ASs that the reachability information traverses, which allows the construction of a connectivity graph.

BGP-4 uses the Transmission Control Protocol (TCP) for greater reliability of communication between ASs. The BGP-4 message header is defined in RFC 1771 [6-4], Section 4.1, and also in Reference [6-5], Section 4.1. This header is 19 octets long and supports one of four message types (Figure 6-5):

- OPEN: initiates the BGP connection.
- UPDATE: used to transfer routing information between BGP peers.
- KEEPALIVE: exchanged on a periodic basis to determine peer reachability.
- NOTIFICATION: sent when an error condition is detected; causes the BGP connection to be closed.

After a TCP connection is established, the first message sent is an OPEN message. If the OPEN is acceptable to the other end of the connection, a KEEPALIVE message is returned in confirmation. Once the OPEN has been confirmed, UPDATE, KEEPALIVE, and NOTIFICATION messages may be exchanged.

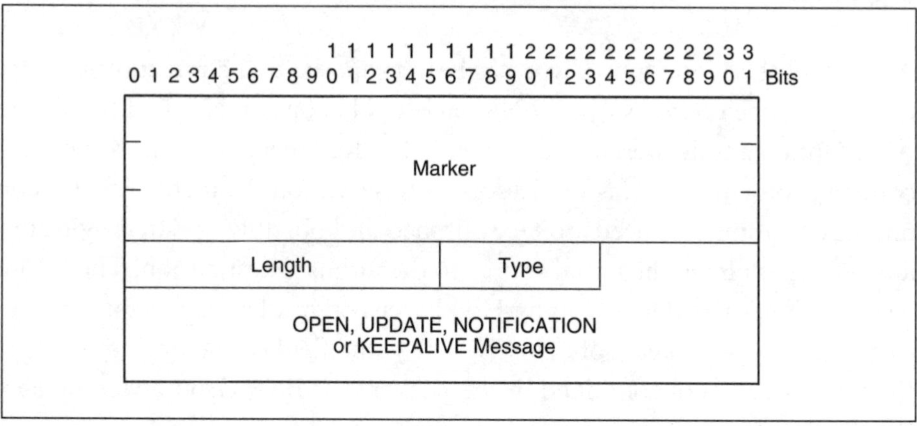

Figure 6-5. BGP-4 message header

Multiprotocol extensions to BGP-4 have been proposed that allow it to carry multiple Network Layer protocols, including IPv6 [6-6]. As with other changes to routing protocols, these BGP-4 extensions must include support for the IPv6 addressing structure, the ability to distinguish between various Network

Layer protocols, and so on. At the time of this writing, this work is still in the preliminary stages.

6.4 Additional Routing Changes Proposed for IPv6

At the present time, several additional routing changes have been proposed in support of IPv6.

A new mechanism called Router Renumbering (RR) allows address prefixes on routers to be easily configured or reconfigured. This mechanism provides a means for a network manager to make updates to the prefixes used and advertised by IPv6 routers throughout a site. The RR process is presently documented in Reference [6-7]. RR messages are a special type of ICMP messages, with two codes: Commands, which are sent to routers; and Results, which are sent by routers. These messages share a common RR header, with distinct message bodies. Command messages include the prefixes to be modified, while the Results messages confirm the prefix operation: add, change or set-global.

A new Hop-by-Hop Option type has been proposed that alerts transit routers to examine the contents of an IPv6 packet. This option is called the Router Alert Option and is presently documented in Reference [6-8]. In some cases, control protocols, such as the Resource Reservation Protocol (RSVP), contain information that needs to be examined and possibly updated by routers along the path from the initial source to the ultimate destination. The Router Alert Option, carried in a Hop-by-Hop Extension header, signals these routers to examine this packet more closely. The value field of the option identifies the type of protocol contained in the packet (ICMPv6 Group Membership, RSVP, etc.) that requires special attention.

6.5 Case Studies

To illustrate some of the various routing protocols and processes, we will use an internetwork configured for both IPv6 and IPv4 that comprises three routers and various workstations (Figure 6-6). Router 1 is a Bay Networks

Inc. router configured for IPv4 and IPv6 on Port 1, and IPv4 on Port 2. Router 2 is also a Bay Networks router, but it is configured for IPv4 on both ports. Router 3 is a Digital Equipment Corp. router configured for IPv4 on Port 1 and IPv6 on Port 2. The internetwork has been divided into four subnets, numbered 242 through 245. Also note that the IPv4 "cloud" in the center of the internetwork simulates the existing Internet infrastructure—an IPv4-only topology.

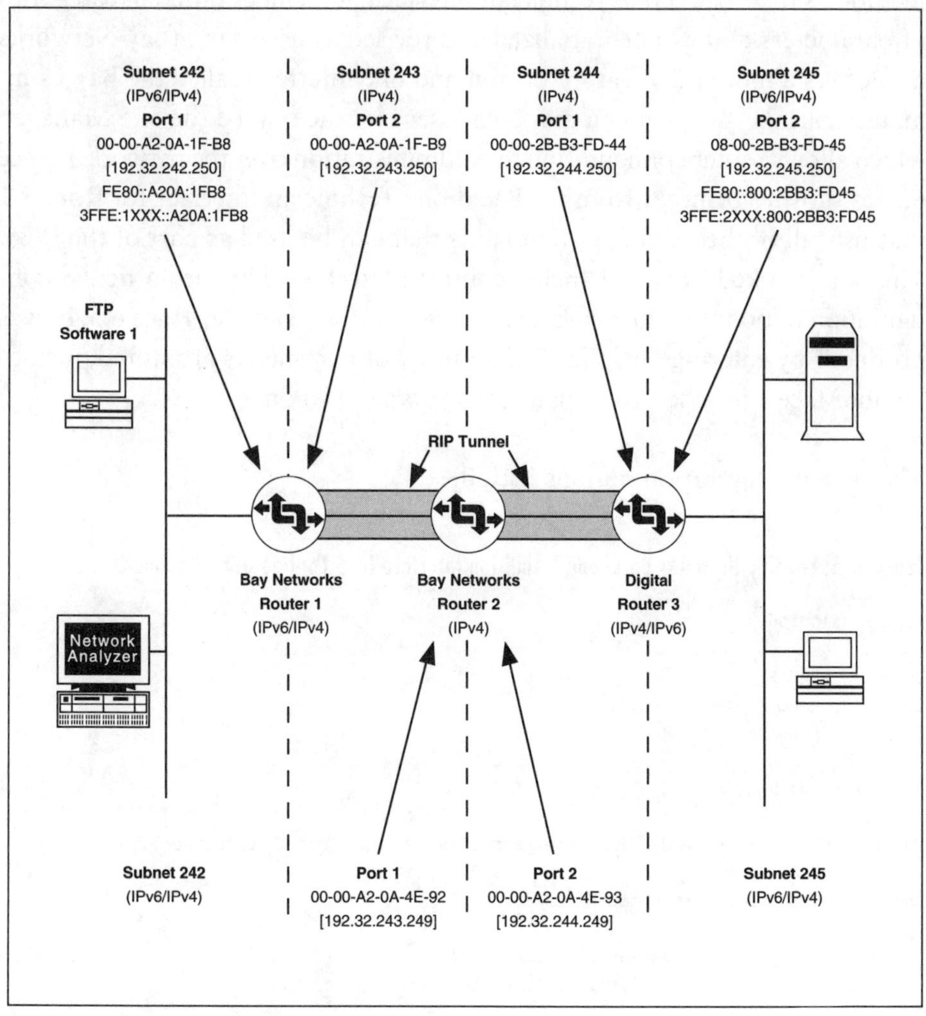

Figure 6-6. IPv6/IPv4 Internetwork with RIP tunnel

In the next three case studies, we will focus on Router 1 (a Bay Networks router) and Router 3 (a Digital router), both running IPv4 and IPv6.

6.5.1 Bay Networks Inc.'s Router Configurations for IPv6

All routers require some degree of configuration prior to operation. Bay Networks, Inc. provides a management console that connects via a serial port to access the router configuration files. Bay Networks refers to this configuration method as their Backbone Technician Interface; it includes different categories of parameters that can be initialized and revised as necessary. (Bay Networks also offers a more fully featured command line interface called the Bay Command Console (BCC), and a graphical user interface called the Site Manager, which allows router configuration and administration over the network.) Trace 6.5.1a shows a printout from the Backbone Technician Interface for Router 1 that lists all of the available commands that can be used as part of the IPv6. This was invoked using the "help" command, followed by the particular configuration option for which help was requested. For example, Trace 6.5.1a was produced by entering "help ip6". A number of parameters are stored, including interface addresses, routing information, and so on.

The IPv6 configuration options include:

Trace 6.5.1a. Bay Networks Backbone Technician Interface IPv6 Configuration Options

```
[1:1]$ help ip6

Usage:
ip6        <sub_command> [<options>]


Privilege: Manager & User

The ip6 (or ipv6) command allows the user to view data from IPv6 protocol.

The following sub_commands can be used:

   routes            - Display the route pool
   stats             - Display interface statistics
```

```
If no optional parameters are provided with 'ip6 stats' command, statistics for all
interfaces are displayed.

The following optional parameters can be used with 'ip6 stats' command:

  <ifindex>                 - display statistics for this interface only.

If no optional parameters are provided with 'ip6 routes' command, all routes in the
route pool are displayed.

The following optional parameters can be used to filter routes:

  <address>                 - all routes which this address matches
  <address>/<pfx. length    - all routes in this prefix range
  -i<ifindex>               - all routes that point out of this interface
  -p<protocol>              - all routes sourced by this protocol, where
                              <protocol> is:
                                 DIRect - directly attached networks
                                 STatic - static network routes
                                 RIP    - RIPv6 routes
                                 ND     - Neighbor Discovery routes
                                 IDRP   - IDRP routes
                                 IF     - local interfaces
                                 SNone  - staticly configured adjacent node
                                          addresses
                                 DNone  - dynanically learned adjacent node
                                          addresses
                                 SYStem - routes installed by the IPv6 kernel
  -n                         - all network routes
  -h                         - all node (host) routes
  -l                         - long display format, i.e. provide more information

Note that dynanically learned adjacent node addresses are only displayed if the '-pDN'
option is explicitly specified.

Example:

 Display all RIPv6routes in 5F00::0000/8 range:

 >  ip6 routes 5F00::0/8 -pRIP
```

For the moment, let's focus on the IPv4 configuration. The IPv4 routes configuration file for Router 1, invoked with the "ip routes" command, is shown in Trace 6.5.1b. Note that two subnets are listed as being Direct routes (192.32.242.0 and 192.32.243.0), and one other route is reachable using RIP information (192.32.244.0). Reviewing Figure 6-6, observe that, for the

192.32.244.0 subnet, the cost is two hops away, and the Next Hop Address is port 1 of Router 2.

Trace 6.5.1b. Router 1 IPv4 Routes Configuration Options

```
[1:1]$ ip routes

Network/Mask        Proto        Age Slot      Cost  NextHop Address     AS
------------------- ------ --------- ---- --------- ---------------- -----
192.32.242.0/24     Direct      1150    1         0 192.32.242.250
192.32.243.0/24     Direct      1150    1         0 192.32.243.250
192.32.244.0/24     RIP           25    1         2 192.32.243.249
```

Next, let's move to the IPv6 configuration options. The IPv6 routes configuration file for Router 1 was invoked using the "ip6 routes" command. Note that two different levels of detail can be provided: a short display and a long display. The short routes listing (Trace 6.5.1c) provides summary information on the various IPv6 routes that have been configured. The Prefix column provides an excellent review of Chapter 3 (and Figure 3-6 on IPv6 Addressing) as it includes the Unspecified, Loopback, Aggregatable Global Unicast, Link-Local, and Multicast address types. Note that the seventh entry is the RIPv6 tunnel to the distant subnet 3FFE:2XXX (we will look at the other end of this tunnel in the next case study). The long routes listing (Trace 6.5.1d) provides further details on the type of address, any related interfaces, and other parameters such as the next hop, when the information was updated, and so on.

Trace 6.5.1c. Router 1 IPv6 Routing Configuration (Short Display Format)

```
[1:1]$ ip6 routes

                                                        Next Hop

             Prefix                         Proto.     Intf.     Weight

------------------------------------------ ---------- ------- ----------
::0.0.0.0/0                                STATIC     5       0x3c00001
::0.0.0.0/128                              SYSTEM     Discard 0x0
::0.0.0.1/128                              SYSTEM     For Me  0x681a0001
3FFE:1XXX::0000/80                         DIRECT     1       0x1
3FFE:1XXX::0000/128                        SYSTEM     1       0x6bda0001
3FFE:1XXX::A20A:1FB8/128                   INTERFACE  1       0x0
3FFE:2XXX::0000/80                         RIPv6      4       0x6b9a0002
3FFE:3XXX::0000/80                         DIRECT     2       0x1
3FFE:3XXX::0000/128                        SYSTEM     2       0x6bda0001
3FFE:3XXX::A20A:1FB9/128                   INTERFACE  2       0x0
FE80::A20A:1FB8/128                        INTERFACE  1       0x0
FE80::A20A:1FB9/128                        INTERFACE  2       0x0
FE80::C020:F3FA/128                        INTERFACE  5       0x0
FE80::C020:F3FA/128                        INTERFACE  4       0x0
FF01::0001/128                             SYSTEM     For Me  0x681a0001
FF01::0002/128                             SYSTEM     For Me  0x681a0001
FF02::0001/128                             SYSTEM     For Me  0x681a0001
FF02::0002/128                             SYSTEM     For Me  0x681a0001
FF02::0009/128                             RIPv6      4       0x6bda0001
FF02::0009/128                             RIPv6      1       0x6bda0001
FF02::0001:A20A:1FB8/128                   SYSTEM     1       0x6bda0001
FF02::0001:A20A:1FB9/128                   SYSTEM     2       0x6bda0001

  Total routes: 22
```

Trace 6.5.1d. Router 1 IPv6 Routing Configuration (Long Display Format)

```
[1:1]$ ip6 routes -l
                                                          Next Hop
                    Prefix                       Proto.    Intf.    Weight
------------------------------------------ ---------- ------- ----------
::0.0.0.0/0                                STATIC     5       0x3c00001
  Forward via Point-to-point link
  Last updated 1338 seconds ago

::0.0.0.0/128                              SYSTEM     Discard 0x0
  Discard packets to this destination
  Last updated 1378 seconds ago

::0.0.0.1/128                              SYSTEM     For Me  0x681a0001
  An address of this router
  Last updated 1378 seconds ago

3FFE:1XXX::0000/80                         DIRECT     1       0x1
  RIPv6 Metric: 1, Prefix on a directly attached link
  Last updated 1346 seconds ago

3FFE:1XXX::0000/128                        SYSTEM     1       0x6bda0001
  An anycast address of this router
  Last updated 1346 seconds ago


3FFE:1XXX::A20A:1FB8/128                   INTERFACE  1       0x0
  An interface address, MAC: 00-00-A2-0A-1F-B8
  Last updated 1348 seconds ago

3FFE:2XXX::0000/80                         RIPv6      4       0x6b9a0002
  RIPv6 Metric: 2, Nexthop: FE80::C020:F4FA
  Last updated 15 seconds ago

3FFE:3XXX::0000/80                         DIRECT     2       0x1
  RIPv6 Metric: 1, Prefix on a directly attached link
  Last updated 1348 seconds ago

3FFE:3XXX::0000/128                        SYSTEM     2       0x6bda0001
  An anycast address of this router

  Last updated 1348 seconds ago

3FFE:3XXX::A20A:1FB9/128                   INTERFACE  2       0x0
  An interface address, MAC: 00-00-A2-0A-1F-B9
  Last updated 1348 seconds ago
```

```
FE80::A20A:1FB8/128                          INTERFACE  1        0x0
  An interface address, MAC: 00-00-A2-0A-1F-B8

  Last updated 1353 seconds ago

FE80::A20A:1FB9/128                          INTERFACE  2        0x0
  An interface address, MAC: 00-00-A2-0A-1F-B9
  Last updated 1355 seconds ago

FE80::C020:F3FA/128                          INTERFACE  5        0x0
  An interface address of this router
  Last updated 1342 seconds ago

FE80::C020:F3FA/128                          INTERFACE  4        0x0
  An interface address of this router
  Last updated 1342 seconds ago

FF01::0001/128                               SYSTEM     For Me   0x681a0001
  An address of this router
  Last updated 1382 seconds ago

FF01::0002/128                               SYSTEM     For Me   0x681a0001
  An address of this router
  Last updated 1382 seconds ago

FF02::0001/128                               SYSTEM     For Me   0x681a0001

  An address of this router
  Last updated 1384 seconds ago

FF02::0002/128                               SYSTEM     For Me   0x681a0001
  An address of this router
  Last updated 1384 seconds ago

FF02::0009/128                               RIPv6      4        0x6bda0001
  An address of this router
  Last updated 1344 seconds ago

FF02::0009/128                               RIPv6      1        0x6bda0001
  An address of this router
  Last updated 1355 seconds ago

FF02::0001:A20A:1FB8/128                     SYSTEM     1        0x6bda0001
  An address of this router
  Last updated 1357 seconds ago
```

```
FF02::0001:A20A:1FB9/128                    SYSTEM     2        0x6bda0001
  An address of this router
  Last updated 1357 seconds ago


  Total routes: 22
```

Another management option, invoked with the command "ip6 stats", provides operational configuration and statistical information on each interface (Trace 6.5.1e). For example, Interface 1 is an Ethernet interface with a Link-Local address of FE80::A20A:1FB8. The ICMP messages are also tabulated, such as the Router Solicitations (RS), Router Advertisements (RA), and so on. Interface 2 is almost identical to Interface 1, with the exception of a different Link-Local address. Interface 4 is a static tunnel across the IPv4 cloud to the Digital router (static tunnels are discussed in Chapter 9). The tunnel entry point is Router 1, port 2 [192.32.243.250], and the tunnel exit point is Router 3, port 1 [192.32.244.250], as shown in Figure 6-6. Interface 5 is an automatic tunnel (automatic tunnels are also discussed in Chapter 9).

Trace 6.5.1e. Router 1 IPv6 Statistics

```
[1:1]$ ip6 stats


Interface 1 (tom) is Up:
  Link: Ethernet at 10000000 bps (circuit 1)
  Neighbor Discovery: On, Router Advertisements: On
  Address(es): FE80::A20A:1FB8 (link-local)
               3FFE:1XXX::A20A:1FB8 (pfx len 80)
  Rx 2, Tx 107, Drop 0, Err 0
  Icmp In: DestUnr 0, TimeExc 0, ParmProb 0, TooBig 0
  Icmp Out: DestUnr 0, TimeExc 0, ParmProb 0, TooBig 0
  Icmp In: Echos 0, EchoRep 0, RS 1, RA 0, NS 1, NA 0
  Icmp Out: Echos 0, EchoRep 0, RS 0, RA 15, NS 2, NA 0
```

```
Interface 2 (bill) is Up:
  Link: Ethernet at 10000000 bps (circuit 2)
  Neighbor Discovery: On, Router Advertisements: On
  Address(es): FE80::A20A:1FB9 (link-local)
               3FFE:3XXX::A20A:1FB9 (pfx len 80)
  Rx 0, Tx 32, Drop 0, Err 0
  Icmp In: DestUnr 0, TimeExc 0, ParmProb 0, TooBig 0
  Icmp Out: DestUnr 0, TimeExc 0, ParmProb 0, TooBig 0
  Icmp In: Echos 0, EchoRep 0, RS 0, RA 0, NS 0, NA 0
  Icmp Out: Echos 0, EchoRep 0, RS 0, RA 30, NS 2, NA 0


Interface 4 (tunnel) is Up:
  Link: IPv4 static tunnel (192.32.243.250->192.32.244.250)
  Neighbor Discovery: Off, Router Advertisements: Off
  Address(es): FE80::C020:F3FA (link-local)
  Rx 11, Tx 91, Drop 0, Err 0
  Icmp In: DestUnr 0, TimeExc 0, ParmProb 0, TooBig 0
  Icmp Out: DestUnr 0, TimeExc 0, ParmProb 0, TooBig 0
  Icmp In: Echos 0, EchoRep 0, RS 0, RA 0, NS 0, NA 0
  Icmp Out: Echos 0, EchoRep 0, RS 0, RA 0, NS 0, NA 0


Interface 5 (auto) is Up:
  Link: IPv4 static tunnel (192.32.243.250->0.0.0.0)
  Neighbor Discovery: Off, Router Advertisements: Off
  Address(es): FE80::C020:F3FA (link-local)
  Rx 0, Tx 0, Drop 0, Err 0
  Icmp In: DestUnr 0, TimeExc 0, ParmProb 0, TooBig 0
  Icmp Out: DestUnr 0, TimeExc 0, ParmProb 0, TooBig 0
  Icmp In: Echos 0, EchoRep 0, RS 0, RA 0, NS 0, NA 0
  Icmp Out: Echos 0, EchoRep 0, RS 0, RA 0, NS 0, NA 0
```

To summarize, the Bay Networks Backbone Technician Interface provides a wealth of information regarding the current configuration and status of the router within either IPv4 or IPv6 environments.

6.5.2 Digital Equipment Corp.'s Router Configurations for IPv6

Digital Equipment Corp.'s RouteAbout Central EW router has an extensive configuration utility that can be accessed via either TELNET or a local console using a serial port connection. Note that the main console screen provides the IP addresses for the ports that have been configured on this router for TELNET access (Trace 6.5.2a).

Trace 6.5.2a. Digital's RouteAbout Central EW Installation Menu

```
==============================================================================

                      RtAbt Cntrl EW/IP INSTALLATION MENU

         * * * * * * * * * * * * * * * * * * * * * * * * * * * * * * *
            To fully manage this device telnet to one of the
            following IP addresses or select item [3] below.
            Out-of-Band: Not Configured
            In-Band     : 192.32.244.250
                          192.32.245.250
         * * * * * * * * * * * * * * * * * * * * * * * * * * * * * * *

                      [1]  Restart with Factory Defaults
                      [2]  Restart with Current Settings
                      [3]  Go to Local Console

==============================================================================

                       Enter selection : 3
```

At the asterisk prompt ("*"), the command "talk 2" is entered to communicate with the monitor process. The Monitor screen provides a summary of the router's current interfaces and routes (Trace 6.5.2b).

Trace 6.5.2b. Digital's RouteAbout Central EW Monitor Screen

```
*talk 2

  GW.001: Copyright 1995-1996 Digital Equipment Corporation
  GW.002: [not configured], RtAbt Cntrl EW/IP,  Brouter: 2 Enet 8T1,HW=1,RO=1,
          #307,SW=T2.0-5 Started
  GW.004: Sys trans q adv alloc 171 excd 188
  GW.005: Bffrs: 400 avail 400 idle   fair 103 low 80
 ETH.047: Eth self-test Operational test fld maintenance failure nt 0 int Eth/0
 ETH.047: Eth self-test Operational test fld maintenance failure nt 1 int Eth/1
  IP.022: add nt 192.32.244.0 int 192.32.244.250 nt 0 int Eth/0
  IP.022: add nt 192.32.245.0 int 192.32.245.250 nt 1 int Eth/1
 RIP.011: updt nt 192.32.242.0 hps 3 via 192.32.244.249
 RIP.011: updt nt 192.32.243.0 hps 2 via 192.32.244.249
  IP.068: routing cache cleared
  IP.070: cache entry 192.32.244.249 cleared
```

The Operator Console screen provides information on the router's current hardware configuration, protocols operational, interface types, and packet statistics (Trace 6.5.2c). This process is invoked by entering "talk 5" at the "*" prompt, followed by "configuration" and "statistics" at the "+" prompt.

Trace 6.5.2c. Digital's RouteAbout Central EW Configuration Screen

```
*talk 5
+configuration

RtAbt Cntrl EW/IP,  Brouter: 2 Enet 8T1,HW=1,RO=1,#307,SW=T2.0-5
Hostname: [not configured]
Boot ROM version  3.4      Watchdog timer enabled     Auto-boot switch enabled

Num Name  Protocol
0   IP    DOD-IP
3   ARP   Address Resolution
11  SNMP  Simple Network Management Protocol
28  IPV6  Internet Protocol Version 6

Num Name  Feature
2   MCF   MAC Filtering

10 Networks:

Net Interface  MAC/Data-Link          Hardware                    State
0   Eth/0      Ethernet/IEEE 802.3    SCC Ethernet                Up
1   Eth/1      Ethernet/IEEE 802.3    SCC Ethernet                Up
2   PPP/0      Point to Point         SCC Serial Line             Down
3   PPP/1      Point to Point         SCC Serial Line             Down
4   PPP/2      Point to Point         SCC Serial Line             Down
5   PPP/3      Point to Point         SCC Serial Line             Down
6   PPP/4      Point to Point         SCC Serial Line             Down
7   PPP/5      Point to Point         SCC Serial Line             Down
8   PPP/6      Point to Point         SCC Serial Line             Down
9   PPP/7      Point to Point         SCC Serial Line             Down
```

```
+statistics

Nt Interface   Unicast  Multicast      Bytes    Packets      Bytes
              Pkts Rcv   Pkts Rcv   Received      Trans      Trans
0  Eth/0             6          2       1930         40       4446
1  Eth/1             2          0       1200         32       3640
2  PPP/0             0          0          0          0          0
3  PPP/1             0          0          0          0          0
4  PPP/2             0          0          0          0          0
5  PPP/3             0          0          0          0          0
6  PPP/4             0          0          0          0          0
7  PPP/5             0          0          0          0          0
8  PPP/6             0          0          0          0          0
9  PPP/7             0          0          0          0          0
```

Information regarding the configured protocols is also available; it is invoked by entering "protocol" at the "+" prompt. For IPv4, the "dump" command at the "IP>" prompt provides a dump of the routing table, and the "interface" command at the "IP>" prompt lists the names and their associated IPv4 addresses (Trace 6.5.2d). Reviewing Figure 6-6, notice that addresses 192.32.244.250 and 192.32.245.250 are associated with interfaces Eth/0 and Eth/1, respectively, and that the other subnets (on the Bay Networks routers) are also shown in the table, but with a higher cost metric (i.e. more hops away).

Trace 6.5.2d. Digital's RouteAbout Central EW IPv4 Protocol Screen

```
+protocol
IP>dump

Type   Dest net          Mask        Cost      Age   Next hop(s)

 RIP   192.32.242.0      FFFFFF00    3         20    192.32.244.249
 RIP   192.32.243.0      FFFFFF00    2         20    192.32.244.249
 Dir*  192.32.244.0      FFFFFF00    1         0     Eth/0
 Dir*  192.32.245.0      FFFFFF00    1         0     Eth/1

Routing table size: 768 nets (61440 bytes), 4 nets known

IP>interface

Interface  IP Address(es)   Mask(s)

   Eth/0   192.32.244.250   255.255.255.0
   Eth/1   192.32.245.250   255.255.255.0
```

One interface on the Digital router is configured for IPv6. This information is identified in the IPv6 protocol screen by the "IPv6" prompt. Options include the IPv6 addresses ("addr"), routing table dump ("dump"), specifics about each interface ("interface"), and the RIP tunnel ("riptunnel") that has been configured (Trace 6.5.2e). Referring again to Figure 6-6, note that the Digital router points to the other end of the tunnel, the Bay Networks router with IP address 192.32.243.250. (Recall that the Bay Networks router pointed to the Digital tunnel endpoint in its configuration file, shown in Section 6.5.1.)

Trace 6.5.2e. Digital's RouteAbout Central EW IPv6 Screen

```
IPV6>addr
Addresses
---------

Interface         =  Eth/1
  Address         =  3FFE:2XXX::0800:2BB3:FD45
  OnLink          =  TRUE
  Autonomous      =  TRUE
  RIP Enabled     =  TRUE


IPV6>dump
Routing table
-------------

Type  Address                                        Cost Next Hop
Dflt  ::0/0                                             1 ::0
 Dir  FE80::0/10                                        1 Link Local Prefix
 Dir  ::0001/128                                        1 Loopback Address
 Dir  ::0/96                                            1 Auto V4 Tunnel
 Dir  FE80::0800:2BB3:FD44/128                          1 Link Local Address
 Dir  ::192.32.244.250/128                              1 Local Address
 Dir  3FFE:2XXX::0/80                                   1 Eth/1
 Dir  3FFE:2XXX::0800:2BB3:FD45/128                     1 Local Address
 Dir  FE80::0800:2BB3:FD45/128                          1 Link Local Address
 Dir  ::192.32.245.250/128                              1 Local Address
 RIP  3FFE:1XXX::0/80                                   2 192.32.243.250
 RIP  3FFE:3XXX::0/80                                   2 192.32.243.250
```

```
IPV6>interface
Interfaces
----------

Interface        =  Eth/0
Enabled          =  TRUE
Default Router   =  TRUE
Send RA          =  TRUE
Managed          =  TRUE
Other            =  TRUE
RIP Enabled      =  TRUE
MTU Size         =   1500
Max Adv Int      =     30
Min Adv Int      =      5
Current Hop      =     64

Interface        =  Eth/1
Enabled          =  TRUE
Default Router   =  TRUE
Send RA          =  TRUE
Managed          =  TRUE
Other            =  TRUE
RIP Enabled      =  TRUE
MTU Size         =  1500
Max Adv Int      =    30
Min Adv Int      =     5
Current Hop      =    64

IPV6>riptunnel
RIP Tunnels
-----------

End Point = 192.32.243.250  State =     UP
```

To summarize, the Digital Local Console provides a number of interface and protocol statistics plus configuration options.

6.5.3 Booting Bay Networks Routers with IPv6

Next, we will use a protocol analyzer to verify the configuration of Bay Networks Router 1 during system initialization. To accomplish this, the analyzer is connected to the same segment as the IPv6 side of the Bay router (Figure 6-6). The analysis is started while the router is running; next, the router is powered down and then restarted. Thus, we will be able to see the router's operation before and after it reinitializes.

Frames 1–8 of Trace 6.5.3a cover the time period prior to router reinitialization. Note that the Bay Networks Breath of Life (BOFL) transmissions have been occurring for some time, as the sequence numbers are relatively high (e.g. Seq = 4025 in Frame 3). Frame 4 is a RIP advertisement showing four routes being advertised. Frames 7 and 8 show a transmission from Workstation FTP Software 1, which is sending a periodic NetWare Service Advertising Protocol (SAP) broadcast.

Between Frame 6 (BOFL Seq = 4027) and Frame 9 (BOFL Seq = 1) the router is reinitialized. Note from the Delta T column in the trace that the total initialization time is about 1.5 minutes. In Frame 10 the router sends an ARP Request, and in Frame 11 we see the Address Autoconfiguration process test the tentative IPv6 address FE80:0:0:0:0:0:A20A:1FB8. In Frame 14, the router starts using an Aggregatable Global Unicast address, with a prefix of 3FFE:1XXX. The first ICMPv6 Router Advertisement message is issued in Frame 16, followed by RIP advertisements in Frames 17 and 27.

The first Router Advertisement in Frame 16 (Trace 6.5.3b), plus others in Frames 22 and 29, carry parameters that we studied in Chapter 5. These include the Source Link Layer Address (00-00-A2-0A-1F-B8, the hardware address of Port 1), an MTU of 1,500 octets (since this port is connected to an Ethernet link), and a prefix of 3FFE:1XXX for that link.

The first RIP packet in Frame 17 (Trace 6.5.3c) identifies only two routes: 192.32.242.0 and 192.32.243.0. Note that these are the two subnets that connect to this router, which is all that this router is aware of at this time. When the next RIP packet is sent in Frame 27 (Trace 6.5.3d), the router has complete knowledge of the network topology and identifies four routes: 192.32.242.0, 192.32.243.0, 192.32.244.0, and 192.32.245.0. A similar RIP packet is sent in Frame 36, indicating that the router's routing table information has become stable at this time.

Trace 6.5.3a. Bay Router Initialization (Summary)

```
--------------        Protocol Summary - bootbay.cap 9/9        --------------

Frame  DeltaTime        Destination          Source        Interpretation

   1                    Bay IPv6 P1      Bay IPv6 P1    BOFL(WF) Seq=4023
   2    5.0 sec         Bay IPv6 P1      Bay IPv6 P1    BOFL(WF) Seq=4024
   3    5.0 sec         Bay IPv6 P1      Bay IPv6 P1    BOFL(WF) Seq=4025
   4    4.0 sec           Broadcast      Bay IPv6 P1    RIP (TCP/IP) Response ID=IP
                                                          Entries=4
   5    1.0 sec         Bay IPv6 P1      Bay IPv6 P1    BOFL(WF) Seq=4026
   6    5.0 sec         Bay IPv6 P1      Bay IPv6 P1    BOFL(WF) Seq=4027
   7    9.1 sec           Broadcast   FTP Software 1    SAP Nearest Service Query
                                                          ServerType=File Server
                                                          (SLIST source)
   8   59.9 sec           Broadcast   FTP Software 1    SAP General Service Query
                                                          ServerType=File Server
                                                          (SLIST source)
   9   23.9 sec         Bay IPv6 P1      Bay IPv6 P1    BOFL(WF) Seq=1
  10  151.6 ms            Broadcast      Bay IPv6 P1    ARP REQUEST
                                                          Desir_Prtcl=192.32.242.250
                                                          Protocol=DOD IP
  11  239.7 ms  33-33-A2-0A-1F-B8        Bay IPv6 P1    ICMPv6 Neighbor Solicitation
                                                          Target_Address=
                                                          FE80:0:0:0:0:0:A20A:1FB8
                                                        Opt=Src Link Layer Addr
  12  119.7 ms  33-33-00-00-00-09        Bay IPv6 P1    RPC FRAME TOO SHORT
  13    2.6 sec           Broadcast      Bay IPv6 P1    ARP REQUEST
                                                          Des_Prtcl=192.32.242.250
                                                          Protocol=DOD IP
  14    1.1 sec  33-33-A2-0A-1F-B8       Bay IPv6 P1    ICMPv6 Neighbor Solicitation
                                                          Target_Address=
                                                          3FFE:1XXX:0:0:0:0:A20A:1FB8
                                                          Opt=Srce Lnk Layer Addr
  15  702.8 ms          Bay IPv6 P1      Bay IPv6 P1    BOFL(WF) Seq=2
  16  297.2 ms  33-33-00-00-00-01        Bay IPv6 P1    ICMPv6 Router Advertisement
                                                          MTU=1500
                                                          Router_Lifetime=1800
                                                          Opt=Src Link Layer Addr
                                                          Prefix=3FFE:1XXX:0:0:0:0:0:0
  17  110.0 ms            Broadcast      Bay IPv6 P1    RIP (TCP/IP) Response ID=IP
                                                          Entries=2
  18    4.6 sec         Bay IPv6 P1      Bay IPv6 P1    BOFL(WF) Seq=3
  19    1.1 sec           Broadcast      Bay IPv6 P1    RPC FRAME TOO SHORT
  20    3.8 sec         Bay IPv6 P1      Bay IPv6 P1    BOFL(WF) Seq=4
  21    5.0 sec         Bay IPv6 P1      Bay IPv6 P1    BOFL(WF) Seq=5
```

```
22    1.1 sec  33-33-00-00-00-01      Bay IPv6 P1  ICMPv6 Router Advertisement
                                                     MTU=1500
                                                     Router_Lifetime=1800
                                                     Opt=Src Link Layer Addr
                                                     Prefix=3FFE:1XXX:0:0:0:0:0:0
23    3.9 sec        Bay IPv6 P1      Bay IPv6 P1  BOFL(WF) Seq=6
24    5.0 sec        Bay IPv6 P1      Bay IPv6 P1  BOFL(WF) Seq=7
25   47.8 ms   33-33-00-00-00-09      Bay IPv6 P1  UDP D=521 S=521 Len=52
26    5.0 sec        Bay IPv6 P1      Bay IPv6 P1  BOFL(WF) Seq=8
27   32.3 ms          Broadcast       Bay IPv6 P1  RIP (TCP/IP) Response ID=IP
                                                     Entries=4
28  559.5 ms          Broadcast     FTP Software 1 SAP Nearest Service Query
                                                     ServerType=File Server
                                                    (SLIST source)
29    1.3 sec  33-33-00-00-00-01      Bay IPv6 P1  ICMPv6 Router Advertisement
                                                     MTU=1500
                                                     Router_Lifetime=1800
                                                     Opt=Src Link Layer Addr
                                                     Prefix=3FFE:1XXX:0:0:0:0:0:0
30    3.1 sec        Bay IPv6 P1      Bay IPv6 P1  BOFL(WF) Seq=9
31    5.0 sec        Bay IPv6 P1      Bay IPv6 P1  BOFL(WF) Seq=10
32    5.0 sec        Bay IPv6 P1      Bay IPv6 P1  BOFL(WF) Seq=11
33    5.0 sec        Bay IPv6 P1      Bay IPv6 P1  BOFL(WF) Seq=12
34    3.7 sec  33-33-00-00-00-09      Bay IPv6 P1  UDP D=521 S=521 Len=72
35    1.3 sec        Bay IPv6 P1      Bay IPv6 P1  BOFL(WF) Seq=13
36    4.7 sec         Broadcast       Bay IPv6 P1  RIP (TCP/IP) Response ID=IP
                                                     Entries=4
37  342.7 ms         Bay IPv6 P1      Bay IPv6 P1  BOFL(WF) Seq=14
38    5.0 sec        Bay IPv6 P1      Bay IPv6 P1  BOFL(WF) Seq=15
39    5.0 sec        Bay IPv6 P1      Bay IPv6 P1  BOFL(WF) Seq=16
40    5.0 sec        Bay IPv6 P1      Bay IPv6 P1  BOFL(WF) Seq=17
```

Trace 6.5.3b. Bay Router Initialization (Router Advertisement Packet)

```
--------------  Frame 16   Size 122   Absolute Time   10:23:26.85005--------------
                         Protocol Detail - bootbay.cap 9/9


IEEE 802.3/Ethernet DIX V2 Header


              Decode Status : -
               Frame Length : 122
        Destination Address : 33-33-00-00-00-01 ( Group, Locally Administered Addr
             Source Address : 00-00-A2-0A-1F-B8,  Bay IPv6 P1 ( OUI = WELLFLEET, U
               Frame Format : Ethernet DIX V2
```

```
            Ethertype : 0x86DD (IPv6)
       Frame Checksum : Good,  Frame Check Sequence : 00 00 00 00


IPv6 - Internet Protocol (Version 6)


        Decode Status : -
       Version Number : 6 (IP Version 6)
                Class : 0x0
           Flow Label : 0x0
       Payload Length : 64
          Next Header : 58 (ICMPv6)
            Hop Limit : 255
       Source Address : FE80:0:0:0:0:0:A20A:1FB8
  Destination Address : FF02:0:0:0:0:0:0:1


ICMPv6 - Internet Control Message Protocol (Version 6)


        Decode Status : -
            ICMP Type : 134 (Router Advertisement)
Router Advertisement Code : 0
             Checksum : 47173
    Current Hop Limit : 64
                Flags : 0x00
                        0... .... = Administered Protocol is not Used for Ad
                        .0.. .... = Administered Protocol is not Used for Au
                        ..00 0000 = Unused
      Router Lifetime : 1800 Seconds(s)
       Reachable Time : 0 Milliseconds(s)
  Retransmission Time : 0 Milliseconds(s)

                              ----- Options -----

               Option : 1 (Source Link Layer Address)
        Option Length : 1
Source Link Layer Address : 00-00-A2-0A-1F-B8,  Bay IPv6 P1
```

```
                Option : 5 (Maximum Transmission Unit)
         Option Length : 1
              Reserved : 0x00
Maximum Transmission Unit : 1500

                Option : 3 (Prefix Information)
         Option Length : 4
         Prefix Length : 80
                 Flags : 0xC0
                         1... .... = Prefix Length Can be Used for On-Link Det
                         .1.. .... = Prefix Length Can be Used for Autonomous
                         ..00 0000 = Unused
        Valid Lifetime : 4294967295 (Infinity)
    Preferred Lifetime : 604800 Seconds(s)
              Reserved : 0x0
                Prefix : 3FFE:1XXX:0:0:0:0:0:0
```

Trace 6.5.3c. Bay Router Initialization (First RIP Packet)

```
-------------- Frame 17  Size 90  Absolute Time  10:23:26.96003--------------
                  Protocol Detail - bootbay.cap 9/9


IEEE 802.3/Ethernet DIX V2 Header


         Decode Status : -
          Frame Length : 90
   Destination Address : FF-FF-FF-FF-FF-FF,  Broadcast ( Group, Locally Admin
        Source Address : 00-00-A2-0A-1F-B8,  Bay IPv6 P1 ( OUI = WELLFLEET, U
          Frame Format : Ethernet DIX V2
             Ethertype : 0x800 (IP)
        Frame Checksum : Good,  Frame Check Sequence : 00 00 00 00
```

```
IP - Internet Protocol


        Decode Status : -
              Version : 4,  Header length : 20
      Type of Service : 0x00
                        000. .... = Routine Precedence
                        ...0 .... = Normal Delay
                        .... 0... = Normal Throughput
                        .... .0.. = Normal Reliability
                        .... ..00 = Reserved
         Total length : 72 bytes
       Identification : 0
     Fragment Control : 0x00
                        0... .... .... .... = Reserved
                        .0.. .... .... .... = May Fragment
                        ..0. .... .... .... = Last Fragment
                        ...0 0000 0000 0000 = Fragment Offset = 0 bytes
         Time to Live : 1 seconds/hops
             Protocol : 17 (UDP)
             Checksum : 0x536A (Checksum Good)
       Source Address : 192.32.242.250
  Destination Address : 192.32.242.255

 No IP options


UDP - User Datagram Protocol


Decode Status : -
          Source Port : 520 (RIP (TCP/IP))
     Destination Port : 520 (RIP (TCP/IP))
           UDP Length : 52
             Checksum : 0x2DF0 (Checksum Good)


RIP (TCP/IP) - Routing Information Protocol


        Decode Status : -
              Command : 2 (Response)
              Version : 1
               Unused : 0x00
```

```
              Entry 1
 Address Family ID : 0x02 (IP)
         Route Tag : 0x00
        IP Address : 192.32.242.0
       Subnet Mask : 0.0.0.0
          Next Hop : 0.0.0.0
            Metric : 0x1

              Entry 2
 Address Family ID : 0x02 (IP)
         Route Tag : 0x00
        IP Address : 192.32.243.0
       Subnet Mask : 0.0.0.0
          Next Hop : 0.0.0.0
            Metric : 0x1
```

Trace 6.5.3d. Bay Router Initialization (Second RIP Packet)

```
--------------  Frame 27   Size 130   Absolute Time   10:23:56.95926--------------
Protocol Detail - bootbay.cap 9/9


IEEE 802.3/Ethernet DIX V2 Header


          Decode Status : -
           Frame Length : 130
    Destination Address : FF-FF-FF-FF-FF-FF,  Broadcast ( Group, Locally Admin
         Source Address : 00-00-A2-0A-1F-B8,  Bay IPv6 P1 ( OUI = WELLFLEET, U
           Frame Format : Ethernet DIX V2
              Ethertype : 0x800 (IP)
         Frame Checksum : Good,  Frame Check Sequence : 00 00 00 00
```

```
IP - Internet Protocol


            Decode Status : -
                  Version : 4,  Header length : 20
          Type of Service : 0x00
                            000. .... = Routine Precedence
                            ...0 .... = Normal Delay
                            .... 0... = Normal Throughput
                            .... .0.. = Normal Reliability
                            .... ..00 = Reserved
             Total length : 112 bytes
           Identification : 7
         Fragment Control : 0x00
                            0... .... .... .... = Reserved
                            .0.. .... .... .... = May Fragment
                            ..0. .... .... .... = Last Fragment
                            ...0 0000 0000 0000 = Fragment Offset = 0 bytes
              Time to Live : 1 seconds/hops
                  Protocol : 17 (UDP)
                  Checksum : 0x533B (Checksum Good)
            Source Address : 192.32.242.250
       Destination Address : 192.32.242.255

 No IP options


UDP - User Datagram Protocol


            Decode Status : -
              Source Port : 520 (RIP (TCP/IP))
         Destination Port : 520 (RIP (TCP/IP))
               UDP Length : 92
                 Checksum : 0xC453 (Checksum Good)
```

```
RIP (TCP/IP) - Routing Information Protocol


        Decode Status : -
              Command : 2 (Response)
              Version : 1
               Unused : 0x00

              Entry 1
    Address Family ID : 0x02 (IP)
            Route Tag : 0x00
           IP Address : 192.32.242.0
          Subnet Mask : 0.0.0.0
             Next Hop : 0.0.0.0
               Metric : 0x1

              Entry 2
    Address Family ID : 0x02 (IP)
            Route Tag : 0x00
           IP Address : 192.32.243.0
          Subnet Mask : 0.0.0.0
             Next Hop : 0.0.0.0
               Metric : 0x1

              Entry 3
    Address Family ID : 0x02 (IP)
            Route Tag : 0x00
           IP Address : 192.32.244.0
          Subnet Mask : 0.0.0.0
             Next Hop : 0.0.0.0
               Metric : 0x2

              Entry 4
    Address Family ID : 0x02 (IP)
            Route Tag : 0x00
           IP Address : 192.32.245.0
          Subnet Mask : 0.0.0.0
             Next Hop : 0.0.0.0
               Metric : 0x3
```

To summarize, IPv6 adds enhancements to most of the major routing protocols, including RIP, OSPF, and BGP. A clear understanding of the internetwork topology and configuration of the routers goes a long way toward a successful routing system implementation. In the next chapter, we will look at the other side of the implementation equation—issues relating to the hosts.

6.6 References

[6-1] Malkin, G., and R. Minnear. "RIPng for IPv6." RFC 2080, January 1997.

[6-2] Moy, J. "OSPF Version 2." RFC 1583, March 1994.

[6-3] Coltun, R., D. Ferguson, and J. Moy. "OSPF for IPv6." Work in progress, March 1997.

[6-4] Rekhter, Y., and T. Li. "A Border Gateway Protocol 4 (BGP-4)." RFC 1771, March 1995.

[6-5] Rekhter, Y., and T. Li. "A Border Gateway Protocol 4 (BGP-4)." Work in progress, June 1997.

[6-6] Bates, Tony, et al. "Multiprotocol Extensions for BGP-4." Work in progress, July 1997.

[6-7] Crawford, Matt, and Robert Hinden. "Router Renumbering for IPv6." Work in progress, July 1997.

[6-8] Katz, Dave, et al. "IPv6 Router Alert Option." Work in progress, July 1997.

7 Host Issues: Upper Layer Protocols, APIs, and Security

The two principle elements of a TCP/IP-based internetwork are routers and hosts. We looked at the issues surrounding IPv6 routing in the previous chapter, and will now turn our attention to host-related concerns. These include changes to operating systems necessary to support IPv6 characteristics, such as larger addresses, changes to the Domain Name System (DNS) that identifies hosts within the Internet, and work in IP Security that provides both authentication and encryption services for IPv6. We will begin our study with issues surrounding the upper layers and operating systems.

7.1 Upper Layer Protocol Issues

Since IP is at the core of the ARPA architecture, changes at the lower layer affect the operation of the upper layers. Four of these upper layer issues are considered in section 8 of the IPv6 Specification [7-1], and in additional work that documents proposed enhancements to that effort [7-2].

7.1.1 Upper Layer Checksums

Both the TCP and UDP headers include a 16-bit checksum field which is used to verify the reliability of the data delivered to the upper layer process. But in addition to the data itself being reliable, that data must be delivered to the correct destination. To incorporate this destination element into the overall checksum calculation, a special header, called a *Pseudo header*, was devised. This Pseudo header includes the source and destination addresses for that packet. The checksum calculation then includes the Pseudo header, the UDP or TCP header, plus the upper layer protocol headers and data in its algorithm (Figure 7-1a). Since the Pseudo header includes the addresses, the destination element is included in the reliability function. In addition, ICMPv6 uses this same Pseudo header in its calculation, unlike ICMP for IPv4.

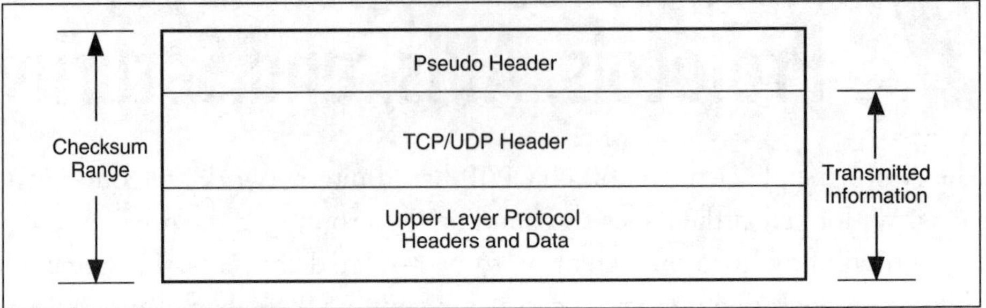

Figure 7-1a. Pseudo header position and checksum range

For IPv6, which uses larger addresses, the Pseudo header format is revised (Figure 7-1b). The IPv6 Pseudo header includes fields for the 128-bit Source and Destination addresses, the Upper Layer Packet Length, and a Next Header field. If the IPv6 packet contains a Routing header, the Destination address field in the Pseudo header contains the final address for that packet. The Upper Layer Packet Length field is the length of the upper layer header (e.g. TCP) plus data. The Next Header field identifies the upper layer protocol, such as TCP (Next Header = 6), UDP (Next Header = 17), or ICMP (Next Header = 58). Note that the contents of this field may not have the same value as the IPv6 header, if extension headers are included in the IPv6 packet.

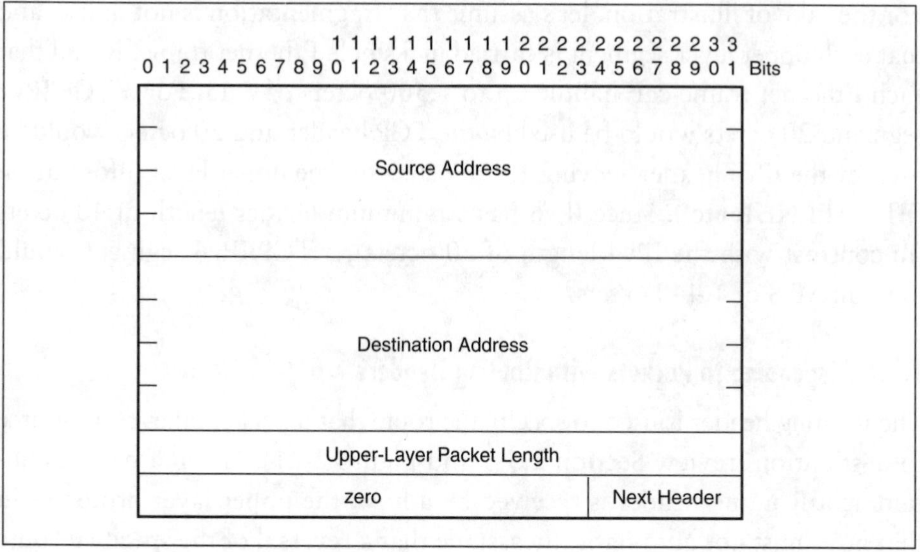

Figure 7-1b. Pseudo header for use with IPv6

7.1.2 Maximum Packet Lifetimes

The IPv4 header included a Time-to-Live field which could be measured in seconds or hops. In IPv6, this function is performed by the Hop Limit field, which is measured only in hops. For IPv4 applications, most implementations measure the Time-to-Live in hops (not seconds); however, any upper layer protocols that need a time basis for measurement will need to be revised, such that some other mechanism is provided to detect and discard obsolete packets.

7.1.3 Maximum Upper Layer Payload Size

The maximum segment size (MSS) is the maximum payload size available for the upper layer data. In some cases, this number may be constrained by lower layer functions, such as the availability of fragmentation (at the OSI Network Layer) or the type of local network being used (at the OSI Data Link Layer).

For the sake of illustration, let's assume that fragmentation is not in use, and that each upper layer segment is carried in a single Ethernet frame. Recall that each Ethernet frame can handle up to 1,500 octets of data. For a TCP/IPv4 segment, 20 octets would be used by the TCP header and 20 octets would be used by the IPv4 header, leaving 1,460 octets for the upper layer information (FTP, TELNET, etc.). Since IPv6 has a minimum header length of 40 octets (in contrast with the IPv4 length of 20 octets), a TCP/IPv6 segment would have an MSS of 1,440 octets.

7.1.4 Responding to Packets with Routing Headers

The Routing header is used to specify the route that a packet takes from source to destination (review Section 2.5.5 and Figure 2-21). When a packet containing a Routing header is received by a host, the upper layer protocols in that host must not automatically assume that a reversal of the specified route is correct and/or appropriate. Depending on the circumstances, there are three possible kinds of response packets that can be sent:

- A response packet that does not contain a Routing header.
- A response packet that contains a Routing header that was not derived by reversing the original route, such as a Routing header that was derived by the responding host itself.
- A response packet that contains a Routing header that was derived by reversing the original route, if the integrity and authenticity of the received Source address and Routing header have been verified.

Additional details on these upper layer issues are found in the IPv6 Specification, RFC 1883 [7-1], and Reference [7-2].

7.2 Domain Name System Extensions

The *Domain Name System*, or *DNS*, is a distributed database that provides a naming hierarchy for machines that are attached to the Internet. DNS has two key functions: a specification for the names themselves, and a method of mapping host names to IP addresses. In specifying machine names, a hierarchy exists that defines a number of top-level domains, such as .com (commercial), .edu (educational), .gov (government), .net (networks), and so on. For example, the host *teal* belongs to the domain *sni.net*, registered by SuperNet, Inc., an Internet Services Provider. The machine name for that host would therefore be *teal.sni.net*. While applications may identify process destinations with machine names, communication protocols require numeric addresses. Therefore the second key function of DNS is to provide a machine name lookup service similar to the telephone white pages. You supply a host name such as *teal.csn.net*, and a DNS server returns an IP address: *128.138.213.22*.

But heretofore, all DNS information has been based on the assumption that IPv4 addresses, called Type A Resource Records, were being stored and retrieved. To support IPv6, enhancements to DNS, which are documented in RFC 1886 [7-3], have been developed. These are:

- A new Resource Record Type (AAAA), which stores a single 128-bit IPv6 address.
- A new special domain, IP6.INT, which is used to look up a host name given its IPv6 address. (These queries are sometimes referred to as *Pointer Queries*.)
- New procedures for existing query types that perform additional section processing. (DNS messages include a field called "Additional Information" which may contain other types of records, such as name server, mail exchange, or mailbox information.) If these additional records are queried, the name server must add any relevant IPv4 addresses and any relevant IPv6 addresses to the response.

Further details on these extensions can be found in RFC 1886 [7-3].

7.3 Application Programming Interfaces

IPv4 is implemented in the Berkeley Software Distribution (BSD) version 4.x of the UNIX operating system, which defines an application programming interface (API) through which TCP/IP-based applications can communicate. This is informally known as the *socket interface*.

In order for the upper layer applications to access and therefore take advantage of the new IPv6 features, the APIs must be enhanced. These API extensions have been defined in two categories: basic and advanced. The Basic Socket Extensions are documented in RFC 2133 [7-4] and include:

- New address data structures that can accommodate the 16-octet IPv6 address (enhanced from the 4-octet IPv4 address), plus support for special addresses such as the IPv4-mapped IPv6 address and IPv6 Loopback address.
- Name-to-address translation functions, including Hostname-to-Address translation with support for the AAAA record type within the DNS, and also Address-to-Hostname translation.
- Address conversion functions, which convert IPv6 addresses between binary and text formats.

The proposed Advanced Socket Extensions are presently documented in Reference [7-5] and include:

- Definitions for IPv6 raw sockets (those that bypass the Transport Layer (UDP or TCP)) that are used for ICMPv6, and are also used for datagrams with a Next Header field that the operating system kernel does not process.
- Packet information that is transferred between the application and the outgoing/received packet, including the source/destination addresses, the outgoing/received interface, the outgoing/received hop limit, and the outgoing next hop address.
- Support for extension header processing, including the Hop-by-Hop, Destination Options, and Routing headers.
- Future requirements, such as support for Flow Labels, Path MTU Discovery and UDP, and Neighbor Discovery and UDP.

One vendor's operating system enhancements are discussed in "Internet Protocol Version 6 and the Digital UNIX Implementation Experience" [7-6], which details many of the enhancements that Digital Equipment Corp. has made to the Digital UNIX operating system in support of IPv6.

At the time of this writing, IPv6 host implementations have been announced by Apple Computer, Bull SA, Dassault Electronique Group, Digital Equipment Corp., DRET, Epilogue Technology Corp., FTP Software, IBM, INRIA Rocquencourt, Linux, Mentat, Novell, Inc., Pacific Softworks, Process Software Corp., SCO, Swedish Institute of Computer Science, Siemens Nixdorf, Silicon Graphics, Sun Microsystems, the University of New Hampshire, the U.S. Naval Research Laboratory, and the WIDE Project. It can be anticipated that similar changes to these operating systems and their APIs will be required to support IPv6.

For a current listing of IPv6 host implementations, see the IPv6 industry web site at http://playground.sun.com/pub/ipng/html/ipng-main.html.

7.4 Security

From our review of the IPv6 architecture in Chapter 2, recall that both Authentication (AH) and Encryption (ESP) extension headers have been defined and are required for a full implementation of IPv6. The Authentication and Encryption headers are part of the ongoing work in IP Security (IPsec), which is addressing applications for both IPv4 and IPv6 [7-7]. The authentication and encryption functions have been separated so that individual implementations can use one or both of the functions as needed by the upper layer applications. Encryption, for example, may be restricted by government regulation; therefore, only authentication is implemented in some cases. References [7-8] through [7-10] are examples of current books and journal articles that provide further background into these security-related issues in general and IP security in particular.

7.4.1 IP Security Architecture

The goal of IP Security (IPsec) is to provide interoperable, cryptographically based security for IPv4 and IPv6. Since these security functions are offered at the IP layer, protection for both IP and any upper layer protocols are provided. IPsec enables a system to select the required security protocols, determine the algorithms that will be used for the security service, and implement any cryptographic keys that are required to provide those services. IPsec may be used to protect the communication paths between two hosts, between two security gateways, or between a host and a security gateway.

The security architecture for IPv6 is defined in RFC 1825 [7-11], with additional work that documents many proposed enhancements to these efforts [7-12]. These documents include the following baseline definitions for the various systems and processes:

- Access Control: The process of preventing unauthorized access to a network resource.
- Authentication: The property of knowing that the data received is the same as the data that was sent and that the claimed sender is in fact the actual sender (also known as *data origin authentication*), plus the property that an individual IP packet has not been altered (*connectionless integrity*).
- Integrity: The property of ensuring that data is transmitted from source to destination without undetected alteration. *Connectionless integrity* is a service that detects modification of an individual IP packet, without regard to the ordering of the packet in a datastream. *Anti-replay integrity* (or *partial sequence integrity*) detects the arrival of duplicate IP packets within a constrained window.
- Confidentiality: The protection of data from unauthorized disclosure.
- Encryption: A mechanism to transform data from an intelligible form (*plaintext*) to an unintelligible form (*ciphertext*), thus providing confidentiality.

- Security Parameters Index (SPI): 32-bit value that is used to distinguish among different Security Associations (SAs) terminating at the same destination and using the same IPsec protocol.
- Security Association (SA): The set of security information relating to a given network connection or set of connections. Both AH and ESP make use of SAs. A key distribution protocol, such as the Internet Secure Association Key Management Protocol (ISAKMP), is used to establish and maintain the SA. The SA is a simplex (one-way) logical connection that provides security services to AH, or to ESP, but not to both. Therefore, if both AH and ESP were to be applied to a stream of traffic, two SAs would be assigned. In addition, authenticated, bi-directional communication sessions between two hosts will have two SAs in use—one in each direction. The SA may include: the authentication algorithm, algorithm mode, and keys; the encryption algorithm, algorithm mode, transform, and keys; lifetime of the key, or time when the key should be changed, etc. Two types of SAs are defined: transport mode and tunnel mode.
- Security Gateway: A system that acts as an intermediate system between two networks. The hosts or networks on the external side of the security gateway are viewed as untrusted systems, while hosts or networks on the internal side are viewed as trusted systems.
- Traffic Analysis: The analysis of network traffic flow for the purpose of deducing information that is useful to an adversary. Examples of such information are frequency of transmission, the identities of the conversing parties, sizes of packets, Flow Identifiers used, etc.
- Trusted Subnetwork: A network that contains hosts and routers that trust each other not to engage in active or passive attacks, and that trust that the underlying communication channel (e.g., an Ethernet) isn't being attacked.
- Transport Mode Security Association: A security association between two hosts, primarily providing security for the upper layer protocols.
- Tunnel Mode Security Association: A security association applied to an IP tunnel, primarily providing security for a tunneled packet.

The following sections discuss the various security associations that are possible, plus the manner in which AH and ESP are implemented within those security associations.

7.4.2 Security Associations

The Security Association (SA) is a *simplex* (or one-way) logical connection that provides security services to the traffic being carried over that connection. These SA services can be provided by either AH or ESP, but not both. Should both AH and ESP be desired, then two SAs are required.

Two types of SAs are defined: transport mode and tunnel mode. The *transport mode* SA exists between two hosts. For transport mode, the security protocol header (AH or ESP) would appear after the IP header and any optional extension headers, and before any upper layer protocol headers such as UDP or TCP. When AH is employed in transport mode, security is provided for portions of the IP header and the upper layer protocols. When ESP is employed in transport mode, security is provided for the upper layer protocols only.

In *tunnel mode*, the security association is applied to a tunnel. Whenever one end of the tunnel is a security gateway, tunnel mode must be used. If both ends of the tunnel are hosts, then either tunnel mode or transport mode may be used. For tunnel mode, there are two IP headers: an outer header that specifies the destination for IPsec processing, and an inner header that specifies the ultimate destination of the packet. When AH is employed in tunnel mode, security is provided for portions of the outer IP header plus all of the inner tunneled packet. When ESP is employed in tunnel mode, security is provided for the inner tunneled packet only.

At the time of this writing, four representative security associations (for either AH or ESP) have been identified, and other scenarios may be developed in the future. End-to-end security between two hosts across the Internet or an intranet may use either transport mode or tunnel mode (Figure 7-2). Virtual private networks that are connected across the Internet use tunnel mode between security gateways (Figure 7-3). Hosts that are attached to those virtual private networks may add transport mode security between the sending and receiving hosts (Figure 7-4). Remote hosts, accessing another host on a distant intranet, would use tunnel mode between the host and the security gateway, and either transport mode or tunnel mode between hosts (Figure 7-5).

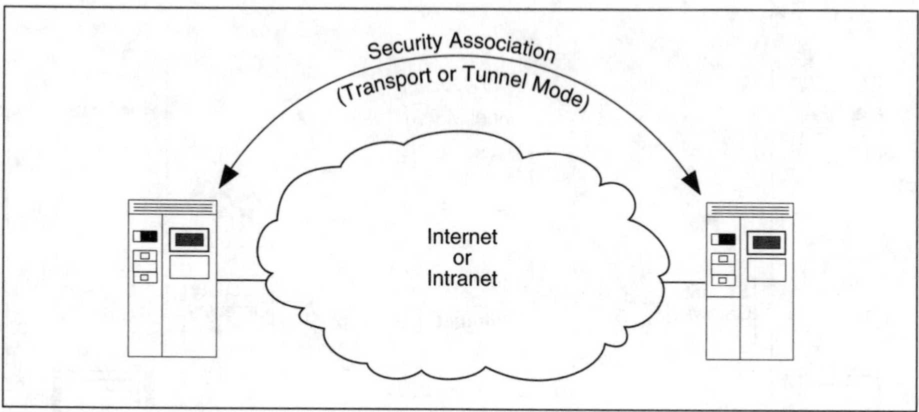

Figure 7-2. Security association between two hosts

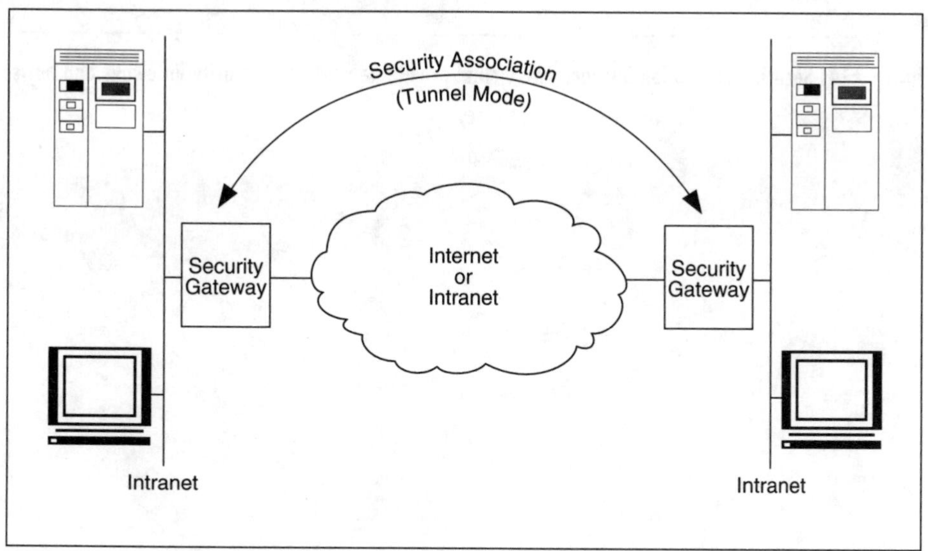

Figure 7-3. Security association between two virtual private networks via security gateways

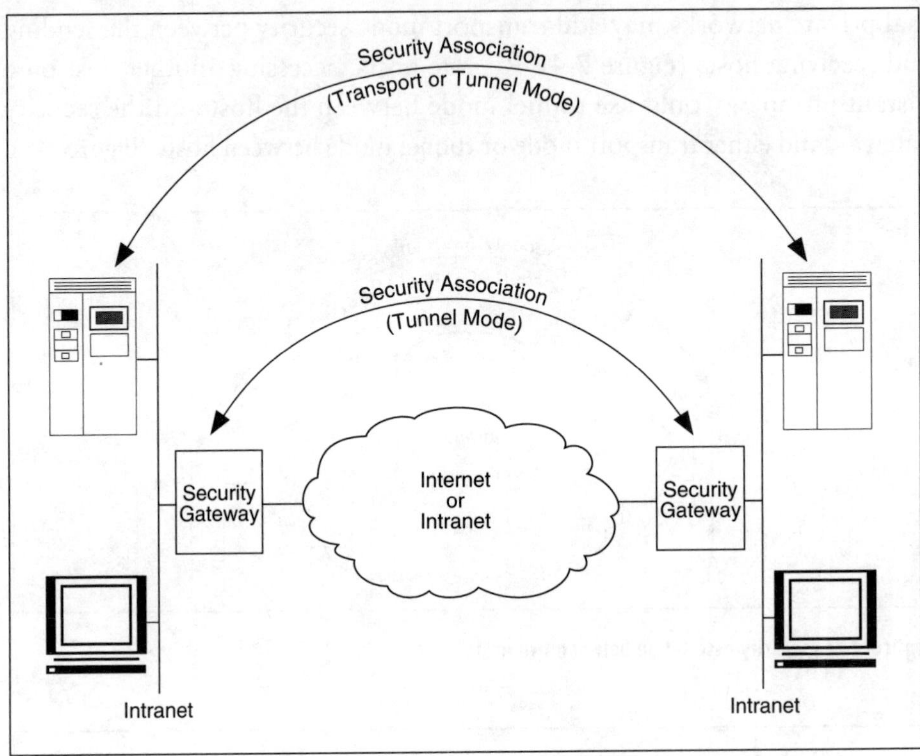

Figure 7-4. Security association between two virtual private networks via security gateways and hosts

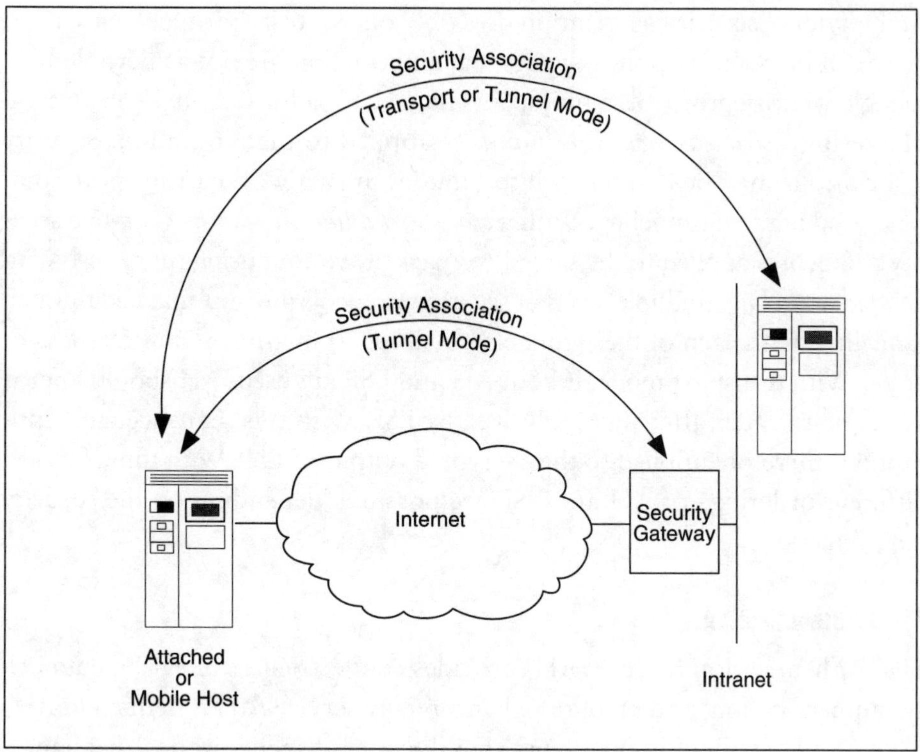

Figure 7-5. Security association for attached or mobile hosts

An individual security association uses only one security protocol: either AH or ESP. If the security policy dictates capabilities that are not achievable with a single security protocol, multiple SAs may be used for that implementation. The term *security association bundle* is applied to that condition. Security associations may be combined into bundles in two ways: a transport adjacency and iterated tunneling. With a *transport adjacency*, more than one security protocol is applied to the same IPv6 packet, without using tunneling. With *iterated tunneling*, multiple levels of security protocols are implemented through tunneling, with each of these tunnels possibly terminating at a different endpoint. With transport mode, if both AH and ESP are used, AH should appear as the first header after IPv6, followed by ESP. With this sequence, authentication is therefore applied to the encrypted output of ESP. With tunnel mode, different orderings of AH and ESP are possible, depending on the security requirements.

7.4.3 Authentication

The Authentication Header (AH) provides connectionless integrity, data origin authentication, and an optional anti-replay service. AH is defined in RFC 1826 [7-13], with additional work that documents many proposed enhancements to these efforts [7-14]. AH may be implemented in two ways: transport mode (between hosts) and tunnel mode (between hosts and security gateways, or between two hosts). AH is an appropriate protocol to implement when confidentiality is not required, or is not permitted (perhaps because of government regulations).

Note that both ESP and AH may provide authentication. The key difference between the authentication services provided by the two protocols is the extent of the coverage. ESP does not protect any IPv6 header fields unless those fields are encapsulated by ESP. In contrast, AH can have a wider range of coverage. (Figures 7-6 through 7-9 will demonstrate this. Note that in these four figures, we illustrate the complete packet by showing all the headers from top to bottom rather than left to right. This is necessary for these figures because of space limitations. No protocol changes are implied by this difference, however.)

In transport mode, AH is considered an end-to-end payload, and therefore should be placed after the hop-by-hop, routing, and fragmentation headers. The Destination Options header(s) could be placed before or after the AH, as required by the specific implementation (Figure 7-6).

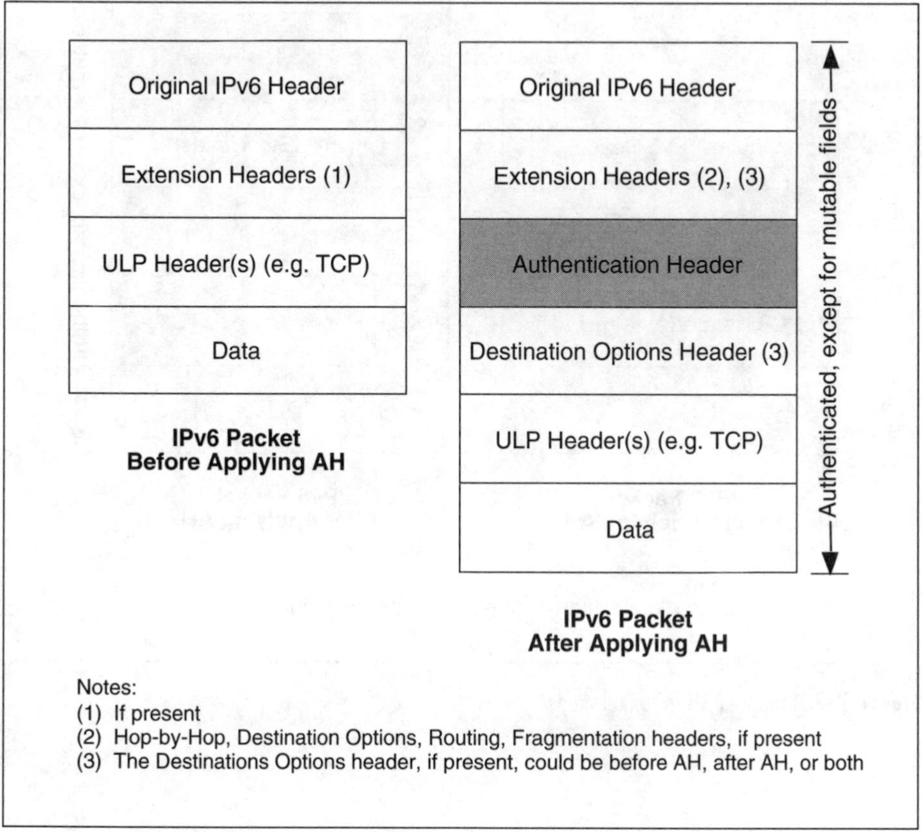

Figure 7-6. Proposed AH in transport mode

Tunnel mode contains both an inner IPv6 packet (heading for the ultimate destination), and an outer IPv6 packet, which may be sent to an intermediate security gateway. In tunnel mode, AH protects the entire inner IP packet, including the entire inner IPv6 packet header (Figure 7-7).

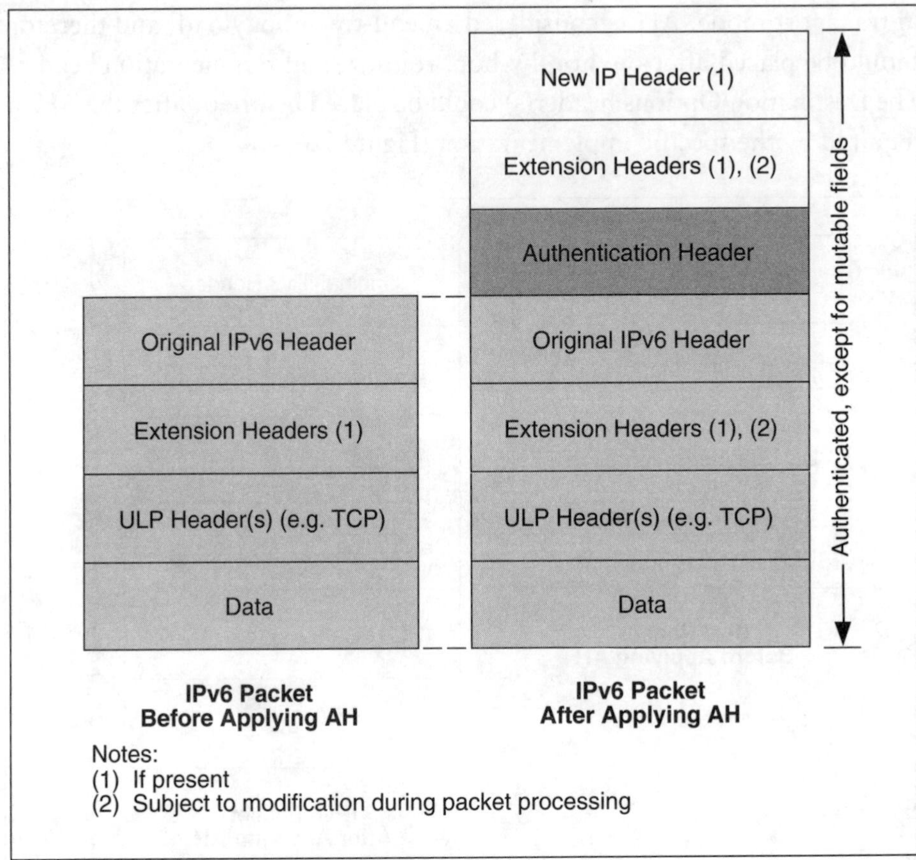

Figure 7-7. Proposed AH in tunnel mode

At the time of this writing, the authentication algorithms that are employed for the Integrity Check Value (ICV) computation, and are mandatory to implement, are the HMAC with SHA-1 (described in RFC 2104 [7-15]) or the HMAC with MD5 (described in RFC 1321 [7-16]). Other algorithms may be supported in certain implementations.

7.4.4 Encryption

The Encapsulating Security Payload (ESP) provides confidentiality (encryption), data origin authentication, connectionless integrity, anti-replay service, and limited traffic flow confidentiality (guarding against traffic analysis). Both AH and ESP may be used for access control, based on the key distribution and traffic flows in use. The scope of the authentication offered by ESP is not as broad as that provided with AH. ESP is defined in RFC 1827 [7-17], with additional work that documents many proposed enhancements to these efforts [7-18].

In transport mode, ESP is considered an end-to-end payload, and therefore should be placed after the hop-by-hop, routing, and fragmentation headers. The Destination Options header(s) could be placed before or after the ESP (Figure 7-8). However, since ESP protects only those fields that come after the ESP header, placing the Destination Options header after ESP may be desirable.

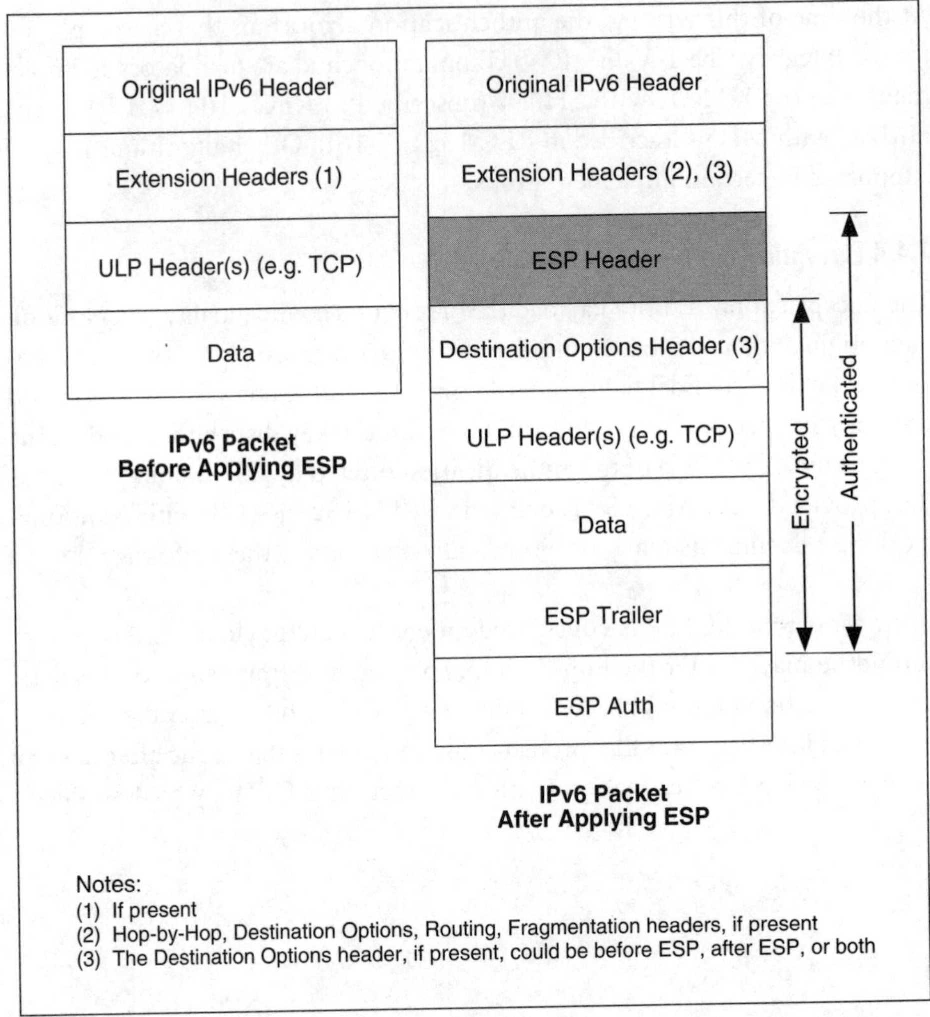

Figure 7-8. Proposed ESP in transport mode

Tunnel mode contains both an inner IPv6 packet, heading for the ultimate destination, and an outer IPv6 packet, which may be sent to an intermediate security gateway. In tunnel mode, ESP protects the entire inner IP packet, including the entire inner IPv6 packet header (Figure 7-9).

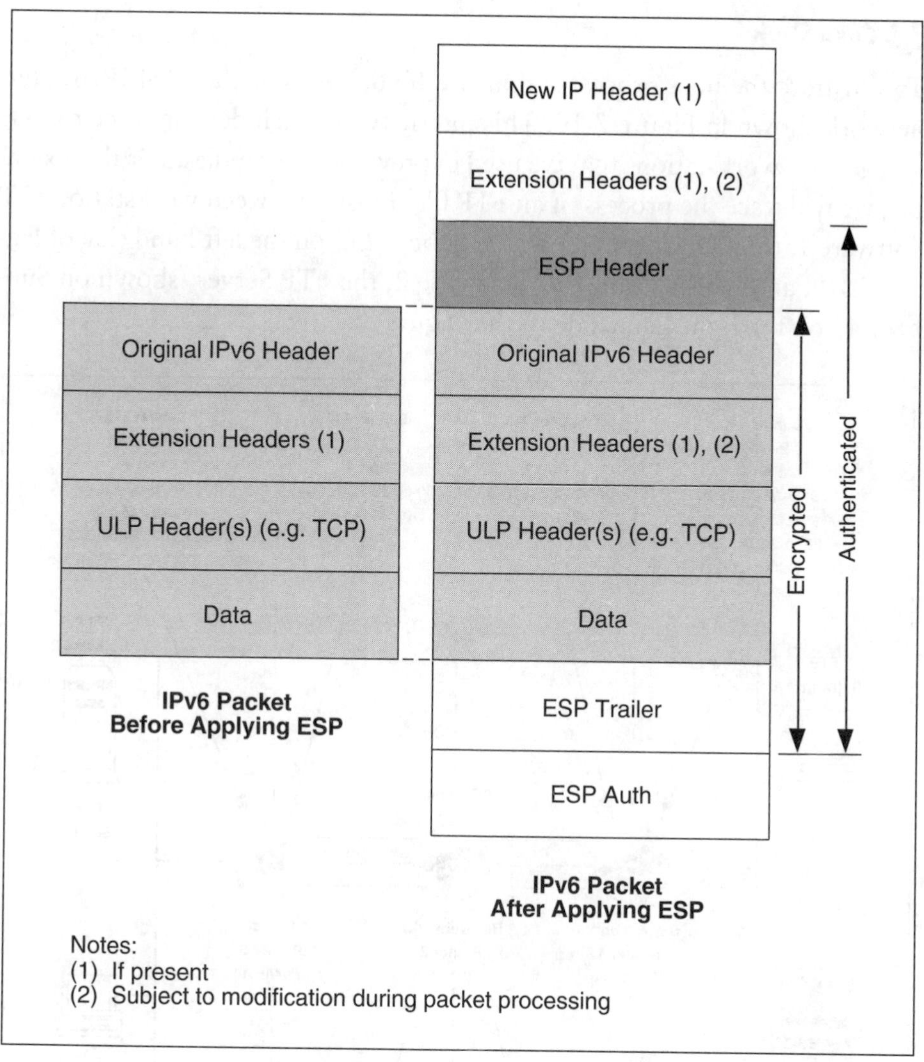

Figure 7-9. Proposed ESP in tunnel mode

At the time of this writing, a compliant ESP implementation must support the following algorithms: DES in CBC mode, described in RFC 1829 [7-19], and HMAC with MD5 or HMAC with SHA-1, described in RFC 2104 [7-13]. Other algorithms may be supported in certain implementations. An excellent reference on network security in general is the "Site Security Handbook," RFC 2196 [7-20].

7.5 Case Study

To illustrate the host processes that use IPv6, consider the IPv4/IPv6 internetwork shown in Figure 7-10. This internetwork includes the three routers and various workstations that we used in previous case studies. For this example, we will trace the process of an FTP file transfer between workstation FTP Software 1, the FTP Client (shown on Subnet 242 on the left-hand side of Figure 7-10), and workstation FTP Software 2, the FTP Server (shown on Subnet 245 on the right-hand side of that figure).

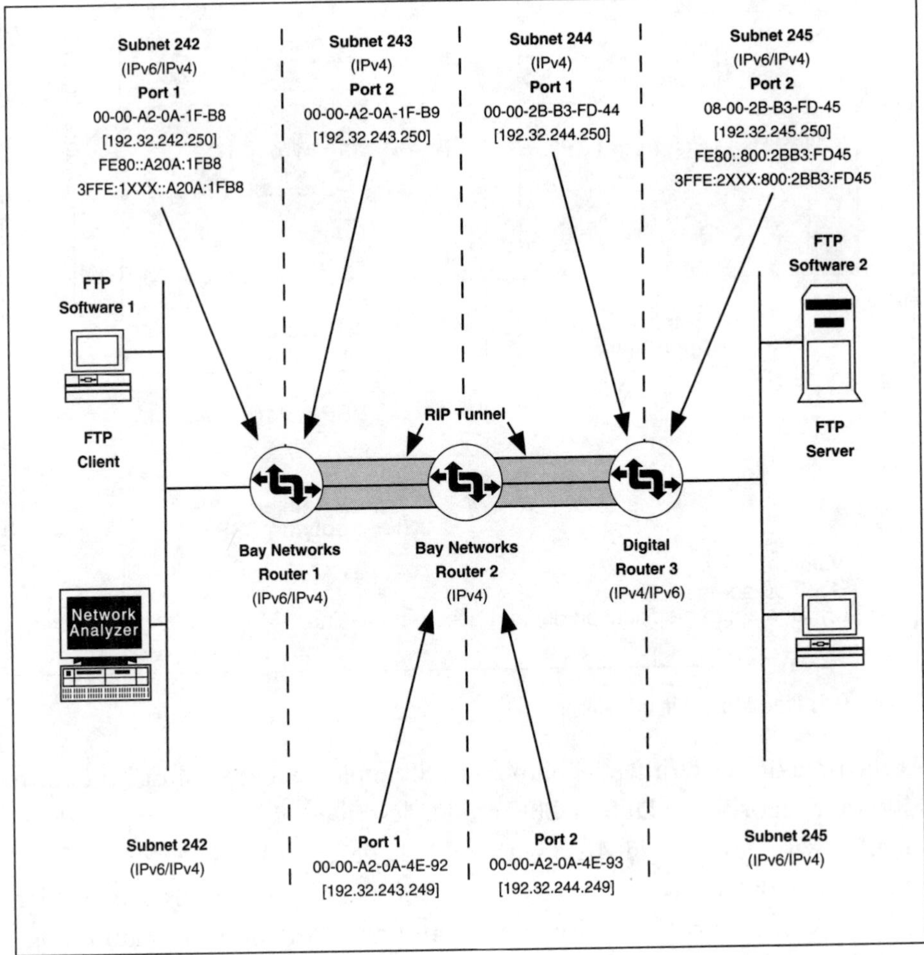

Figure 7-10. IPv6/IPv4 Internetwork

The server contains an archive of RFC documents; one of these documents will be transferred across the IPv4/IPv6 internetwork. Reviewing Figure 7-10, note that a RIP tunnel exists between the Bay Networks router (shown as Router 1 in the figure) and the Digital router (shown as Router 3 in the figure). In Section 6.5, we studied the configuration of this tunnel and discovered the various parameters that were established for its configuration.

In this case study, we will go step by step across the internetwork, tracing the packet encapsulation at each subnet that the information goes through. Our initial result, shown in Trace 7.5a, is taken with the network analyzer on Subnet 242; it shows a summary of all frames sent from the FTP Client and then returned (via Router 1) from the FTP Server. A summary of the protocol operations is:

Frames	Operation
1–4	Breath of Life (BOFL) transmission from router, confirming operational status of transmission media; NetWare Service Advertising Protocol (SAP) broadcast from the workstation, looking for NetWare servers; and Routing Information Protocol (RIP) broadcast from router advertising available routes.
5–7	Initiate connection from client to server with the synchronize (SYN) command (from the FTP Control port, port 21), using TCP 3-way handshake. Note that the client selects port 1556.
8–17	Login to server using anonymous FTP.
18–52	Request root directory information from server.
53–65	Initiate connection from server to client using TCP 3-way handshake, return directory information, and close connection. Note that in Frame 53 the server is now using the FTP Data port (port 20) and sending to a different port on the client (port 1557).
71–74	Neighbor Solicitation/Neighbor Advertisement exchange.
66–101	Request listing of /RFC directory, initiate TCP connection, transfer data, close connection. Note that in Frame 89 the server is still using the FTP Data port (port 20), but is now sending to another port on the client (port 1558).
102	Breath of Life (BOFL) transmission from router.

103–137	Request listing of /RFC/RFC18XX directory, initiate TCP connection, transfer data, close connection. Note that in Frame 123 the server is still using the FTP Data port (port 20), but is now sending to another port on the client (port 1559).
138–171	Retrieve file /RFC/RFC18XX/RFC1897.TXT, initiate TCP connection, transfer data, close connection. Note that in Frame 154 the server is still using the FTP Data port (port 20), but is now sending to another port on the client (port 1560).
172–177	BOFL, RIP, User Datagram Protocol (UDP) messages.
178–185	Terminate (QUIT) FTP session and close the connection. Note that in Frames 182 and 184 the server is once again using the FTP Control port (port 21), and the client is using the port (1556) that was originally established for FTP Control messages (review Frames 5–7).

Trace 7.5a. File Transfer Summary

```
--------------          Protocol Summary - ftp1.cap 9/18          --------------

Frame      DeltaTime       Destination        Source        Interpretation

     1                     Bay 1 P1           Bay 1 P1      BOFL(WF) Seq=487
     2   2.3 sec           Broadcast     FTP Software 1     SAP General Service Query
     3   2.6 sec           Bay 1 P1           Bay 1 P1      BOFL(WF) Seq=488
     4   407.2 ms          Broadcast          Bay 1 P1      RIP (TCP/IP) Response
                                                              ID=IP Entries=4
     5   637.1 ms          Bay 1 P1      FTP Software 1     TCP D=FTP S=1556 SYN
                                                              Seq=317875309
                                                              Len=0 Win=8192
     6     5.7 ms    FTP Software 1           Bay 1 P1      TCP D=1556 S=FTP SYN
                                                              Ack=317875310
                                                              Seq=325083126
                                                              Len=0 Win=21420
     7     1.7 ms          Bay 1 P1      FTP Software 1     TCP D=FTP S=1556
                                                              Ack=325083127
                                                              Seq=317875310
                                                              Len=0 Win=8568
     8   121.2 ms    FTP Software 1           Bay 1 P1      FTP Command=220
                                                              FTP Software, Inc. Win32
                                                              FTP Server 3,0,0,117 ready
                                                              <0D><0A>
```

```
 9     1.5 ms        Bay 1 P1     FTP Software 1   TCP D=FTP S=1556
                                                     Ack=325083185
                                                     Seq=317875310
                                                     Len=0 Win=8568
10   134.3 ms        Bay 1 P1     FTP Software 1   FTP Command=USER
                                                     anonymous<0D><0A>
11     4.9 ms  FTP Software 1           Bay 1 P1   TCP D=1556 S=FTP
                                                     Ack=317875326
                                                     Seq=325083185
                                                     Len=0 Win=21420
12    63.6 ms  FTP Software 1           Bay 1 P1   FTP Command=331
                                                     Guest login ok,
                                                     please send your email
                                                     address as a password.
                                                     <0D><0A>
13     1.7 ms        Bay 1 P1     FTP Software 1   TCP D=FTP S=1556
                                                     Ack=325083252
                                                     Seq=317875326
                                                     Len=0 Win=8568
14    21.5 ms        Bay 1 P1     FTP Software 1   FTP Command=PASS
                                                     guest<0D><0A>
15     4.7 ms  FTP Software 1           Bay 1 P1   TCP D=1556 S=FTP
                                                     Ack=317875338
                                                     Seq=325083252
                                                     Len=0 Win=21420
16   135.0 ms  FTP Software 1           Bay 1 P1   FTP Command=230
                                                     Guest login ok,
                                                     access restrictions apply.
                                                     <0D><0A>
17     1.6 ms        Bay 1 P1     FTP Software 1   TCP D=FTP S=1556
                                                     Ack=325083300
                                                     Seq=317875338
                                                     Len=0 Win=8568
18    21.3 ms        Bay 1 P1     FTP Software 1   FTP Command=TYPE I<0D><0A>
19     4.6 ms  FTP Software 1           Bay 1 P1   TCP D=1556 S=FTP
                                                     Ack=317875346
                                                     Seq=325083300
                                                     Len=0 Win=21420
20   865.1 ms  FTP Software 1           Bay 1 P1   FTP Command=200
                                                     Type set to I.<0D><0A>
21     1.5 ms        Bay 1 P1     FTP Software 1   TCP D=FTP S=1556
                                                     Ack=325083320
                                                     Seq=317875346
                                                     Len=0 Win=8568
22    31.0 ms        Bay 1 P1     FTP Software 1   FTP Command=SYST<0D><0A>
23     4.6 ms  FTP Software 1           Bay 1 P1   TCP D=1556 S=FTP
                                                     Ack=317875352
                                                     Seq=325083320
                                                     Len=0 Win=21420
```

```
24    6.1 ms   FTP Software 1           Bay 1 P1   FTP Command=215
                                                     Windows_NT version 4.0
                                                     (build 67109814) <0D><0A>
25    1.5 ms        Bay 1 P1      FTP Software 1   TCP D=FTP S=1556
                                                     Ack=325083366
                                                     Seq=317875352
                                                     Len=0 Win=8568
26   32.8 ms        Bay 1 P1      FTP Software 1   FTP Command=SITE
                                                     DIRSTYLE<0D><0A>
27    4.7 ms   FTP Software 1           Bay 1 P1   TCP D=1556 S=FTP
                                                     Ack=317875367
                                                     Seq=325083366
                                                     Len=0 Win=21420
28    7.8 ms   FTP Software 1           Bay 1 P1   FTP Command=200
                                                     MSDOS-like directory
                                                     output is off<0D><0A>
29    1.5 ms        Bay 1 P1      FTP Software 1   TCP D=FTP S=1556
                                                     Ack=325083406
                                                     Seq=317875367
                                                     Len=0 Win=8568
30   17.9 ms        Bay 1 P1      FTP Software 1   FTP Command=SITE
                                                     DIRSTYLE<0D><0A>
31    4.7 ms   FTP Software 1           Bay 1 P1   TCP D=1556 S=FTP
                                                     Ack=317875382
                                                     Seq=325083406
                                                     Len=0 Win=21420
32    6.4 ms   FTP Software 1           Bay 1 P1   FTP Command=200
                                                     MSDOS-like directory
                                                     output is on<0D><0A>
33    1.5 ms        Bay 1 P1      FTP Software 1   TCP D=FTP S=1556
                                                     Ack=325083445
                                                     Seq=317875382
                                                     Len=0 Win=8568
34   18.5 ms        Bay 1 P1      FTP Software 1   FTP Command=PWD<0D><0A>
35    4.6 ms   FTP Software 1           Bay 1 P1   TCP D=1556 S=FTP
                                                     Ack=317875387
                                                     Seq=325083445
                                                     Len=0 Win=21420
36    6.0 ms   FTP Software 1           Bay 1 P1   FTP Command=257
                                                     "\" is the current working
                                                     directory.<0D><0A>
37    1.4 ms        Bay 1 P1      FTP Software 1   TCP D=FTP S=1556
                                                     Ack=325083488
                                                     Seq=317875387
                                                     Len=0 Win=8568
38   71.9 ms  33-33-00-00-00-09         Bay 1 P1   UDP D=521 S=521 Len=72
39  262.6 ms        Bay 1 P1      FTP Software 1   FTP Command=CWD /<0D><0A>
```

```
40    4.7 ms    FTP Software 1        Bay 1 P1        TCP D=1556 S=FTP
                                                        Ack=317875394
                                                        Seq=325083488
                                                        Len=0 Win=21420
41   41.2 ms    FTP Software 1        Bay 1 P1        FTP Command=250
                                                        CWD command successful.
                                                        Current Working Directory
                                                        is: '\'<0D><0A>
42    1.5 ms          Bay 1 P1   FTP Software 1       TCP D=FTP S=1556
                                                        Ack=325083551
                                                        Seq=317875394
                                                        Len=0 Win=8568
43    6.5 ms          Bay 1 P1   FTP Software 1       FTP Command=TYPE A N<0D><0A>
44    4.6 ms    FTP Software 1        Bay 1 P1        TCP D=1556 S=FTP
                                                        Ack=317875404
                                                        Seq=325083551
                                                        Len=0 Win=21420
45    5.9 ms    FTP Software 1        Bay 1 P1        FTP Command=200
                                                        Type set to A.<0D><0A>
46    1.5 ms          Bay 1 P1   FTP Software 1       TCP D=FTP S=1556
                                                        Ack=325083571
                                                        Seq=317875404
                                                        Len=0 Win=8568
47   20.3 ms          Bay 1 P1   FTP Software 1       FTP Command=LPRT
                                                        6,16,95,0,0,1,0,0,0,0,0,0,
                                                        0,128,199,95,159,61,2,6,21
                                                        <0D><0A>
48    4.6 ms    FTP Software 1        Bay 1 P1        TCP D=1556 S=FTP
                                                        Ack=317875463
                                                        Seq=325083571
                                                        Len=0 Win=21420
49    7.7 ms    FTP Software 1        Bay 1 P1        FTP Command=200
                                                        LPRT command successful.
                                                        <0D><0A>
50    1.5 ms          Bay 1 P1   FTP Software 1       TCP D=FTP S=1556
                                                        Ack=325083601
                                                        Seq=317875463
                                                        Len=0 Win=8568
51   22.9 ms          Bay 1 P1   FTP Software 1       FTP Command=LIST<0D><0A>
52    4.5 ms    FTP Software 1        Bay 1 P1        TCP D=1556 S=FTP
                                                        Ack=317875469
                                                        Seq=325083601
                                                        Len=0 Win=21420
53   15.3 ms    FTP Software 1        Bay 1 P1        TCP D=1557 S=FTP Data SYN
                                                        Seq=325428363
                                                        Len=0 Win=20480
```

```
54   1.9 ms       Bay 1 P1       FTP Software 1   TCP D=FTP Data S=1557 SYN
                                                    Ack=325428364
                                                    Seq=318240639
                                                    Len=0 Win=8568
55   4.8 ms   FTP Software 1     Bay 1 P1         TCP D=1557 S=FTP Data
                                                    Ack=318240640
                                                    Seq=325428364
                                                    Len=0 Win=21420
56   27.6 ms  FTP Software 1     Bay 1 P1         FTP Command=150
                                                    Opening ASCII mode data
                                                    connection for /bin/ls.
                                                    <0D><0A>
57   1.5 ms       Bay 1 P1       FTP Software 1   TCP D=FTP S=1556
                                                    Ack=325083654
                                                    Seq=317875469
                                                    Len=0 Win=8568
58   17.0 ms  FTP Software 1     Bay 1 P1         FTP Data Data=[410 byte(s)]
59   1.2 ms   FTP Software 1     Bay 1 P1         FTP Command=226
                                                    File transfer complete.
                                                    <0D><0A>
60   770 us       Bay 1 P1       FTP Software 1   TCP D=FTP Data S=1557
                                                    Ack=325428774
                                                    Seq=318240640
                                                    Len=0 Win=8568
61   1.3 ms       Bay 1 P1       FTP Software 1   TCP D=FTP S=1556
                                                    Ack=325083683
                                                    Seq=317875469
                                                    Len=0 Win=8568
62   1.0 ms   FTP Software 1     Bay 1 P1         TCP D=1557 S=FTP Data FIN
                                                    Ack=318240640
                                                    Seq=325428774
                                                    Len=0 Win=21420
63   1.4 ms       Bay 1 P1       FTP Software 1   TCP D=FTP Data S=1557
                                                    Ack=325428775
                                                    Seq=318240640
                                                    Len=0 Win=8568
64   17.3 ms      Bay 1 P1       FTP Software 1   TCP D=FTP Data S=1557 FIN
                                                    Ack=325428775
                                                    Seq=318240640
                                                    Len=0 Win=8568
65   4.6 ms   FTP Software 1     Bay 1 P1         TCP D=1557 S=FTP Data
                                                    Ack=318240641
                                                    Seq=325428775
                                                    Len=0 Win=21419
66   670 us       Bay 1 P1       FTP Software 1   FTP Command=TYPE I<0D><0A>
67   4.5 ms   FTP Software 1     Bay 1 P1         TCP D=1556 S=FTP
                                                    Ack=317875477
                                                    Seq=325083683
                                                    Len=0 Win=21420
```

```
68    5.9 ms      FTP Software 1          Bay 1 P1   FTP Command=200
                                                       Type set to I.<0D><0A>
69    1.5 ms            Bay 1 P1    FTP Software 1   TCP D=FTP S=1556
                                                       Ack=325083703
                                                       Seq=317875477
                                                       Len=0 Win=8568
70    1.8 sec           Bay 1 P1          Bay 1 P1   BOFL(WF) Seq=489
71    1.0 sec  33-33-A2-0A-1F-B8    FTP Software 1   ICMPv6 Neighbor Solicitation
                                                       Target_Address=
                                                       FE80:0:0:0:0:0:A20A:1FB8
                                                       Opt = Src Link Layer Addr
72    930 us      FTP Software 1          Bay 1 P1   ICMPv6 Neighbor Advertisemen
                                                       Target_Address=
                                                       FE80:0:0:0:0:0:A20A:1FB8
                                                       Opt = Tgt Link Layer Addr
73  171.2 ms      FTP Software 1          Bay 1 P1   ICMPv6 Neighbor Solicitation
                                                       Target_Address=
                                                       3FFE:1XXX::80:C75F:9F3D
                                                       Opt = Src Link Layer Addr
74    1.3 ms            Bay 1 P1    FTP Software 1   ICMPv6 Neighbor Advertisemen
                                                       Target_Address=
                                                       3FFE:1::80:C75F:9F3D
                                                       Opt = Tgt Link Layer Addr
75    3.5 sec           Bay 1 P1    FTP Software 1   FTP Command=CWD /RFC<0D><0A>
76    4.8 ms      FTP Software 1          Bay 1 P1   TCP D=1556 S=FTP
                                                       Ack=317875487
                                                       Seq=325083703
                                                       Len=0 Win=21420
77   10.9 ms      FTP Software 1          Bay 1 P1   FTP Command=250
                                                       CWD command successful.
                                                       Current Working Directory
                                                       is: '\RFC'<0D><0A>
78    1.6 ms            Bay 1 P1    FTP Software 1   TCP D=FTP S=1556
                                                       Ack=325083769
                                                       Seq=317875487
                                                       Len=0 Win=8568
79   10.2 ms            Bay 1 P1    FTP Software 1   FTP Command=TYPE A N<0D><0A>
80    4.6 ms      FTP Software 1          Bay 1 P1   TCP D=1556 S=FTP
                                                       Ack=317875497
                                                       Seq=325083769
                                                       Len=0 Win=21420
81    6.0 ms      FTP Software 1          Bay 1 P1   FTP Command=200
                                                       Type set to A.<0D><0A>
82    1.5 ms            Bay 1 P1    FTP Software 1   TCP D=FTP S=1556
                                                       Ack=325083789
                                                       Seq=317875497
                                                       Len=0 Win=8568
```

```
83   20.3 ms          Bay 1 P1       FTP Software 1   FTP Command=LPRT
                                                        6,16,95,0,0,1,0,0,0,0,0,
                                                        0,0,128,199,95,159,61,2,
                                                        6,22<0D><0A>
84    5.0 ms    FTP Software 1           Bay 1 P1   TCP D=1556 S=FTP
                                                        Ack=317875556
                                                        Seq=325083789
                                                        Len=0 Win=21420
85    6.8 ms    FTP Software 1           Bay 1 P1   FTP Command=200
                                                        LPRT command successful.
                                                        <0D><0A>
86    1.5 ms          Bay 1 P1       FTP Software 1   TCP D=FTP S=1556
                                                        Ack=325083819
                                                        Seq=317875556
                                                        Len=0 Win=8568
87   21.9 ms          Bay 1 P1       FTP Software 1   FTP Command=LIST<0D><0A>
88    4.6 ms    FTP Software 1           Bay 1 P1   TCP D=1556 S=FTP
                                                        Ack=317875562
                                                        Seq=325083819
                                                        Len=0 Win=21420
89   14.3 ms    FTP Software 1           Bay 1 P1   TCP D=1558 S=FTP Data SYN
                                                        Seq=326413970
                                                        Len=0 Win=20480
90    1.9 ms          Bay 1 P1       FTP Software 1   TCP D=FTP Data S=1558 SYN
                                                        Ack=326413971
                                                        Seq=319249386
                                                        Len=0 Win=8568
91   12.1 ms    FTP Software 1           Bay 1 P1   TCP D=1558 S=FTP Data
                                                        Ack=319249387
                                                        Seq=326413971
                                                        Len=0 Win=21420
92    7.2 ms    FTP Software 1           Bay 1 P1   FTP Command=150
                                                        Opening ASCII mode
                                                        data connection for
                                                        /bin/ls.<0D><0A>
93    1.5 ms          Bay 1 P1       FTP Software 1   TCP D=FTP S=1556
                                                        Ack=325083872
                                                        Seq=317875562
                                                        Len=0 Win=8568
94   21.7 ms    FTP Software 1           Bay 1 P1   FTP Data
                                                          Data=[664 byte(s)]
95    450 us    FTP Software 1           Bay 1 P1   FTP Command=226
                                                        File transfer complete.
                                                        <0D><0A>
96    2.5 ms          Bay 1 P1       FTP Software 1   TCP D=FTP Data S=1558
                                                        Ack=326414635
                                                        Seq=319249387
                                                        Len=0 Win=8568
```

```
 97    160 us    FTP Software 1          Bay 1 P1   TCP D=1558 S=FTP Data FIN
                                                      Ack=319249387
                                                      Seq=326414635
                                                      Len=0 Win=21420
 98    670 us          Bay 1 P1    FTP Software 1   TCP D=FTP S=1556
                                                      Ack=325083901
                                                      Seq=317875562
                                                      Len=0 Win=8568
 99    1.7 ms          Bay 1 P1    FTP Software 1   TCP D=FTP Data S=1558
                                                      Ack=326414636
                                                      Seq=319249387
                                                      Len=0 Win=8568
100   21.8 ms          Bay 1 P1    FTP Software 1   TCP D=FTP Data S=1558 FIN
                                                      Ack=326414636
                                                      Seq=319249387
                                                      Len=0 Win=8568
101    4.7 ms    FTP Software 1          Bay 1 P1   TCP D=1558 S=FTP
                                                      Data Ack=319249388
                                                      Seq=326414636
                                                      Len=0 Win=21419
102   11.9 ms          Bay 1 P1          Bay 1 P1   BOFL(WF) Seq=490
103   17.9 ms          Bay 1 P1    FTP Software 1   FTP Command=TYPE I<0D><0A>
104    4.6 ms    FTP Software 1          Bay 1 P1   TCP D=1556 S=FTP
                                                      Ack=317875570
                                                      Seq=325083901
                                                      Len=0 Win=21420
105    5.9 ms    FTP Software 1          Bay 1 P1   FTP Command=200
                                                      Type set to I.<0D><0A>
106    1.5 ms          Bay 1 P1    FTP Software 1   TCP D=FTP S=1556
                                                      Ack=325083921
                                                      Seq=317875570
                                                      Len=0 Win=8568
107    4.9 sec         Bay 1 P1          Bay 1 P1   BOFL(WF) Seq=491
108    3.3 sec         Bay 1 P1    FTP Software 1   FTP Command=CWD
                                                       /RFC/RFC18XX<0D><0A>
109    5.0 ms    FTP Software 1          Bay 1 P1   TCP D=1556 S=FTP
                                                      Ack=317875588
                                                      Seq=325083921
                                                      Len=0 Win=21420
110   13.9 ms    FTP Software 1          Bay 1 P1   FTP Command=250
                                                      CWD command successful.
                                                      Current Working Directory
                                                      is:'\RFC\RFC18XX'<0D><0A>
111    1.6 ms          Bay 1 P1    FTP Software 1   TCP D=FTP S=1556
                                                      Ack=325083995
                                                      Seq=317875588
                                                      Len=0 Win=8568
112    8.5 ms          Bay 1 P1    FTP Software 1   FTP Command=TYPE A N<0D><0A>
```

```
113    4.6 ms    FTP Software 1         Bay 1 P1    TCP D=1556 S=FTP
                                                      Ack=317875598
                                                      Seq=325083995
                                                      Len=0 Win=21420
114    5.8 ms    FTP Software 1         Bay 1 P1    FTP Command=200
                                                      Type set to A.<0D><0A>
115    1.6 ms         Bay 1 P1    FTP Software 1    TCP D=FTP S=1556
                                                      Ack=325084015
                                                      Seq=317875598
                                                      Len=0 Win=8568
116   19.7 ms         Bay 1 P1    FTP Software 1    FTP Command=LPRT
                                                      6,16,95,0,0,1,0,0,0,0,0,
                                                      0,0,128,199,95,159,61,2,
                                                      6,23<0D><0A>
117    5.0 ms    FTP Software 1         Bay 1 P1    TCP D=1556 S=FTP
                                                      Ack=317875657
                                                      Seq=325084015
                                                      Len=0 Win=21420
118    6.2 ms    FTP Software 1         Bay 1 P1    FTP Command=200
                                                      LPRT command successful.
                                                      <0D><0A>
119    1.5 ms         Bay 1 P1    FTP Software 1    TCP D=FTP S=1556
                                                      Ack=325084045
                                                      Seq=317875657
                                                      Len=0 Win=8568
120   24.6 ms         Bay 1 P1    FTP Software 1    FTP Command=LIST<0D><0A>
121    4.6 ms    FTP Software 1         Bay 1 P1    TCP D=1556 S=FTP
                                                      Ack=317875663
                                                      Seq=325084045
                                                      Len=0 Win=21420
122   15.1 ms    FTP Software 1         Bay 1 P1    TCP D=1559 S=FTP Data SYN
                                                      Seq=327707960
                                                      Len=0 Win=20480
123    1.9 ms         Bay 1 P1    FTP Software 1    TCP D=FTP Data S=1559 SYN
                                                      Ack=327707961
                                                      Seq=320537611
                                                      Len=0 Win=8568
124   12.0 ms    FTP Software 1         Bay 1 P1    TCP D=1559 S=FTP Data
                                                      Ack=320537612
                                                      Seq=327707961
                                                      Len=0 Win=21420
125    7.8 ms    FTP Software 1         Bay 1 P1    FTP Command=150
                                                      Opening ASCII mode
                                                      data connection for
                                                      /bin/ls.<0D><0A>
126    1.5 ms         Bay 1 P1    FTP Software 1    TCP D=FTP S=1556
                                                      Ack=325084098
                                                      Seq=317875663
                                                      Len=0 Win=8568
```

```
127   101.6 ms   FTP Software 1        Bay 1 P1   FTP Data Data=[1428 byte(s)]
128    11.5 ms   FTP Software 1        Bay 1 P1   FTP Command=226
                                                    File transfer complete.
                                                    <0D><0A>
129     1.4 ms         Bay 1 P1  FTP Software 1   TCP D=FTP S=1556
                                                    Ack=325084127
                                                    Seq=317875663
                                                    Len=0 Win=8568
130    86.5 ms         Bay 1 P1  FTP Software 1   TCP D=FTP Data S=1559
                                                    Ack=327709389
                                                    Seq=320537612
                                                    Len=0 Win=8568
131    13.2 ms   FTP Software 1        Bay 1 P1   FTP Data Data=[1428 byte(s)]
132     2.9 ms   FTP Software 1        Bay 1 P1   FTP Data Data=[1428 byte(s)]
133     480 us   FTP Software 1        Bay 1 P1   FTP Data Data=[491 byte(s)]
134     4.2 ms         Bay 1 P1  FTP Software 1   TCP D=FTP Data S=1559
                                                    Ack=327712245
                                                    Seq=320537612
                                                    Len=0 Win=8568
135     830 us         Bay 1 P1  FTP Software 1   TCP D=FTP Data S=1559
                                                    Ack=327712737
                                                    Seq=320537612
                                                    Len=0 Win=8568
136    30.7 ms         Bay 1 P1  FTP Software 1   TCP D=FTP Data S=1559 FIN
                                                    Ack=327712737
                                                    Seq=320537612
                                                    Len=0 Win=8568
137     4.6 ms   FTP Software 1        Bay 1 P1   TCP D=1559 S=FTP Data
                                                    Ack=320537613
                                                    Seq=327712737
                                                    Len=0 Win=21419
138     1.0 ms         Bay 1 P1  FTP Software 1   FTP Command=TYPE I<0D><0A>
139     4.6 ms   FTP Software 1        Bay 1 P1   TCP D=1556 S=FTP
                                                    Ack=317875671
                                                    Seq=325084127
                                                    Len=0 Win=21420
140     6.0 ms   FTP Software 1        Bay 1 P1   FTP Command=200
                                                    Type set to I.<0D><0A>
141     1.5 ms         Bay 1 P1  FTP Software 1   TCP D=FTP S=1556
                                                    Ack=325084147
                                                    Seq=317875671
                                                    Len=0 Win=8568
142     1.2 sec        Bay 1 P1        Bay 1 P1   BOFL(WF) Seq=492
143     4.9 sec        Bay 1 P1        Bay 1 P1   BOFL(WF) Seq=493
144     3.1 sec        Bay 1 P1  FTP Software 1   FTP Command=TYPE I<0D><0A>
145     5.0 ms   FTP Software 1        Bay 1 P1   TCP D=1556 S=FTP
                                                    Ack=317875679
                                                    Seq=325084147
                                                    Len=0 Win=21420
```

146	6.0 ms	FTP Software 1	Bay 1 P1	FTP Command=200 Type set to I.<0D><0A>
147	1.7 ms	Bay 1 P1	FTP Software 1	TCP D=FTP S=1556 Ack=325084167 Seq=317875679 Len=0 Win=8568
148	202.6 ms	Bay 1 P1	FTP Software 1	FTP Command=LPRT 6,16,95,0,0,1,0,0,0,0,0, 0,0,128,199,95,159,61,2, 6,24<0D><0A>
149	5.0 ms	FTP Software 1	Bay 1 P1	TCP D=1556 S=FTP Ack=317875738 Seq=325084167 Len=0 Win=21420
150	6.3 ms	FTP Software 1	Bay 1 P1	FTP Command=200 LPRT command successful. <0D><0A>
151	1.5 ms	Bay 1 P1	FTP Software 1	TCP D=FTP S=1556 Ack=325084197 Seq=317875738 Len=0 Win=8568
152	60.3 ms	Bay 1 P1	FTP Software 1	FTP Command=RETR /RFC/RFC18XX/RFC1897.TXT <0D><0A>
153	4.7 ms	FTP Software 1	Bay 1 P1	TCP D=1556 S=FTP Ack=317875769 Seq=325084197 Len=0 Win=21420
154	336.3 ms	FTP Software 1	Bay 1 P1	TCP D=1560 S=FTP Data SYN Seq=329222757 Len=0 Win=20480
155	1.9 ms	Bay 1 P1	FTP Software 1	TCP D=FTP Data S=1560 SYN Ack=329222758 Seq=322045373 Len=0 Win=8568
156	1.1 ms	FTP Software 1	Bay 1 P1	FTP Command=150 Opening BINARY mode data connection for \RFC\RFC18XX\RFC1897.TXT (687 (more)
157	1.5 ms	Bay 1 P1	FTP Software 1	TCP D=FTP S=1556 Ack=325084281 Seq=317875769 Len=0 Win=8568
158	2.0 ms	FTP Software 1	Bay 1 P1	TCP D=1560 S=FTP Data Ack=322045374 Seq=329222758 Len=0 Win=21420

```
159   20.5 ms    FTP Software 1          Bay 1 P1   FTP Data Data=[1428 byte(s)]
160    100 us    FTP Software 1          Bay 1 P1   FTP Command=226
                                                      File transfer complete.
                                                      <0D><0A>
161    3.9 ms          Bay 1 P1    FTP Software 1   TCP D=FTP S=1556
                                                      Ack=325084310
                                                      Seq=317875769
                                                      Len=0 Win=8568
162  134.1 ms          Bay 1 P1    FTP Software 1   TCP D=FTP Data S=1560
                                                      Ack=329224186
                                                      Seq=322045374
                                                      Len=0 Win=8568
163   13.3 ms    FTP Software 1          Bay 1 P1   FTP Data Data=[1428 byte(s)]
164    3.9 ms    FTP Software 1          Bay 1 P1   FTP Data Data=[1428 byte(s)]
165    1.2 ms    FTP Software 1          Bay 1 P1   FTP Data Data=[1158 byte(s)]
166    3.2 ms    FTP Software 1          Bay 1 P1   FTP Data Data=[1428 byte(s)]
167    3.1 ms          Bay 1 P1    FTP Software 1   TCP D=FTP Data S=1560
                                                      Ack=329227042
                                                      Seq=322045374
                                                      Len=0 Win=8568
168    900 us          Bay 1 P1    FTP Software 1   TCP D=FTP Data S=1560
                                                      Ack=329227042
                                                      Seq=322045374
                                                      Len=0 Win=8568
169    700 us          Bay 1 P1    FTP Software 1   TCP D=FTP Data S=1560
                                                      Ack=329229629
                                                      Seq=322045374
                                                      Len=0 Win=8568
170   79.5 ms          Bay 1 P1    FTP Software 1   TCP D=FTP Data S=1560 FIN
                                                      Ack=329229629
                                                      Seq=322045374
                                                      Len=0 Win=8568
171    4.7 ms    FTP Software 1          Bay 1 P1   TCP D=1560 S=FTP Data
                                                      Ack=322045375
                                                      Seq=329229629
                                                      Len=0 Win=21419
172  927.6 ms          Bay 1 P1          Bay 1 P1   BOFL(WF) Seq=494
173  407.2 ms         Broadcast          Bay 1 P1   RIP (TCP/IP) Response
                                                      ID=IP Entries=4
174    1.2 sec 33-33-00-00-00-09         Bay 1 P1   UDP D=521 S=521 Len=72
175    3.3 sec         Bay 1 P1          Bay 1 P1   BOFL(WF) Seq=495
176    4.9 sec         Bay 1 P1          Bay 1 P1   BOFL(WF) Seq=496
177    4.9 sec         Bay 1 P1          Bay 1 P1   BOFL(WF) Seq=497
178    1.9 sec         Bay 1 P1    FTP Software 1   FTP Command=QUIT<0D><0A>
179    5.0 ms    FTP Software 1          Bay 1 P1   TCP D=1556 S=FTP
                                                      Ack=317875775
                                                      Seq=325084310
                                                      Len=0 Win=21420
```

```
180    5.9 ms    FTP Software 1          Bay 1 P1    FTP Command=221
                                                       Service closing control
                                                       connection.<0D><0A>
181    1.5 ms        Bay 1 P1       FTP Software 1   TCP D=FTP S=1556
                                                       Ack=325084351
                                                       Seq=317875775
                                                       Len=0 Win=8568
182    1.8 ms    FTP Software 1          Bay 1 P1    TCP D=1556 S=FTP FIN
                                                       Ack=317875775
                                                       Seq=325084351
                                                       Len=0 Win=21420
183    1.4 ms        Bay 1 P1       FTP Software 1   TCP D=FTP S=1556
                                                       Ack=325084352
                                                       Seq=317875775
                                                       Len=0 Win=8568
184   26.1 ms        Bay 1 P1       FTP Software 1   TCP D=FTP S=1556 FIN
                                                       Ack=325084352
                                                       Seq=317875775
                                                       Len=0 Win=8568
185    4.6 ms    FTP Software 1          Bay 1 P1    TCP D=1556 S=FTP
                                                       Ack=317875776
                                                       Seq=325084352
                                                       Len=0 Win=21419
```

Now let's turn our attention to the IPv6 packets that are sent from the FTP Client to the FTP Server via the internetwork, by tracing the formats and encapsulation of the FTP messages along the way. To do so, we will repeat the same file transfer four times, moving the analyzer from Subnet 242 to Subnet 243, to Subnet 244, and finally to Subnet 245. Figures 7-11a through 7-11d illustrate these four analyzer positions. Figures 7-12a through 7-12d illustrate the packet encapsulations at the same relative positions. (Note that in the trace files that follow, the frames of interest do *not* have the same frame number. This is because other protocols, such as BOFL, ICMPv6, and RIP are active on this internetwork; transmissions from these protocols may come at different times, changing the numerical sequence of the FTP messages that we are interested in. In addition, the FTP Client's port numbers, which we discussed above, will not be consistent throughout. This is because the Client is assigning these ports sequentially, and we are repeating the experiment four times. Therefore, with each pass of the experiment, we see the port numbers increment.)

Let's focus on one identifiable message, the command from the FTP Client to the FTP Server to retrieve the file RFC1897.TXT.

With the analyzer on Subnet 242 (Figure 7-11a), we can see the FTP RETR message that is encapsulated inside an IPv6 packet (Figure 7-12a). Of particular interest are the addresses that are used (Trace 7.5b). Note that the Ethernet addresses go from the FTP Client, shown as FTP Software 1 in the trace (00-80-C7-5F-9F-3D), to Port 1 on the Bay Networks Router (00-00-A2-0A-1F-B8). The IPv6 addresses go from end-to-end: the FTP Client (3FFE:1XXX:0:0:0:80:C75F:9F3D) to the FTP Server, shown as FTP Software 2 in the trace (3FFE:2XXX:0:0:0:0:C0A9:82B2). The TCP segments go from the Client port (1556) to the Server port (21). Finally, the FTP message identifies the file being retrieved: /RFC/RFC18XX/RFC1897.TXT. (Note that the ASCII characters <0D><0A> follow this and many other commands/responses in this case study. These are the hexadecimal representations of the carriage return and line feed characters, respectively.)

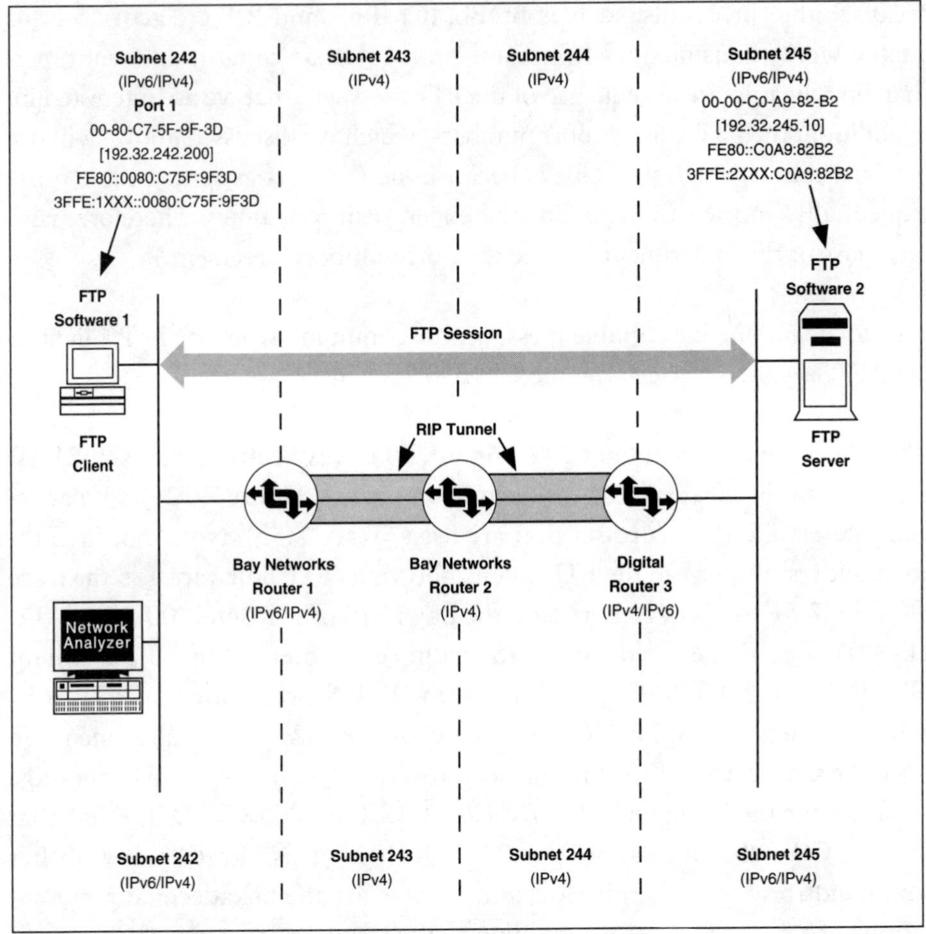

Figure 7-11a. Analyzer on Subnet 242

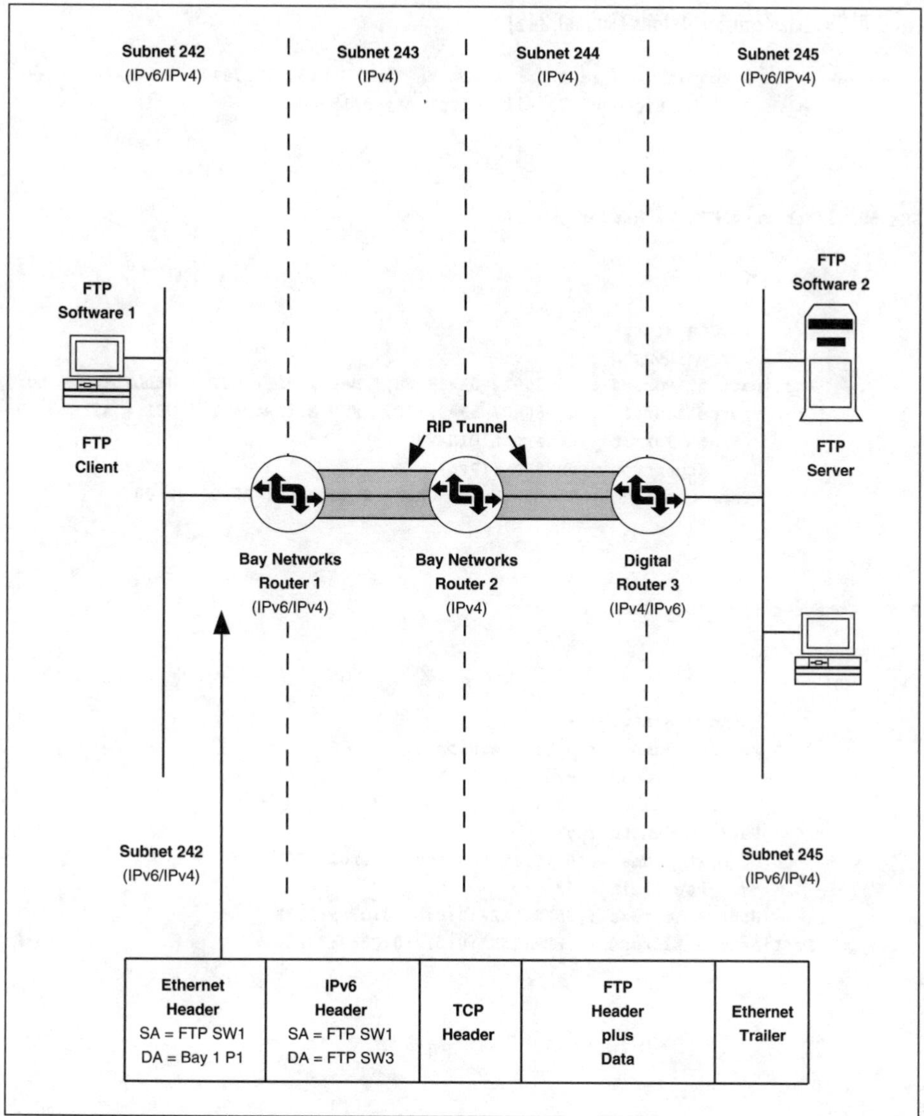

Figure 7-12a. Ethernet frame on Subnet 242

Trace 7.5b. File Transfer Details (Subnet 242)

```
--------------  Frame 152   Size 121   Absolute Time   5:50:33.78400   -------------
                        Protocol Detail - ftp1.cap 9/18


IEEE 802.3/Ethernet DIX V2 Header


             Decode Status : -
              Frame Length : 121
       Destination Address : 00-00-A2-0A-1F-B8,  Bay 1 P1 ( OUI = WELLFLEET, Indi
            Source Address : 00-80-C7-5F-9F-3D,  FTP Software 1 ( OUI = XIRCOM, U
              Frame Format : Ethernet DIX V2
                 Ethertype : 0x86DD (IPv6)
            Frame Checksum : Good,  Frame Check Sequence : 00 00 00 00


IPv6 - Internet Protocol (Version 6)


             Decode Status : -
            Version Number : 6 (IP Version 6)
                     Class : 0x0
                Flow Label : 0x0
            Payload Length : 63
               Next Header : 6 (Transmission Control (TCP))
                 Hop Limit : 63
            Source Address : 3FFE:1XXX:0:0:0:80:C75F:9F3D
       Destination Address : 3FFE:2XXX:0:0:0:0:C0A9:82B2
```

```
TCP - Transport Control Protocol


                Decode Status : -
                  Source Port : 1556 (Unknown)
             Destination Port : 21 (FTP)
              Sequence Number : 317875738
        Acknowledgement Number : 325084197
                  Data Offset : 0x80
                                1000 .... = Header length = 32
                        Flags : 0x18
                                ..0. .... = No Urgent pointer
                                ...1 .... = Acknowledgement
                                .... 1... = Push
                                .... .0.. = No Reset
                                .... ..0. = No Synchronize Sequence numbers
                                .... ...0 = No End of data flow from sender
                       Window : 8568
                     Checksum : 0x991B (Checksum Good)
               Urgent pointer : 0
                         Kind : 1 (No-Operation)
                         Kind : 1 (No-Operation)
                         Kind : 8 (Unknown option)
                      Padding : 0A 00 00 11 72 00 00 11 D9


FTP - File Transfer Protocol


                Decode Status : -
                      Command : RETR /RFC/RFC18XX/RFC1897.TXT<0D><0A>
```

Moving the analyzer to Subnet 243 (Figure 7-11b), we can see the FTP RETR message that is encapsulated inside an IPv6 packet, and then further encapsulated inside an IPv4 datagram (Figure 7-12b). Reviewing the topology of this internetwork, recall that an IPv4 tunnel exists between Bay Router 1, Port 2, and the Digital Router, Port 1. To cross this tunnel, IPv4 encapsulation is required.

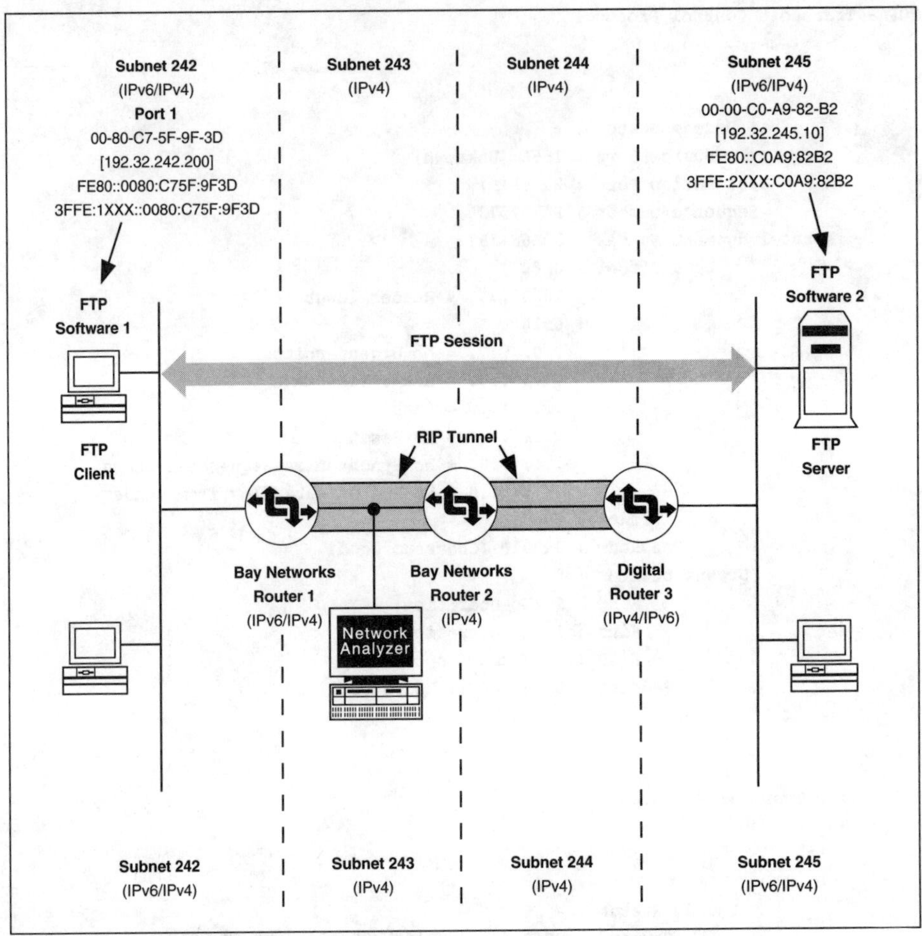

Figure 7-11b. Analyzer on Subnet 243

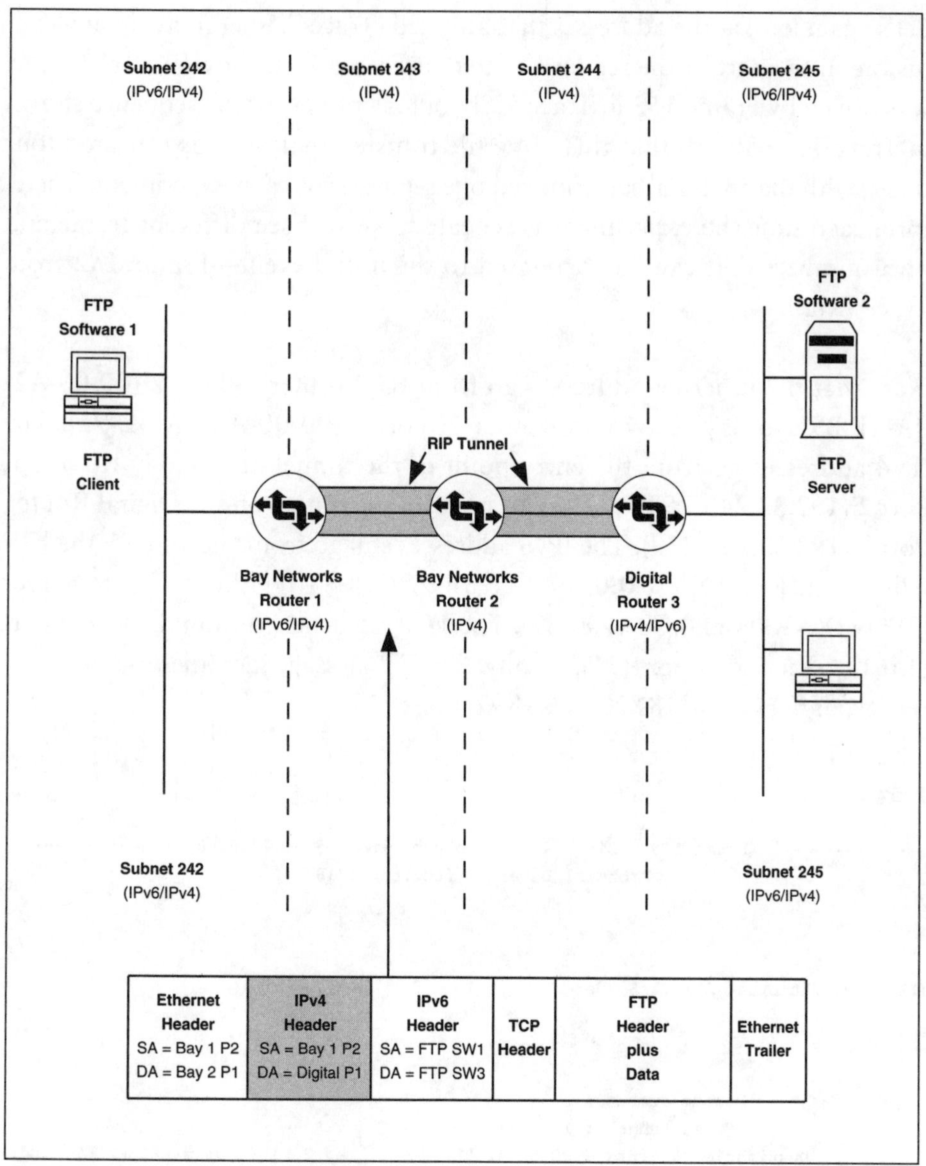

Figure 7-12b. Ethernet frame on Subnet 243

Let's again look at the addresses that are used (Trace 7.5c). (To avoid any confusion on the part of the readers, note that Frame 168, shown in Trace 7.5c, was driven by Frame 152 in Trace 7.5b, but is not part of the sequence shown in Trace 7.5a. Recall that this same file transfer analysis was repeated four times, with the analyzer being moved one segment for each experiment. Therefore, each time the experiment is repeated, we will see different frame and port numbers that can be correlated to the initial event—Frame 152 from Trace 7.5a.)

Note that the Ethernet addresses go from Bay Router 1, Port 2 (00-00-A2-0A-1F-B9), to Bay Networks Router 2, Port 1 (00-00-A2-0A-4E-92). The IPv4 addresses go from the entry point of the tunnel on the Bay Router 1, Port 2 (192.32.243.250), to the exit point of the tunnel on the Digital Router, Port 1 (192.32.244.250). The IPv6 addresses still go from end-to-end: the FTP Client (3FFE:1XXX:0:0:0:80:C75F:9F3D) to the FTP Server (3FFE:2XXX:0:0:0:0:C0A9:82B2). The TCP segments go from the Client port (1561) to the Server port (21). Finally, the FTP message identifies the file being retrieved: /RFC/RFC18XX/RFC1897.TXT.

Trace 7.5c. File Transfer Details (Subnet 243)

```
-------------- Frame 168   Size 141   Absolute Time   5:52:47.56605--------------
                          Protocol Detail - ftp2.cap 9/18


IEEE 802.3/Ethernet DIX V2 Header


           Decode Status : -
            Frame Length : 141
     Destination Address : 00-00-A2-0A-4E-92,  Bay 2 P1 ( OUI = WELLFLEET, Indi
          Source Address : 00-00-A2-0A-1F-B9,  Bay 1 P2 ( OUI = WELLFLEET, Univ
            Frame Format : Ethernet DIX V2
               Ethertype : 0x800 (IP)
          Frame Checksum : Good,  Frame Check Sequence : 00 00 00 00
```

```
IP - Internet Protocol


           Decode Status : -
                 Version : 4,  Header length : 20
         Type of Service : 0x00
                           000. .... = Routine Precedence
                           ...0 .... = Normal Delay
                           .... 0... = Normal Throughput
                           .... .0.. = Normal Reliability
                           .... ..00 = Reserved
            Total length : 123 bytes
          Identification : 1931
        Fragment Control : 0x00
                           0... .... .... .... = Reserved
                           .0.. .... .... .... = May Fragment
                           ..0. .... .... .... = Last Fragment
                           ...0 0000 0000 0000 = Fragment Offset = 0 bytes
            Time to Live : 30 seconds/hops
                Protocol : 41 (IPv6)
                Checksum : 0x2B99 (Checksum Good)
          Source Address : 192.32.243.250
     Destination Address : 192.32.244.250
 No IP options


IPv6 - Internet Protocol (Version 6)


           Decode Status : -
          Version Number : 6 (IP Version 6)
                   Class : 0x0
              Flow Label : 0x0
          Payload Length : 63
             Next Header : 6 (Transmission Control (TCP))
               Hop Limit : 62
          Source Address : 3FFE:1XXX:0:0:0:80:C75F:9F3D
     Destination Address : 3FFE:2XXX:0:0:0:0:C0A9:82B2
```

```
TCP - Transport Control Protocol


             Decode Status : -
               Source Port : 1561 (Unknown)
          Destination Port : 21 (FTP)
           Sequence Number : 338729387
    Acknowledgement Number : 345907340
               Data Offset : 0x80
                             1000 .... = Header length = 32
                     Flags : 0x18
                             ..0. .... = No Urgent pointer
                             ...1 .... = Acknowledgement
                             .... 1... = Push
                             .... .0.. = No Reset
                             .... ..0. = No Synchronize Sequence numbers
                             .... ...0 = No End of data flow from sender
                    Window : 8568
                  Checksum : 0xA494 (Checksum Good)
            Urgent pointer : 0
                      Kind : 1 (No-Operation)
                      Kind : 1 (No-Operation)
                      Kind : 8 (Unknown option)
                   Padding : 0A 00 00 12 79 00 00 12 E0


FTP - File Transfer Protocol


             Decode Status : -
                   Command : RETR /RFC/RFC18XX/RFC1897.TXT<0D><0A>
```

Moving the analyzer to Subnet 244 (Figure 7-11c), we can see the FTP RETR message that is again encapsulated inside an IPv6 packet, and then further encapsulated inside an IPv4 datagram (Figure 7-12c). Reviewing the topology of this internetwork, recall that an IPv4 tunnel exists between Bay Router 1, Port 2, and the Digital Router, Port 1. To cross this tunnel, IPv4 encapsulation is required.

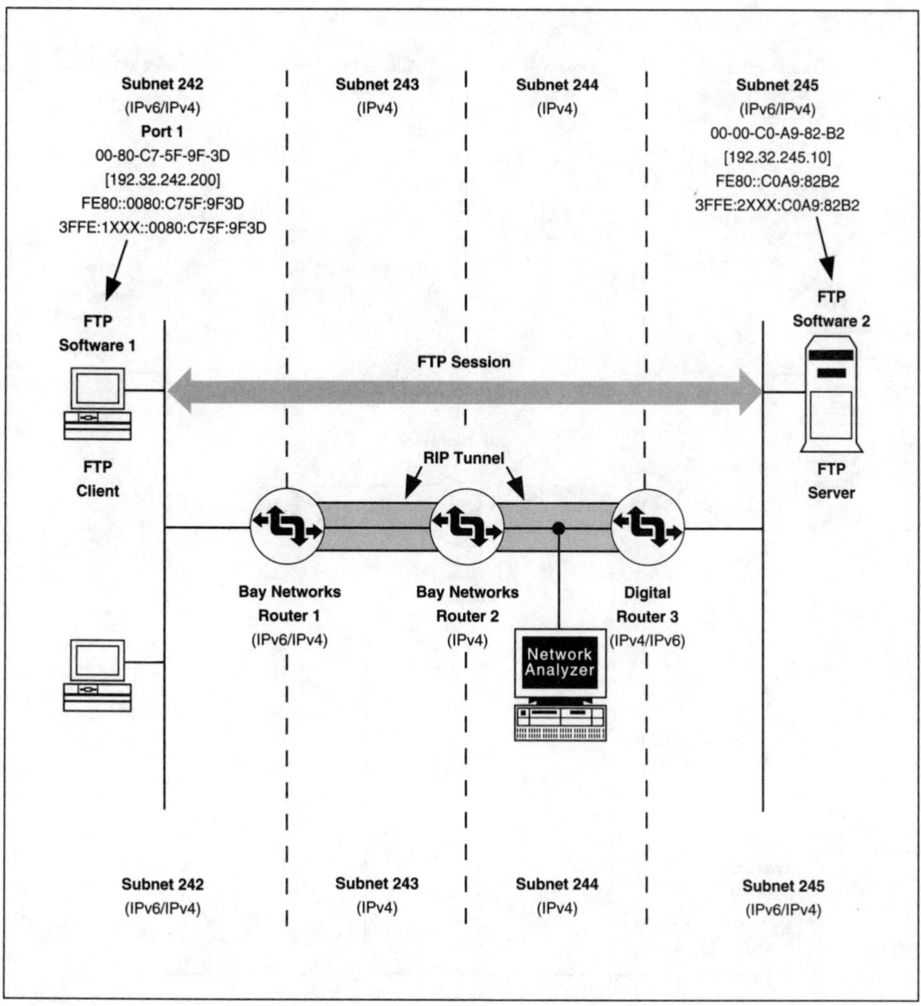

Figure 7-11c. Analyzer on Subnet 244

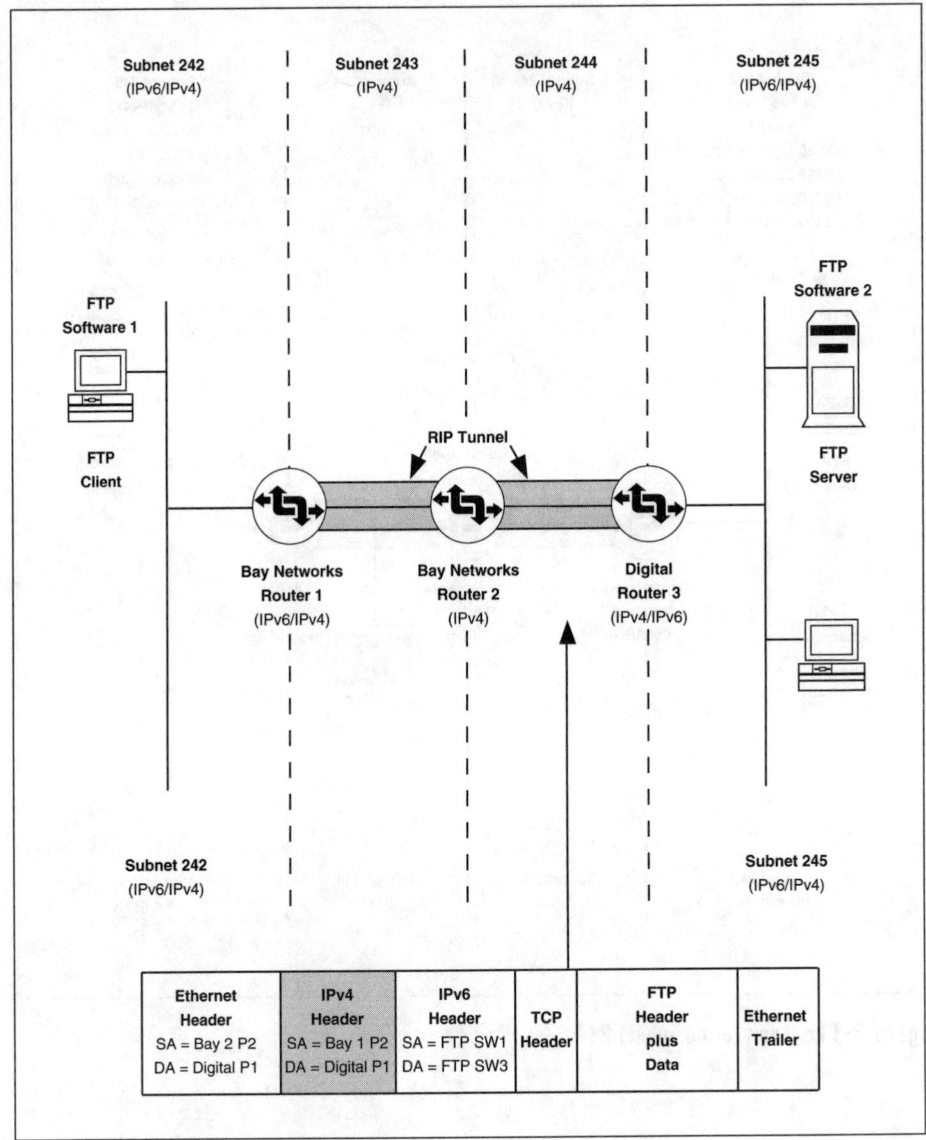

Figure 7-12c. Ethernet frame on Subnet 244

Let's again look at the addresses that are used (Trace 7.5d). (As before, Frame 169 in Trace 7.5d was driven by Frame 152 in Trace 7.5a.)

Note that the Ethernet addresses go from Bay Router 2, Port 2 (00-00-A2-0A-4E-93), to the Digital Router, Port 1 (08-00-2B-B3-FD-44). The IPv4 addresses still go from the entry point of the tunnel on the Bay Router 1, Port 2 (192.32.243.250), to the exit point of the tunnel on the Digital Router, Port 1 (192.32.244.250). The IPv6 addresses still go from end-to-end: the FTP Client (3FFE:1XXX:0:0:0:80:C75F:9F3D) to the FTP Server (3FFE:2XXX:0:0:0:0:C0A9:82B2). The TCP segments go from the Client port (1566) to the Server port (21). Finally, the FTP message identifies the file being retrieved: /RFC/RFC18XX/RFC1897.TXT.

Trace 7.5d. File Transfer Details (Subnet 244)

```
-------------    Frame 169    Size 141    Absolute Time    5:54:44.95517-------------
                         Protocol Detail - ftp3.cap 9/18


IEEE 802.3/Ethernet DIX V2 Header


                Decode Status : -
                 Frame Length : 141
          Destination Address : 08-00-2B-B3-FD-44,  Digital P1 ( OUI = DEC, Individu
               Source Address : 00-00-A2-0A-4E-93,  Bay 2 P2 ( OUI = WELLFLEET, Univ
                 Frame Format : Ethernet DIX V2
                    Ethertype : 0x800 (IP)
               Frame Checksum : Good,  Frame Check Sequence : 00 00 00 00
```

```
IP - Internet Protocol


              Decode Status : -
                    Version : 4,  Header length : 20
            Type of Service : 0x00
                              000. .... = Routine Precedence
                              ...0 .... = Normal Delay
                              .... 0... = Normal Throughput
                              .... .0.. = Normal Reliability
                              .... ..00 = Reserved
               Total length : 123 bytes
             Identification : 2023
           Fragment Control : 0x00
                              0... .... .... .... = Reserved
                              .0.. .... .... .... = May Fragment
                              ..0. .... .... .... = Last Fragment
                              ...0 0000 0000 0000 = Fragment Offset = 0 bytes
               Time to Live : 29 seconds/hops
                   Protocol : 41 (IPv6)
                   Checksum : 0x2C3D (Checksum Good)
             Source Address : 192.32.243.250
        Destination Address : 192.32.244.250
 No IP options


IPv6 - Internet Protocol (Version 6)


              Decode Status : -
             Version Number : 6 (IP Version 6)
                      Class : 0x0
                 Flow Label : 0x0
             Payload Length : 63
                Next Header : 6 (Transmission Control (TCP))
                  Hop Limit : 62
             Source Address : 3FFE:1XXX:0:0:0:80:C75F:9F3D
        Destination Address : 3FFE:2XXX:0:0:0:0:C0A9:82B2
```

```
TCP - Transport Control Protocol


              Decode Status : -
                Source Port : 1566 (Unknown)
           Destination Port : 21 (FTP)
            Sequence Number : 356015910
     Acknowledgement Number : 363118230
                Data Offset : 0x80
                              1000 .... = Header length = 32
                      Flags : 0x18
                              ..0. .... = No Urgent pointer
                              ...1 .... = Acknowledgement
                              .... 1... = Push
                              .... .0.. = No Reset
                              .... ..0. = No Synchronize Sequence numbers
                              .... ...0 = No End of data flow from sender
                     Window : 8568
                   Checksum : 0x3D2E (Checksum Good)
             Urgent pointer : 0
                       Kind : 1 (No-Operation)
                       Kind : 1 (No-Operation)
                       Kind : 8 (Unknown option)
                    Padding : 0A 00 00 13 60 00 00 13 C7


FTP - File Transfer Protocol


              Decode Status : -
                    Command : RETR /RFC/RFC18XX/RFC1897.TXT<0D><0A>
```

Moving the analyzer to Subnet 245 (Figure 7-11d), we can see the FTP RETR message that is again encapsulated inside an IPv6 packet, but no longer encapsulated inside an IPv4 datagram (Figure 7-12d). The Digital Router, seeing the end of the tunnel, has decapsulated the IPv6 packet, removing the IPv4 header.

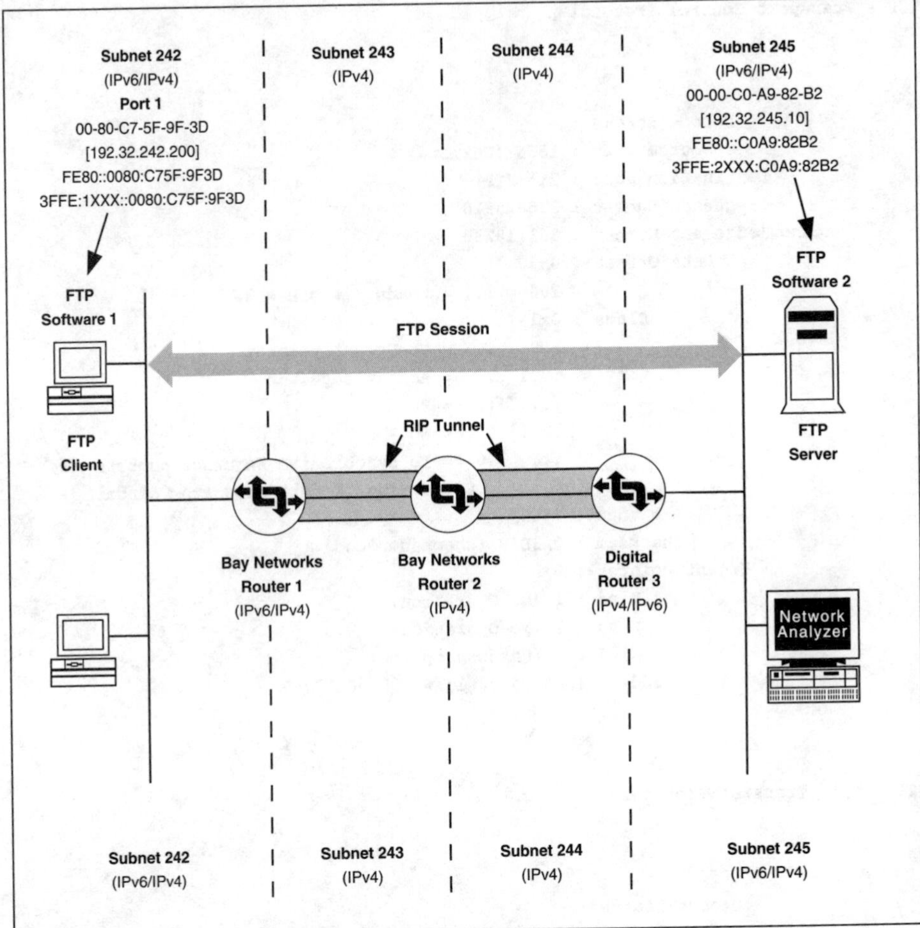

Figure 7-11d. Analyzer on Subnet 245

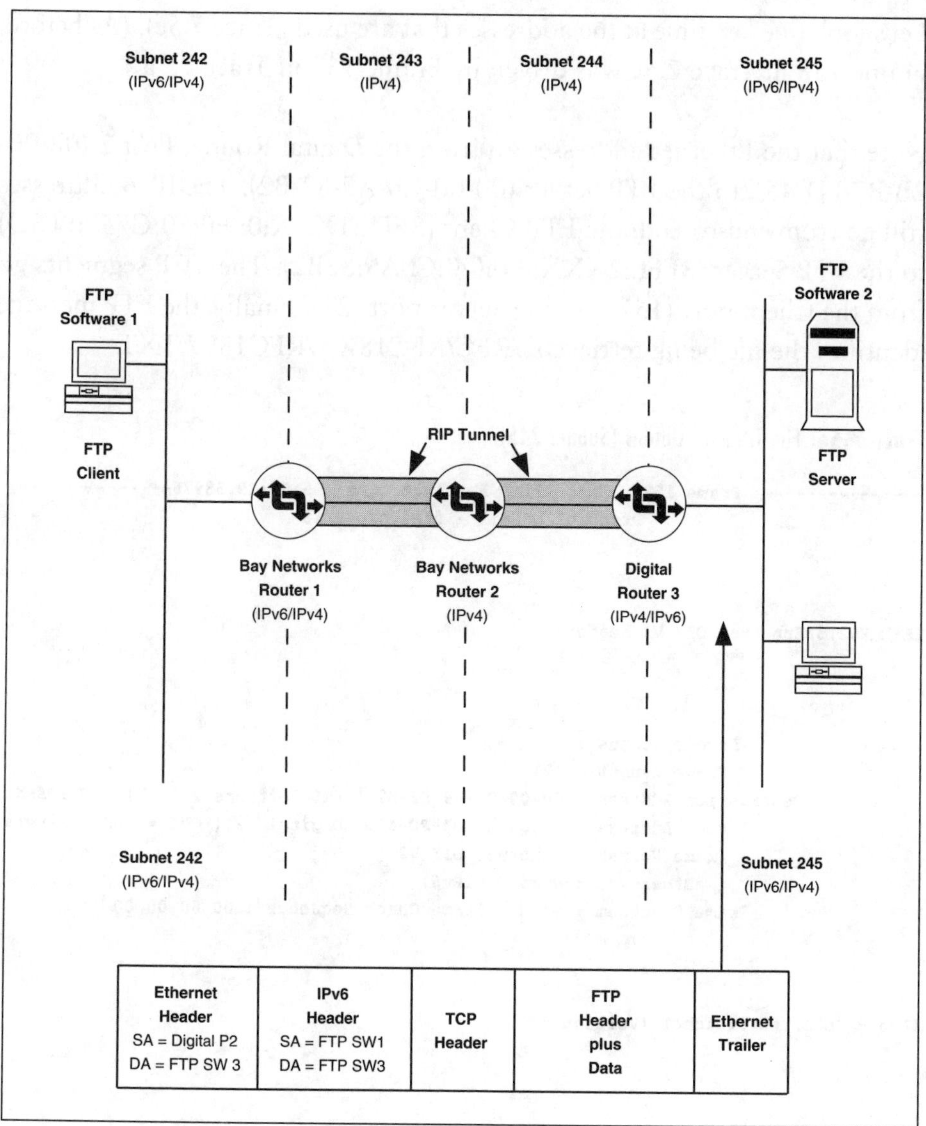

Figure 7-12d. Ethernet frame on Subnet 245

Let's look one last time at the addresses that are used (Trace 7.5e). (As before, Frame 158 in Trace 7.5e was driven by Frame 152 in Trace 7.5a.)

Note that the Ethernet addresses go from the Digital Router, Port 2 (08-00-2B-B3-FD-45), to the FTP Server (00-00-C0-A9-82-B2). The IPv6 addresses still go from end-to-end: the FTP Client (3FFE:1XXX:0:0:0:80:C75F:9F3D) to the FTP Server (3FFE:2XXX:0:0:0:0:C0A9:82B2). The TCP segments go from the Client port (1571) to the Server port (21). Finally, the FTP message identifies the file being retrieved: /RFC/RFC18XX/RFC1897.TXT.

Trace 7.5e. File Transfer Details (Subnet 245)

```
-------------    Frame 158   Size 121   Absolute Time   5:56:29.58976-------------
                          Protocol Detail - ftp4.cap 9/18


IEEE 802.3/Ethernet DIX V2 Header


              Decode Status : -
               Frame Length : 121
        Destination Address : 00-00-C0-A9-82-B2,  FTP Software 2 ( OUI = WESTERN D
             Source Address : 08-00-2B-B3-FD-45,  Digital P2 ( OUI = DEC, Universa
               Frame Format : Ethernet DIX V2
                  Ethertype : 0x86DD (IPv6)
             Frame Checksum : Good,  Frame Check Sequence : 00 00 00 00


IPv6 - Internet Protocol (Version 6)


              Decode Status : -
             Version Number : 6 (IP Version 6)
                      Class : 0x0
                 Flow Label : 0x0
             Payload Length : 63
                Next Header : 6 (Transmission Control (TCP))
                  Hop Limit : 61
             Source Address : 3FFE:1XXX:0:0:0:80:C75F:9F3D
        Destination Address : 3FFE:2XXX:0:0:0:0:C0A9:82B2
```

```
TCP - Transport Control Protocol


            Decode Status : -
              Source Port : 1571 (Unknown)
         Destination Port : 21 (FTP)
          Sequence Number : 371029497
   Acknowledgement Number : 377962809
              Data Offset : 0x80
                            1000 .... = Header length = 32
                    Flags : 0x18
                            ..0. .... = No Urgent pointer
                            ...1 .... = Acknowledgement
                            .... 1... = Push
                            .... .0.. = No Reset
                            .... ..0. = No Synchronize Sequence numbers
                            .... ...0 = No End of data flow from sender
                   Window : 8568
                 Checksum : 0xA04E (Checksum Good)
           Urgent pointer : 0
                     Kind : 1 (No-Operation)
                     Kind : 1 (No-Operation)
                     Kind : 8 (Unknown option)
                  Padding : 0A 00 00 14 2E 00 00 14 96


FTP - File Transfer Protocol


            Decode Status : -
                  Command : RETR /RFC/RFC18XX/RFC1897.TXT<0D><0A>
```

In this chapter, we have studied a number of the mechanisms that support IPv6 on hosts. Perhaps of greatest interest here are the issues concerning IP security, which are being driven, in part, by the commercial use of the Internet and the need for secure transmissions of banking information, credit card orders, and so on. This is one area that is also the subject of a great deal of research. It is expected that the ongoing work in AH and ESP may enhance some of the proposed packet formats described in this chapter. Interested readers should keep abreast of these topics by monitoring the IP Security Mailing List [7-7], and by obtaining the most recent RFC and Internet Draft documents in this subject area.

In our next chapter, we will consider the network management tools that have been developed in support of IPv6.

7.6 References

[7-1] Deering, S., and R. Hinden. "Internet Protocol, Version 6 (IPv6) Specification." RFC 1883, Date.

[7-2] Deering, S. and R. Hinden. "Internet Protocol, Version 6 (IPv6) Specification." Work in progress, July 30, 1997.

[7-3] Thomson, S., and C. Huitema. "DNS Extensions to Support IP Version 6." RFC 1886, December 1995.

[7-4] Gilligan, R., et al. "Basic Socket Interface Extensions for IPv6." RFC 2133, April 1997.

[7-5] Stevens, W. Richard and Matt Thomas. Advanced Sockets API for IPv6. Work in progress, July 21, 1997.

[7-6] Harrington, Daniel T., et al. "Internet Protocol Version 6 and the Digital UNIX Implementation Experience." *Digital Technical Journal*, Volume 8, Number 3, 1996 (5–22).

[7-7] The IP Security Mailing List is sponsored by the IP Security Working Group, which is an open forum for discussing the standards efforts regarding IP security. The list address is ipsec@.tis.com. To subscribe, send email to: *majordomo@tis.com*, with the following in the message body: *subscribe ipsec*.

[7-8] Kaufman, Charlie, Radia Perlman, and Mike Speciner. *Network Security—Private Communication in a Public World*. Englewood Cliffs, NJ: PTR Prentice Hall, 1995.

[7-9] Smith, Richard E. *Internet Cryptography*. Reading, Massachusetts: Addison Wesley, 1997.

[7-10] Hudgins-Bonafield, Christy. "Mapping the Rocky Road to Authentication." *Network Computing* (July 15, 1997): 26–27.

[7-11] Atkinson, R. "Security Architecture for the Internet Protocol." RFC 1825, August 1995.

[7-12] Kent, Stephen, and Randall Atkinson. "Security Architecture for the Internet Protocol." Work in progress, July 30, 1997.

[7-13] Atkinson, R. "IP Authentication Header." RFC 1826, August 1995.

[7-14] Kent, Stephen, and Randall Atkinson. "IP Authentication Header." Work in progress, October 2, 1997.

[7-15] Krawczyk, Hugo, et al. "HMAC: Keyed-Hashing for Message Authentication." RFC 2104, February 1997.

[7-16] Rivest, Ronald. "The MD5 Message Digest Algorithm." RFC 1321, April 1992.

[7-17] Atkinson, R. "IP Encapsulating Security Payload (ESP)." RFC 1827, August 1995.

[7-18] Kent, Stephen, and Randall Atkinson. "IP Encapsulating Security Payload (ESP)." Work in progress, October 2, 1997.

[7-19] Karn, P., et al. "The ESP DES-CBC Transform." RFC 1829, August 1995.

[7-20] Fraser, B., editor. "Site Security Handbook." RFC 2196, September 1997.

8 Managing IPv6 Internetworks

As we have studied thus far, the enhancements that IPv6 brings to internetworks also bring increased levels of network management complexities. Fortunately, the Internet community has enhanced the network management support processes at the same time. These enhancements are based upon the Simple Network Management Protocol (SNMP), with the addition of new Management Information Bases, or MIBs, that support IPv6 processes. But before we look at these enhancements, let's have a quick review of network management concepts in general, and SNMP in particular. Readers unfamiliar with SNMP may find a companion volume, *Managing Internetworks with SNMP*, Second edition [8-1] to be helpful.

8.1 The Agent/Manager Paradigm

Internet-based network management systems are designed around the concept of an Agent/Manager paradigm, as shown in Figure 8-1. The purpose of the Agent/Manager system is to manage *objects*, which are various elements of the system being managed. For example, a workstation would have objects describing its processor, memory, storage capabilities, display, peripheral ports, and so on, plus possibly past or current status information concerning those various objects.

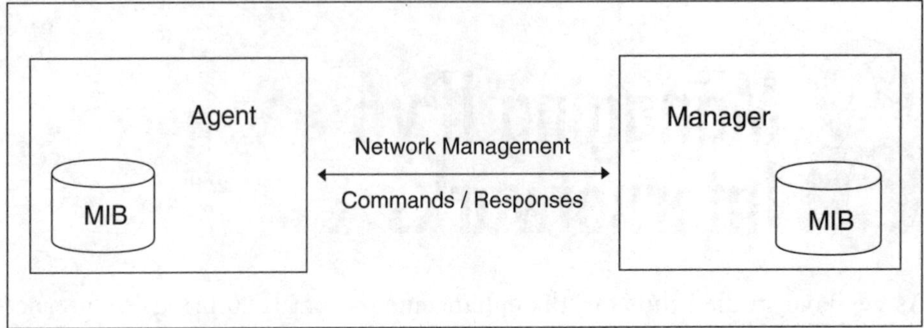

Figure 8-1. The Agent/Manager model

The *Agent*, which typically resides inside a hardware device, such as a router, server, or host, implements the network management process at that device. Its purpose is to report the various objects' current statuses to the Manager. The *Manager*, or console, is the system that is controlling the network management functions and maintaining global knowledge of the entire internetwork. In most cases, the Agent is a rather simple process, designed so that it does not place a processing burden on the single device that it is residing in, such as a router or a server. In contrast, most Managers have extensive processing capabilities, and are typically UNIX or Windows NT workstations designed to handle information concerning hundreds, or possibly thousands of Agents, and to manipulate and graphically display network information (data) in a way easily understood by human users.

The Agent/Manager model operates using three architectural elements: the Structure of Management Information (SMI); the Management Information Base, or MIB; and the Protocol, or SNMP. The SMI identifies the structures that describe the management information; the MIB is a virtual information store that describes and stores the objects being managed; and the SNMP provides a communication mechanism between Agent and Manager.

Taken together, the SMI, the MIB, and the Protocol are called the Internet Network Management Framework. To date, two versions of this framework have been published, supporting SNMPv1 and SNMPv2. The relevant documents are:

Internet Network Management Framework	SMI RFCs	MIB RFCs	Protocol RFCs
SNMPv1	1155	1213	1157
SNMPv2	1902	1907	1905

At the time of this writing, work is underway on a third version of the Internet Network Management Framework, called SNMPv3.

In the following sections, we will discuss the SMI, the MIB, and the SNMP within the context of support for IPv6.

8.2 The Structure of Management Information

Since internetworks can be quite large and can maintain voluminous amounts of information about each device, network managers need a way to organize and manage that information. The SMI provides a mechanism to name and organize objects. The MIB then stores the information about each managed object.

The SMI uses a conceptual tree, with various objects representing the leaves, to help users visualize the structure of the Internet. The objects are represented using the concepts from an ISO message description standard known as Abstract Syntax Notation—1 (ASN.1). The SMI assigns each object a sequence of integers, known as an *Object Identifier*, to locate its position on the tree (Figure 8-2).

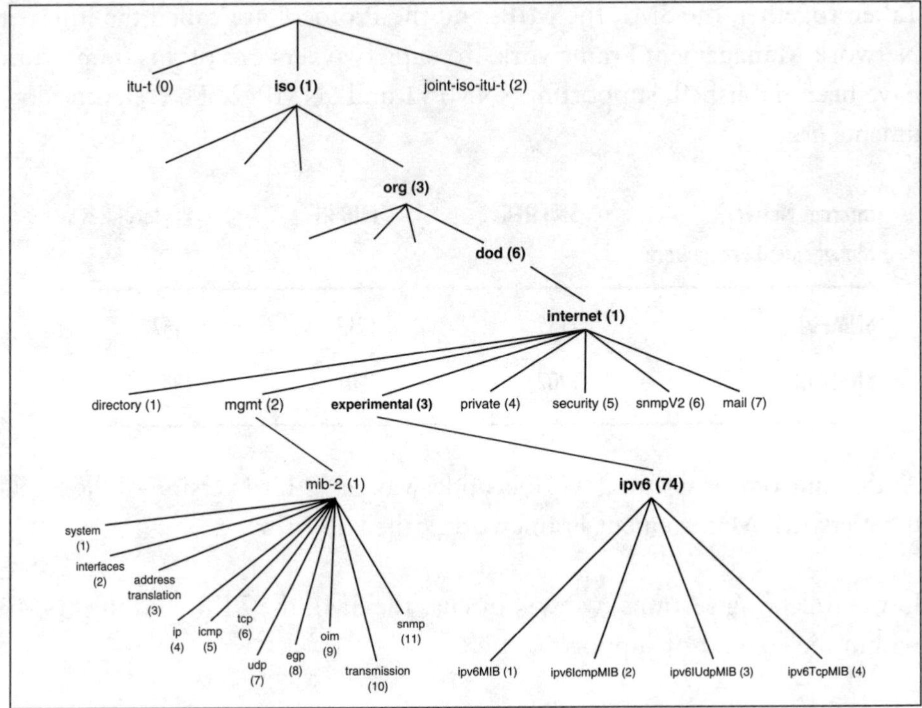

Figure 8-2. Internet OID tree and the proposed IPv6 branch

The root of the tree has no name, but it has three branches, or arcs. Different standards bodies administer different branches: the ITU-T is in charge of Branch 0; ISO administers Branch 1; ITU-T and ISO jointly administer Branch 2.

ISO designates its branch for several organizations. For example, it has given Branch 3 to other international organizations. ISO gives Branch 1 to the U.S. Department of Defense (designated *dod*), which uses it for the Internet objects. So far in the Internet branch, all Object Identifiers begin with {1.3.6.1}, which means that their path from the root is *iso*, *org*, *dod*, *internet*. Historically, Object Identifiers have been enclosed in curly braces to designate them as such.

Under the Internet branch are seven arcs: *directory* (1), *mgmt* (2), *experimental* (3), *private* (4), *security* (5), *SNMPV2* (6), and *mail* (7). *Directory* is planned for the OSI Directory; *mgmt* is used for objects defined in the Internet Activities Board (IAB)-approved documents; *experimental* is used for Internet experiments; *private* is used to define vendor-specific (or private MIB) objects; *security* is for management security; *SNMPV2* contains SNMPv2-specific objects; and *mail* is for mail-related objects.

The Internet Assigned Numbers Authority (IANA) administers the *experimental* and *private* branches, and documents these administrations in the Assigned Numbers document (currently RFC 1700). The *experimental* branch is the area where MIBs for new technologies (such as IPv6) are initially assigned. After some implementation experience, these experimental MIB branches are moved elsewhere, such as under the *mgmt* branch.

IANA designates Branch 1 under the *private* branch for enterprises and assigns vendors an enterprise branch to identify their various devices. For example, an Object Identifier associated with the ABC Company would be designated {1.3.6.1.4.1.a}. The {1.3.6.1} designates the *internet* branch; 4.1 indicates a *private, enterprise* branch; and *a* is assigned to the ABC Company. The ABC Company could further assign identifiers for its bridges, routers, NICs, and so on; for example, {1.3.6.1.4.1.a.1.1}.

In addition to the Object Identifier, the SMI defines the manner in which the data within each object will be represented and stored. These formats are called *datatypes*, or simply *types*. For example, the IpAddress type represents a 32-bit IPv4 address, while the IPv6Address type represents a 128-bit IPv6 address. Further explanations about the syntax and usage of the types are given in the baseline SMI document, RFC 1902 [8-2].

8.3 The Management Information Base

While the SMI defines the tree structure for the Object Identifiers, the MIB defines information about the actual objects being managed and/or controlled. For example, the MIB might store an IP routing table and its table entries.

Two versions of the Internet MIB for SNMPv1 have been published: MIB-1, RFC 1156; and the enhanced MIB-2, RFCs 1212 and 1213 [8-3]. MIB-2 has rendered the Address Translation (at) group obsolete and added the Transmission and SNMP groups. MIB-2 has also added new values, variables, tables, columns, and so on to other groups. For SNMPv2, a separate MIB, documented in RFC 1907, is defined. At the time of this writing, the SNMPv1 MIB is the most widely implemented.

Within each MIB, the objects are divided into various groups. Grouping the objects accomplishes two objectives: it allows a more orderly assignment of Object Identifiers, and it defines the objects that the Agents must implement. The currently defined groups include:

Group	Object ID	Description
system	mib-2 1	Description of that entity.
interfaces	mib-2 2	Number of network interfaces that can send/receive IP datagrams.
at	mib-2 3	Tables of Network Address to Physical Address translations.
ip	mib-2 4	IP routing and datagram statistics.
icmp	mib-2 5	ICMP I/O statistics.
tcp	mib-2 6	TCP connection parameters and statistics.
udp	mib-2 7	UDP traffic statistics and datagram delivery problems.
egp	mib-2 8	EGP traffic, neighbors, and states.
transmission	mib-2 10	Transmission media information (future use).
snmp	mib-2 11	SNMP-related objects.

Note that the mib-2 9 group is no longer used.

MIB modules are collections of objects into convenient groups. For example, MIB modules have been written in support of Ethernet objects (RFC 1650), token ring objects (RFC 1743), frame relay objects (RFC 1315), parallel printer objects (RFC 1660), and many others. These modules are sometimes called *MIB extensions*; they are given a unique branch in the OID tree, typically under mib-2.

The MIB modules written in support of IPv6 are divided into four groups: General, ICMP, UDP, and TCP (review Figure 8-2). Each of these object groups contains multiple objects, many of which are organized into tables. As a minimum, the General and ICMP groups must be implemented. Other groups are implemented as necessary, with the understanding that if a group is implemented, all objects in that group must be implemented.

The following sections will discuss these four groups separately.

8.3.1 IPv6 General Group

The IPv6 General Group is the MIB module for entities that implement the IPv6 protocol. This module is proposed in Reference [8-4] and is comprised of six tables (Figure 8-3):

- ipv6IfTable, which contains information on the entity's IPv6 interfaces
- ipv6IfStatsTable, which contains information on the traffic statistics of the entity's IPv6 interfaces
- ipv6AddrPrefixTable, which contains information on Address Prefixes that are associated with the entity's IPv6 interfaces
- ipv6AddrTable, which contains the addressing information relevant to the entity's IPv6 interfaces
- ipv6RouteTable, which contains an entry for each valid IPv6 unicast route that can be used for packet forwarding determination
- ipv6NetToMediaTable, which is an IPv6 address translation table that contains the IPv6 address to physical address equivalencies

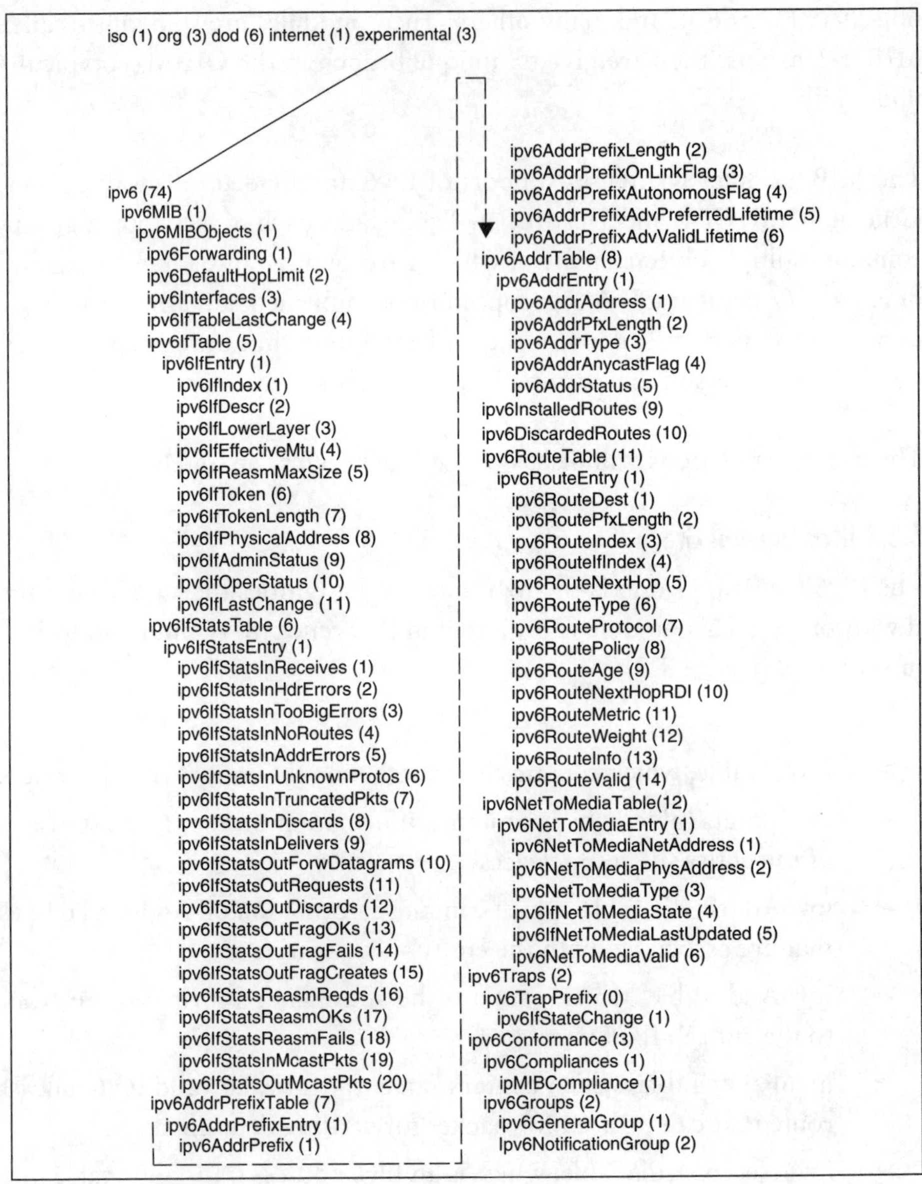
iso (1) org (3) dod (6) internet (1) experimental (3)
ipv6 (74)
ipv6MIB (1)
ipv6MIBObjects (1)
ipv6Forwarding (1)
ipv6DefaultHopLimit (2)
ipv6Interfaces (3)
ipv6IfTableLastChange (4)
ipv6IfTable (5)
ipv6IfEntry (1)
ipv6IfIndex (1)
ipv6IfDescr (2)
ipv6IfLowerLayer (3)
ipv6IfEffectiveMtu (4)
ipv6IfReasmMaxSize (5)
ipv6IfToken (6)
ipv6IfTokenLength (7)
ipv6IfPhysicalAddress (8)
ipv6IfAdminStatus (9)
ipv6IfOperStatus (10)
ipv6IfLastChange (11)
ipv6IfStatsTable (6)
ipv6IfStatsEntry (1)
ipv6IfStatsInReceives (1)
ipv6IfStatsInHdrErrors (2)
ipv6IfStatsInTooBigErrors (3)
ipv6IfStatsInNoRoutes (4)
ipv6IfStatsInAddrErrors (5)
ipv6IfStatsInUnknownProtos (6)
ipv6IfStatsInTruncatedPkts (7)
ipv6IfStatsInDiscards (8)
ipv6IfStatsInDelivers (9)
ipv6IfStatsOutForwDatagrams (10)
ipv6IfStatsOutRequests (11)
ipv6IfStatsOutDiscards (12)
ipv6IfStatsOutFragOKs (13)
ipv6IfStatsOutFragFails (14)
ipv6IfStatsOutFragCreates (15)
ipv6IfStatsReasmReqds (16)
ipv6IfStatsReasmOKs (17)
ipv6IfStatsReasmFails (18)
ipv6IfStatsInMcastPkts (19)
ipv6IfStatsOutMcastPkts (20)
ipv6AddrPrefixTable (7)
ipv6AddrPrefixEntry (1)
ipv6AddrPrefix (1)
ipv6AddrPrefixLength (2)
ipv6AddrPrefixOnLinkFlag (3)
ipv6AddrPrefixAutonomousFlag (4)
ipv6AddrPrefixAdvPreferredLifetime (5)
ipv6AddrPrefixAdvValidLifetime (6)
ipv6AddrTable (8)
ipv6AddrEntry (1)
ipv6AddrAddress (1)
ipv6AddrPfxLength (2)
ipv6AddrType (3)
ipv6AddrAnycastFlag (4)
ipv6AddrStatus (5)
ipv6InstalledRoutes (9)
ipv6DiscardedRoutes (10)
ipv6RouteTable (11)
ipv6RouteEntry (1)
ipv6RouteDest (1)
ipv6RoutePfxLength (2)
ipv6RouteIndex (3)
ipv6RouteIfIndex (4)
ipv6RouteNextHop (5)
ipv6RouteType (6)
ipv6RouteProtocol (7)
ipv6RoutePolicy (8)
ipv6RouteAge (9)
ipv6RouteNextHopRDI (10)
ipv6RouteMetric (11)
ipv6RouteWeight (12)
ipv6RouteInfo (13)
ipv6RouteValid (14)
ipv6NetToMediaTable(12)
ipv6NetToMediaEntry (1)
ipv6NetToMediaNetAddress (1)
ipv6NetToMediaPhysAddress (2)
ipv6NetToMediaType (3)
ipv6IfNetToMediaState (4)
ipv6IfNetToMediaLastUpdated (5)
ipv6NetToMediaValid (6)
ipv6Traps (2)
ipv6TrapPrefix (0)
ipv6IfStateChange (1)
ipv6Conformance (3)
ipv6Compliances (1)
ipMIBCompliance (1)
ipv6Groups (2)
ipv6GeneralGroup (1)
Ipv6NotificationGroup (2)

Figure 8-3. Proposed IPv6 General Group

8.3.2 IPv6 ICMP Group

The IPv6 ICMP Group is the MIB module for entities that implement the ICMPv6 protocol. This module is proposed in Reference [8-5] and is comprised of one large table, the ipv6IcmpTable (Figure 8-4). This table compiles statistics on a per-interface basis, for both incoming and outgoing messages.

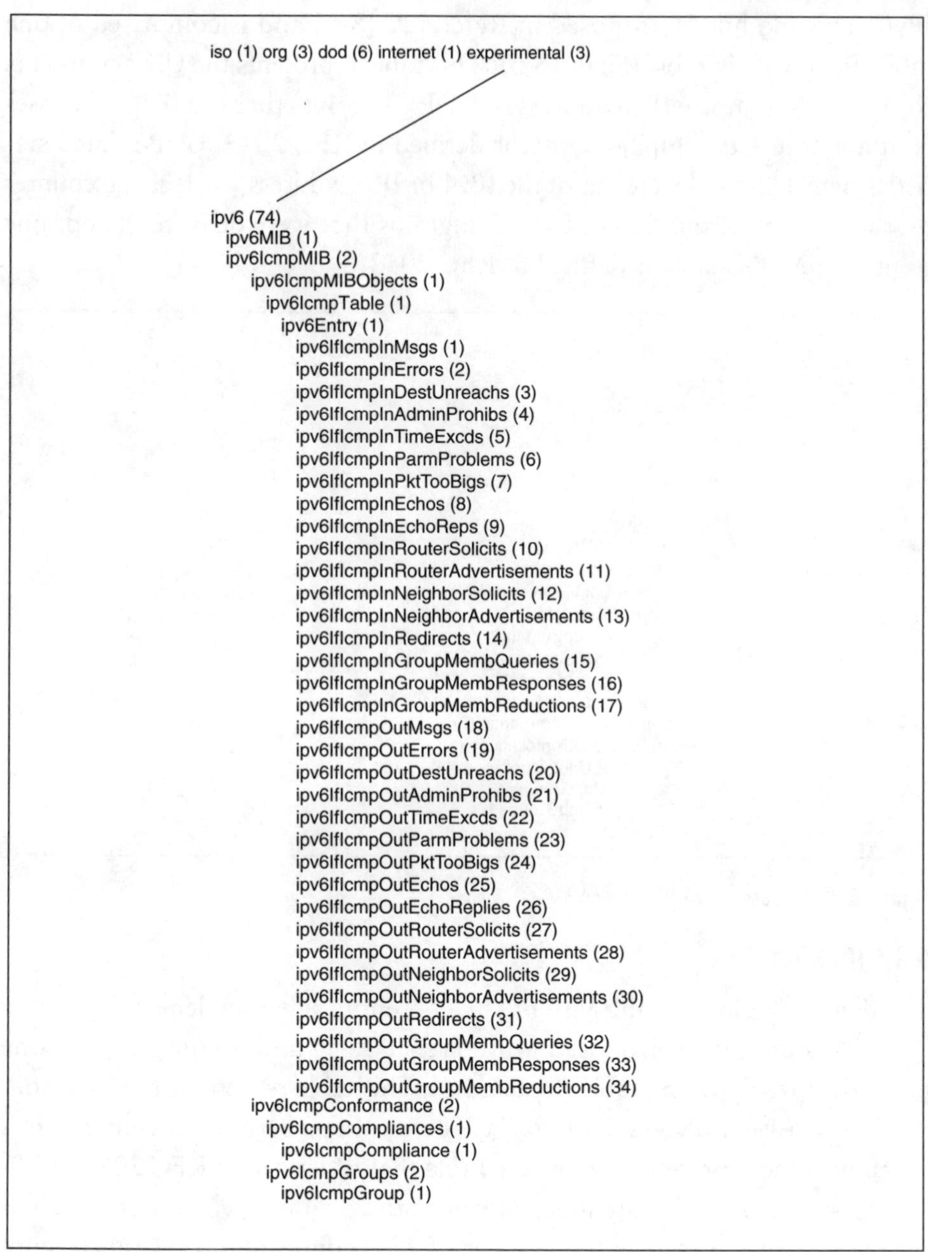

Figure 8-4. Proposed IPv6 ICMP Group

8.3.3 IPv6 UDP Group

The IPv6 UDP Group is the MIB module for entities that implement UDP over IPv6. This module is proposed in Reference [8-6] and is comprised of one table, the ipv6UdpTable (Figure 8-5). This table represents the UDP endpoints (or listeners) that use IPv6 addresses. UDP endpoints that use IPv4 addresses continue to use the udpTable that is defined in RFC 2013. UDP-related statistics, which are independent of the IPv4 or IPv6 address (such as the counter that measures the number of UDP datagrams that were delivered), continue to use the MIB-2 objects defined in RFC 2013.

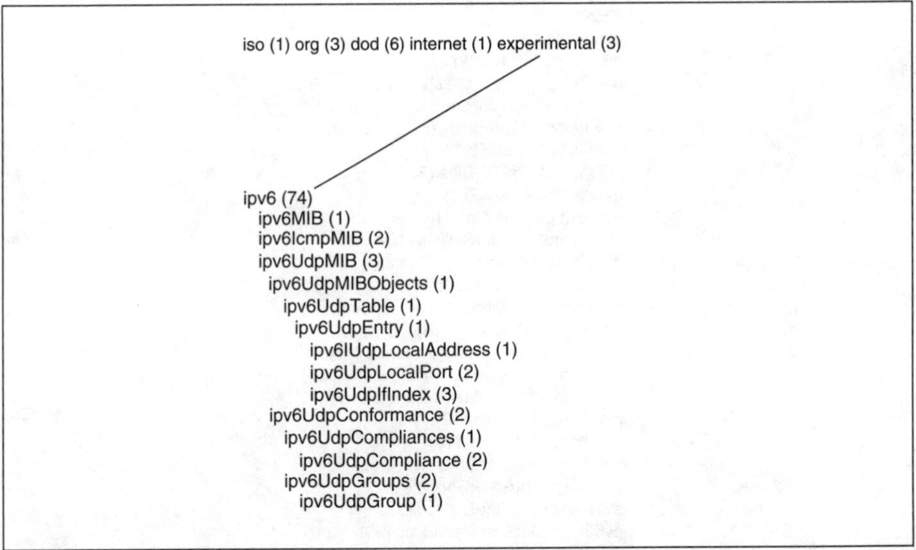

Figure 8-5. Proposed IPv6 UDP Group

8.3.4 IPv6 TCP Group

The IPv6 TCP Group is the MIB module for entities that implement TCP over IPv6. This module is proposed in Reference [8-7] and is comprised of one table, the ipv6TcpConnTable (Figure 8-6). This table represents the TCP connections between IPv6 endpoints. TCP connections between IPv4 endpoints continue to be represented in the tcpTable that is defined in RFC 2012. TCP-related statistics, which are independent of the IPv4 or IPv6 address (such as the counter that measures the number of TCP connection transitions), continue to use the MIB-2 objects defined in RFC 2012.

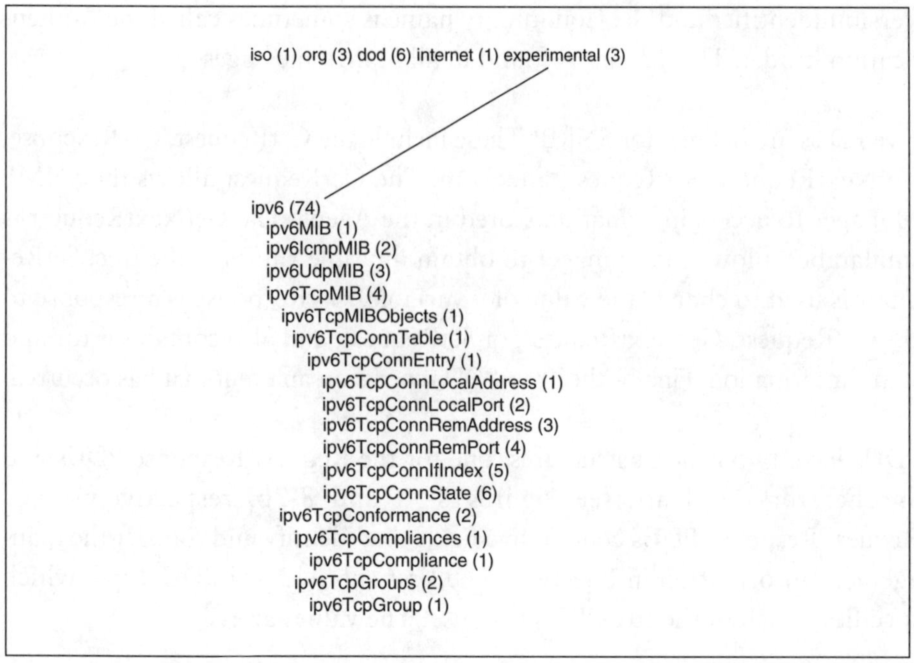

Figure 8-6. Proposed IPv6 TCP Group

8.4 Simple Network Management Protocol

The third element of the Internet Network Management Framework is the protocol SNMP. Two versions, SNMPv1 and SNMPv2, are currently defined, and a third version, SNMPv3, is under development. Since the syntax of SNMPv1 and SNMPv2 differ, we will consider them separately in the next sections.

8.4.1 SNMPv1

SNMPv1 is the protocol used for Agent/Manager communication; it is defined in RFC 1157 [8-8]. The SNMP message consists of a Version Identifier, an SNMP Community name, and the SNMP Protocol Data Units (PDUs). The Version Identifier ensures that both SNMP endpoints use the same version of the protocol. The Community name is encoded as a string of octets and used for authentication; it ensures the proper relationship between the requesting SNMP Manager and the responding SNMP Agent. The combination of the

Version Identifier and the Community name is sometimes called the Authentication header. This header is found in all SNMP messages.

Five PDUs are defined for SNMP. These include the GetRequest, GetResponse, GetNextRequest, SetRequest, and Trap. The GetRequest allows the SNMP Manager to access information stored in the Agent. The GetNextRequest is similar, but allows the Manager to obtain multiple values in the tree. SetRequest is used to change the value of a variable. GetResponse is a response to the GetRequest, GetNextRequest, or SetRequest, and also contains error and status information. Finally, the Trap PDU reports on an event that has occurred.

PDUs have two general structures: one for the Request/Response PDUs and another for the Trap (see Figures 8-7a and 8-7b, respectively). The Request/Response PDUs contain five fields that identify and transfer the management information in question. The first subfield is a PDU Type, which specifies which of the five PDUs is in use. The values are:

Value	PDU Type
0	GetRequest
1	GetNextRequest
2	GetResponse
3	SetRequest
4	Trap

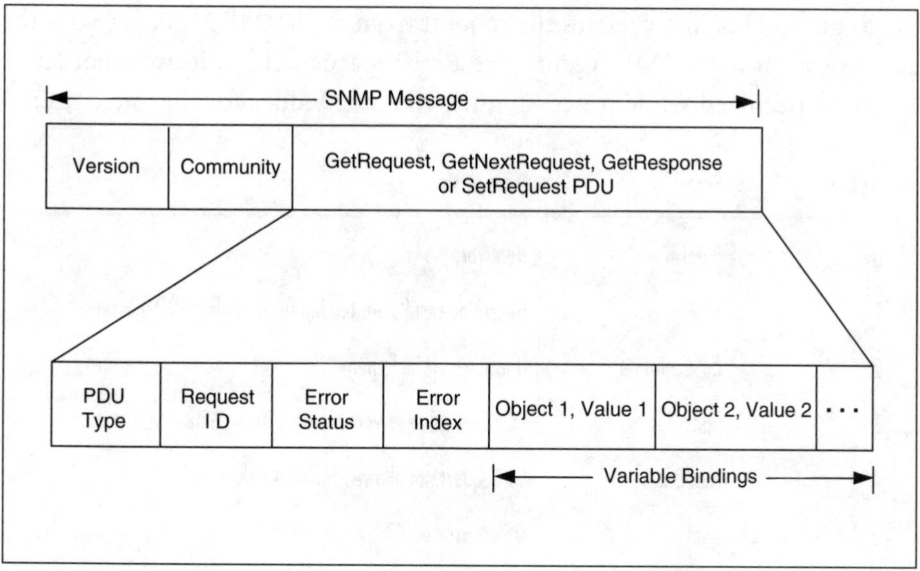

Figure 8-7a. The SNMPv1 GetRequest, GetNextRequest, GetResponse, and SetRequest PDU structures

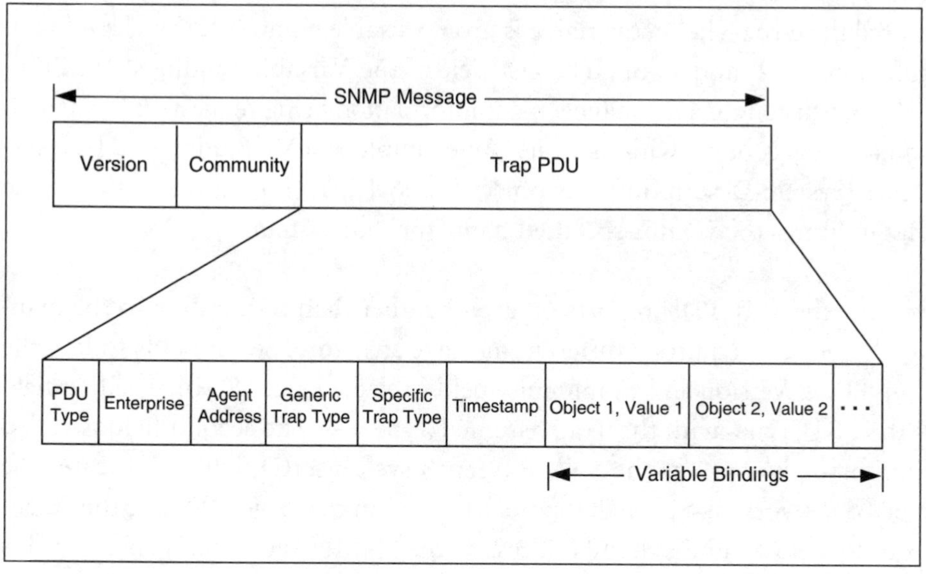

Figure 8-7b. The SNMPv1 Trap PDU structure

The Request ID field correlates the request from the SNMP Manager with the response from the SNMP Agent. The Error Status field indicates that some exception occurred while processing the request. Values for that field are:

Value	Error	Description
0	noError	No error.
1	tooBig	Operation results are too big for a single SNMP message.
2	noSuchName	Unknown variable name.
3	badValue	Incorrect value or variable when using SetRequest.
4	readOnly	SetRequest not allowed for read-only variable.
5	genErr	Other error.

The Error Index field points to the variable in the Variable Bindings field that caused the error. The first variable is given variable number 1, the second variable number 2, and so on. The last field is the Variable Bindings (VarBind) field, which contains the management information being requested. A VarBind pairs an object name with its value. An example of a VarBind would be a sysDescr (System Description) for object {1.3.6.1.2.1.1.1}, paired with a value that indicates the vendor-specified name for that system.

Because the Trap PDU reports on events rather than responding to the manager's query, it requires a different message structure. Seven fields follow the Trap PDU's Version and Community fields (review Figure 8-7b). The first field is the PDU Type, with the Trap assigned Type = 4. The second field is called Enterprise; it contains the SNMP Agent's sysObjectID, which indicates the type of network management system located in that Agent. Next, the Agent Address field contains the IP address of the SNMP Agent that generated this trap. The Generic Trap Type specifies the exact type of message. There are seven possible values for this field:

Value	Trap	Description
0	coldStart	The sending protocol entity is reinitializing; the agent configuration or protocol entity implementation may be altered.
1	warmStart	The sending protocol entity is reinitializing; however, no alterations have been made.
2	linkDown	Communication link in the Agent has failed.
3	linkUp	Communication link in the Agent is now up.
4	Authentication Failure	The sending protocol entity has received an improperly authenticated message.
5	egpNeighborLoss	An EGP peer is down.
6	enterpriseSpecific	An enterprise-specific event has occurred, as defined in the Enterprise field that follows.

The Specific Trap Type elaborates on the type of trap indicated. The Timestamp field transmits the current value of the Agent's sysUpTime object, indicating when the indicated event occurred. As with the Request/Response PDUs, the Variable Bindings contain pairs of object names and values.

8.4.2 SNMPv2

SNMPv2 is defined in RFCs 1901–1908, with the protocol operations documented in RFC 1905 [8-9]. SNMPv2 defines eight PDU types, three of which were added to those defined in SNMPv1: the GetBulkRequest, the InformRequest, and the Report. The GetBulkRequest retrieves a large amount of data, such as the contents of a large table. The InformRequest allows one Manager to communicate information in its MIB view to another Manager. The Report is included in SNMPv2, but its usage is not defined in RFC 1905. It is expected that any Administrative Framework that makes use of this PDU would define its usage and semantics (see RFC 1905, page 6). In addition, the

SNMPv2-Trap PDU format has been revised from the SNMPv1 Trap to conform to the format and structure of the other PDUs (recall that in SNMPv1, the Trap PDU had a unique format).

All SNMPv2 messages have a common structure, as shown in Figure 8-8. Note that the message begins with the Version and Community fields, followed by a PDU Type field. The values for the SNMPv2 PDU Types are:

Value	PDU Type
0	GetRequest
1	GetNextRequest
2	GetResponse
3	SetRequest
4	Obsolete
5	GetBulkRequest
6	InformRequest
7	SNMPv2-Trap
8	Report

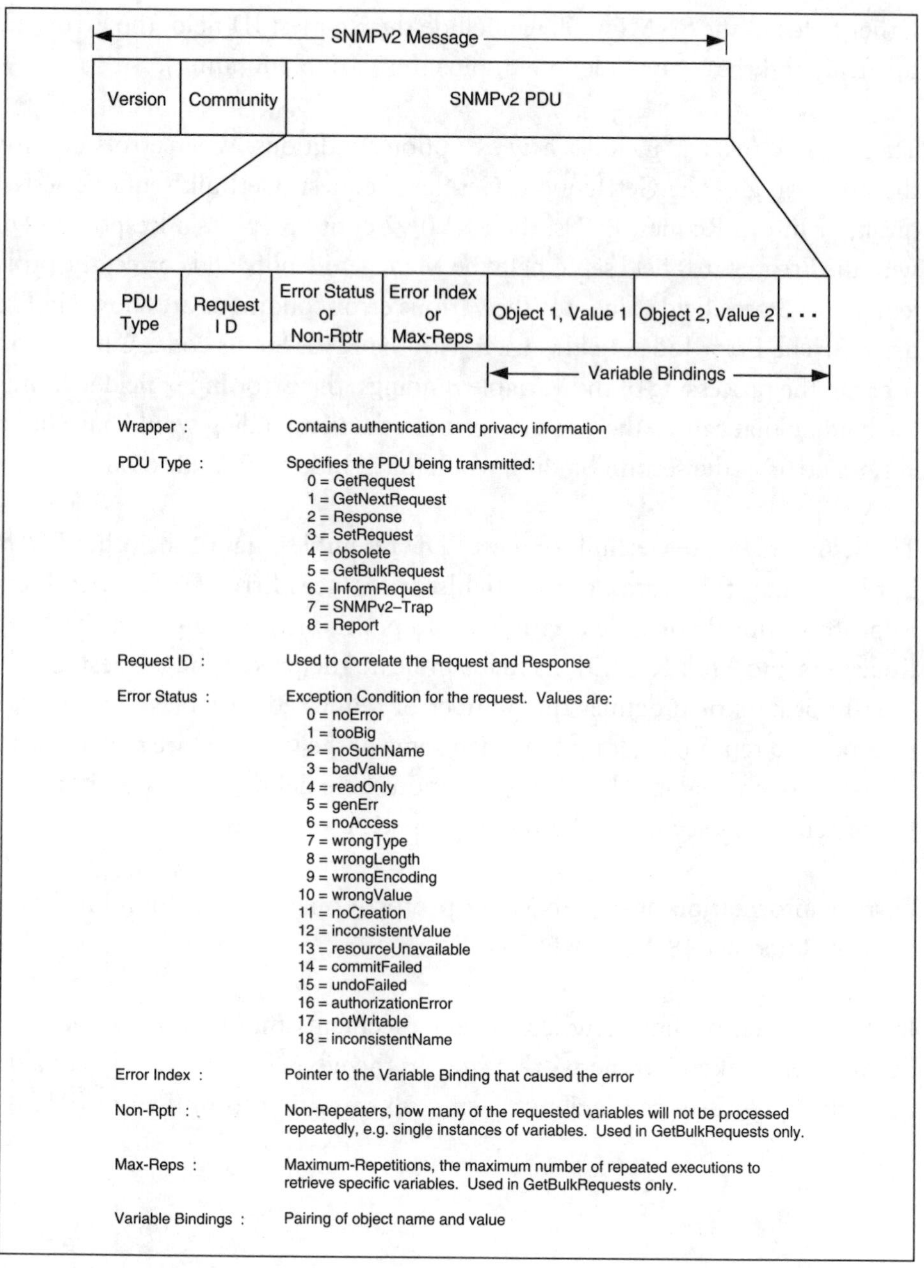

Figure 8-8. SNMPv2 PDU structure

Other fields in the SNMPv2 PDU include the Request ID field, the Error Status field, and the Error Index field, plus the Variable Bindings.

The Error Status field includes new exception conditions. When errors occur in the processing of the GetRequest, GetNextRequest, GetBulkRequest, SetRequest, or InformRequest PDUs, the SNMPv2 entity prepares a Response PDU with the Error Status field set to help the Manager identify and correct the problem. Error Status field values for the various error conditions are shown in Figure 8-8. The Error Index field is used with the Error Status code. When errors occur in the processing of the Variable Bindings, the Error Index field identifies the binding that caused the error. An error in the first binding would have Index = 1, an error in the second binding would have Index = 2, and so on.

The structure of the GetBulkRequest PDU resembles that of the other PDUs, but it changes the syntax of two fields. It replaces Error Status with Non-Repeaters, and Error Index with Max-Repetitions. The values of the Non-Repeaters and Max Repetitions fields indicate the processing requested. The Non-Repeaters field defines the number of requested variables that will not be processed repeatedly; it is used when some of the variables are scalar objects with only one variable. The Max-Repetitions field defines the maximum number of repeated executions that retrieve specific variables.

Further information on the SNMPv2 protocol operations is found in Chapter 5 of Reference [8-1], or RFC 1905.

In this chapter, we have studied the enhancements that will make the management of an IPv6 internetwork easier. In the next chapter, we will consider how these processes can facilitate a smooth transition from IPv4 to IPv6.

8.5 References

[8-1] Miller, Mark A. *Managing Internetworks with SNMP*, Second edition. New York: M&T Books, Inc., 1997

[8-2] Case, J., et al. "Structure of Management Information for Version 2 of the Simple Network Management Protocol (SNMPv2)."

[8-3] McCloghrie, K., et al. "Management Information Base for Network Management of TCP/IP-based Internets: MIB-II." RFC 1213, March 1991.

[8-4] Haskin, D., and S. Onishi. "Management Information Base for IP Version 6: Textual Conventions and General Group." Work in progress, June 1997.

[8-5] Haskin, D., and S. Onishi. "Management Information Base for IP Version 6: ICMPv6 Group." Work in progress, March 1997.

[8-6] Daniele, Mike. "IP Version 6 Management Information Base for the User Datagram Protocol." Work in progress, June 1997.

[8-7] Daniele, Mike. "IP Version 6 Management Information Base for the Transmission Control Protocol." Work in progress, June 1997.

[8-8] Case, J., et al. "Simple Network Management Protocol (SNMP)." RFC 1157, May 1990.

[8-9] Case, J., et al. "Protocol Operations for Version 2 of the Simple Network Management Protocol (SNMPv2)." RFC 1905, January 1996.

Transition Strategies

Just as Rome was not built in a day, neither corporate internetworks nor the global Internet will immediately move from IPv4 to IPv6. Instead, an orderly transition plan must be developed. This is the charter of the IETF's Next Generation Transition (ngtrans) Working Group [9-1]. The group's efforts fall into three areas: defining the processes through which the Internet will be transitioned from IPv4 to IPv6, defining the mechanisms that will be incorporated into routers and hosts that will facilitate this transition, and developing an operating plan for the Internet's transition from IPv4 to IPv6.

As we studied in Chapter 1, RFC 1752, "The Recommendation for the IP Next Generation Protocol," described four key transition criteria:

- Incremental upgrade—Allowing existing IPv4 hosts to be upgraded at any time without a dependency on other hosts or routers being upgraded.
- Incremental deployment—New IPv6 hosts and routers can be installed at any time without any prerequisites.
- Easy addressing—When existing installed IPv4 hosts or routers are upgraded to IPv6, they may continue to use their existing address, without needing new assigned addresses.
- Low start-up costs—Little or no preparation work is needed in order to upgrade existing IPv4 systems to IPv6, or to deploy new IPv6 systems.

In this chapter, we will look at the processes and mechanisms that are designed to facilitate these criteria, and will also consider various scenarios that may occur in the process.

9.1 Transition Definitions

The benefits derived from a new protocol must also be balanced with the costs associated with making a transition from the existing systems. These logistical and technical issues have been addressed in a document entitled "Transition Mechanisms for IPv6 Hosts and Routers," RFC 1933 [9-2]. Transition issues specific to routing infrastructures are addressed in another document, "Routing Aspects of IPv6 Transition," RFC 2185 [9-3].

The developers of IPv6 recognized that not all systems would upgrade from IPv4 to IPv6 in the immediate future, and that for some, that upgrade might not be for years. To complicate matters, most internetworks are heterogeneous systems, with various routers, hosts, etc. manufactured by different vendors. If such a multivendor system were to be upgraded at one time, IPv6 capabilities would be required on all of the individual elements before the larger project could be attempted. Another (much larger) issue becomes the worldwide Internet, which operates across 24 different time zones. Upgrading this system in a single process would be even more difficult.

Given the above constraints, it therefore becomes necessary to develop strategies for IPv4 and IPv6 to coexist, until such time as IPv6 becomes the preferred option. At the time of this writing, two mechanisms for this coexistence have been proposed: a dual IP layer and IPv6 over IPv4 tunneling. These two complementary technologies will be discussed in the following sections.

The following terms, which relate to nodes and addresses for use in the transition architectures, are defined in RFC 1933:

- *IPv4-only node*: A host or router that implements only IPv4 and does not understand IPv6. The installed base of IPv4 hosts and routers existing before the transition begins are IPv4-only nodes.
- *IPv6/IPv4 node*: A host or router that implements both IPv4 and IPv6.
- *IPv6-only node*: A host or router that implements IPv6 and does not implement IPv4.

- *IPv6 node*: Any host or router that implements IPv6. IPv6/IPv4 and IPv6-only nodes are both IPv6 nodes.
- *IPv4 node*: Any host or router that implements IPv4. IPv6/IPv4 and IPv4-only nodes are both IPv4 nodes.
- *IPv4-compatible IPv6 address*: An IPv6 address, assigned to an IPv6/IPv4 node, which bears the high-order 96-bit prefix 0:0:0:0:0:0 and an IPv4 address in the low-order 32-bits. IPv4-compatible addresses are used by the automatic tunneling mechanism.
- *IPv6-only address*: The remainder of the IPv6 address space. An IPv6 address that bears a prefix other than 0:0:0:0:0:0.

9.2 Transition Mechanisms

The transition mechanisms provide the ways and means of implementing a transition strategy. RFC 1933 considers two mechanisms: a dual IP layer and IPv6 over IPv4 tunneling. For the tunneling mechanism, there are two alternatives: configured tunneling and automatic tunneling. With *configured tunneling*, the tunnel endpoint is determined by configuration information that exists at the tunnel entry point (or encapsulating node). For *automatic tunneling*, a special address, the IPv4-compatible IPv6 address, is used to derive the tunnel endpoint. We will see examples of these two alternatives in the sections that follow.

9.2.1 Dual IP Stacks

The simplest mechanism for IPv4 and IPv6 coexistence is for both of the protocol stacks to be implemented on the same device. That device, which could be either a host or a router, is then referred to as an IPv6/IPv4 node. The IPv6/IPv4 node has the capability to send and receive both IPv4 and IPv6 packets, and can therefore interoperate with an IPv4 device using IPv4 packets and interoperate with an IPv6 packet using IPv6 packets (Figure 9-1). The dual IP stacks may also work in conjunction with the two tunneling techniques described above.

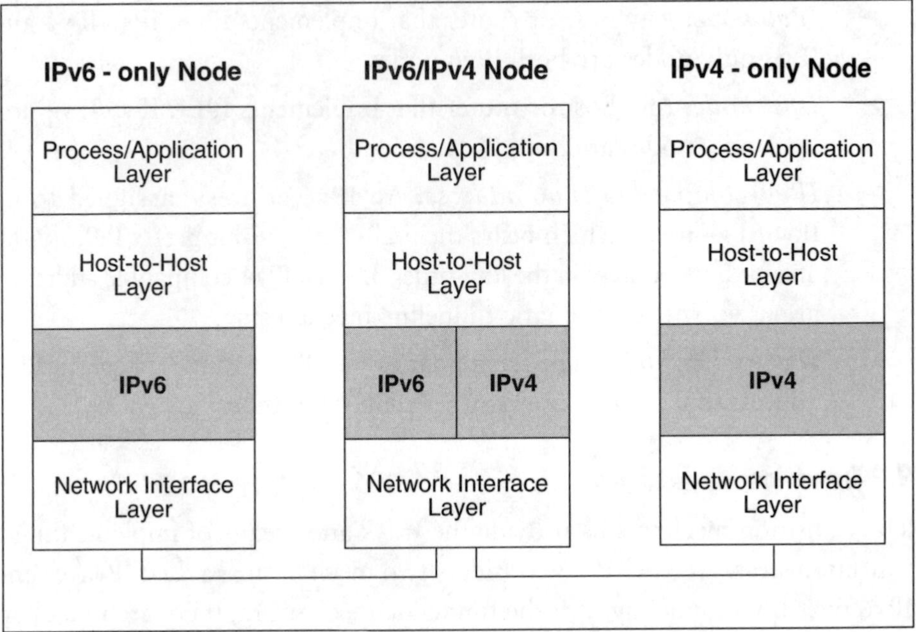

Figure 9-1. Dual IP stack architecture

The IPv6/IPv4 node would be configured with addresses that support both protocols, and those addresses may or may not be related to each other. Other address-related functions, such as the Dynamic Host Configuration Protocol (DHCP), or the Bootstrap Protocol (BOOTP), may also be involved in this process. In addition, an IPv6/IPv4 node must support both the A and AAAA resource record types within the Domain Name System (DNS).

9.2.2 Tunneling

Tunneling is a process whereby information from one protocol is encapsulated inside the frame or packet of another architecture, thus enabling the original data to be carried over that second architecture. The tunneling scenarios for IPv6/IPv4 are designed to enable an existing IPv4 infrastructure to carry IPv6 packets by encapsulating the IPv6 information inside IPv4 datagrams. Note that the major emphasis of the transition mechanisms is on tunneling IPv6 packets over an existing IPv4 infrastructure, since the majority of today's networks are IPv4 systems. As the transition process matures, however, it is expected that some IPv4-only systems may then tunnel packets over newly installed IPv6 infrastructures. But for most of us, this second scenario is a few years off.

The *encapsulation* process is illustrated in Figure 9-2a. Note that the resulting IPv4 datagram contains both an IPv4 header and an IPv6 header, plus all of the upper layer information, such as the TCP header, application data, and so on. The reverse process, *decapsulation*, is illustrated in Figure 9-2b. In this case, the IPv4 header is removed, leaving only the IPv6 packet. Within the IPv4 header, the Protocol field would have a value of 41, identifying an IPv6 payload.

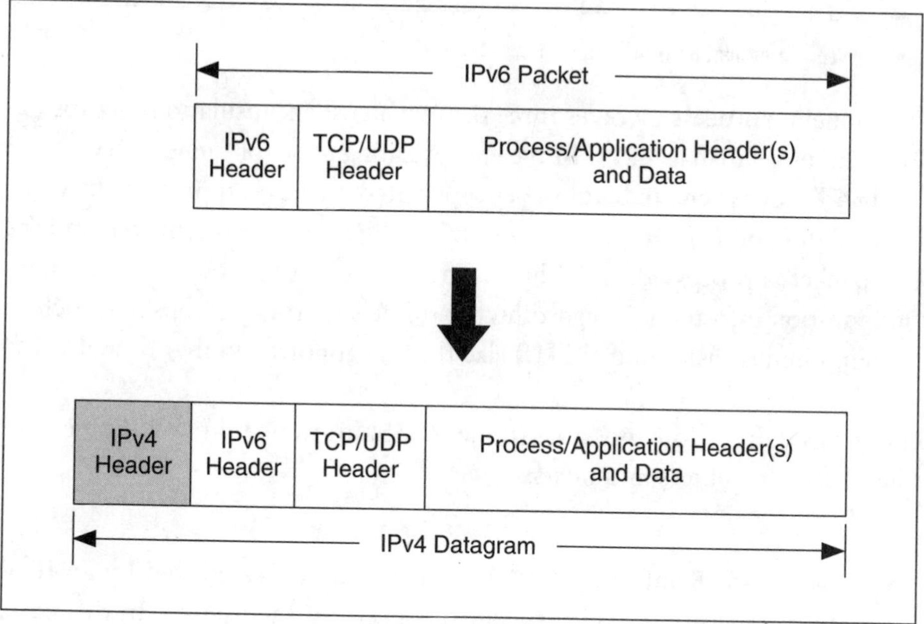

Figure 9-2a. Encapsulating IPv6 in IPv4

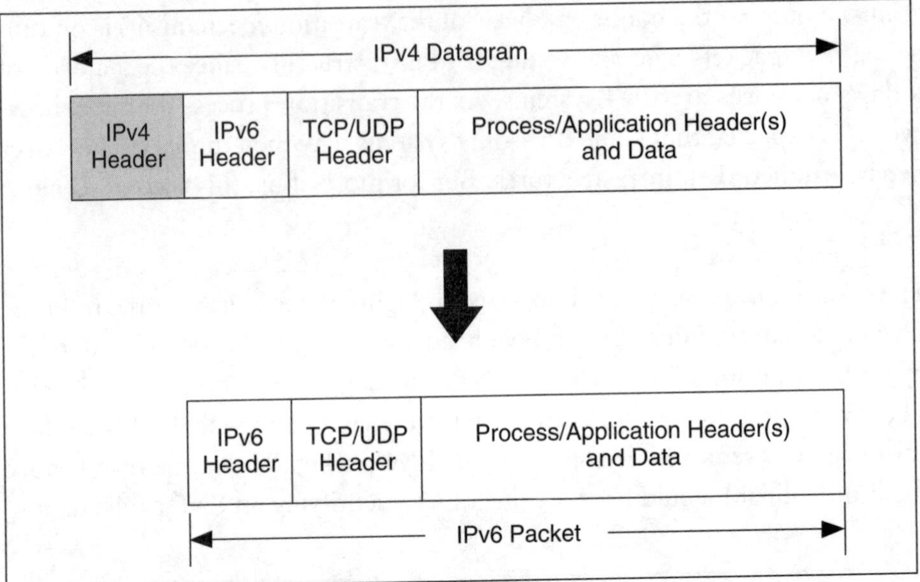

Figure 9-2b. Decapsulating IPv6 from IPv4

The tunneling process involves three distinct steps: encapsulation, decapsulation, and tunnel management. At the encapsulating node (or tunnel entry point), the IPv4 header is created and the encapsulated packet is transmitted. At the decapsulating node (or tunnel exit point), the IPv4 header is removed and the IPv6 packet is processed. In addition, the encapsulating node may maintain configuration information regarding the tunnels that are established, such as the maximum transfer unit (MTU) size that is supported in that tunnel.

RFC 1933 defines four possible tunnel configurations that could be established between routers and hosts:

- Router-to-Router: IPv6/IPv4 routers that are separated by an IPv4 infrastructure tunnel IPv6 packets between themselves. In this case, the tunnel would span one segment of the packet's end-to-end path.
- Host-to-Router: An IPv6/IPv4 host tunnels IPv6 packets to an IPv6/IPv4 router that is reachable via an IPv4 infrastructure. In this case, the tunnel would span the first segment of the packet's end-to-end path.

- Host-to-Host: IPv6/IPv4 hosts that are interconnected by an IPv4 infrastructure can tunnel IPv6 packets across the IPv4 infrastructure. In this case, the tunnel spans the packet's entire end-to-end path.
- Router-to-Host: IPv6/IPv4 routers can tunnel IPv6 packets to an IPv6/IPv4 host which is the final destination. In this case, the tunnel would span only the final segment of the packet's end-to-end path.

For a tunnel to operate, addresses of both the tunnel endpoint and the packet's destination must be known, and these two addresses are not necessarily the same. The manner in which the tunnel endpoint address is determined defines one of two types of tunnels: an automatic tunnel or a configured tunnel. These alternatives will be explored in the following sections.

9.2.2.1 Configured Tunneling

As described in RFC 1933, tunneling techniques are classified according to the mechanism by which the encapsulating node determines the address of the node at the end of the tunnel. From the four tunneling scenarios that were discussed previously, the router-to-router and host-to-router terminate on a router, which then decapsulates the information and forwards the IPv6 packet to its final destination. Note that the tunnel endpoint address is different from the final destination endpoint address. This requires that the node performing the tunneling determine the tunnel endpoint from some configuration information. For this reason, this type of tunneling is called configured tunneling.

Let's look at the various scenarios individually. The first case occurs when two IPv6 hosts are separated by an IPv4 infrastructure (Figure 9-3). The source host, H_1, is an IPv6 node configured for either IPv6-only or IPv6/v4. H_1 generates an IPv6 packet and sends that packet to the first router, R_1, a dual node. A configured tunnel exists across the IPv4 infrastructure between R_1 and R_2. When the entry router sees the IPv6 destination address, it encapsulates the IPv6 packet inside an IPv4 datagram and sends it across the IPv4 internetwork. At the tunnel endpoint, the exit router decapsulates the IPv6 packet and sends it to the final destination, H_2. (This was the scenario that we studied in Section 7.5.)

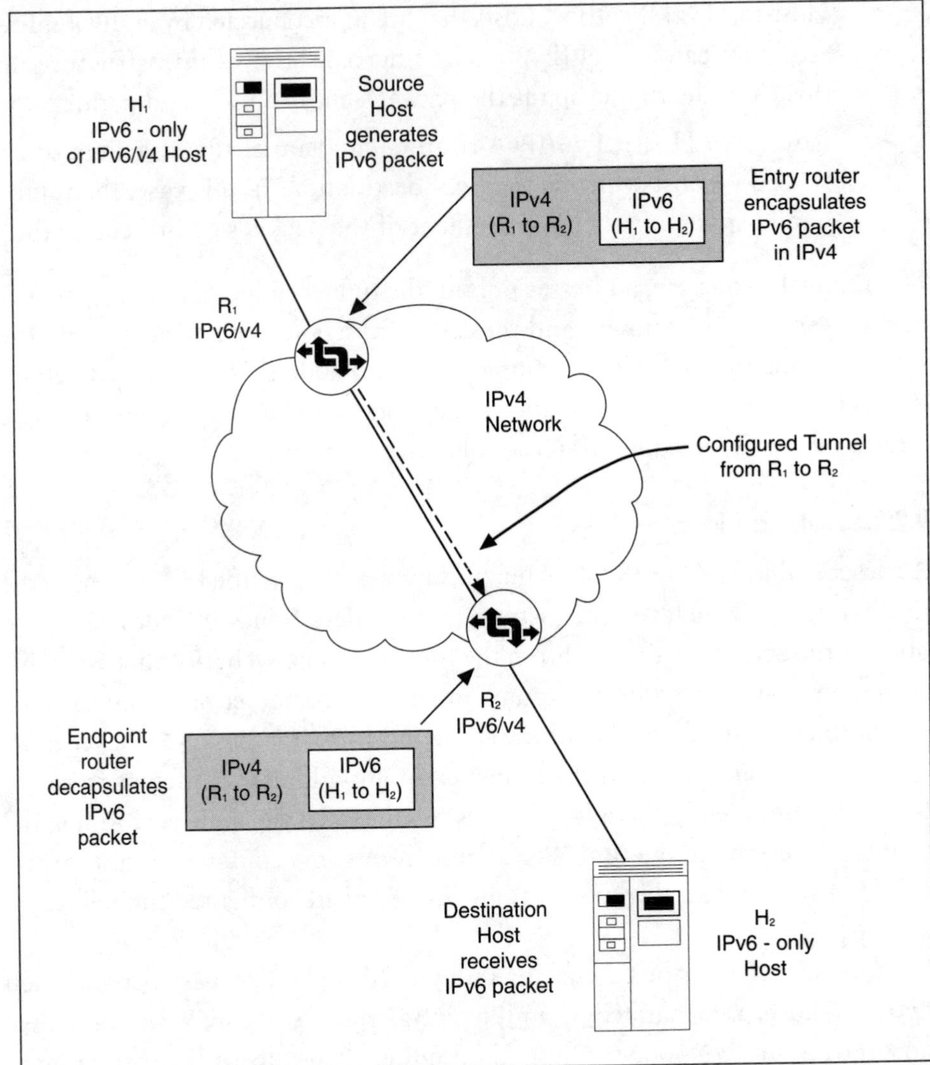

Figure 9-3. Router-to-router configured tunnel

The internetwork could also be configured such that the tunnel entry point is at the originating host (Figure 9-4). In this case, the source host, H_1, must be a dual host, and the tunnel is configured between H_1 and R_2. The encapsulation occurs at the source host, H_1, and decapsulation occurs at the tunnel endpoint, R_2. (In this case, the destination host, H_2, does not have an IPv4-compatible address available.)

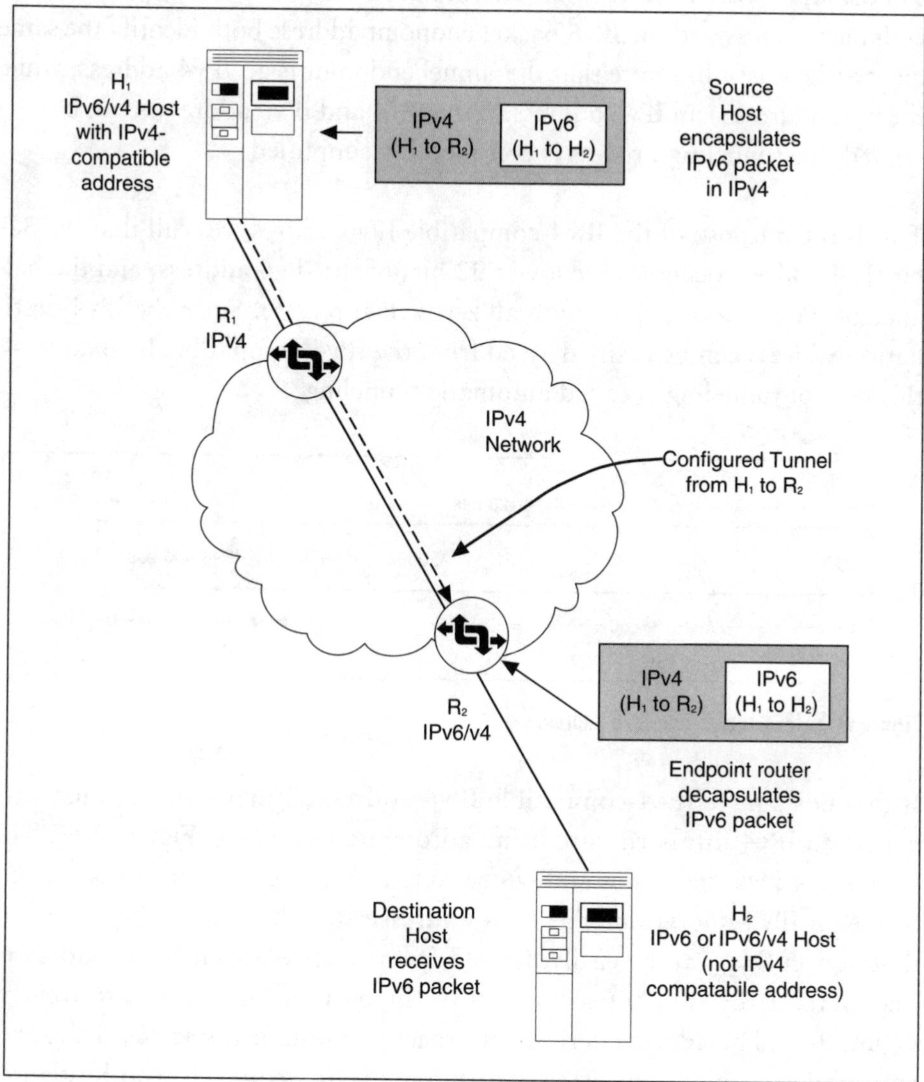

Figure 9-4. Host-to-router configured tunnel

9.2.2.2 Automatic Tunneling

From the four tunneling scenarios that were discussed previously, the host-to-host and router-to-host tunnels terminate on a host. Note that the tunnel endpoint address and the IPv6 packet endpoint address both identify the same device (the host). But note that the tunnel endpoint is an IPv4 address, while the host address is an IPv6 address. If the IPv4 and IPv6 addresses can be correlated, the tunneling process is considerably simplified.

This is the purpose of the IPv4-compatible IPv6 address. Recall that the 32-bit IPv4 address occupies the lower 32 bits of the IPv6 address, and the balance of the address is filled with all zeros (Figure 9-5). Since the IPv4 destination address can be easily derived from the IPv4-compatible IPv6 address, this type of tunneling is called automatic tunneling.

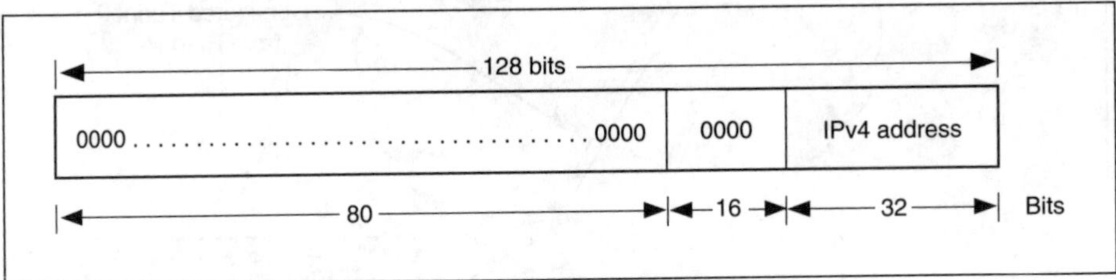

Figure 9-5. IPv4-compatible IPv6 address

If two hosts have IPv4-compatible IPv6 addresses, they can communicate across an IPv4 infrastructure using automatic tunneling (Figure 9-6). The source host, H1, generates an IPv6 packet, and also encapsulates that packet inside an IPv4 datagram. The IPv4 addresses for the source (H_1) and the destination (H_2) can be easily derived from the IPv4-compatible addresses known to H_1 by simply masking off the high order 96 bits of zero (review Figure 9-5). The address derivation process automatically yields the tunnel entry and exit points, hence the term *automatic tunneling*. Host-to-host automatic tunneling allows IPv6 to be deployed on the hosts with no changes required to the routing infrastructure.

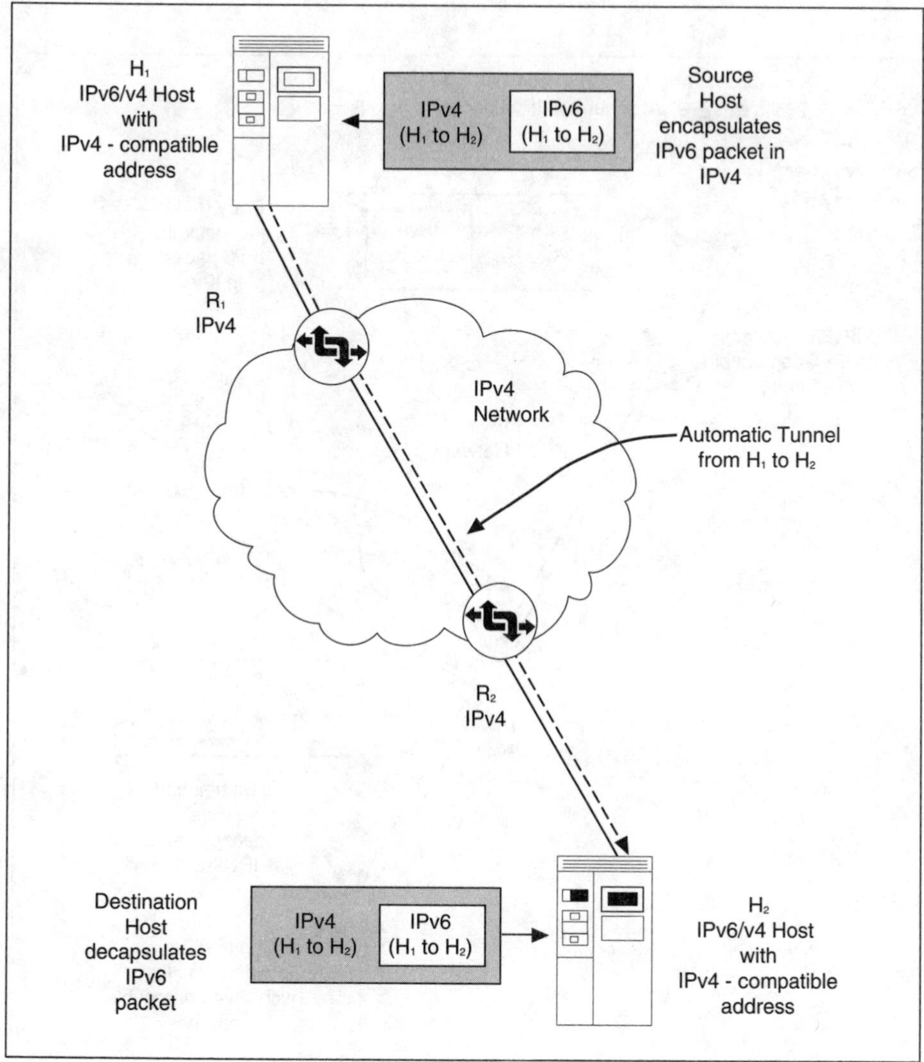

Figure 9-6. Host-to-host automatic tunnel

In a similar manner, a dual router, upon receiving an IPv6 packet destined for a host with an IPv4-compatible address, can automatically tunnel that packet to its endpoint (Figure 9-7).

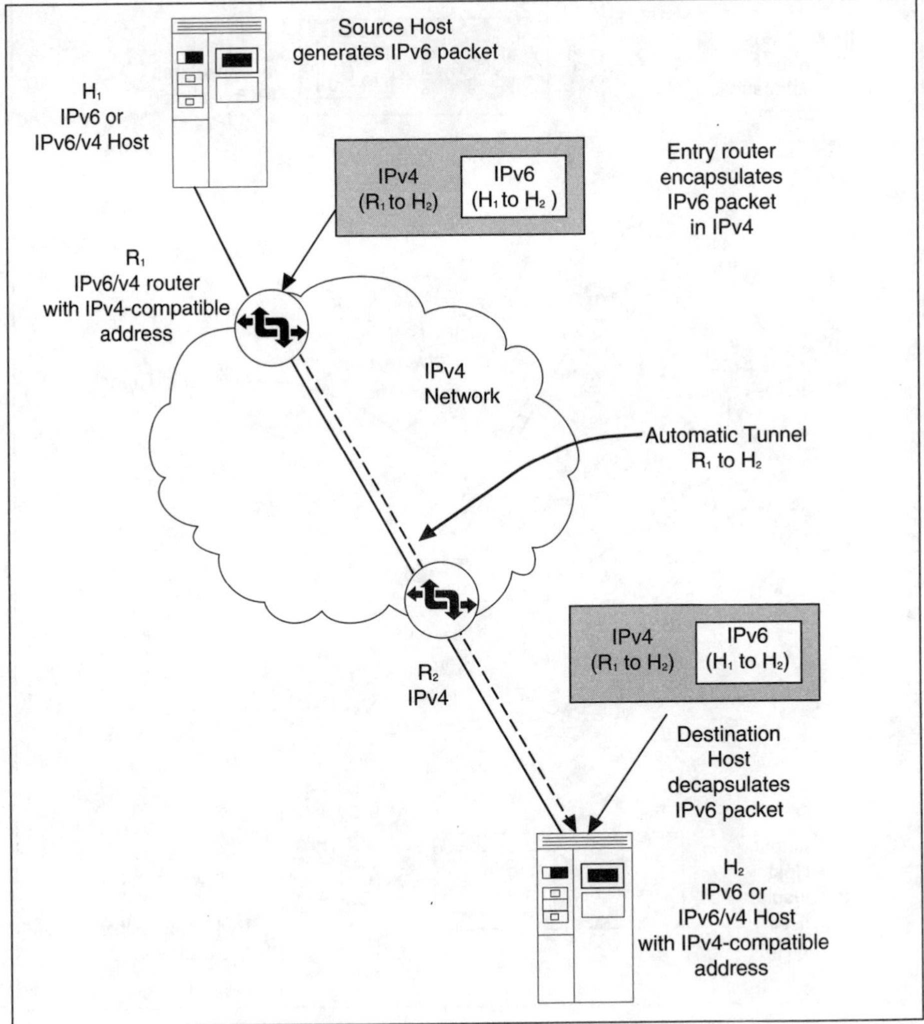

Figure 9-7. Router-to-host automatic tunnel

9.2.2.3 Combined Tunnels

RFC 2185 also discusses tunneling, but from the perspective of a tunnel's interaction with neighboring routers [9-3]. In addition, that document discusses various combinations of automatic tunnels so that communication can be achieved in both directions. (Recall from Figures 9-3, 9-4, 9-6, and 9-7 that our focus was on one-way communication.) RFC 2185 summarizes the various communication paths that are possible between two hosts, A and B (Figure 9-8).

Host A	Host B	Communication Paths
IPv4-compatible addr. no local IPv6 router	IPv4-compatible addr. no local IPv6 router	Host-to-Host tunneling in both directions
IPv4-compatible addr. no local IPv6 router	IPv4-compatible addr. local IPv6 router	A->B: Host-to-Host tunneling B->A: IPv6 forwarding plus Router-to-Host tunnel
IPv4-compatible addr. no local IPv6 router	Incompatible addr. local IPv6 router	A->B: Host-to-Router tunnel plus IPv6 forwarding B->A: IPv6 forwarding plus Router-to-Host tunnel
IPv4-compatible addr. local IPv6 router	IPv4-compatible addr. local IPv6 router	End-to-End native IPv6 in both directions
IPv4-compatible addr. local IPv6 router	Incompatible addr. local IPv6 router	End-to-End native IPv6 in both directions
Incompatible addr. local IPv6 router	Incompatible addr. local IPv6 router	End-to-End native IPv6 in both directions

Figure 9-8. Automatic tunneling combinations

Two key assumptions are made for this figure: when possible, native IPv6 communication is preferred over tunneling, and if tunneling is needed, host-to-host tunneling (going end-to-end) is preferred over host-to-router tunneling.

Referring to Figure 9-8, if two hosts have IPv4-compatible addresses, and no local IPv6 routers are available, then host-to-host tunneling should be used in both directions (review Figure 9-6). If one of these hosts has a local IPv6 router, then a host-to-host tunnel can be used in one direction (Figure 9-6), and a router-to-host tunnel in the other (Figure 9-7). If one host has an IPv4-compatible address and the other does not, then a host-to-router tunnel may be used in one direction (Figure 9-4), and a router-to-host tunnel in the other direction (Figure 9-7). Anytime that an IPv6 router is available, regardless of the type of IPv6 address used (IPv4-compatible or not), native IPv6 packets are sent in both directions.

9.2.3 Default Sending Algorithm

RFC 1933 includes a sending algorithm that enables implementers to determine which type of packet to send (IPv4 or IPv6), based on the type of address of the end node, the presence or absence of routers on that link, and so on. A summary of that algorithm, also from RFC 1933, is shown in Figure 9-9. Let's look at a few examples from that algorithm.

End Node Address Type	End Node on Link?	IPv4 Router on Link?	IPv6 Router on Link?	Packet Format To Send	IPv6 Dest Addr	IPv4 Dest Addr	Data Link Dest Addr
IPv4	Yes	N/A	N/A	IPv4	N/A	E4	EL
IPv4	No	Yes	N/A	IPv4	N/A	E4	RL
IPv4	No	No	N/A	UNRCH	N/A	N/A	N/A
IPv4 - compat	Yes	N/A	N/A	IPv6	E6	N/A	EL
IPv4 - compat	No	Yes	N/A	IPv6/4	E6	E4	RL
IPv4 - compat	No	No	Yes	IPv6	E6	N/A	RL
IPv4 - compat	No	No	No	UNRCH	N/A	N/A	N/A
IPv6 - only	Yes	N/A	N/A	IPv6	E6	N/A	EL
IPv6 - only	No	N/A	Yes	IPv6	E6	N/A	RL
IPv6 - only	No	Yes	No	IPv6/4	E6	T4	RL
IPv6 - only	No	No	No	UNRCH	N/A	N/A	N/A

Notes:

N/A: Not applicable or does not matter
E6: IPv6 address of end node
E4: IPv4 address of end node (low-order 32-bits of IPv4-compatible address)
EL: Data link address of end node
T4: IPv4 address of the tunnel endpoint
R6: IPv6 address of router
R4: IPv4 address of router
RL: Data link address of router
IPv4: IPv4 packet format
IPv6: IPv6 packet format
IPv6/4: IPv6 encapsulated in IPv4 packet format
UNRCH: Destination is unreachable - Don't send a packet

Figure 9-9. IPv4 and IPv6 sending rules

Row 1 of Figure 9-9 is the case where an IPv6/IPv4 node wishes to send to another IPv4 node on the same link. In that situation, an IPv4 packet would be used with the IPv4 destination address of the end node (shown as E4), and the Data Link Layer destination address also of the end node (shown as EL).

Row 2 considers the case where the IPv4 destination node is not on the same link, but an IPv4 router is available. The IPv4 packet is then sent to the Data Link Layer address of the router on that link (RL).

Row 3 considers the case where the destination node is not on the same link, but a router is not available. Without a router, the destination is unreachable (UNRCH).

The middle section of Figure 9-9 deals with end nodes that have IPv4-compatible IPv6 addresses. If the destination node is on the same link, then an IPv6 packet may be sent without encapsulation (Row 4). If the destination node is off link and an IPv4 router exists, then automatic tunneling may be used (Row 5). If the destination node is off link, and an IPv6 router exists, then an IPv6 packet may be sent (Row 6). If the destination node is off link and no routers exist, then the destination is unreachable (Row 7).

The final section of Figure 9-9 deals with end nodes that have IPv6-only addresses. If the destination node is on the same link, then an IPv6 packet may be sent natively (Row 8). Similarly, if the destination node is off link and an IPv6 router exists, then an IPv6 packet can also be sent natively and then forwarded by the IPv6 router (Row 9). If an IPv4 router exists and the destination is reachable via a configured tunnel, then send the IPv6 packet encapsulated in an IPv4 datagram (Row 10). Finally, if the destination is off link and no routers exist, then the destination is unreachable (Row 11).

The next section will discuss the routing conditions in greater detail.

9.3 Transition Routing

A number of routing issues affect IPv4 to IPv6 transitions; these are described in RFC 2185. The following terms, which relate to transition routing architectures, are defined in that document:

- *Border router*: A router that forwards packets across routing domain boundaries.
- *Routing domain*: A collection of routers that coordinate routing knowledge using a single routing protocol.
- *Routing region* (or *region*): Collection of routers interconnected by a single Internet protocol (e.g., IPv6) and coordinating their routing knowledge using routing protocols from a single Internet protocol stack. A routing region may be a superset of a routing domain.
- *Tunneling*: Encapsulation of protocol A within protocol B, such that A treats B as though it were a Data Link layer.
- *Reachability information* (or *reachability*): Information describing the set of reachable destinations that can be used for packet forwarding decisions.
- *Address prefix*: The high-order bits in an address.
- *Routing prefix*: Address prefix that expresses destinations that have addresses with the matching address prefixes. The routing prefix is used by routers to advertise what systems they are capable of reaching.
- *Route leaking*: Advertisement of network layer reachability information across routing region boundaries.

Some of the issues described in this document are: the routing for IPv4 datagrams (using IPv4 addresses), the routing of IPv6 packets (using IPv6-native or IPv4-compatible addresses), the operation of configured tunnels, and the operation of automatic tunnels. It is assumed that dual routers may independently support IPv4 and IPv6 (i.e. two instances of RIP or two instances of OSPF, with each instance supporting one version of the protocol). It would be conceivable for a single routing protocol to support both IPv4 and IPv6, although, to date, none of these have been developed. When required, one protocol may inject routing information into another protocol's region to facilitate tunnel configurations or other routing decisions.

9.4 Transition Scenarios

RFC 2185 provides several examples that illustrate routing scenarios for packet transmission between two regions: A, which contains IPv6/IPv4 routers, and B, which contains IPv4-only routers (Figure 9-10a). Some of the hosts in each region are dual hosts; others support IPv4 only.

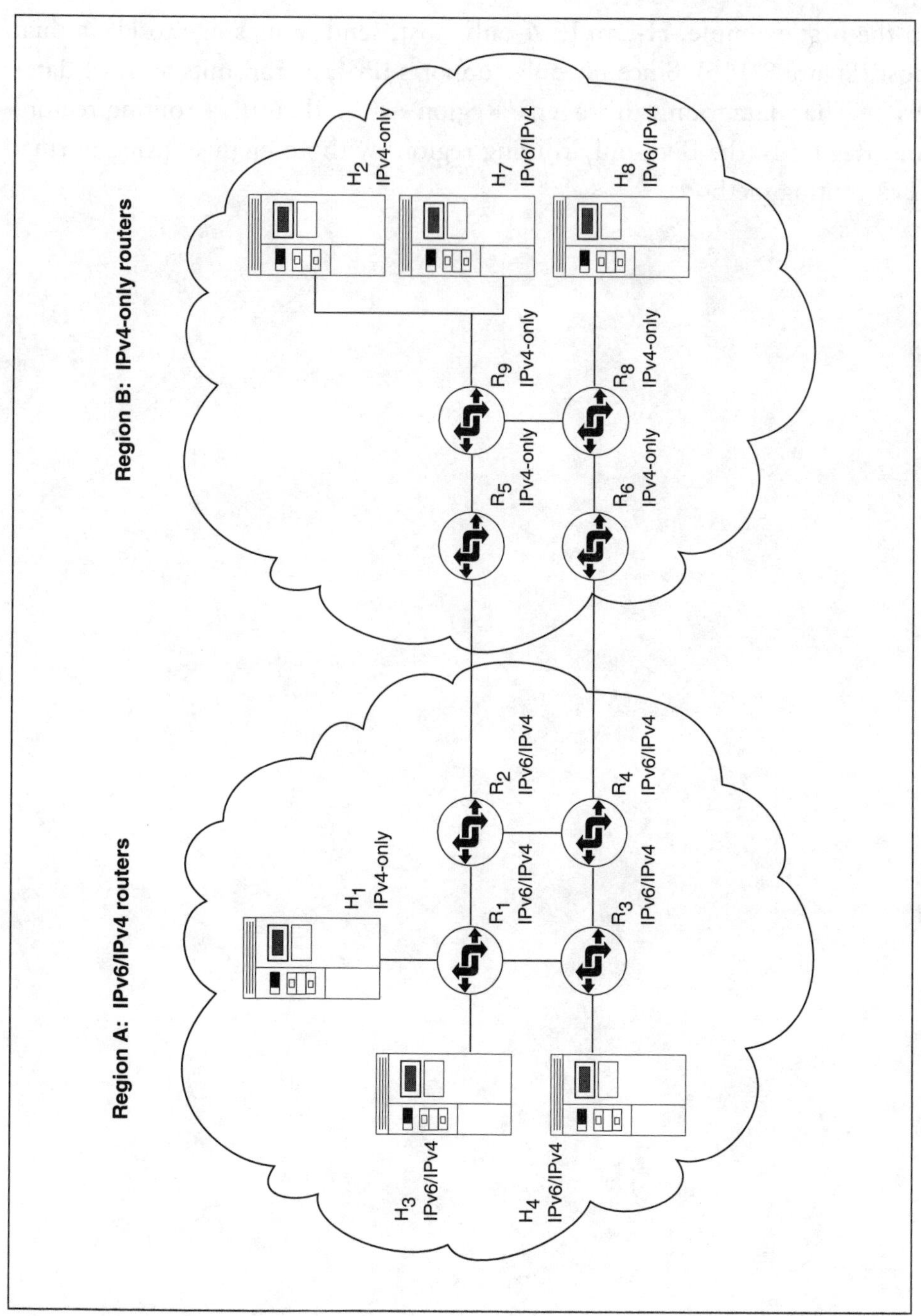

Figure 9-10a. Routing example

In the first example, H_1, an IPv4-only host, sends a message to H_8, a dual host (Figure 9-10b). Since H_1 only supports IPv4, it transmits an IPv4 datagram. That datagram can traverse Region A (the IPv6/IPv4 routing region) and Region B (the IPv4-only routing region) with no change, using normal IPv4 routing methods.

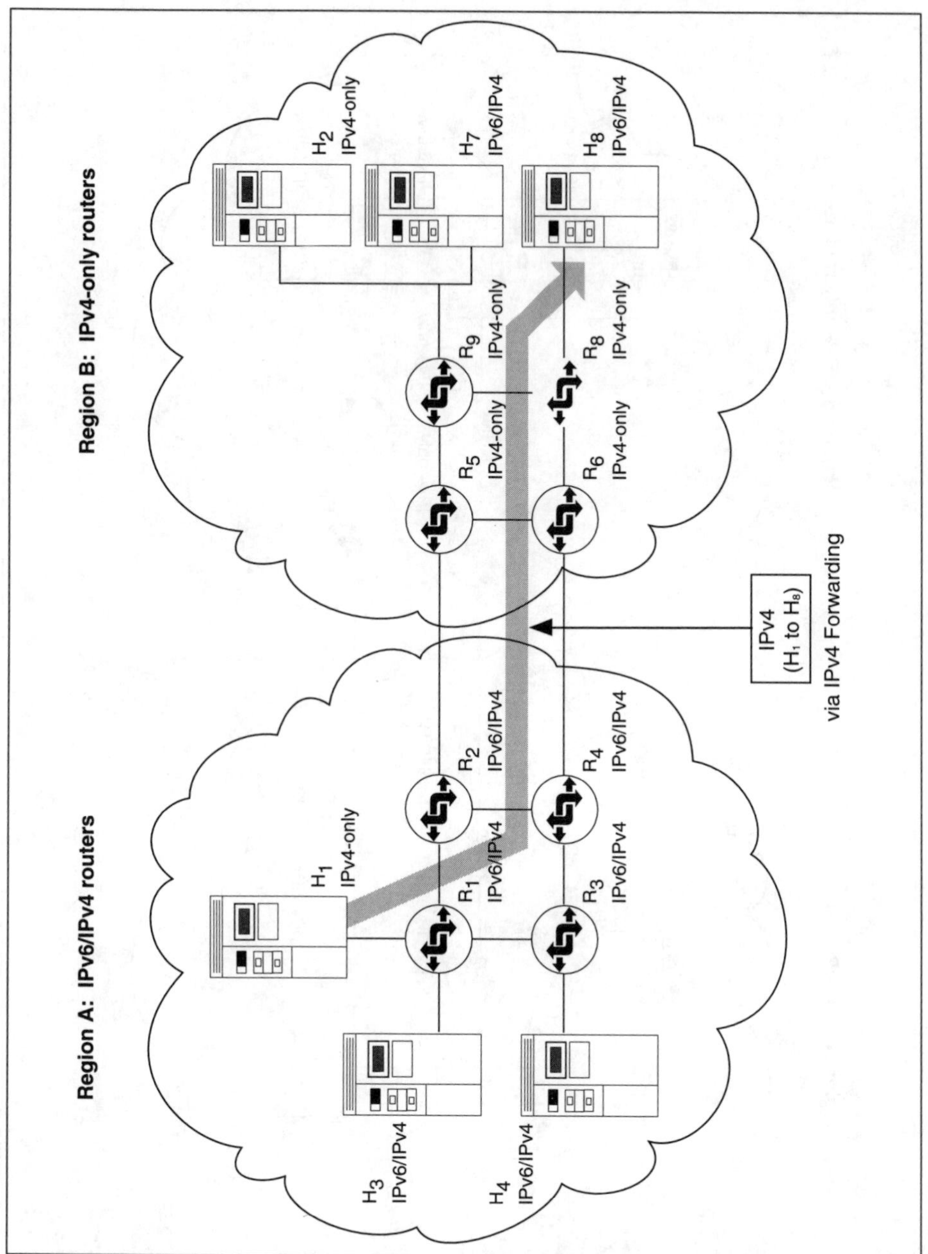

Figure 9-10b. Routing example: IPv4 datagram from H_1 to H_8 (via IPv4 forwarding)

A return message, from H_8 to H_1, would also be transmitted as an IPv4 datagram and would also use the IPv4 routing infrastructure (Figure 9-10c).

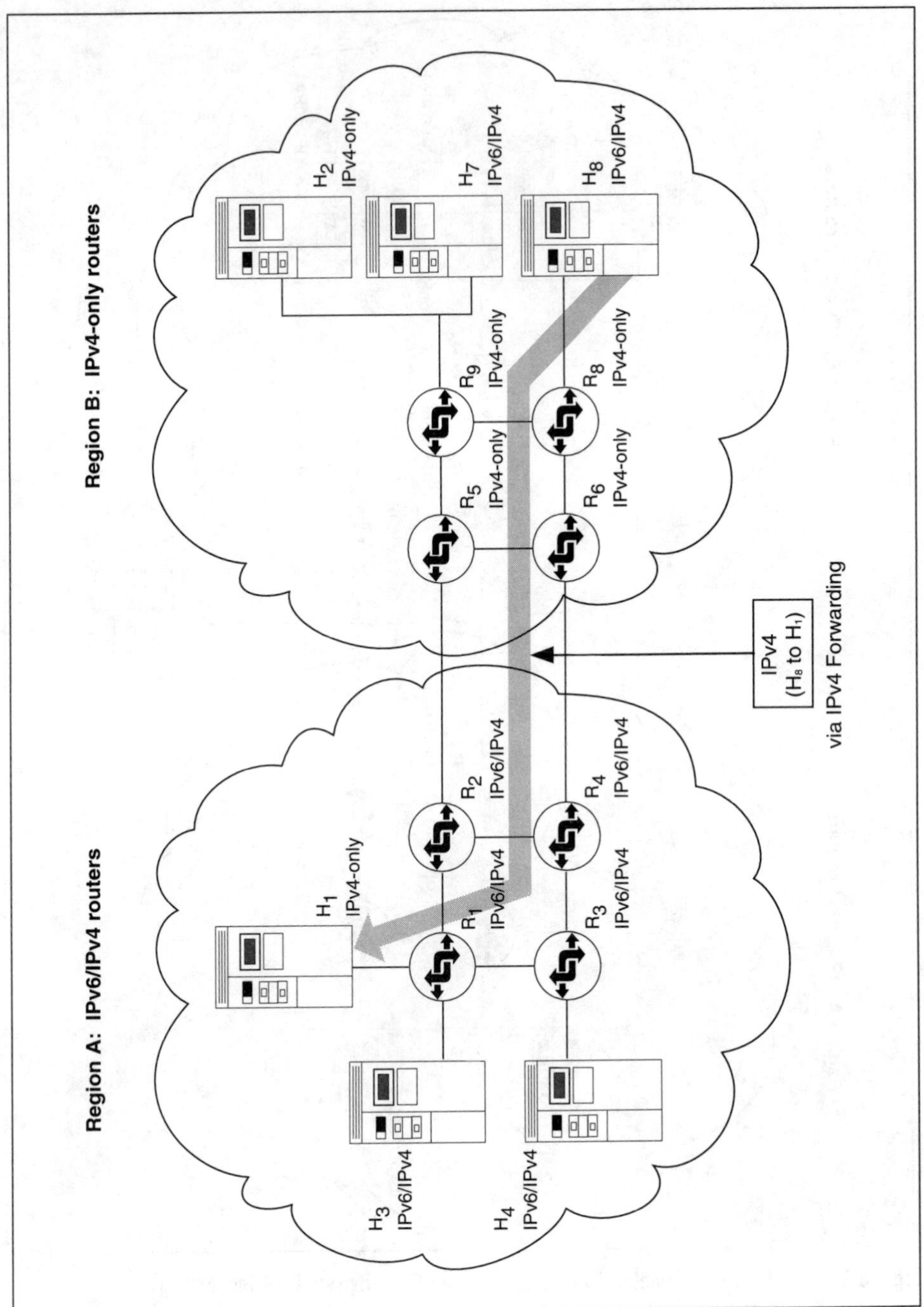

Figure 9-10c. Routing example: IPv4 datagram from H_8 to H_1 (via IPv4 forwarding)

Now assume a message from H_3 to H_8 (Figure 9-10d). Since H_8 is a dual host, but resident in an IPv4-only domain, it should have an IPv4-compatible address assigned. Since both H_3 and H_8 have IPv6 capabilities, H_3 can send an IPv6 packet as far as a boundary router (R2 or R4). At that point, it is encapsulated inside an IPv4 packet and sent via a Router-to-Host tunnel to the final destination, H_8.

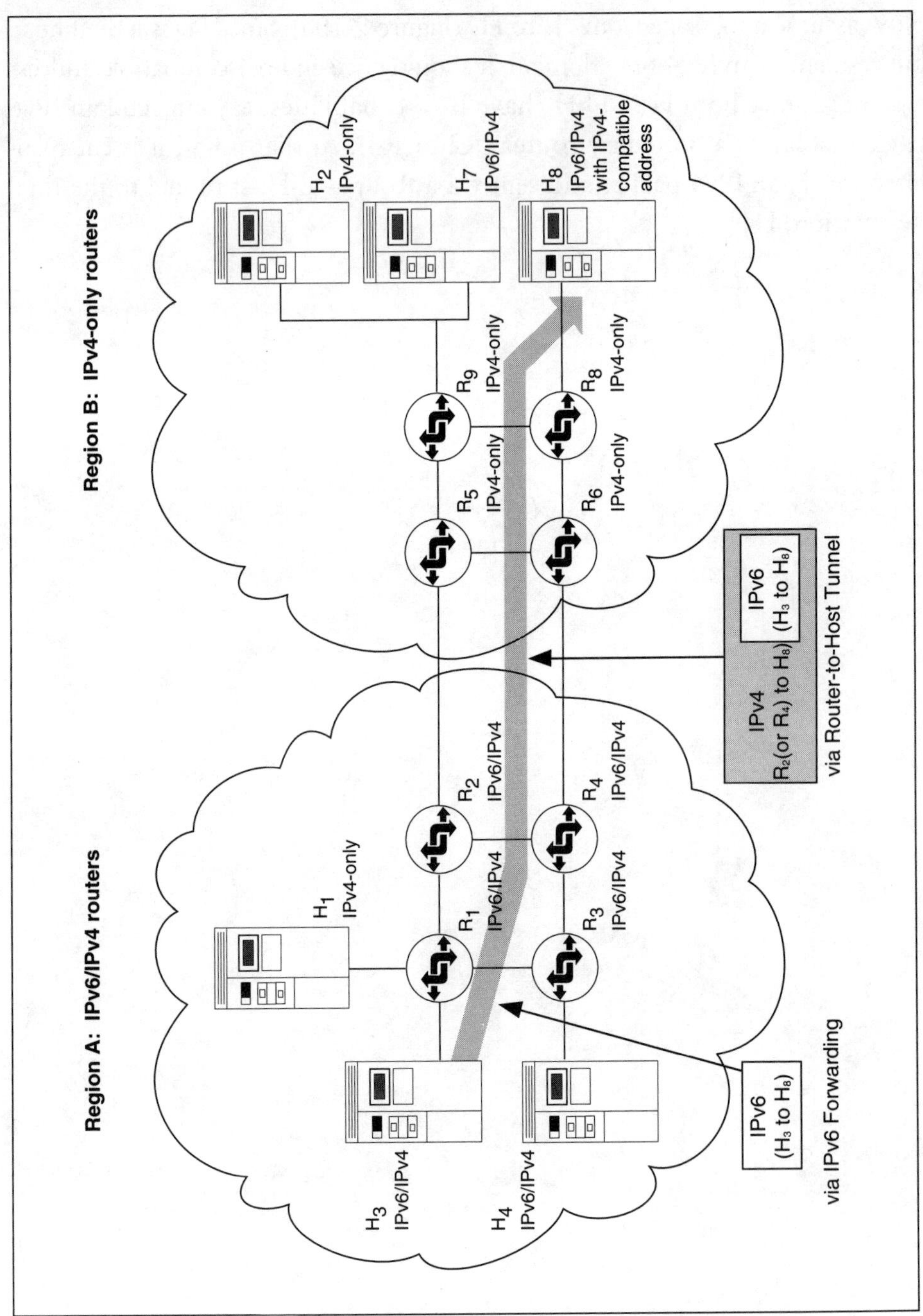

Figure 9-10d. Routing example: IPv6 packet from H_3 to H_8 (via Router-to-Host tunnel)

The return path from H_8 to H_3 may utilize one of two possible tunnels, depending on the type of address that is assigned to H_3. If H_3 has an IPv4-compatible address, and we continue to assume that H_8 also has an IPv4-compatible address (since it is in an IPv4-only region), then Host-to-Host automatic tunneling may be used (Figure 9-10e).

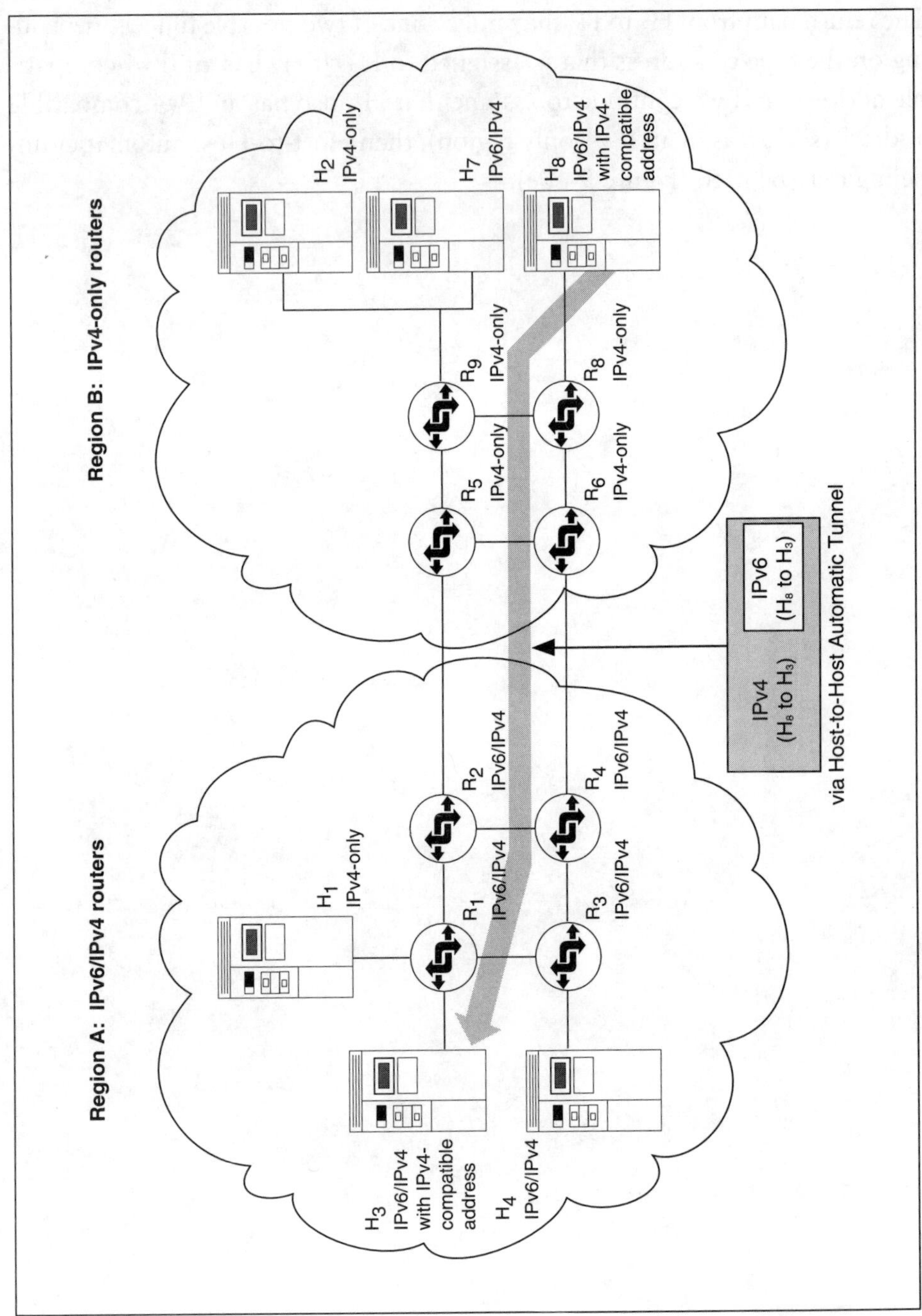

Figure 9-10e. Routing example: IPv6 packet from H_8 to H_3 (via Host-to-Host automatic tunnel)

If H_3 has an IPv6-only address (i.e. not IPv4-compatible), then the Host-to-Host automatic tunnel will not work, since the IPv4 destination address cannot be derived from the IPv6 address. A Host-to-Router configured tunnel from H_8 to a Region A border router (R_2 or R_4) will be used instead (Figure 9-10f). Source Host H_8 will generate an IPv6 packet, encapsulate it in an IPv4 datagram, and send it via a configured tunnel to Region A (R_2 or R_4). One of those dual routers will decapsulate the IPv6 packet, discard the IPv4 header, and send it to its final destination, H_3.

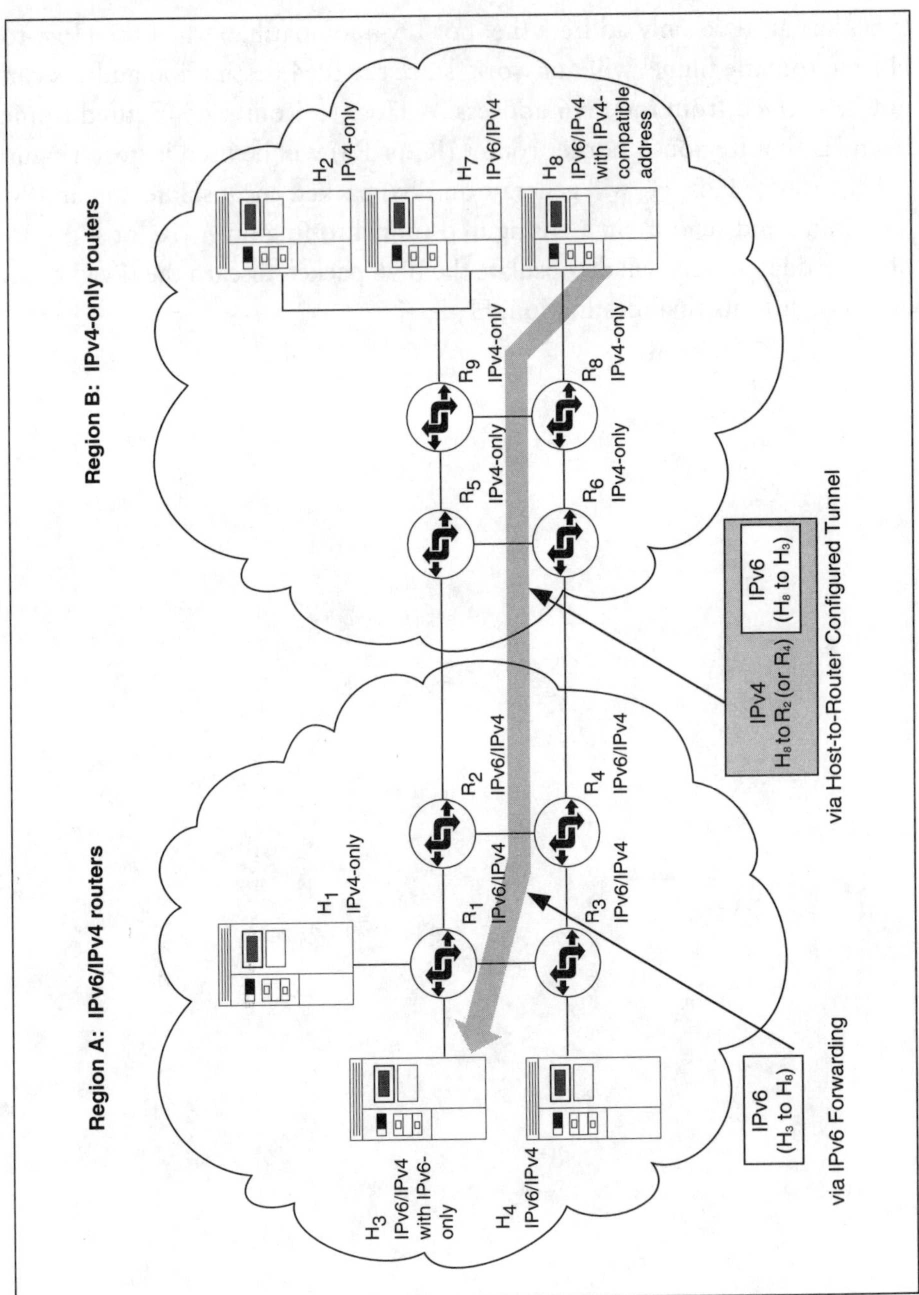

Figure 9-10f. Routing example: IPv6 packet from H_8 to H_3 (via Host-to-Router configured tunnel)

9.5 Implementing IPv6

Perhaps more so with IPv6 than with other network or systems implementations, the axiom *proper preparation prevents poor performance* rings true. A phased approach works best for most cases [9-4]. With IPv6, this may include setting up a test lab to experiment with IPv6 under very controlled conditions, connecting to the global 6Bone network to gain experience with links to other locations, and finally implementing IPv6 on your own internetwork or intranetwork. At some point in the implementation, installing IPv6 on a production network will occur; the key to that part of the upgrade is to avoid disruption to both systems and end users, thus keeping the required IPv4 services operational.

As we have seen, the IPv6 enhancements fall into two general categories: routing enhancements and host enhancements. The routing enhancements would include packet prioritization, flow labeling, tunneling mechanisms, and so on. The host enhancements include address autoconfiguration, authentication, encryption, multicast packet transmission, plus real-time application support (by initiating packet prioritization and flow labeling). Thus, by defining your objective for implementing IPv6—to leverage the router-based enhancements, host-based enhancements, or both—you can get a clearer picture of your objective.

A next step would be to survey the vendors that are currently supplying your internetworking hardware and software to ascertain their progress with IPv6. In many cases, you will need to upgrade your operating system or application programs to take advantage of the IPv6 capabilities such as security or multicasting. The IPv6 Industry Web Site (http://playground.sun.com/pub/ipng) is a good source of this information. Appendix C lists many of the manufacturers that have indicated support for IPv6-related products.

Planning the implementation must include a study of both the physical and logical topologies of your internetwork. From Chapter 4, we saw that both IPv4 and IPv6 can operate on the same Physical and Data Link Layer infrastructure; however, support for IPv6-specific functions, such as multicasting and address autoconfiguration, may be desired and should be verified as part of the implementation process.

Careful attention to the IPv6 addressing scheme, a key element of your logical topology, will also be an important step, as most devices that run IPv6 will be assigned multiple IPv6 addresses of different types (unicast, multicast, and so on). In addition, your Domain Name Server (DNS) will need to be upgraded to add support for the AAAA record type that is required for IPv6, and it may require additional memory.

Give special consideration to dual stack host software that supports IPv4-compatible IPv6 addresses, as this will enable Host-to-Host tunneling over your existing IPv4-based routing infrastructure. Once the DNS has been upgraded and the hosts have been enabled with software supporting automatic tunneling, your entry-level IPv6 internetwork is operational.

Upgrading the routing infrastructure may take a little more time. In addition, an upgrade to the routing infrastructure will require the cooperation of your Internet Service Provider (ISP), which will assign your organization an IPv6 address prefix.

Keep in mind that the existing IPv4-only routing infrastructure must be maintained as you progress to a dual IPv6/IPv4 system. According to RFC 2185, IPv4 and IPv6 presently have separate routing systems, with reachability from one system advertised into the other (route leaking). In the design of the IPv6 implementation, it is therefore important to verify connectivity between the IPv4 and IPv6/IPv4 domains. In many cases, configured tunnels will be required to span IPv4 segments between routers.

As the IPv6 protocol becomes more widespread and the industry as a whole matures, the interest in transition strategies and methods will necessarily increase. To keep up to date on these current events, monitor the ngtrans mailing list and check for any recently released Internet Drafts with the term *ngtrans* in the filename. Information on obtaining both RFC and Internet Draft documents can be found in Appendix D.

9.6 References

[9-1] The ngtrans mailing list is sponsored by the Next Generation Transition Working Group, which is an open forum for discussing the mechanisms and procedures to support the transition from IPv4 to IPv6. The list address is ngtrans@.sunroof.eng.com. To subscribe, send email to: *majordomo@eng.sun.com*, with the following in the message body: *subscribe ngtrans.*

[9-2] Gilligan, R., and E. Nordmark. "Transition Mechanisms for IPv6 Hosts and Routers." RFC 1933, April 1996.

[9-3] Callon, R., and D. Haskin. "Routing Aspects of IPv6 Transition." RFC 2185, September 1997.

[9-4] Miller, Mark A. "Making the Move—"The Path for an Orderly Transition from IPv4 to IPv6." *Network World* (January 20, 1997): 37–42.

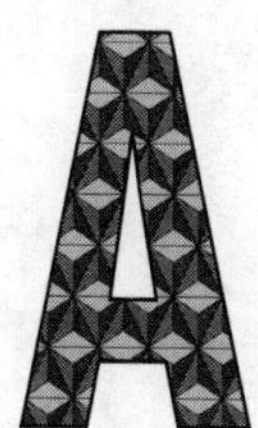

Addresses of Standards Organizations

ANSI STANDARDS

American National Standards Institute
11 West 42nd Street
New York, NY 10036
Telephone (212) 354-3300
Sales Department (212) 642-4900
URL: http://www.ansi.org

ATIS PUBLICATIONS

Alliance for Telecommunications Industry Solutions
(formerly the Exchange Carriers Standards Association)
1200 G Street N.W., Suite 500
Washington, DC 20005
Tel: (202) 628-6380
Fax: (202) 393-5453
URL: http://www.atis.org

AT&T PUBLICATIONS

Lucent Technologies
P.O. Box 19901
Indianapolis, IN 46219
Tel: (317) 322-6557 or (888) 582-3688
Fax: (800) 566-9568
URL: http://www.lucentdocs.com

BELLCORE STANDARDS

Bell Communications Research
Information Management Services
8 Corporate Place, Room 3A-184
Piscataway, NJ 08854-4196
Tel: (908) 699-5800 or (800) 521-2673
Fax: (732) 336-2559
URL: http://www.bellcore.com

CSA STANDARDS

Canadian Standards Association
178 Rexdale Boulevard
Etobicoke, ONT M9W 1R3
Canada
Tel: (416) 747-4363
Fax: (416) 747-2473

DDN STANDARDS

DoD Network Information Center
Boeing Corporation
7990 Boeing Court, M/S CV-50
Vienna, VA 22183-7000
Tel: (703) 821-6266 or (800) 365-3642
Fax: (703) 821-6161
URL: http://www.nic.mil

DISA STANDARDS

Defense Information Systems Agency
URL: http://www.itsi.disa.mil

ECMA STANDARDS

European Computer Manufacturers Association
114 Rue de Rhone
CH-1204 Geneva
Switzerland
Tel: 41 22 849 60 00
Fax: 41 22 849 60 01
E-mail: helpdesk@ecma.ch
URL: http://www.ecma.ch

EIA STANDARDS

Electronic Industries Association
2500 Wilson Blvd.
Arlington, VA 22201
Tel: (703) 907-7500
Fax: (703) 907-7501
URL: http://www.eia.org

ETSI STANDARDS

European Telecommunications Standards Institute
ETSI Publications Office
06921 Sophia Antipolis Cedex
France
Tel: 33 (0) 492 94 42 41
Fax: 33 (0) 493 95 81 33
E-mail: anja.mulder@etsi.fr
URL: http://www.etsi.fr

FEDERAL INFORMATION PROCESSING STANDARDS (FIPS)

U.S. Department of Commerce
National Technical Information Service
5285 Port Royal Road
Springfield, VA 22161
Tel: (703) 487-4650
URL: http://www.ntis.gov

IEC STANDARDS

International Electrotechnical Commission
IEC Central Office
3, rue de Verenbe
P.O. Box 131
1211 Geneva 20
Switzerland
Tel: 41 22 919 02 11
Fax: 41 22 919 03 00
E-mail: dn@iec.ch
URL: http://www.hike.te.chiba-u.ac.jp/ikeda/IEC

IEEE STANDARDS

Institute of Electrical and Electronics Engineers
445 Hoes Lane
Piscataway, NJ 08855-1331
Tel: (908) 981-1393 or (800) 678-IEEE
Fax: (908) 562-1571
URL: http://www.ieee.org

INTERNET STANDARDS

Internet Society International
12020 Sunrise Valley Drive, Suite 210
Reston, VA 22191-3429
Tel: (703) 648-9888
Fax: (703) 648-9887
E-mail: isoc@isoc.org
URL: http://www.isoc.org

ISO STANDARDS

International Organization for Standardization

1, Rue de Varembe

Case Postale 56

CH-1211 Geneva 20

Switzerland

Tel: 41 22 749 01 11

Fax: 41 22 733 34 30

E-mail: central@isocs.iso.ch

URL: http://www.iso.ch

ITU STANDARDS

International Telecommunications Union

Information Services Department

Place des Nations

1211 Geneva 20

Switzerland

Tel: 41 22 730 5111 or 733 7256

E-mail: itumail@itu.int

URL: http://www.itu.ch

NATIONAL INSTITUTE OF STANDARDS AND TECHNOLOGY

Technology Building 820, NIST N, Room B-562

Gaithersburg, MD 20899

Tel: (301) 975-2000

Fax: (301) 948 6213

URL: http://www.ncsl.nist.gov

WWW STANDARDS

World Wide Web Consortium
Massachusetts Institute of Technology
Laboratory for Computer Science
545 Technology Square, 3rd Floor
Cambridge, MA 02139
Tel: (617) 253-2613
Fax: (617) 258-5999
E-mail: www-request@w3.org
URL: http://www.w3.org

Many of the above standards may be purchased from:

Global Engineering Documents
15 Inverness Way East
Englewood, CO 80112
Tel: (303) 790-0600 or (800) 854-7179
Fax: (303) 397-2740
URL: http://global.ihs.com

Phillips Business Information, Inc.
1201 Seven Locks Road, Suite 300
Potomac, MD 20854-2957
Tel: (301) 424-3338 or (800) 777-5006
Fax: (301) 309-3847
E-mail: clientservices.pbi@phillips.com
URL: http//www.phillips.com

Broadband Technology Forums

ATM Forum

Worldwide Headquarters

2570 W. El Camino Rio, Suite 304

Mountain View, CA 94040

Tel: (650) 949-6700

Fax: (650) 949-6705

E-mail: info@atmforum.com

URL: http://www.atmforum.com

ATM Forum

European Office

Boulevard Saint Michel 78

1040 Brussels, Belgium

Tel: 32 2 732 8505

Fax: 32 2 732 8408

Frame Relay Forum
North American Office
39355 California Street, Suite 307
Fremont, CA 94538
Tel: (510) 608-5920
Fax: (510) 608-5917
E-mail frf@frforum.com
FTP: ftp://frforum.com
URL: http://www.frforum.com

Frame Relay Forum
Asia/Pacific Office
Bldg. Hamamatsucho
Suzuki Bldg. 3F
1-2-11, Hamamatsucho,
Minato-ku Tokyo, 105, Japan
Tel: 81 3 3438 3694
Fax: 81 3 3438 3698

Frame Relay Forum
European Office
c/o OST, BP 158
Z1 Sud Est rue du bas Village
35510 Cesson Sevigne Cedex
France
Tel: 33 99 51 76 55
Fax: 33 99 41 71 75

SMDS Interest Group

303 Vintage Park Drive

Foster City, CA 94404

Tel: (415) 578-6979

Fax: (415) 525-0182

Faxback: (415) 688-4314

E-mail: sig@interop.com

URL: ftp://ftp.acc.com/pub/protocols/smds

Selected Manufacturers of IPv6-Related Internetworking Products

Apple Computer, Inc.
20525 Mariani Avenue
Cupertino, CA 95014
Tel: (408) 996-1010
(800) 776-2333
Fax: (408) 974-6726
http://www.apple.com

Bay Networks, Inc.
P.O. Box 58185
4401 Great America Parkway
Santa Clara, CA 95052-8185
Tel: (408) 988-2400
Fax: (408) 495-1194
http://www.baynetworks.com

Cisco Systems, Inc.
170 W. Tasman Drive
San Jose, CA 95134
Tel: (408) 526-4000
(800) 553-6387
Fax: (408) 526-4100
http://www.cisco.com

Digital Equipment Corporation
129 Parker Street
Maynard, MA 01754
Tel: (508) 467-4120
(800) 344-4825
Fax: (508) 467-3166
http://www.digital.com/info/ipv6

Epiloque Technology Corporation
201 Moffett Park Drive
Sunnyvale, CA 94089
Tel: (408) 542-1500
Fax: (408) 542-1961
E-mail: info@epilogue.com
http://www.epilogue.com

FTP Software, Inc.
2 High Street
North Andover, MA 01845
Tel: (978) 685-4000
(800) 282-4287
Fax: (978) 794-4488
http://www.ftp.com
info@ftp.com

Hitachi, Ltd.

810 Simo-imaizumi
Ebina-shi
Kanagawa-ken
243-04 Japan
Tel: 81 462 35 8259
E-mail: info-net@comp.hitachi.co.jp

IBM

11400 Burnet Road
Austin, TX 78758
(800) 426-3333
Fax: (800) 426-4329
E-mail: askibm@info.ibm.com
http://www.rs6000.ibm.com/ipv6

INRIA

French National Institute for Research in Computer Science and Control
Tel: 33 1 39 63 52 44
Fax: 33 1 39 63 59 60
http://www.inria.fr

Ipsilon Networks, Inc.

232 Java Drive
Sunnyvale, CA 94089-1318
Tel: (408) 990-2000
Fax: (408) 743-5675
E-mail: sales@ipsilon.com
http://www.ipsilon.com

Mentat, Inc.
1145 Gayley Avenue, Suite 315
Los Angeles, CA 90024
Tel: (310) 208-2650
Fax: (310) 208-3724
E-mail: info@mentat.com
http://www.mentat.com/ipv6.html

Novell, Inc.
2080 Fortune Dr.
San Jose, CA 95131
Tel: (408) 434-2300
(800) 638-9273
Fax: (408) 259-0778
http://www.novell.com

Pacific Softworks, Inc.
4000 Via Pescador
Camarillo, CA 93012
Tel: (805) 484-2128
(800) 541-9508
Fax: (805) 484-3929
E-mail: sales@pacificsw.com
http://www.pacificsw.com

Process Software Corporation
959 Concord Street
Framingham, MA 01701
Tel: (508) 879-6994
(800) 722-7770
Fax: (508) 879-0042
E-mail: info@process.com
http://www.process.com/ipv6

Santa Cruz Operation (SCO)
400 Encinal Street
Santa Cruz, CA 95060
Tel: (408) 425-7222
(800) 726-8649
Fax: (408) 458-4227
info@sco.com
http://www.sco.com

Siemens Nixdorf Informationssysteme AG
Otto-Hahn-Ring 6
D-81730
Munich, Germany
Tel: 49 89 636-01
Fax: 49 89 636-52
E-mail: uk-www.group@mch.sni.de
http://www.sni.de

Silicon Graphics, Inc.
2011 N. Shoreline Boulevard
Mountain View, CA 94043-1389
Tel: (650) 933-8000
(800) 800-7441
Fax: (650) 960-0197
http://www.sgi.com

Sumitomo Electric USA, Inc.
3235 Kifer Road, Suite 150
Santa Clara, CA 95051-0815
Tel: (408) 737-8517
Fax: (408) 737-0134
E-mail: info@sumitomo.com
http://www.sumitomo.com

Sun Microsystems, Inc.
2550 Garcia Avenue
Mountain View, CA 94043
Tel: (415) 960-1300
(800) 622-4786
Fax: (415) 968-9506
E-mail: sun-ipv6-info@sunroof.sun.com
http://www.playground.sun.com/pub/solaris2-ipv6

Telebit Communications A/S

Skanderborgvej 234

DK-8260 Viby J

Denmark

Tel: 45 86 28 81 76

Fax: 45 86 28 81 86

E-mail: info@tbit.dk

http://www.tbit.dk/MAY97/ipv6.html

3Com Corporation

5400 Bayfront Plaza

Santa Clara, CA 95052

Tel: (408) 764-5000

(800) 638-3266

Fax: (408) 764-5001

http://www.3com.com/nsc/ipv6.html

Wandel & Goltermann, Inc.

1030 Swabia Court

Research Triangle Park, NC 27709-3585

Tel: (919) 941-5730

(800) 729-9441

Fax: (919) 941-5751

http://www.wg.com

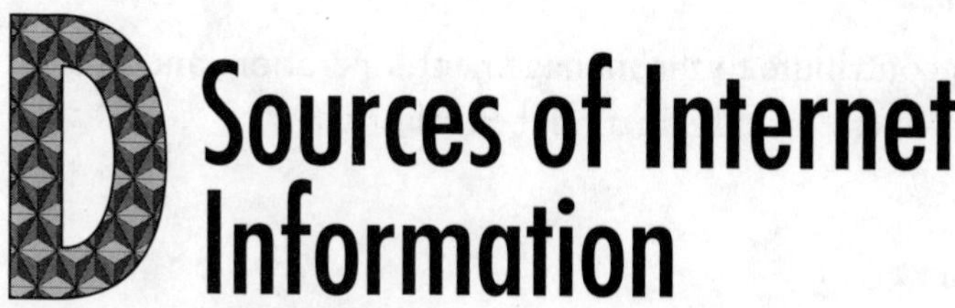

D Sources of Internet Information

Many of the adminstrative functions for the Internet are handled by the InterNIC. Directory and Database services are handled by AT&T, while Registration Services are handled by Network Solutions, Inc. Addresses for these organizations are listed below.

Internet Directory and Database Services

AT&T

Tel: (908) 668-6587 or (800) 862-0677

E-mail: admin@ds.internic.net

URL: ftp://ds.internic.net

Registration Services

Network Solutions, Inc.

Attn.: InterNIC Registration Services

505 Huntmar Park Drive

Herndon, VA 22070

Tel: (703) 742-4777

E-mail: admin@rs.internic.net

URL: http://rs.internic.net

Internet Organizations

A number of groups contribute to the management, operation, and proliferation of the Internet. These include (in alphabetical order):

CommerceNet
URL: http://www.commerce.net
E-mail: info@commerce.net

Commercial Internet Exchange Association
Tel: (703) 709-8200
URL: http://www.cix.org
E-mail: helpdesk@cix.org

Internet Architecture Board
URL: http://www.iab.org
E-mail: iab-contact@isi.edu

Internet Assigned Numbers Authority
URL: http://www.iana.org
E-mail: iana@isi.edu

Internet Engineering Task Force
URL: http://www.ietf.cnri.reston.va.us
E-mail: ietf-web@ietf.org

Internet Society
Tel: (703) 648-9888
URL: http://www.isoc.org
E-mail: isoc@isoc.org

World Wide Web Consortium
URL: http://www.w3.org
E-mail: admin@w3.org

Obtaining RFCs

The following is an excerpt from the file *rfc-retrieval.txt,* which is available from many of the RFC repositories listed below. This information is subject to change; obtain the current version of the rfc-retrieval file if problems occur. Also note that each RFC site may have instructions for file retrieval (such as a particular subdirectory) that are unique to that location.

RFCs may be obtained via e-mail or FTP from many RFC repositories. The primary repositories will have the RFC available when it is first announced, as will many secondary repositories. Some secondary repositories may take a few days to make available the most recent RFCs.

Many of these repositories also now have World Wide Web servers. Try the following URL as a starting point:

http://www.isi.edu/rfc-editor/

Primary Repositories

RFCs can be obtained via FTP from DS.INTERNIC.NET, NIS.NSF.NET, NISC.JVNC.NET, FTP.ISI.EDU, WUARCHIVE.WUSTL.EDU, SRC.DOC.IC.AC.UK, FTP.NCREN.NET, FTP.SESQUI.NET, NIS.GARR.IT, or FTP.IMAG.FR.

1. DS.INTERNIC.NET—InterNIC Directory and Database Services

   RFCs may be obtained from DS.INTERNIC.NET via FTP, WAIS, and electronic mail. Through FTP, RFCs are stored as rfc/rfcnnnn.txt or rfc/rfcnnnn.ps where "nnnn" is the RFC number. Login as "anonymous" and provide your e-mail address as the password. Through WAIS, you may use either your local WAIS client or telnet to DS.INTERNIC.NET and login as "wais" (no password required) to access a WAIS client. Help information and a tutorial for using WAIS are available online. The WAIS database to search is "rfcs."

   Directory and Database Services also provides a mail server interface. Send a mail message to mailserv@ds.internic.net and include any of the following commands in the message body:

document-by-name rfcnnnn	where "nnnn" is the RFC number. The text version is sent.
file /ftp/rfc/rfcnnnn.yyy	where "nnnn" is the RFC number and "yyy" is "txt" or "ps."
help	to get information on how to use the mailserver.

   The InterNIC Directory and Database Services Collection of Resource Listings, Internet Documents such as RFCs, FYIs, STDs, and Internet Drafts, and Publically Accessible Databases are also now available via Gopher. All our collections are WAIS-indexed and can be searched from the Gopher menu.

   To access the InterNIC Gopher servers, please connect to "internic.net" port 70.

   Contact: admin@ds.internic.net

2. NIS.NSF.NET

   To obtain RFCs from NIS.NSF.NET via FTP, login with username "anonymous" and password "guest"; then connect to the directory of RFCs with cd /internet/documents/rfc. The filename is of the form rfcnnnn.txt (where "nnnn" refers to the RFC number).

For sites without FTP capability, electronic mail query is available from NIS.NSF.NET. Address the request to NIS-INFO@NIS.NSF.NET and leave the subject field of the message blank. The first text line of the message must be "send rfcnnnn.txt" where "nnnn" is the RFC number.

Contact: rfc-mgr@merit.edu

3. NISC.JVNC.NET

RFCs can also be obtained via FTP from NISC.JVNC.NET, with the pathname rfc/rfcNNNN.txt (where "NNNN" refers to the number of the RFC). An index can be obtained with the pathname rfc/rfc-index.txt.

JvNCnet also provides a mail service for sites that cannot use FTP. Address the request to "SENDRFC@NISC.JVNC.NET" and in the subject field of the message indicate the RFC number, as in "Subject: rfcNNNN" (where "NNNN" is the RFC number). Please note that RFCs numbered less than 1000 need not place a leading "0" (for example, RFC932 is fine). For a complete index to the RFC library, enter "rfc-index" in the subject field, as in "Subject: rfc-index". No text in the body of the message is needed.

Contact: rfc-admin@nisc.jvnc.net

4. FTP.ISI.EDU

RFCs can be obtained via FTP from FTP.ISI.EDU, with the pathname in-notes/rfcnnnn.txt (where "nnnn" refers to the number of the RFC). Login with FTP username "anonymous" and password "name@host.domain."

RFCs can also be obtained via electronic mail from ISI.EDU by using the RFC-INFO service. Address the request to "rfc-info@isi.edu" with a message body of:

```
Retrieve: RFC
    Doc-ID: RFCnnnn
```

where "nnnn" refers to the number of the RFC (always use four digits; for example, the DOC-ID of RFC 822 is "RFC0822"). The RFC-INFO@ISI.EDU server provides other ways of selecting RFCs based on keywords and such; for more information send a message to "rfc-info@isi.edu" with the message body "help: help. "

Contact: RFC-Manager@ISI.EDU

5. WUARCHIVE.WUSTL.EDU

   RFCs can also be obtained via FTP from WUARCHIVE.WUSTL.EDU, with the pathname info/rfc/rfcnnnn.txt.Z (where "nnnn" refers to the number of the RFC and "Z" indicates that the document is in compressed form).

   At WUARCHIVE.WUSTL.EDU the RFCs are in an "archive" file system and various archives can be mounted as part of an NFS file system. Please contact Chris Myers (chris@wugate.wustl.edu) if you want to mount this file system in your NFS.

   Contact: chris@wugate.wustl.edu

6. SRC.DOC.IC.AC.UK

   RFCs can be obtained via FTP from SRC.DOC.IC.AC.UK with the pathname rfc/rfcnnnn.txt.gz or rfc/rfcnnnn.ps.gz (where "nnnn" refers to the number of the RFC). Login with FTP username "anonymous" and password "your-email-address". To obtain the RFC index, use the pathname rfc/rfc-index.txt.gz. (The trailing .gz indicates that the document is in compressed form.)

   SRC.DOC.IC.AC.UK also provides an automatic mail service for sites in the UK that cannot use FTP. Address the request to info-server@doc.ic.ac.uk with a subject line of "wanted" and a message body of:

   ```
   request sources
   topic path rfc/rfcnnnn.txt.gz
   request end
   ```

where "nnnn" refers to the number of the RFC. Multiple requests may be included in the same message by giving multiple "topic path" commands on separate lines. To request the RFC index, the command should read "topic path rfc/rfc-index.txt.gz."

The archive is also available using NIFTP and the ISO FTAM system.

Contact: ukuug-soft@doc.ic.ac.uk

7. FTP.NCREN.NET

To obtain RFCs from FTP.NCREN.NET via FTP, login with username "anonymous" and your Internet e-mail address as password. The RFCs can be found in the directory /rfc, with file names of the form:

rfcNNNN.txt or rfcNNNN.ps

where NNNN refers to the RFC number.

This repository is also accessible via WAIS and the Internet Gopher.

Contact: rfc-mgr@ncren.net

8. FTP.SESQUI.NET

RFCs can be obtained via FTP from FTP.SESQUI.NET, with the pathname pub/rfc/rfcnnnn.xxx (where "nnnn" refers to the number of the RFC and "xxx" indicates the document form, "txt" for ASCII and "ps" for Postscript).

At FTP.SESQUI.NET the RFCs are in an "archive" file system and various archives can be mounted as part of an NFS file system. Please contact RFC-maintainer (rfc-maint@sesqui.net) if you want to mount this file system in your NFS.

Contact: rfc-maint@sesqui.net

9. NIS.GARR.IT

RFCs can be obtained from NIS.GARR.IT FTP archive with the pathname mirrors/RFC/rfcnnnn.txt (where "nnnn" refers to the number of the RFC). Login with FTP, username "anonymous" and password "guest."

Summary of ways to get RFC from GARR-NIS FTP archive:

Via ftp:	ftp.nis.garr.it directory mirrors/RFC
Via gopher:	gopher.nis.garr.it folders
GARR-NIS anonymous FTP	
	"ftp.nis.garr.it"
	mirrors
	RFC
Via WWW:	ftp://ftp.nis.garr.it/mirrors/RFC
Via e-mail:	send a mail to dbserv@nis.garr.it whose body contains "get mirrors/ RFC/rfc<number>.[txt,ps]."

To get a file in the FTP archive via e-mail, put the get <fullpathname> command either in the subject or as a mail body line of a mail message sent to dbserv@nis.garr.it. <fullpathname> must be the concatenation of two strings, the directory path and the filename.

Remember to use uppercase and lowercase exactly! The directory path is listed at the beginning of each block of files.

Example: to get RFC1004... the command should be:

get mirrors/RFC/rfc1004.txt.

10. FTP.IMAG.FR

RFCs can be obtained via FTP from ftp.imag.fr with the pathname /pub/archive/IETF/rfc/rfcnnnn.txt (where ìnnnnî refers to the number of the RFC).

Login with FTP username ìanonymousî and password ìyour-email-address.î To obtain the RFC Index, use the pathname /pub/archive/IETF/rfc/rfc-index.txt.

Internet drafts and other IETF-related documents are also mirrored in the /pub/archive/IETF directory.

Contact: rfc-adm@imag.fr.

Secondary Repositories

Australia and Pacific Rim

Site:	munnari
Contact:	Robert Elz <kre@cs.mu.OZ.AU>
Host:	munnari.oz.au
Directory:	rfc
Notes:	RFCs in compressed format rfcNNNN.Z; postscript RFCs rfcNNNN.ps.Z

Site:	The Programmers' Society
z	University of Technology, Sydney
Contact:	ftp@progsoc.uts.edu.au
Host:	ftp.progsoc.uts.edu.au
Directory:	rfc (or std). Both are stored uncompressed.

Denmark

Site:	University of Copenhagen
Host:	ftp.denet.dk
Directory:	rfc

Finland

Site:	FUNET
Host:	nic.funet.fi
Directory:	index/RFC
Directory:	/pub/netinfo/rfc
Notes:	RFCs in compressed format. Also provides e-mail

access by sending mail to archive-server@nic.funet.fi.

France

Site: Centre d'Informatique Scientifique et Medicale (CISM)

Contact: ftpmaint@univ-lyon1.fr

Host: ftp.univ-lyon1.fr

Directories: pub/rfc/* Classified by hundreds

pub/mirrors/rfc Mirror of Internic

Notes: Files compressed with gzip. Online decompression done by the FTP server.

Site: Institut National de la Recherche en Informatique et Automatique (INRIA)

Address: info-server@inria.fr

Notes: RFCs are available via e-mail to the above address. Info Server manager is Mireille Yamajako (yamajako@inria.fr).

Germany

Site: EUnet Germany

Host: ftp.Germany.EU.net

Directory: pub/documents/rfc

Netherlands

Site:	EUnet
Host:	mcsun.eu.net
Directory:	rfc
Notes:	RFCs in compressed format.

Norway

Host:	ugle.unit.no
Directory:	pub/rfc

South Africa

Site:	The Internet Solution
Contact:	ftp-admin@is.co.za
Host:	ftp.is.co.za
Directory:	internet/in-notes/rfc

Sweden

Host:	sunic.sunet.se
Directory:	rfc
Host:	chalmers.se
Directory:	rfc

United States

Site:	cerfnet
Contact:	help@cerf.net
Host:	nic.cerf.net
Directory:	netinfo/rfc
Site:	NASA NAIC
Contact:	rfc-updates@naic.nasa.gov
Host:	naic.nasa.gov
Directory:	files/rfc
Site:	NIC.DDN.MIL (DoD users only)
Contact:	NIC@nic.ddn.mil
Host:	NIC.DDN.MIL
Directory:	rfc/rfcnnnn.txt
Note:	DOD users only may obtain RFCs via FTP from NIC.DDN.MIL. Internet users should *not* use this source due to inadequate connectivity.
Site:	uunet
Contact:	James Revell <revell@uunet.uu.net>
Host:	ftp.uu.net
Directory:	inet/rfc

The RFC-Info Service

The following describes the RFC-Info Service, which is an Internet document and information retrieval service. The text that follows describes in detail the service, which was obtained by using "Help:Help" as discussed below.

RFC-Info is an e-mail based service to help in locating and retrieving RFCs, FYIs, STDs, and IMRs. Users can ask for "lists" of all RFCs, FYIs, STDs, and IMRs having certain attributes such as their ID number, keywords, title, author, issuing organization, and date.

To use the service send e-mail to RFC-INFO@ISI.EDU with your requests in the body of the message. Feel free to put anything in the SUBJECT, the system ignores it. The body of the message is processed with case independence.

To get started you may send a message to RFC-INFO@ISI.EDU with requests such as in the following examples (without the explanation between []):

Help: Help	[to get this information page]
List: FYI	[list the FYI notes]
List: RFC	[list RFCs with window as keyword or in title] keywords: window
List: FYI	[list FYIs about windows] Keywords: window
List: *	[list all documents by Cooper] Author: Cooper
List: RFC	[list RFCs about ARPANET, ARPA NETWORK, etc.] title: ARPA*NET

List: RFC [list RFCs issued by MITRE, dated 7+8/1991]
Organization: MITRE
Dated-after: Jul-01-1991
Dated-before: Aug-31-1991

List: RFC [list RFCs obsoleting a given RFC]
Obsoletes: RFC0010

List: RFC [list RFCs by authors starting with "Bracken"]
Author: Bracken* [* is a wildcard matching all endings]

List: IMR [list the IMRs for the first 6 months of 92]
Dated-after: Dec-31-1991
Dated-before: Jul-01-1992

Retrieve: RFC [retrieve RFC 822]
Doc-ID: RFC0822 [note, always 4 digits in RFC#]

Retrieve: FYI [retrieve FYI 4]
Doc-ID: FYI0004 [note, always 4 digits in FYI#]

Retrieve: STD [retrieve STD 1]
Doc-ID: STD0001 [note, always 4 digits in STD#]

Retrieve: IMR [retrieve May 1992 Internet Monthly Report]

Doc-ID: IMR9205 [note, always 4 digits = YYMM]

Help: Manual [to retrieve the long user manual, 30+ pages]
Help: List [how to use the LIST request]
Help: Retrieve [how to use the RETRIEVE request]
Help: Topics [list topics for which help is available]
Help: Dates ["Dates" is such a topic]

List: keywords [list the keywords in use]

List: organizations [list the organizations known to the system]

A useful way to test this service is to retrieve the file "Where and how to get new RFCs" (which is also the file rfc-retrieval.txt noted above in the section "Obtaining RFCs"). Place the following in the message body:

```
Help: ways_to_get_rfcs
```

Internet Mailing Lists

A number of mailing lists are maintained on the Internet for the purposes of soliciting information and discussions on specific subjects. In addition, a number of the Internet Engineering Task Force (IETF) working groups maintain a list for the exchange of information specific to that group.

For example, the IETF maintains two lists: the IETF General Discussion list and the IETF Announcement list. To join the IETF Announcement list, send a request to:

ietf-announce-request@ietf.org

To join the IETF General Discussion, send a request to:

ietf-request@ietf.org

A number of other mailing lists are available. To join a mailing list, send a message to the associated request list:

listname-request@listhost (for example, *snmp-request@psi.com*)

With the following as the message body:

subscribe listname (for example, *subscribe snmp*)

A complete listing of the current IETF working groups and their respective mailing lists is available at:

http://www.ietf.cnri.reston.va.us/mailinglists.html

IPv6-Related RFCs

This appendix contains a listing of IPv6-related Request for Comments (RFC) documents, available via the Internet. This information was retrieved using the RFC Info Service, as described in Appendix D, using the keywords *IPng* and *IPv6*. For each entry, there are notations for author(s), publication date, and so on; most importantly, there are other RFCs that may either update or make obsolete a particular listing. In the event that the RFC you are researching has been updated or madde obsolete, go to the new RFC for more current information.

TYPE: RFC
DOC-ID: **RFC1454**
TITLE: Comparison of Proposals for Next Version of IP
AUTHORS: T. Dixon
DATE: May 1993
KEYWORDS: IPng, PIP, TUBA, SIP
ORGANIZATION: RARE Secretariat
FORMAT: ASCII
CHAR-COUNT: 35064
STATUS: INFORMATIONAL

TYPE: RFC
DOC-ID: **RFC1475**
TITLE: TP/IX: The Next Internet
AUTHORS: R. Ullmann
DATE: June 1993
KEYWORDS: IPv7, IPng
ORGANIZATION: Process Software Corporation
FORMAT: ASCII
CHAR-COUNT: 77854
STATUS: EXPERIMENTAL

TYPE: RFC
DOC-ID: **RFC1550**
TITLE: IP: Next Generation (IPng) White Paper Solicitation
AUTHORS: S. Bradner and A. Mankin
DATE: December 1993
ORGANIZATION: Harvard University, Naval Research Laboratory
FORMAT: ASCII
CHAR-COUNT: 12472
STATUS: INFORMATIONAL

TYPE: RFC
DOC-ID: **RFC1621**
TITLE: Pip Near-term Architecture
AUTHORS: P. Francis
DATE: May 1994
KEYWORDS: Internet Protocol, IPng

ORGANIZATION: NTT Software Lab
FORMAT: ASCII
CHAR-COUNT: 128905
STATUS: INFORMATIONAL

TYPE: RFC
DOC-ID: **RFC1622**
TITLE: Pip Header Processing
AUTHORS: P. Francis
DATE: May 1994
KEYWORDS: Internet Protocol, IPng
ORGANIZATION: NTT Software Lab
FORMAT: ASCII
CHAR-COUNT: 34837
STATUS: INFORMATIONAL

TYPE: RFC
DOC-ID: **RFC1667**
TITLE: Modeling and Simulation Requirements for IPng
AUTHORS: S. Symington, D. Wood, and M. Pullen
DATE: August 1994
KEYWORDS: White, Paper
ORGANIZATION: MITRE Corporation, George Mason University
FORMAT: ASCII
CHAR-COUNT: 17291
STATUS: INFORMATIONAL

TYPE: RFC

DOC-ID: **RFC1668**

TITLE: Unified Routing Requirements for IPng

AUTHORS: D. Estrin, T. Li, and Y. Rekhter

DATE: August 1994

KEYWORDS: White, Paper

ORGANIZATION: University of Southern California, Cisco Systems, Inc., T.J. Watson Research Center IBM Corporation

FORMAT: ASCII

CHAR-COUNT: 5106

STATUS: INFORMATIONAL

TYPE: RFC

DOC-ID: **RFC1669**

TITLE: Market Viability as a IPng Criteria

AUTHORS: J. Curran

DATE: August 1994

KEYWORDS: White, Paper

ORGANIZATION: BBN Technology Services, Inc.

FORMAT: ASCII

CHAR-COUNT: 8099

STATUS: INFORMATIONAL

TYPE: RFC

DOC-ID: **RFC1670**

TITLE: Input to IPng Engineering Considerations

AUTHORS: D. Heagerty

DATE: August 1994
KEYWORDS: White, Paper
ORGANIZATION: CERN
FORMAT: ASCII
CHAR-COUNT: 5350
STATUS: INFORMATIONAL

TYPE: RFC
DOC-ID: **RFC1671**
TITLE: IPng White Paper on Transition and Other Considerations
AUTHORS: B. Carpenter
DATE: August 1994
ORGANIZATION: CERN
FORMAT: ASCII
CHAR-COUNT: 17631
STATUS: INFORMATIONAL

TYPE: RFC
DOC-ID: **RFC1672**
TITLE: Accounting Requirements for IPng
AUTHORS: N. Brownlee
DATE: August 1994
KEYWORDS: White, Paper
ORGANIZATION: The University of Auckland
FORMAT: ASCII
CHAR-COUNT: 6185
STATUS: INFORMATIONAL

TYPE: RFC
DOC-ID: **RFC1673**
TITLE: Electric Power Research Institute Comments on IPng
AUTHORS: R. Skelton
DATE: August 1994
KEYWORDS: White, Paper
ORGANIZATION: EPRI
FORMAT: ASCII
CHAR-COUNT: 7476
STATUS: INFORMATIONAL

TYPE: RFC
DOC-ID: **RFC1674**
TITLE: A Cellular Industry View of IPng
AUTHORS: M. Taylor
DATE: August 1994
KEYWORDS: White, Paper
ORGANIZATION: McCaw Cellular Communications, Inc.
FORMAT: ASCII
CHAR-COUNT: 6157
STATUS: INFORMATIONAL

TYPE: RFC
DOC-ID: **RFC1675**
TITLE: Security Concerns for IPng
AUTHORS: S. Bellovin
DATE: August 1994

KEYWORDS: White, Paper

ORGANIZATION: AT&T Bell Laboratories

FORMAT: ASCII

CHAR-COUNT: 8290

STATUS: INFORMATIONAL

TYPE: RFC

DOC-ID: **RFC1676**

TITLE: INFN Requirements for an IPng

AUTHORS: A. Ghiselli, D. Salomoni, and C. Vistoli

DATE: August 1994

KEYWORDS: White, Paper

ORGANIZATION: INFN-CNAF

FORMAT: ASCII

CHAR-COUNT: 8493

STATUS: INFORMATIONAL

TYPE: RFC

DOC-ID: **RFC1677**

TITLE: Tactical Radio Frequency Communication Requirments for IPng

AUTHORS: B. Adamson

DATE: August 1994

KEYWORDS: White, Paper

ORGANIZATION: Naval Research Laboratory

FORMAT: ASCII

CHAR-COUNT: 24065

STATUS: INFORMATIONAL

TYPE: RFC
DOC-ID: **RFC1678**
TITLE: IPng Requirements of Large Corporate Networks
AUTHORS: E. Britton and J. Tavs
DATE: August 1994
KEYWORDS: White, Paper
ORGANIZATION: IBM Corp.
FORMAT: ASCII
CHAR-COUNT: 18650
STATUS: INFORMATIONAL

TYPE: RFC
DOC-ID: **RFC1679**
TITLE: HPN Working Group Input to the IPng Requirements Solicitation
AUTHORS: D. Green, P. Irey, D. Marlow, and K. O'Donoghue
DATE: August 1994
KEYWORDS: White, Paper
ORGANIZATION: NSWC-DD
FORMAT: ASCII
CHAR-COUNT: 22974
STATUS: INFORMATIONAL

TYPE: RFC
DOC-ID: **RFC1680**
TITLE: IPng Support for ATM Services
AUTHORS: C. Brazdziunas
DATE: August 1994

KEYWORDS: White, Paper

ORGANIZATION: Bellcore

FORMAT: ASCII

CHAR-COUNT: 17846

STATUS: INFORMATIONAL

TYPE: RFC

DOC-ID: **RFC1682**

TITLE: IPng BSD Host Implementation Analysis

AUTHORS: J. Bound

DATE: August 1994

KEYWORDS: White, Paper, Unix

ORGANIZATION: Digital Equipment Corporation

FORMAT: ASCII

CHAR-COUNT: 22295

STATUS: INFORMATIONAL

TYPE: RFC

DOC-ID: **RFC1683**

TITLE: Multiprotocol Interoperability In IPng

AUTHORS: R. Clark, M. Ammar, and K. Calvert

DATE: August 1994

KEYWORDS: White, Paper

ORGANIZATION: College of Computing Georgia Institute of Technology

FORMAT: ASCII

CHAR-COUNT: 28201

STATUS: INFORMATIONAL

TYPE: RFC
DOC-ID: **RFC1686**
TITLE: IPng Requirements: A Cable Television Industry Viewpoint
AUTHORS: M. Vecchi
DATE: August 1994
KEYWORDS: White, Paper
ORGANIZATION: Time Warner Cable
FORMAT: ASCII
CHAR-COUNT: 39052
STATUS: INFORMATIONAL

TYPE: RFC
DOC-ID: **RFC1687**
TITLE: A Large Corporate User's View of IPng
AUTHORS: E. Fleischman
DATE: August 1994
KEYWORDS: White, Paper
ORGANIZATION: Boeing Computer Services
FORMAT: ASCII
CHAR-COUNT: 34120
STATUS: INFORMATIONAL

TYPE: RFC
DOC-ID: **RFC1688**
TITLE: IPng Mobility Considerations
AUTHORS: W. Simpson
DATE: August 1994

KEYWORDS: White, Paper
ORGANIZATION: Daydreamer
FORMAT: ASCII
CHAR-COUNT: 19151
STATUS: INFORMATIONAL

TYPE: RFC
DOC-ID: **RFC1705**
TITLE: Six Virtual Inches to the Left: The Problem with IPng
AUTHORS: R. Carlson and D. Ficarella
DATE: October 1994
KEYWORDS: IPng, White paper
ORGANIZATION: Argonne National Laboratory, Motorola
FORMAT: ASCII
CHAR-COUNT: 65222
STATUS: INFORMATIONAL

TYPE: RFC
DOC-ID: **RFC1707**
TITLE: CATNIP: Common Architecture for the Internet
AUTHORS: M. McGovern and R. Ullmann
DATE: October 1994
KEYWORDS: IPng, White, Paper, IPv7
ORGANIZATION: Sunspot Graphics, Lotus Development Corporation
FORMAT: ASCII
CHAR-COUNT: 37568
STATUS: INFORMATIONAL

TYPE: RFC
DOC-ID: **RFC1710**
TITLE: Simple Internet Protocol Plus White Paper
AUTHORS: R. Hinden
DATE: October 1994
KEYWORDS: SIPP, IPng
ORGANIZATION: Sun Microsystems, Inc.
FORMAT: ASCII
CHAR-COUNT: 56910
STATUS: INFORMATIONAL

TYPE: RFC
DOC-ID: **RFC1715**
TITLE: The H Ratio for Address Assignment Efficiency
AUTHORS: C. Huitema
DATE: November 1994
KEYWORDS: IPng, White, Paper
ORGANIZATION: INRIA, Sophia-Antipolis
FORMAT: ASCII
CHAR-COUNT: 7392
STATUS: INFORMATIONAL

TYPE: RFC
DOC-ID: **RFC1719**
TITLE: A Direction for IPng
AUTHORS: P. Gross
DATE: December 1994

KEYWORDS: IPng, White, Paper, Internet, Protocol
ORGANIZATION: MCI
FORMAT: ASCII
CHAR-COUNT: 11118
STATUS: INFORMATIONAL

TYPE: RFC
DOC-ID: **RFC1726**
TITLE: Technical Criteria for Choosing IP The Next Generation (IPng)
AUTHORS: C. Partridge and F. Kastenholz
DATE: December 1994
KEYWORDS: IPng, White, Paper, Internet, Protocol
ORGANIZATION: BBN, FTP Software, Inc.
FORMAT: ASCII
CHAR-COUNT: 74109
STATUS: INFORMATIONAL

TYPE: RFC
DOC-ID: **RFC1752**
TITLE: The Recommendation for the IP Next Generation Protocol
AUTHORS: S. Bradner and A. Mankin
DATE: January 1995
KEYWORDS: IPng, Internet
ORGANIZATION: Harvard University, USC/Information Sciences Institute
FORMAT: ASCII
CHAR-COUNT: 127784
STATUS: PROPOSED STANDARD

TYPE: RFC

DOC-ID: **RFC1753**

TITLE: IPng Technical Requirements Of the Nimrod Routing and Addressing Architecture

AUTHORS: N. Chiappa

DATE: December 1994

KEYWORDS: IPng, White, Paper, Internet, Protocol

FORMAT: ASCII

CHAR-COUNT: 46586

STATUS: INFORMATIONAL

TYPE: RFC

DOC-ID: **RFC1776**

TITLE: The Address is the Message

AUTHORS: S. Crocker

DATE: March 1995

KEYWORDS: IPng

ORGANIZATION: CyberCash, Inc.

FORMAT: ASCII

CHAR-COUNT: 2051

STATUS: INFORMATIONAL

TYPE: RFC

DOC-ID: **RFC1809**

TITLE: Using the Flow Label Field in IPv6

AUTHORS: C. Partridge

DATE: June 1995

ORGANIZATION: BBN Systems and Technologies
FORMAT: ASCII
CHAR-COUNT: 13591
STATUS: INFORMATIONAL

TYPE: RFC
DOC-ID: **RFC1810**
TITLE: Report on MD5 Performance
AUTHORS: J. Touch
DATE: June 1995
KEYWORDS: IPv6, Message, Digest, Algorithm, Authentication
ORGANIZATION: USC/Information Sciences Institute
FORMAT: ASCII
CHAR-COUNT: 16607
STATUS: INFORMATIONAL

TYPE: RFC

TYPE: RFC
DOC-ID: **RFC1825**
TITLE: Security Architecture for the Internet Protocol
AUTHORS: R. Atkinson
DATE: August 1995
KEYWORDS: IPv4, IPv6, IP-layer
ORGANIZATION: Naval Research Laboratory
FORMAT: ASCII
CHAR-COUNT: 56772
STATUS: PROPOSED STANDARD

TYPE: RFC
DOC-ID: **RFC1826**
TITLE: IP Authentication Header
AUTHORS: R. Atkinson
DATE: August 1995
KEYWORDS: Internet, Protocol, AH, security, IPv4, IPv6
ORGANIZATION: Naval Research Laboratory
FORMAT: ASCII
CHAR-COUNT: 27583
STATUS: PROPOSED STANDARD

TYPE: RFC
DOC-ID: **RFC1827**
TITLE: IP Encapsulating Security Payload (ESP)
AUTHORS: R. Atkinson
DATE: August 1995
KEYWORDS: Internet, Protocol, IPv4, IPv6
ORGANIZATION: Naval Research Laboratory
FORMAT: ASCII
CHAR-COUNT: 30278
STATUS: PROPOSED STANDARD

TYPE: RFC
DOC-ID: **RFC1881**
TITLE: IPv6 Address Allocation Management
AUTHORS: IAB and IESG
DATE: December 1995
KEYWORDS: IANA, Internet, Assigned, Numbers, Authority
ORGANIZATION: Internet Architecture Board, Internet Engineering Steering Group
FORMAT: ASCII
CHAR-COUNT: 3215
STATUS: INFORMATIONAL

TYPE: RFC
DOC-ID: **RFC1883**
TITLE: Internet Protocol, Version 6 (IPv6) Specification
AUTHORS: S. Deering and R. Hinden
DATE: December 1995
KEYWORDS: IP, Next, Generation, IPng
ORGANIZATION: Xerox Palo Alto Research Center, Ipsilon Networks, Inc.
FORMAT: ASCII
CHAR-COUNT: 82089
STATUS: PROPOSED STANDARD

TYPE: RFC

DOC-ID: **RFC1885**

TITLE: Internet Control Message Protocol (ICMPv6) for the Internet Protocol Version 6 (IPv6)

AUTHORS: A. Conta and S. Deering

DATE: December 1995

KEYWORDS: IP, Next, Generation, IPng, Internet, Group, Management, IGMP

ORGANIZATION: Digital Equipment Corporation, Xerox Palo Alto Research Center

FORMAT: ASCII

CHAR-COUNT: 32214

STATUS: PROPOSED STANDARD

TYPE: RFC

DOC-ID: **RFC1887**

TITLE: An Architecture for IPv6 Unicast Address Allocation

AUTHORS: Y. Rekhter and T. Li, editors

DATE: December 1995

KEYWORDS: IP, Next, Generation, IPng

ORGANIZATION: cisco Systems, Inc.

FORMAT: ASCII

CHAR-COUNT: 66066

STATUS: INFORMATIONAL

TYPE: RFC

DOC-ID: **RFC1888**

TITLE: OSI NSAPs and IPv6

AUTHORS: J. Bound, B. Carpenter, D. Harrington, J. Houldsworth, and A. Lloyd

DATE: August 1996

KEYWORDS: Internet, Protocol, Open, Systems, Interconnection

ORGANIZATION: Digital Equipment Corporation, CERN, Datacraft Technologies

FORMAT: ASCII

CHAR-COUNT: 36469

STATUS: EXPERIMENTAL

DOC-ID: **RFC1883**

TITLE: Internet Protocol, Version 6 (IPv6) Specification

AUTHORS: S. Deering and R. Hinden

DATE: December 1995

KEYWORDS: IP, Next, Generation, IPng

ORGANIZATION: Xerox Palo Alto Research Center, Ipsilon Networks, Inc.

FORMAT: ASCII

CHAR-COUNT: 82089

STATUS: PROPOSED STANDARD

TYPE: RFC

DOC-ID: **RFC1884**

TITLE: IP Version 6 Addressing Architecture

AUTHORS: R. Hinden and S. Deering, editors

DATE: December 1995

KEYWORDS: IP, Next, Generation, IPng

ORGANIZATION: Xerox Palo Alto Research Center, Ipsilon Networks, Inc.

FORMAT: ASCII

CHAR-COUNT: 37860

STATUS: PROPOSED STANDARD

TYPE: RFC

DOC-ID: **RFC1885**

TITLE: Internet Control Message Protocol (ICMPv6) for the Internet Protocol Version 6 (IPv6)

AUTHORS: A. Conta, S. Deering

DATE: December 1995

KEYWORDS: IP, Next, Generation, IPng, Internet, Group, Management, IGMP

ORGANIZATION: Digital Equipment Corporation, Xerox Palo Alto Research Center

FORMAT: ASCII

CHAR-COUNT: 32214

STATUS: PROPOSED STANDARD

TYPE: RFC

DOC-ID: **RFC1886**

TITLE: DNS Extensions to support IP version 6

AUTHORS: S. Thomson and C. Huitema

DATE: December 1995

KEYWORDS: IP, Next, Generation, IPng, Domain, Name, System

FORMAT: ASCII

CHAR-COUNT: 6424

STATUS: PROPOSED STANDARD

TYPE: RFC

DOC-ID: **RFC1887**

TITLE: An Architecture for IPv6 Unicast Address Allocation

AUTHORS: Y. Rekhter and T. Li, editors

DATE: December 1995

KEYWORDS: IP, Next, Generation, IPng,

ORGANIZATION: cisco Systems, Inc.

FORMAT: ASCII

CHAR-COUNT: 66066

STATUS: INFORMATIONAL

TYPE: RFC

DOC-ID: **RFC1897**

TITLE: IPv6 Testing Address Allocation

AUTHORS: R. Hinden and J. Postel

DATE: January 1996

KEYWORDS: Internet, Protocol, prototype, software

ORGANIZATION: Ipsilon Networks, Inc., Information Sciences Institute

FORMAT: ASCII

CHAR-COUNT: 6643

STATUS: EXPERIMENTAL

TYPE: RFC

DOC-ID: **RFC1924**

TITLE: A Compact Representation of IPv6 Addresses

AUTHORS: R. Elz

DATE: April 1996

KEYWORDS: encoding

ORGANIZATION: University of Melbourne

FORMAT: ASCII

CHAR-COUNT: 10409

STATUS: INFORMATIONAL

TYPE: RFC
DOC-ID: **RFC1933**
TITLE: Transition Mechanisms for IPv6 Hosts and Routers
AUTHORS: R. Gilligan and E. Nordmark
DATE: April 1996
KEYWORDS: IPv4
ORGANIZATION: Sun Microsystems, Inc.
FORMAT: ASCII
CHAR-COUNT: 47005
STATUS: PROPOSED STANDARD

TYPE: RFC
DOC-ID: **RFC1955**
TITLE: New Scheme for Internet Routing and Addressing (ENCAPS) for IPNG
AUTHORS: R. Hinden
DATE: June 1996
KEYWORDS: IPNG, addressing, routing
ORGANIZATION: Ipsilon Networks, Inc.
FORMAT: ASCII
CHAR-COUNT: 10115
STATUS: INFORMATIONAL

TYPE: RFC
DOC-ID: **RFC1970**
TITLE: Neighbor Discovery for IP Version 6 (IPv6)
AUTHORS: T. Narten, E. Nordmark, and W. Simpson
DATE: August 1996
KEYWORDS: Internet, Protocol

ORGANIZATION: Sun Microsystems, Inc., IBM Corporation, Daydreamer

FORMAT: ASCII

CHAR-COUNT: 197632

STATUS: PROPOSED STANDARD

TYPE: RFC

DOC-ID: **RFC1971**

TITLE: IPv6 Stateless Address Autoconfiguration

AUTHORS: S. Thomson and T. Narten

DATE: August 1996

KEYWORDS: Internet, Protocol, link-local, address, Duplicate, Address, Detection, procedure

ORGANIZATION: Bellcore, IBM Corporation,

FORMAT: ASCII

CHAR-COUNT: 56890

STATUS: PROPOSED STANDARD

TYPE: RFC

DOC-ID: **RFC1972**

TITLE: A Method for the Transmission of IPv6 Packets over Ethernet Networks

AUTHORS: M. Crawford

DATE: August 1996

KEYWORDS: Internet, Protocol, frame, format, transmission

ORGANIZATION: Fermilab MS 368

FORMAT: ASCII

CHAR-COUNT: 6353

STATUS: PROPOSED STANDARD

TYPE: RFC
DOC-ID: **RFC2019**
TITLE: Transmission of IPv6 Packets Over FDDI
AUTHORS: M. Crawford
DATE: October 1996
KEYWORDS: frame, format, Fiber, Distributed, Data, Interface
ORGANIZATION: Fermilab
FORMAT: ASCII
CHAR-COUNT: 12344
STATUS: PROPOSED STANDARD

TYPE: RFC
DOC-ID: **RFC2023**
TITLE: IP Version 6 over PPP
AUTHORS: D. Haskin, E. Allen
DATE: October 1996
KEYWORDS: Internet, Protocol, Point, IPv6
ORGANIZATION: Bay Networks, Inc.
FORMAT: ASCII
CHAR-COUNT: 20275
STATUS: PROPOSED STANDARD

TYPE: RFC
DOC-ID: **RFC2030**
TITLE: Simple Network Time Protocol (SNTP) Version 4 for IPv4, IPv6 and OSI
AUTHORS: D. Mills
DATE: October 1996
KEYWORDS: computer, clocks, synchronization

ORGANIZATION: University of Delaware

FORMAT: ASCII

CHAR-COUNT: 48620

OBSOLETES: RFC1769

STATUS: INFORMATIONAL

TYPE: RFC

DOC-ID: **RFC2073**

TITLE: An IPv6 Provider-Based Unicast Address Format

AUTHORS: Y. Rekhter, P. Lothberg, R. Hinden, S. Deering, and J. Postel

DATE: January 1997

ORGANIZATION: Cisco Systems, Inc., STUPI.AB, Ipsilon Networks, Inc., Xerox Palo Alto Research Center, Information Sciences Institute

FORMAT: ASCII

CHAR-COUNT: 15549

STATUS: PROPOSED STANDARD

TYPE: RFC

DOC-ID: **RFC2080**

TITLE: RIPng for IPv6

AUTHORS: G. Malkin and R. Minnear

DATE: January 1997

KEYWORDS: Routing, Information, Protocol, Internet

ORGANIZATION: Xylogics, Inc., Ipsilon Networks, Inc.

FORMAT: ASCII

CHAR-COUNT: 47534

STATUS: PROPOSED STANDARD

TYPE: RFC

DOC-ID: **RFC2133**

TITLE: Basic Socket Interface Extensions for IPv6

AUTHORS: R. Gilligan, S. Thomson, J. Bound, and W. Stevens

DATE: April 1997

KEYWORDS: application, program, interface, API, Internet, Protocol, addresses

ORGANIZATION: Freegate Corporation, Bell Communications Research, Digital Equipment Corporation,

FORMAT: ASCII

CHAR-COUNT: 69737

STATUS: INFORMATIONAL

TYPE: RFC

DOC-ID: **RFC2147**

TITLE: TCP and UDP over IPv6 Jumbograms

AUTHORS: D. Borman

DATE: May 1997

KEYWORDS: User, Datagram, Protocol, Terminal, Control, Internet

ORGANIZATION: Berkeley Software Design, Inc.

FORMAT: ASCII

CHAR-COUNT: 1883

STATUS: PROPOSED STANDARD

TYPE: RFC

DOC-ID: **RFC2185**

TITLE: Routing Aspects of IPv6 Transition

AUTHORS: R. Callon and D. Haskin

DATE: September 1997

KEYWORDS: address, network, tunneling

ORGANIZATION: Cascade Communications Co., Bay Networks, Inc.

FORMAT: ASCII

CHAR-COUNT: 31281

STATUS: INFORMATIONAL

IPv6 Parameters

The Internet Assigned Numbers Authority (IANA) periodically publishes a (very lengthy) RFC entitled "Assigned Numbers" (currently RFC 1700). The various sections of this document are also updated periodically in an online archive:

ftp://ftp.isi.edu/in-notes/iana/assignments

The sections below were retrieved from that archive and are reproduced here for the benefit of the reader. Note that the various RFC references (shown in brackets, e.g., [RFC1888]) that this information is based upon may be updated and may become obsolete. Therefore, the information below may become obsolete as well. For the most current information, consult the FTP server noted above. The filenames are included at the end of each section.

F.1 IP Version 6 Parameters

Note that the information below is based upon the IPv6 Specification given in RFC 1883.

```
1. Version Number = 6

2. Priority

        0 - uncharacterized
        1 - filler
        2 - unattended
        3 - (reserved)
        4 - attended bulk
        5 - (reserved)
        6 - interactive
        7 - internet control
```

3. Payload Length

4. Flow Label

5. Next Header

5.a. Header types

```
00 - Hop-by-Hop Options
43 - Routing
44 - Fragment
51 - Authentication
60 - Destination Options
50 - Encapsulating Security Payload
xx - Upper Layer Header
58 - Internet Control Message Protocol (ICMP)
59 - no next header
```

For the "xx" values see the list of protocol numbers (see the file: protocol-numbers).

5.b. Options

The options have a type, length. value (TLV) structure.

The type is a 2-bit action code, a 1-bit change code, and a 5-bit operation code.

The action codes are:

```
00 - skip
01 - discard
10 - discard and report
11 - discard and report if not multicast
```

The change codes are:

```
0 - no change en-route
1 - change allowed en-route
```

The operation codes are:

```
0 - Pad 1 (special case: this option is just this one octet)
1 - Pad N
2 - Jumbo Payload Length
3 - NSAP Address                                 [RFC1888]
4 - Endpoint Identifier for Nimrod
```

```
5.c. Routing Types

        0 - Source Route
        1 - Nimrod

6. Hop Limit

7. Source Address

8. Destination Address
```

Filename: ftp://ftp.isi.edu/in-notes/iana/assignments/ipv6-parameters

F.2 Protocol Numbers

In the Internet Protocol version 4 (IPv4) [RFC791] there is a field called "Protocol"that is used to identify the next level protocol. This is an 8-bit field. In Internet Protocol version 6 (IPv6) [RFC1883], this field is called the "Next Header" field.

Decimal	Keyword	Protocol
0	HOPOPT	IPv6 Hop-by-Hop Option
1	ICMP	Internet Control Message
2	IGMP	Internet Group Management
3	GGP	Gateway-to-Gateway
4	IP	IP in IP (encapsulation)
5	ST	Stream
6	TCP	Transmission Control
7	CBT	CBT
8	EGP	Exterior Gateway Protocol
9	IGP	any private interior gateway
10	BBN-RCC-MON	BBN RCC Monitoring
11	NVP-II	Network Voice Protocol
12	PUP	PUP
13	ARGUS	ARGUS
14	EMCON	EMCON
15	XNET	Cross Net Debugger
16	CHAOS	Chaos
17	UDP	User Datagram
18	MUX	Multiplexing
19	DCN-MEAS	DCN Measurement Subsystems
20	HMP	Host Monitoring
21	PRM	Packet Radio Measurement
22	XNS-IDP	XEROX NS IDP

23	TRUNK-1	Trunk-1
24	TRUNK-2	Trunk-2
25	LEAF-1	Leaf-1
26	LEAF-2	Leaf-2
27	RDP	Reliable Data Protocol
28	IRTP	Internet Reliable Transaction
29	ISO-TP4	ISO Transport Protocol Class 4
30	NETBLT	Bulk Data Transfer Protocol
31	MFE-NSP	MFE Network Services Protocol
32	MERIT-INP	MERIT Internodal Protocol
33	SEP	Sequential Exchange Protocol
34	3PC	Third Party Connect Protocol
35	IDPR	Inter-Domain Policy Routing Protocol
36	XTP	XTP
37	DDP	Datagram Delivery Protocol
38	IDPR-CMTP	IDPR Control Message Transport Protocol
39	TP++	TP++ Transport Protocol
40	IL	IL Transport Protocol
41	IPv6	IPv6
42	SDRP	Source Demand Routing Protocol
43	IPv6-Route	Routing Header for IPv6
44	IPv6-Frag	Fragment Header for IPv6
45	IDRP	Inter-Domain Routing Protocol
46	RSVP	Reservation Protocol
47	GRE	General Routing Encapsulation
48	MHRP	Mobile Host Routing Protocol
49	BNA	BNA
50	ESP	Encapsulating Security Payload for IPv6
51	AH	Authentication Header for IPv6
52	I-NLSP	Integrated Net Layer Security
53	SWIPE	IP with Encryption
54	NARP	NBMA Address Resolution Protocol
55	MOBILE	IP Mobility
56	TLSP	Transport Layer Security Protocol
57	SKIP	SKIP
58	IPv6-ICMP	ICMP for IPv6
59	IPv6-NoNxt	No Next Header for IPv6
60	IPv6-Opts	Destination Options for IPv6
61	any host internal protocol	
62	CFTP	CFTP
63	any local network	
64	SAT-EXPAK	SATNET and Backroom EXPAK
65	KRYPTOLAN	Kryptolan
66	RVD	MIT Remote Virtual Disk Protocol
67	IPPC	Internet Pluribus Packet Core
68	any distributed file system	

69	SAT-MON	SATNET Monitoring
70	VISA	VISA Protocol
71	IPCV	Internet Packet Core Utility
72	CPNX	Computer Protocol Network Executive
73	CPHB	Computer Protocol Heart Beat
74	WSN	Wang Span Network
75	PVP	Packet Video Protocol
76	BR-SAT-MON	Backroom SATNET Monitoring
77	SUN-ND	SUN ND PROTOCOL-Temporary
78	WB-MON	WIDEBAND Monitoring
79	WB-EXPAK	WIDEBAND EXPAK
80	ISO-IP	ISO Internet Protocol
81	VMTP	VMTP
82	SECURE-VMTP	SECURE-VMTP
83	VINES	VINES
84	TTP	TTP
85	NSFNET-IGP	NSFNET-IGP
86	DGP	Dissimilar Gateway Protocol
87	TCF	TCF
88	EIGRP	EIGRP
89	OSPFIGP	OSPFIGP
90	Sprite-RPC	Sprite RPC Protocol
91	LARP	Locus Address Resolution Protocol
92	MTP	Multicast Transport Protocol
93	AX.25	AX.25 Frames
94	IPIP	IP-within-IP Encapsulation Protocol
95	MICP	Mobile Internetworking Control Protocol
96	SCC-SP	Semaphore Communications Sec. Protocol
97	ETHERIP	Ethernet-within-IP Encapsulation
98	ENCAP	Encapsulation Header
99	any private encryption scheme	
100	GMTP	GMTP
101	IFMP	Ipsilon Flow Management Protocol
102	PNNI	PNNI over IP
103	PIM	Protocol Independent Multicast
104	ARIS	ARIS
105	SCPS	SCPS
106	QNX	QNX
107	A/N	Active Networks
108	IPPCP	IP Payload Compression Protocol
109	SNP	Sitara Networks Protocol
110	Compaq-Peer	Compaq Peer Protocol
111-254	Unassigned	
255	Reserved	

Filename: ftp://ftp.isi.edu/in-notes/iana/assignments/protocol-numbers

F.3 IP Version 6 Address Space

The allocation of Internet Protocol version 6 (IPv6) address space to various uses listed here [RFC1884].

Allocation	Prefix (binary)	Fraction of Address Space	Reference
Reserved	0000 0000	1/256	
the "unspecified"address	0:0:0:0:0:0:0:0		[RFC1970]
Unassigned	0000 0001	1/256	
Reserved for NSAP Allocation	0000 001	1/128	
Reserved for IPX Allocation	0000 010	1/128	
Unassigned	0000 011	1/128	
Unassigned	0000 1	1/32	
Unassigned	0001	1/16	
Unassigned	001	1/8	
Provider-Based Unicast Address	010	1/8	
Multi-Regional (IANA)	010 10000	1/256	
Europe (RIPE-NCC)	010 01000	1/256	
North America (ARIN)	010 11000	1/256	
Asia-Pacific (APNIC)	010 00100	1/256	
IPv6 Testing Address Block	010 11111	1/256	[RFC1897]
Unassigned	011	1/8	
Reserved for Geographic-Based Unicast Addresses	100	1/8	
Unassigned	101	1/8	
Unassigned	110	1/8	
Unassigned	1110	1/16	
Unassigned	1111 0	1/32	
Unassigned	1111 10	1/64	
Unassigned	1111 110	1/128	
Unassigned	1111 1110 0	1/512	
Link Local Use Addresses	1111 1110 10	1/1024	
link local	FE80		[RFC1971]
Site Local Use Addresses	1111 1110 11	1/1024	
site local	FE90		

```
Multicast Addresses              1111 1111      1/256
```

An IPv6 multicast address is an identifier for a group of nodes. A node may belong to any number of multicast groups. Multicast addresses have the following format:

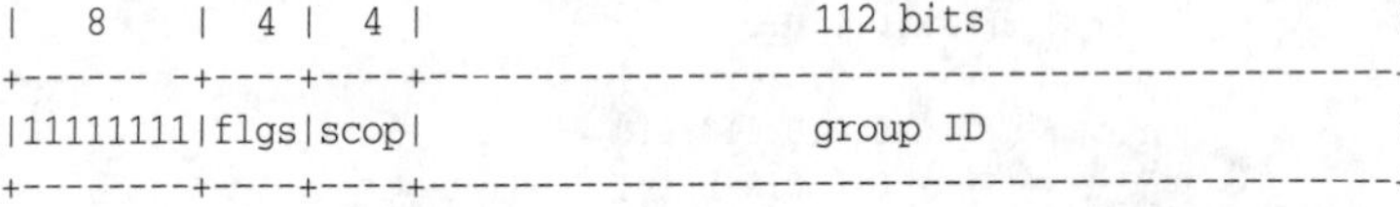

```
|   8    |  4 |  4 |                  112 bits                   |
+------ -+----+----+---------------------------------------------+
|11111111|flgs|scop|                  group ID                   |
+--------+----+----+---------------------------------------------+
```

11111111 at the start of the address identifies the address as being a multicast address.

```
                                  +-+-+-+-+
flgs is a set of 4 flags:         |0|0|0|T|
                                  +-+-+-+-+
```

The high-order 3 flags are reserved, and must be initialized to 0.

T = 0 indicates a permanently-assigned ("well-known") multicast address, assigned by the global internet numbering authority.

T = 1 indicates a non-permanently-assigned ("transient") multicast address.

scop is a 4-bit multicast scope value used to limit the scope of the multicast group. The values are:

```
0  reserved
1  node-local scope
2  link-local scope
3  (unassigned)
4  (unassigned)
5  site-local scope
6  (unassigned)
7  (unassigned)
8  organization-local scope
9  (unassigned)
A  (unassigned)
B  (unassigned)
C  (unassigned)
D  (unassigned)
E  global scope
F  reserved
```

```
group ID identifies the multicast group, either permanent or transient,
within the given scope.

So here we assign only the group ID part of the address (the low order 112 bits).

all-nodes                     FFxx:0:0:0:0:0:0:1
all-routers                   FFxx:0:0:0:0:0:0:2
all-rip-routers               FFxx:0:0:0:0:0:0:9
all-cbt-routers               FFxx:0:0:0:0:0:0:10
reserved                      FFxx:0:0:0:0:0:1:0
linkname                      FFxx:0:0:0:0:0:1:1
all-dhcp-agents               FFxx:0:0:0:0:0:1:2
all-dhcp-servers              FFxx:0:0:0:0:0:1:3
all-dhcp-relays               FFxx:0:0:0:0:0:1:4
solicited-nodes               FFxx:0:0:0:0:1:0:0              [RFC1970]

multicast address            FFxx::1:0:0 to FFxx::1:FFFF:FFFF

Note: The "unspecified address" the loopback address, and the IPv6 Addresses with
Embedded IPv4 Addresses, are assigned out of the 0000 0000 format prefix space.
```

Filename: ftp://ftp.isi.edu/in-notes/iana/assignments/ipv6-address-space

F.4 ICMP Version 6 Parameters

The Internet Control Message Protocol (ICMPv6) has many messages that are identified by a "type" field [RFC1885].

Type	Name	Reference
1	Destination Unreachable	[RFC1885]
2	Packet Too Big	[RFC1885]
3	Time Exceeded	[RFC1885]
4	Parameter Problem	[RFC1885]
128	Echo Request	[RFC1885]
129	Echo Reply	[RFC1885]
130	Group Membership Query	[RFC1885]
131	Group Membership Report	[RFC1885]
132	Group Membership Reduction	[RFC1885]

```
Many of these ICMP types have a "code" field.  Here we list the types again with
their assigned code fields.
```

```
Type     Name                                           Reference

  1        Destination Unreachable                      [RFC1885]

  Code          0 - no route to destination
                1 - communication with destination
                      administratively prohibited
                2 - not a neighbor
                3 - address unreachable
                4 - port unreachable

  2        Packet Too Big                               [RFC1885]

  Code          0

  3        Time Exceeded                                [RFC1885]

  Code          0 - hop limit exceeded in transit
                1 - fragment reassembly time exceeded

  4        Parameter Problem                            [RFC1885]

  Code          0 - erroneous header field encountered
                1 - unrecognized Next Header type encountered
                2 - unrecognized IPv6 option encountered

128        Echo Request                                 [RFC1885]

  Code          0

129        Echo Reply                                   [RFC1885]

  Code          0

130        Group Membership Query                       [RFC1885]

  Code          0

131        Group Membership Report                      [RFC1885]

  Code          0
```

```
132        Group Membership Reduction                  [RFC1885]

  Code          0

133        Router Solicitation                         [RFC1970]

  Code          0

134        Router Advertisement                        [RFC1970]

  Code          0

135        Neighbor Solicitation                       [RFC1970]

  Code          0

136        Neighbor Advertisement                      [RFC1970]

  Code          0

137        Redirect Message                            [RFC1970]

  Code          0
```

Filename: ftp://ftp.isi.edu/in-notes/iana/assignments/ipv6-address-space

G Acronyms and Abbreviations

A	ampere
AARP	AppleTalk Address Resolution Protocol
ABP	alternate bipolar
ACK	acknowledgement
ACS	asynchronous communication server
ACTLU	activate logical unit
ACTPU	activate physical unit
ADSP	AppleTalk Data Stream Protocol
AEP	AppleTalk Echo Protocol
AFI	authority and format identifier
AFP	AppleTalk Filing Protocol
AFRP	ARCNET Fragmentation Protocol
AGS	asynchronous gateway server
AH	authentication header
AI	artificial intelligence
AMI	alternate mark inversion
AMT	address mapping table
ANSI	American National Standards Institute

API	applications program interface
APPC	Advanced Program-to-Program Communication
ARE	all routes explorer
ARI	address recognized indicator bit
ARM	administrative runtime module
ARP	Address Resolution Protocol
ARPA	Advanced Research Projects Agency
ARPANET	Advanced Research Projects Agency Network
ASCE	Association Control Service Element
ASCII	American Standard Code for Information Interchange
ASN.1	Abstract Syntax Notation One
ASP	AppleTalk Session Protocol
ATM	Asynchronous Transfer Mode
ATP	AppleTalk Transaction Protocol
AUP	acceptable use policy
AVM	administrative view module
B8ZS	bipolar with 8 ZERO substitution
BC	block check
BER	Basic Encoding Rules
BIOS	Basic Input/Output System
BITNET	Because It's Time NETwork
BIU	basic information unit

BOC	Bell Operating Company
BOFL	Breath of Life
BOOTP	Bootstrap Protocol
BPDU	bridge protocol data unit
bps	bits per second
BPV	bipolar violations
BRI	basic rate interface
BSC	binary synchronous communication
BSD	Berkeley Software Distribution
BTU	basic transmission unit
BUI	browser user interface
CATNIP	Common Architecture for Next Generation Internet Protocol
CCIS	common channel interoffice signaling
CCITT	International Telegraph and Telephone Consultative Committee
CCR	commitment, concurrency, and recovery
CICS	customer information communication system
CIDR	classless interdomain routing
CLNP	Connectionless Network Protocol
CLNS	Connectionless-mode Network Services
CLTP	Connectionless Transport Protocol
CMIP	Common Management Information Protocol
CMIS	Common Management Information Service

CMISE	Common Management Information Service Element
CMOL	CMIP on IEEE 802.2 Logical Link Control
CMOT	Common Management Information Protocol over TCP/IP
CONS	Connection-mode Network Services
CORBA	Common Object Request Broker Architecture
COS	Corporation for Open Systems
CPE	customer premises equipment
CPE	convergence protocol entity
CRC	cyclic redundancy check
CREN	The Corporation for Research and Educational Networking
CRS	configuration report server
CSMA/CD	Carrier Sense Multiple Access with Collision Detection
CSNET	computer+science network
CSU	channel service unit
CTERM	Command Terminal Protocol
DA	destination address
DAP	Data Access Protocol
DARPA	Defense Advanced Research Projects Agency
DAT	duplicate address test
DCA	Defense Communications Agency
DCC	Data Country Code
DCE	data circuit-terminating equipment

DDCMP	Digital Data Communications Message Protocol
DDN	Defense Data Network
DDP	Datagram Delivery Protocol
DECmcc	DEC Management Control Center
DEMPR	DEC multiport repeater
DHCP	Dynamic Host Configuration Protocol
DIX	DEC, Intel, and Xerox
DL	data link
DLC	data link control
DMA	direct memory access
DMI	Desktop Management Interface
DMTF	Desktop Management Task Force
DNIC	Data Network Identification Code
DNS	Domain Name System
DOD	Department of Defense
DPA	demand protocol architecture
DRP	DECnet Routing Protocol
DSAP	destination service access point
DSU	data service unit
DSU/CSU	Data service unit/channel service unit
DTE	data terminal equipment
DTR	data terminal ready

EBCDIC	Extended Binary Coded Decimal Interchange Code
ECL	End Communication layer
ECSA	Exchange Carriers Standards Association
EDI	electronic data interchange
EGA	enhanced graphics array
EGP	Exterior Gateway Protocol
EIA	Electronic Industries Association
ELAP	EtherTalk Link Access Protocol
EOT	end of transmission
ESF	extended superframe format
ES-IS	End System to Intermediate System Protocol
ESP	encapsulating security payload
FAL	file access listener
FAT	file access table
FCC	Federal Communications Commission
FCI	frame copied indicator bit
FCS	frame check sequence
FDDI	fiber data distributed interface
FDM	frequency division multiplexing
FID	format identifer
FIPS	Federal Information Processing Standard
FM	function management

FMD	function management data
FT1	fractional T1
FTAM	File Transfer Access and Management
FTP	File Transfer Protocol
G	giga-
GB	gigabyte
GHz	gigahertz
GOSIP	Government OSI profile
GUI	graphical user interface
HA	hardware address
HDLC	high-level data link control
HEMS	high-level entity management system
HLLAPI	High-level language API
HMMO	Hypermedia Managed Object
HMOM	Hypermedia Object Manager
HMMP	Hypermedia Management Protocol
HMMS	Hypermedia Management Schema
HTML	Hypertext Markup Language
HTTP	Hypertext Transfer Protocol
Hz	hertz
IAB	Internet Activities Board
IANA	Internet Assigned Numbers Authority

ICD	international code designator
ICMP	Internet Control Message Protocol
ICP	Internet Control Protocol
IDI	initial domain indicator
IDP	Internetwork Datagram Protocol
IDRP	Interdomain Routing Protocol
IEEE	Institute of Electrical and Electronics Engineers
IETF	Internet Engineering Task Force
I/G	individual/group
IGMP	Internet Group Management Protocol
IGP	Interior Gateway Protocol
IGRP	Internet Gateway Routing Protocol
IMPS	interface message processors
I/O	input/output
IOC	interoffice channel
IP	Internet Protocol
IPng	Internet Protocol, next generation
IPv6	Internet Protocol, version 6
IPv6CP	Internet Protocol version 6 Control Protocol
IPC	Interprocess Communications Protocol
IP sec	Internet Protocol security
IPX	Internetwork Packet Exchange Protocol

IR	Internet router
IRTF	Internet Research Task Force
ISAKMP	Internet Secure Association Key Management Protocol
ISDN	Integrated Services Digital Network
IS-IS	Intermediate System to Intermediate System Protocol
ISN	initial sequence number
ISO	International Organization for Standardization
ISODE	ISO Development Environment
ITU	International Telecommunication Union
IXC	inter-exchange carrier
JDBC	Java Database Connectivity
JMAPI	Java Management Application Programming Interface
Kbps	kilo bits per second
KHz	kilohertz
LAA	locally administered address
LAN	local area network
LAP	link access procedure
LAPB	Link Access Procedure Balanced
LAPD	Link Access Procedure D Channel
LAT	Local Area Transport
LATA	local access transport area
LAVC	local area VAX cluster

LCP	Link Control Protocol
LDAP	Lightweight Directory Access Protocol
LEC	local exchange carrier
LEN	length
LF	largest frame
LLAP	LocalTalk Link Access Protocol
LLC	Logical Link Control
LME	layer management entity
LMI	layer management interface
LMMP	LAN/MAN Management Protocol
LMMPE	LAN/MAN Management Protocol Entity
LMMS	LAN/MAN Management Service
LMMU	LAN/MAN Management User
LPP	Lightweight Presentation Protocol
LSB	least significant bit
LSL	Link Support layer
MAC	medium access control
MAN	metropolitan area network
Mbps	megabits per second
MHS	message handling service
MHz	megahertz
MIB	management information base

MILNET	MILitary NETwork
MIOX	Multiprotocol Interconnect over X.25
MIPS	millions instructions per second
MIS	management information systems
MLID	multiple link interface driver
MNP	Microcom Networking Protocol
MOP	Maintenance Operations Protocol
MSAU	multistation access unit
MSB	most significant bit
MSS	maximum segment size
MTA	message transfer agent
MTBF	mean time between failures
MTTR	mean time to repair
MTU	maximum transmission unit
MUX	multiplex, multiplexor
NACS	NetWare Asynchronous Communications Server
NAK	negative acknowledg-ment
NASI	NetWare Asynchronous Service Interface
NAU	network addressable unit
NAUN	nearest active upstream neighbor
NBP	Name Binding Protocol
NCP	Network Control Program

NCP	Network Control Protocol
NCP	NetWare Core Protocol
NCSI	network communications services interface
NDIS	Network Driver Interface Standard
NetBEUI	NetBIOS Extended User Interface
NetBIOS	Network Basic Input/Output System
NFS	Network File System
NIC	network information center
NIC	network interface card
NICE	network information and control exchange
NIS	names information socket
NIST	National Institute of Standards and Technology
NLA	next-level aggregation identifier
NLM	netware loadable module
NMS	network management station
NOC	network operations center
NOS	network operating system
NSAP	Network Service Access Point
NSF	National Science Foundation
NSP	Network Services Protocol
NT	network termination
OC1	optical carrier, level 1

ODI	Open Data Link Interface
OID	object identifier
OIM	OSI Internet management
OSF	Open Software Foundation
OSI	Open Systems Interconnection
OSI-RM	Open Systems Interconnection Reference Model
OSPF	Open Shortest Path First
PA	protocol address
PABX	private automatic branch exchange
PAD	packet assembler and disassembler
PAP	Printer Access Protocol
PBX	private branch exchange
PCI	protocol control information
PCM	pulse code modulation
PDN	public data network
PDU	protocol data unit
PEP	Packet Exchange Protocol
PLEN	protocol length
PMTU	path maximum transmission unit
POP	point of presence
POSIX	Portable Operating System Interface-UNIX
POTS	plain old telephone service

PPP	Point-to-Point Protocol
PSN	packet switch node
PSP	presentation services process
PSPDN	packet switched public data network
PTP	point-to-point
PUC	Public Utility Commission
RARP	Reverse Address Resolution Protocol
RBOC	Regional Bell Operating Company
RC	routing control
RD	route descriptor
RFC	request for comments
RFS	remote file system
RH	request/response header
RI	routing information
RII	route information indicator
RIP	Routing Information Protocol
RJE	remote job entry
ROSE	Remote Operations Service Element
RMI	Remote Method Invocation
RMON	remote monitoring
RPC	remote procedure call
RPS	ring parameter server

RSX	Realtime Resource-Sharing eXecutive
RT	routing type
RU	request/response unit
SA	source address
SA	security association
SABME	set asynchronous balanced mode extended
SAP	service access point
SAP	Service Advertising Protocol
SCS	system communication services
SDLC	Synchronous Data Link Control
SDN	software defined network
SEQ	sequence
SGMP	Simple Gateway Management Protocol
SIPP	Simple Internet Protocol Plus
SKIP	Simple Key Management for the Internet Protocol.
S/L	strict/loose bits
SLA	site-level aggregation identifier
SLIP	Serial Line IP
SMB	server message block
SMDS	Switched Multimegabit Data Service
SMI	structure of management information
SMI	system management interface

SMTP	Simple Mail Transfer Protocol
SNA	System Network Architecture
SNADS	Systems Network Architecture Distribution Services
SNAP	subnetwork access protocol
SNMP	Simple Network Management Protocol
SOH	start of header
SONET	Synchronous Optical Network
SPI	security parameters index
SPP	Sequenced Packet Protocol
SPX	Sequenced Packet Exchange protocol
SR	source routing
SRF	specifically routed frame
SRI	Stanford Research Institute
SRT	source routing transparent
SSAP	source service access point
STE	spanning tree explorer
SUA	stored upstream address
SVC	switched virtual circuit
TB	terabyte
TCP	Transmission Control Protocol
TCP/IP	Transmission Control Protocol/Internet Protocol
TDM	time division multiplexing

TELNET	Telecommunications Network Protocol
TFTP	Trivial File Transfer Protocol
TH	transmission header
TLA	top-level aggregation identifier
TLAP	TokenTalk Link Access Protocol
TLI	Transport Layer Interface
TLV	Type-Length-Value encoding
TP	Transport Protocol
TSR	terminate-and-stay resident
TTL	time to live
TUBA	TCP/UDP with Bigger Addresses
UA	unnumbered acknowledgement
UA	user agent
UDP	User Datagram Protocol
U/L	universal/local
ULP	Upper Layer Protocols
UNMA	unified network management architecture
UT	universal time
UTP	unshielded twisted pair
UUCP	UNIX to UNIX copy program
V	volt
VAN	value-added network

VAP	value-added process
VARP	VINES Address Resolution Protocol
VFRP	VINES Fragmentation Protocol
VGA	video graphics array
VICP	VINES Internet Control Protocol
VINES	Virtual Networking System
VIP	VINES Internet Protocol
VIPC	VINES Interprocess Communications
VLSI	very large-scale integration
VMS	virtual memory system
VRTP	VINES Routing Update Protocol
VSPP	VINES Sequenced Packet Protocol
VT	virtual terminal
WAN	wide area network
WBEM	Web-based Enterprise Management
WIN	window
XDR	External data representation
XID	exchange identification
XMP	X/Open Management Protocol
XNS	Xerox Network System
ZIP	Zone Information Protocol
ZIS	Zone Information Socket
ZIT	Zone Information Table

Trademarks

PostScript is a trademark of Adobe Systems

Apple, the Apple logo, AppleTalk, EtherTalk, LocalTalk, Macintosh, and TokenTalk are registered trademarks of Apple Computer, Inc.

Bay Networks is a trademark of Bay Networks, Inc.

DigiNet is a trademark of Digital Network Corporation, registered in the Turks and Caicos Islands, British West Indies.

DEC, DECmcc, DECnet, Digital, LAT, LAVC, Micro-VAX, MOP, POLY-CENTER, ThinWire, Ultrix, VAX, and VAX Cluster are trademarks, and Ethernet is a registered trademark of Digital Equipment Corporation.

PC/TCP and LANWatch are registered trademarks of FTP Software, Inc.

Ethernet are registered trademarks of Intel Corporation.

IBM PC LAN, PC/AT, PC/XT, SNA, System/370, MicroChannel, NetBIOS, SAA, and System View are trademarks of International Business Machines Corporation; and AIX, AT, IBM, NetView, and PS/2 are registered trademarks of International Business Machines Corporation.

EUI-64 is a trademark of the Institute of Electrical and Electronics Engineers. Inc.

Microsoft, MS-DOS, LAN Manager, Windows and Windows NT are registered trademarks of Microsoft Corporation.

IPX, ManageWise, NetWare, NetWare 386, Novell, and SPX are trademarks, and Novell is a registered trademark of Novell, Inc.

BSD is a trademark of the Regents of the University of California.

Java, Network File System, NFS, Sun, Sun Microsystems Inc., Sun Microsystems, SunNet, SunOS and SunSoft are trademarks or registered trademarks of Sun Microsystems, Inc. SPARC is a registered trademark of SPARC International, Inc., licensed to Sun Microsystems, Inc.

Domino and WG Examine are trademarks, and Wandel & Goltermann is a registered Trademark or Wandel & Goltermann, Inc.

UNIX is a registered trademark of X/Open Company Ltd.

Ethernet and Xerox are registered trademarks of Xerox Corporation.

All other trademarks are the property of their respective owners.

Index

J

L